Organic Gardener's
Edible Plants

Rosalind Creasy

Illustrations by Marcia Hawthorne

Van Patten Publishing

Portland, Oregon

Organic Gardener's Edible Plants is an updated edition of *Gardener's Encyclopedia of Edible Plants* ISBN: 0-87156-758-X (hardcover) ISBN: 0-87156-756-8 (paperback) published by Sierra Club Books in 1986.

Organic Gardener's Edible Plants is one of the books in Van Patten's Organic Gardener's Series.

Text Copyright C 1986, 1993 by Rosalind Creasy
Drawings Copyright C 1986, 1993 Marcia Hawthorne

Printed in the United States of America

Van Patten Publishing

ISBN: 1-878823-07-8 Trade Paperback
ISBN: 1-878823-12-4 Hard Cover

Library of Congress Cataloging in Publication Data

Publisher's Cataloging in Publication
(Prepared by Quality Books Inc.)

Creasy, Rosalind
    Organic gardener's edible plants/ Rosalind Creasy
    p. cm. -- (Organic gardener's series ; 5)
    Includes bibliographical references and index
    ISBN: 1-878823-07-8 (trade paper)
    ISBN: 1-878823-12-4 (hardcover)

    1. Plants, Edible--Encyclopedias. 2. Organic Gardening -- Encyclopedias. I. Title. II. Series
SB453.4.C74 1993   635'.048'4
                         QB193-20015

Jacket/cover design by Peter Callis, Linda Provost
Cover photo: Rosalind Creasy
Back cover photos: *The Oregonian*
Editor: Maggie Gage
Artwork: Marcia Hawthorne

Layout & Design: PC Design
Typesetting: Linoman

10 9 8 7 6 5 4 3 2 1

Distributed by   **Login Publisher's Consortium**
                  1436 West Randolph Street
                  Chicago, IL 60607
                  1-800-626-4330

Table of Contents

Acknowledgements

THIS BOOK IS adapted from *The Complete Book of Edible Landscaping*. Numerous talented people helped me bring it to fruition. The majority of the effort was expended by Marcia Hawthorne, my illustrator, and Maggie Gage, who did much of the original editing. In addition, my heartfelt thanks go to: Alice Reeves, Donna Breed, Ann Clifton, Sheldon Edelman, Jamie Jobb, James W. Wilson, William Olkowski, Charles Konigsberg, William Patterson, Robert Will, Ken Arutunian, Klaus Hertzer, Robert Kourik, Craig Dremann, Daniel Hawthorne, Richard Turner, Nate Gage, Walter Doty, Nancy Garrison, Karla Patterson, Raymond Ten, Timmie Gallagher, Dave Smith, Paul Hawken, Ruth Troetschler, Larry Breed, David Burmaster, Jeff Cox, Marie Giasi, Richard Goodwin, William Niering, Charles Gould, Ed Carman, Al Cieslak, Corwin Davis, Henry Leuthart, Louis Lipofsky, Frank Reid, John Stephenson, Burpee Seed Company, Geo. W. Park Seed Company, Tsang and Ma International, Vermont Hardy Bean Seed Company, Renee Shepherd, Jan Blum, John Riley, Joe and Katherine Massidda, Paul Jackson, Penney Logem an, Adelma Simmons, Suzanne Lipsett, Anita Walker Scott, Eileen Max, Diana Landau, Gene Coan, John and Joan Creasy, Nancy and Richard olds, David and Jennifer Reeves, Gail and John Gallagher, Jeannette and Philip Valence, Ruth and Richard White, Don Hatfield, Paul and Carolyn Kuckein, Arvind and Bhadra Fancy, Margaret Creasy, Alberta Lee, Jane McKendall, and my husband, Robert, and son and daughter, Bob and Laura Creasy.

This handbook was given extra attention by Wendy Krupnik, Dayna Breeden, Mary Anne Stewart, Nancy Warner, Susan Ristow, and Linda Gunnarson.

Foreword

For about twenty years I lived just a few miles from Ros Creasy's home in northern California and looked in on her garden every now and then. Every year, it seemed, she was growing some new variety of vegetable, berry or herb that I had never before seen, often several of them. And she grew everything well, so well that her "edibles" were highly ornamental.

I didn't realize it then, but Ros was on her way to becoming the most respected authority in the field of edible ornamentals, thanks to her insistence on personally growing and learning how to prepare every new plant before she ventured to write or lecture about it. At one point she had such a backlog that she had to enlist the aid of good gardening friends to grow certain kinds for her to observe and use. After all, she had long since jumped the fence into her front yard and had eliminated every scrap of lawn to make room for her trial rows.

Ros's new book, *Organic Gardener's Edible Plants*, describes nearly one hundred edible species that thrive under organic gardening practices. Gardeners in all but favored parts of Florida and California may be momentarily puzzled by Surinam cherry, but this book is of national scope. No one will be misled by the descriptions; they state plainly the climate limitations for each species. Nor will they be misled into trying species that are difficult to grow; Ros has included an "Effort Scale" rating for each species.

This isn't a book of rare or unusual vegetables, fruits and berries. You won't find in it descriptions of garbanzo beans, gherkins or naranjillo, for example. Ros has included only the species that are the most popular, or that have the potential for popularity, as with paw paw, for example. Yes, paw paw' not papaya, but the native American shrub/small tree that bears fruit so aromatic and delicious that you have to race the raccoons and the possums for the ripening fruit.

This is a book from which you can learn, no matter your level of expertise in vegetables, tree fruits or berries. Ros is a talented and determined researcher who knows where to find the leading specialists in each plant specialty, and how to pick their brains for information that can make plants easier and more rewarding to grow.

I can guarantee that you won't get far into this book before you will find yourself exclaiming, "I didn't know that!," or "Well, I'll be jiggered!" And you can count on what you read as accurate, such is the depth of Ros's research.

I'm not easily impressed by new books on edible plants because so many of them plow old ground. Upon reading the first few words of a paragraph in such a dreary book, I can pretty well predict the rest of it. Not so with *Organic Gardener's Edible Plants*; its descriptions are strewn with fresh new facts about plants and how to grow them.

Last but not least, the price is right, You get a lot for your money!

Jim Wilson
Host of the PBS *Victory Garden*

INTRODUCTION

Welcome to the World of Edible Plants

JOHNNY APPLESEED would be pleased. Americans are planting more apple trees, and we are also rediscovering other home-grown produce: peaches so full of juice that it runs down your chin, velvety Bibb lettuce served with fresh basil, and just-picked strawberries so flavorful they taste like the volume has been turned up. We walk out our front door and enjoy apple blossoms falling on the entranceway, open the windows to savor fragrant citrus and plum blossoms, and enjoy compliments from neighbors who admire the amethyst bouquets of ornamental kale decorating our flower borders. Long imprisoned in houses surrounded by lawns and a mustache of evergreen shrubs, we are breaking out of the confining tradition of using strictly ornamental plants in our yards. After a hundred years of being hidden behind the garage, fruit trees and vegetable plants are being accepted as landscape material. Surely, the 1980's mark the renaissance of the edible garden.

For the last century a number of sociological phenomena had directed American garden design away from edible plants. Our grandparents' migration from the farm made most of us city folk, and efficient agriculture, inexpensive oil, and advanced technology made food cheap and readily available. Add to these factors an inherited European landscaping style that included no edible plants—whose very point was that an ornamental landscape proved to the world that you had so much land, so many servants, and so much wealth that, in fact, you could cover your soil with nonproductive plants—and it was a rare hobby gar-

dener who grew his or her own food. Nurseries, landscape designers, and garden books and magazines reflected this bias against edible plants; so, if you wanted to place an apple or plum tree in your yard, you were hard pressed to find design information.

But times have changed, and with them our priorities. During the last decade, my work as a professional landscape designer and teacher has involved a critical look at our dependency, for food, on commercial agriculture—with its attendant high food prices and potential pesticide and chemical health hazards—and at our expenditure of precious water, soil, and fossil-fuel resources to create and maintain purely decorative landscapes. As a consequence of my concerns, my professional and home gardening efforts have been devoted to finding ways to revise standard landscaping practices to meet three goals: to provide delicious, healthful food for the table; to curtail practices that waste water, soil, and energy; and-most important, since it provides incentive for the rest-to create beautiful, well-planned landscapes with the use of edible plants.

The information in *Organic Gardeners Edible Plants* was assembled to fill the need for a systematic approach to choosing edible plants for your landscape. The book is adapted from my earlier publication *The Complete Book of Edible Landscaping*. I felt the encyclopedic information should be made available to home gardeners without the historical and "how-to" chapters on landscaping contained in the earlier book; so the complete edible Plant listings are included here, with comprehensive updating and revision—especially regarding sources—and with some new entries, along with information on planting and maintaining these edibles. Basic landscaping information for individual edibles is included in each encyclopedic entry.

I cannot overemphasize the potential for beauty that landscaping with edibles holds, since many people still have difficulty accepting this notion. I came to understand this potential by experimenting in my own yard, in the process relearning the joys of eating fresh-picked peas, vine-ripened tomatoes, and sun-warmed apricots. I purchased dozens of different varieties of vegetables-not only to plant in my food garden, but also to interplant in my flower garden. Red cabbage with its colorful foliage, string beans with purple flowers, the many varieties of lettuce with their interesting leaf patterns, artichokes with their gray-green, fernlike foliage and magnificent blue thistles, and heavenly purple eggplants were extremely effective in my standard flower bed. Since my first tentative experiments, I developed and thoroughly researched ornamental edible plants that can be grown in different areas of the United States. The plants selected range from the exotic water chestnut to the familiar apple. I also discovered some unusually attractive varieties: string beans with large, showy, white flowers; bush cucumbers with compact vines; peaches with showy, pink, double blossoms; and plum trees with delicious fruit and red foliage. I found that some standard food-growing practices—for example, staking bean vines with an odd assortment of poles, or "caging" tomatoes—could be replaced by less intrusive, more aesthetically pleasing techniques. I found, too, that some edible plants were hard to manage in a landscape situation; so these were not included in this book.

A word about how this book is organized. Part One is an encyclopedia describing more than 80 edible ornamental plants. Each entry describes a plant or related group of plants; identifies the zones in which it will grow; assesses the effort required to grow the plant; describes its uses both in the kitchen and in the landscape; and provides relevant information on growing, purchasing, and preserving.

Part Two provides the specific information you need to get your plantings off to a good start and to keep them in good shape. Though some yards take less work than others, no residential landscape is completely maintenance-free, and many of the popular edible plants require a considerable amount of care. This section also discusses composting and pruning, as well as environmentally healthful methods of watering, fertilizing, and pest control.

Part Three is a resource and reference section that contains several appendices. The first is a list of 225 edible plants, many of which are not covered in the encyclopedia but which might be used in a yard; basic information about each plant is given in table form. Appendix B includes an annotated list of nurseries from which the plants can be obtained. Appendix C lists sources of information: organizations, periodicals, and the like. Following the appendices are a glossary and an annotated bibliography.

The book's comprehensive edible listings, landscaping guidelines, and resource information are intended to help you choose the edible plants best suited to a home garden. And an edible garden means delicious eating, a boost to your budget, and a beautiful yard. Nowhere is it written: Thou shalt landscape only with barren ornamentals. So—welcome to the world of edible plants!

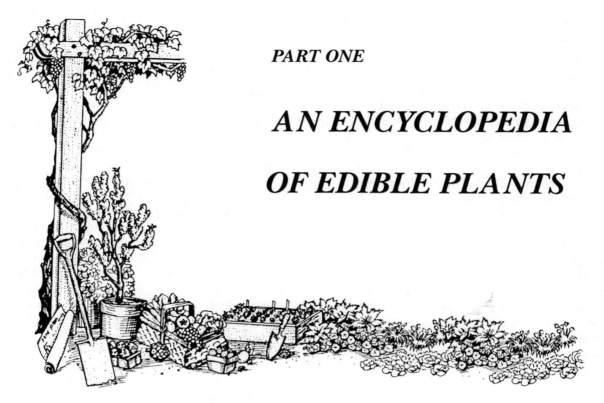

PART ONE

AN ENCYCLOPEDIA

OF EDIBLE PLANTS

EUELL GIBBONS went into the wilds to discover edible plants. I went into my well-stocked pantry to discover which foods I could grow. It is possible that my pantry includes more edible exotica than most, owing to my lifelong interest in cooking, my family's adventurous collective palate, and my inability to resist the blandishments of seed catalogues. Still, with few exceptions, the foods I am concerned with and describe here could be called "domesticated." That is, they have been long used in the cuisine of many cultures. They are not wild edibles such as milkweed, cattails, or acorns.

In this encyclopedia I have described species of edible or food-bearing plants that both provide delicious food and beautify the home landscape. Selecting plants for aesthetic qualities took some doing, since edible species often come in many varieties, some more decorative than others—they may have showier blossoms, more attractive foliage, or more interesting forms. Few reference books emphasize the beauty inherent in edible plants or direct you to these varieties, of course, beauty was not the only criterion for my final selection of edibles to be covered here. Flavor and disease resistance are also stressed. With a few exceptions, sources are noted for most of the varieties mentioned in the encyclopedia.

In compiling the encyclopedia, I systematically examined domesticated edibles with an eye to their place in the landscape. The entries were gleaned from a more extensive list of edibles documented in Appendix A. All plants covered in the encyclopedia fall into one of the following categories:

1. Popular, familiar edibles such as apples, oranges, and plums. These were chosen because they are the most loved. People know what they look like and how they taste, but often do not know how to use them in a landscaping situation. Farmers grow food and landscape designers tend to plan for ornamentation only; to combine these functions long seemed forbidden.

2. Common edibles from particular cuisines, often available in foreign food markets or in large suburban produce markets but otherwise difficult to find. Such items as sugar peas, water chestnuts, and Alpine strawberries were largely unknown to our parents, but we have traveled more and our tastes have grown more sophisticated. We have learned to enjoy these delights from other lands.

3. Newly popular edibles such as kiwi, sugar snap peas, and carob.

4. Edibles that are local favorite—for example, pawpaw in the Midwest, beach plum on the East Coast, and sea grape in Florida. These attractive plants produce foods that have never been commercially grown but are appreciated by local residents. Their territories can and should be expanded for more people's pleasure. They are tasty, beautiful, and generally easy to grow. With encroaching subdivisions, lawns, and streets, some of these plants have become endangered, so it is important that they be grown purposefully in people's yards.

All the encyclopedia entries contain information on how hard a plant is to grow, its growing zones, its uses in the kitchen and the landscape, information on buying and growing it, and usually one or more recipes or suggested methods of preserving it. See the outline of a typical entry, below, for a more detailed explanation.

With more common plants, I have chosen not to present the available information in toto. If you can't find here your favorite apple variety, or the worst pest you have on your tomatoes, or a recipe for grape jam, it is because I feel that ample material already exists on these topics. If you need or wish to pursue such matters in detail, consult the books in the bibliography. Also, I encourage you to talk to your neighbors, join local garden societies, get to know your local agricultural agent, and seek assistance from university extension services. They provide much information that is both up-to-date and specific to your area, and it is usually free.

Guidelines for Buying Edibles

Late winter and early spring are the times to buy most edible plants. This is when nurseries offer the greatest variety of deciduous trees and shrubs, bare-root fruit trees, shrubs, vines, and herbaceous perennials. The largest selection of vegetable seed is also available in spring, as are the tender evergreens for mild-winter regions, such as citrus fruits, avocado, and guava.

It is still uncommon for local nurseries to carry a large selection of edible plants, other than the standard vegetable seeds and fruit trees, and when you go looking for more unusual edibles you are likely to encounter some common pitfalls. First, beware of non-vining varieties: there are peach trees that don't bear edible peaches and flowering almond trees that don't produce almonds. I once had a student who had moved into a new house. Her neighbor had told her there was a peach tree in her front yard, so for two years my student watched her tree bloom and waited for the juicy peach—but none appeared. When she brought a flowering branch to class, I had to give her the sad news that her peach tree was only a flowering peach and would never bear fruit. She looked at me wide-eyed and said, "Why would anyone plant a peach tree that doesn't bear fruit?" Why, indeed! There are flowering plums, crabapples, quince, pomegranates, pears, currants, gooseberries—all flowers, no fruit. As my father would say, "Big noise at the head of the stairs, but no one comes down." Thus, when you shop for edibles, stress the words *edible* and *fruiting*.

E.1. Old, spreading apple tree at Sturbridge Village, Massachusetts.

The pistachios you find in the nursery is the fruitless form. Again, make sure you are buying a fruiting plant.

To get a predictable product most people buy selected named varieties of fruit trees instead of growing them from seed: 'Concord' grape, say, or an 'Allred' plum. Most of the fruit trees you can buy are grafted varieties (or budded ones, the results of a similar method). These plants are the result of joining together two plants. The bottom of the plant is called the rootstock, and the top is called the scion. (See Figure 2.15.) Grafted or budded fruit trees are used for a number of reasons.

1. The scion contains genetic material that will guarantee a similar product for every tree, shrub, or vine onto which it is grafted—in other words, a clone. For example, all 'Concord' grapes will be deep purple and have a similar taste; every 'Allred' plum will have red foliage and red plums.
2. Fruits are generally produced a year or two earlier than on non-grafted varieties.
3. Rootstocks can be developed for specific soil conditions, such as heavy clay or sand, or for disease or pest resistance.
4. Grafted plants are usually more economical for nurseries to produce.
5. Grafting certain scions onto known rootstocks can produce a dwarfing effect on the plant. The resultant dwarf trees have a number of advantages over full-size trees (see the sidebar titled "What Size Fruit Tree" under APPLE AND CRABAPPLE in the encyclopedia for more on dwarf trees).
6. Grafting is necessary to reproduce members of the plant world that produce no seed, such as some grape, fig, or orange varieties.
7. Some plants are grafted to improve resistance to specific diseases.

Although the use of named, usually grafted, varieties has been emphasized in this book, (Or, in the case of annual fruits and vegetables, hybrids have been stressed. For more on the subject of hybrids, see Appendix B.) for the reasons just enumerated, growing fruit trees from seed is a viable alternative with most species. The results are fairly reliable; depending on the species, the chance of a seed you plant producing a tree and fruit similar to the parent could be 75-80 percent. (Among the notable exceptions are two well-known edibles, apple and almond; neither produces reliable products from seed.) However, growing fruit trees from seed has some advantages of its own. To summarize:

1. The initial investment for seed is low.

2. Most viruses are not transmitted by seed, so you are less apt to lose a fruit tree to these diseases than with a grafted variety.
3. Often seedling trees adapt better to their environment.
4. A number of species of unusual fruits are available only as seed.
5. If the resultant seedling-grown tree does not have good fruits, you can always graft onto it scion wood that does.
6. One of the strongest reasons for planting fruit trees from seed is to keep the genetic pool strong. The continued production of cloned fruit trees can produce large numbers of trees susceptible to the same diseases, and in addition gives us fewer naturally occurring variations to choose from for breeding material..

Growing your own fruit trees from seed can be a rewarding alternative to using commercially produced plant materials. For more information on the subject join the fruit- and nut-growing societies mentioned in Appendix C.

Further information on acquiring edibles is given in Appendix B and in the individual encyclopedia entries.

A Typical Encyclopedia Entry

Entry Title

Plants are listed alphabetically, generally under their most often used common name. In some cases, alternate common names are given in parentheses. Sometimes, too, the heading is for a compound entry, such as PEACH AND NECTARINE, or for a group of closely related plants, such as the cucurbits (cucumber, squash, and melon). All plants grouped together have similar landscaping uses and growing conditions.

The common names of plants can be confusing: blueberry to you may be huckleberry to me, my okra may be your gumbo, and papaya is often called pawpaw. Because common names can vary regionally, I have included the Botanical, or Latin, name in each entry, so there will be no question as to the plant's identity. It is found after the entry title. If the entry title comprises more than one species, the common and botanical names of most or all of them are included.

Botanical names are not always agreed upon, however. I have used the third edition of *Hortus*, the major reference of many American horticulturists, as the authority for names and spellings. In a few cases, based on other resource material, I have disagreed and used a different botanical name.

The botanical name includes genus, species (and

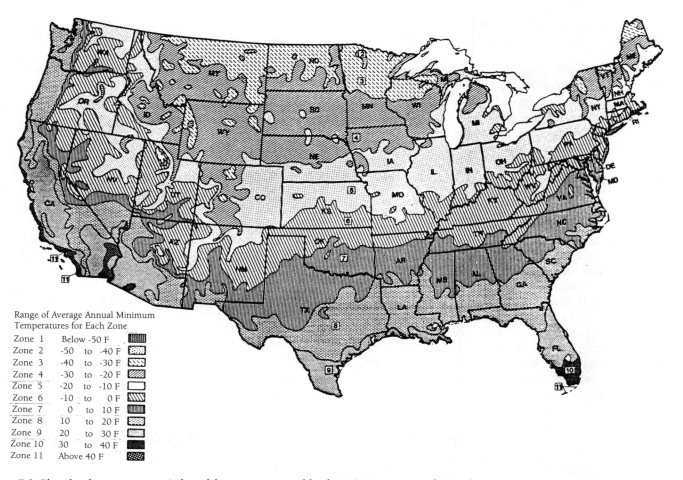

E.2. Plant hardiness zone map (adapted from map prepared by the U.S. Department of Agriculture).

Range of Average Annual Minimum
Temperatures for Each Zone

Zone 1	Below -50 F
Zone 2	-50 to -40 F
Zone 3	-40 to -30 F
Zone 4	-30 to -20 F
Zone 5	-20 to -10 F
Zone 6	-10 to 0 F
Zone 7	0 to 10 F
Zone 8	10 to 20 F
Zone 9	20 to 30 F
Zone 10	30 to 40 F
Zone 11	Above 40 F

sometimes subspecies), variety or horticultural variety (also known as a clone or cultivar).

A genus is a definable group of plants that are related and share certain characteristics. The genus name is always the first of the Latin names commonly given that constitute a plant's botanical name. The genus name for all pears, for example, is *Pyrus*. As you use the encyclopedia, you will notice that often several seemingly distinct groups of plants will share the same genus name, e.g., almonds, peaches, and plums all belong to the genus *Prunus*. Other examples are the genus *Brassica*, which includes mustard, kale, or cabbage; and *Vaccinium*, which includes cranberries and blueberries. Knowing a plant's genus helps you know more about a plant. For example, almonds, peaches, and plums are often bothered by the same pests. Cranberries and blueberries need similar soil acidity and moisture.

The second word in the botanical name indicates its species. Put simply, the species indicates an even closer relationship between plants in the same genus. A particular species of pear, then, would be *Pyrus communis*.

Further differentiation is indicated by the name of a particular variety, horticultural variety, hybrid, or strain. The form most often encountered in this book is the horticultural variety. These are usually choice varieties selected by horticulturists for special qualities and are designated by single quotation marks, e.g., the 'Bartlett' pear. Thus the full botanical name of this pear is *Pyrus communis* 'Bartlett'.

Effort Scale

The degree of effort involved in growing and using edibles varies widely. To keep you from overburdening yourself and to help you have a successful gardening experience, the effort scale has been devised. My experience with students and clients has shown that newcomers to edible gardening sometimes get carried away. Overextension often leads to discouragement, and that is why I have tried to quantify the size of the project you are taking on. The effort scale is designed to eliminate unpleasant surprises—it tells you ahead of time what each plant will require from you in effort, time, and skill.

The effort scale is a simple 1-5 ranking. The ranking assigned to each plant represents the sum of a combination of factors: obtaining the plant; planting, growing, harvesting, and handling it; and processing the product. A ranking of No. 1 indicates that the plant requires minimal effort—perhaps as little as picking the fruit; while a No. 5 was assigned to plants that require both high maintenance and considerable effort to process the product.

Here are a few examples of the variables that affect a plant's effort ranking. If you live where olive trees grow well, you will find them easy to take care of. They have few pests and provide beauty with a minimum of effort. Of course, if you want the tree to develop a certain form, or if you want the wonderfully gnarled trunk to show, some pruning will be required, but basically the olive is simple to grow. The processing of its fruits, on the other hand, is difficult: it requires much harvesting time, usually the use of lye, fermenting the fruits, and canning, or else the pressing and clarifying of olive oil—so the effort for the olive becomes high, and consequently it was assigned a ranking of No. 4. On the other hand, citrus fruit trees take some work in pruning, mulching, fertilizing, watering, and disease control; but the fruits are easy to pick, most varieties do not have to be picked immediately, and are generally eaten fresh. Thus, citrus trees were ranked No. 3 on the effort scale. The ranking for basil as number 2 was chosen because transplanting of an annual, spring fertilizing, and harvesting leaves takes some time. Finally, the pomegranate, which is easy to grow, needs little watering, can be eaten fresh, has no major pests or diseases, and is easy to obtain in the areas where it grows. Hence it was ranked on the scale as No. 1.

The effort scale ranking assumes that you have selected a plant variety appropriate for your area. For example, a quince planted in the warm, humid Southeast will have more diseases than if it were grown in a cool, dry climate. Combating those troubles would obviously result in an increase in effort.

In some entries I supplied two effort scale rankings for the same plant, indicating that growing requirements differ significantly from region to region or that different types of the same plant are easier to grow than others. However, I have supplied a dual reference only where a discrepancy can be quantified. Two examples will suffice for these dual rankings. Avocados are easier to grow in California (where they are ranked No. 2 on the effort scale) than in Florida (No. 3), where the moist climate leads to diseases not present in the drier heat of California. And *genetic dwarf* peaches (No. 3) are generally easier to grow everywhere than are standard-size peach trees (No. 5).

Finally, it is important to note that the effort scale is approximate and is meant to serve as a guide only. Different households, yards, and climates add to the variables involved.

Zones

The ratings in individual entries correspond to the climatic zone map on page 12, adapted from one compiled by the United States Department of Agriculture. Any map of this kind is only an approximation, since many factors that cannot be represented will influence the microclimate of a particular property.

Each zone on the map corresponds to a temperature range in increments of $10^{\circ}F$. These 10 ranges represent the lowest temperature to which a plant is hardy. For example, a plant designated for zone 4 is hardy above $-30^{\circ}F$ to $-20^{\circ}F$, and a zone 7 plant is hardy above $0F$ to $10^{\circ}F$. Most of the plants in the encyclopedia are designated as growable within a range of several zones. The lowest-numbered zone in the range is a simple measure of the plant's hardiness, but the top end of the range may be determined by any of a number of factors: that the plant needs winter chilling, for instance, or that it does poorly in too much summer heat. The range assigned to gooseberries, for example, is zones 3-8, indicating that they are hardy to zone 3 temperatures but do not do well in zones 9 and 10 because they need winter chilling and dislike long, hot summers.

Again, zone numbers are meant only as rough guides, and further investigation on your part is required to assess a plant's needs. For that reason I urge you to study your yard, talk to your neighbors, question the nurseries of your choice, and check with your local university extension service. The information and experience you can glean in this way can help you decide which plant materials will be successful in your gardening space. In general I have been conservative when assigning zone numbers.

The following list describes some of the factors not reflected in the zone designation that will make a difference in the choice of plants that you can grow:

1. Wind. Cold winds are chilling; hot winds are drying. So even though a plant is designated zone 8, if you live in a part of zone 8 where desert conditions prevails—as opposed to a part of zone 8 in the humid Southeast—a plant adapted to humid conditions will need special protection from drying winds or may not grow at all.
2. Hillsides. Cold air drains off hillsides and collects at the bottom of a hill. A tree planted at the bottom of a hill in zone 5 could actually be exposed to colder temperatures than a tree planted on the side of a hill in zone 4.

3. Proximity of water. Large bodies of water maintain heat in the winter, thereby bringing some warmer air to nearby areas. A garden near a lake or the ocean would be warmer than one farther south but located some distance from a body of water.

4. Length of summer-heat conditions. Certain plants need a great deal of heat. For particular areas, this is usually defined in terms of the numbers of hours the location receives temperatures of over 65°F. The amount of heat required is pertinent to two groups of plants mentioned in the encyclopedia: warm-season annuals, such as peanuts and most melons, and heat-requiring perennials, such as jujube, most citrus and pistachio. These plants might grow adequately in less than optimum zones but will produce few or inferior fruits and nuts.

5. Humidity. The olive exemplifies the effect of humidity. Where the humidity is too high, the tree will grow well but the fruit will not form. Avocados will bear good fruit but develop many diseases in climates that are moist, while many plants, such as artichokes, flourish in humidity.

6. Length of winter-cold conditions. Plants that need many hours of winter cold do not do well in many warm, mid-winter southern climates. For example, pears, peaches, and apples require a certain number of hours of temperatures under approximately 45F (known as "chilling requirement" or "winter chill factor") before their dormancy will be broken. Mother Nature has some sophisticated survival mechanisms and this is one of them. If an apple tree started blooming or leafed out after a few freakish warm days in December, at the very least it would lose its chance to fruit, and the tree would probably die when winter weather returned. The chilling requirement combats this problem. Many temperate-zone plants do not grow well in southern Florida, southern California, the Gulf Coast, and the lower elevations of Hawaii. Plant breeders have tried to modify this situation by breeding plants with low chilling requirements for the areas with warmer winters. Varieties of many species now exist that have been developed for different climates—for example, a peach that will grow well in parts of Florida, and another particularly suited to Connecticut. Each has a different chilling requirement. It is imperative that you choose a variety suited for your climate.

7. High summer-heat conditions. A different problem involves the intensity of summer heat. Peas, spinach, and plants in the cabbage family, for example, are called cool-season annuals and cannot take high temperatures. Also, certain perennial plants, such as gooseberries, currants, and arti-chokes, will not thrive in the heat of the most southern latitudes.

Careful study of your property could increase your options. Even though you are in zone 4 on the map, you might have a warm, sheltered spot that would be perfect for a peach tree that is designated hardy only to zone 5. Conversely, you may be in zone 5 on the map but get so much winter wind that a peach tree could not survive. Also, find out the exact composition of your seasons. If you don't have 110 days of summer heat, don't plan to grow peanuts.

Note that only perennial plants have been given a zone number. Annuals are more flexible—their growing season can be extended if they are started indoors and protected from frost—so no zone number is supplied for them. Most can be grown throughout most of the United States. Check with your local weather service to find out the average dates of first and last frosts. In selecting annuals, you need only distinguish between cool-season and warm-season annuals. This information is given under "How to Grow" in each entry.

Thumbnail Sketch

Each entry begins with a brief sketch to allow you to see quickly the pertinent landscaping features and possibilities of each plant. This sketch will prove particularly useful when you are selecting your plant materials.

How to Use

In the Kitchen

A number of the plants included in the encyclopedia are somewhat unusual, so a brief description of each plant's edible portion has been given as well as suggestions for serving. For common edibles, a wide range of uses is indicated.

In the Landscape

In this section the plant or plants are briefly described and their landscaping uses detailed.

Caution: In many cases, I have suggested ways of combining plants, including inedible species. If a plant is not on the list in Appendix A, consider it inedible until you have given it much extra study.

How to Grow

Here I have supplemented material found in Part Two. Pertinent facts are supplied that will enable you to grow relatively simple annual food crops and perennial herbs. The more complicated work of growing demanding annuals and perennials, including woody shrubs and trees, is covered in an outline format, in which information on climate, exposure, soil, fertilizing, watering, pruning, pests and diseases, and harvesting can be quickly researched. Sometimes special material is featured, such as the planting techniques for asparagus, a list of the sources for "antique" varieties of apples, or discussions of dwarf trees under the entries for APPLE AND CRABAPPLE and PEACH AND NECTARINE.

Climate

The broad subject of climate is discussed in the zones section. Under "Climate" appears specific information on the weather limitations of individual plants, as well as information on where they grow best.

Exposure

Most edible plants require full sun. Some plants can grow in filtered sun, though, and an occasional plant requires shade. All instances are noted.

Soil

Under the "Soil" heading, soil pH and salinity are covered wherever they are factors that need to be considered for the successful growing of a particular plant. Special drainage needs are also noted here. A more general discussion of soil is found in Part Two.

Fertilizing

The fertilizing requirements of individual plants are briefly described. Where mulching is especially helpful, this fact is noted. A general discussion of fertilizing is found in Part Two.

Watering

Watering needs specific to each entry are handled in this section. These needs are more critical in arid and hot parts of the country, but during drought years this information is relevant nationwide. I recommend using plants with the lowest water requirements wherever possible. Part Two gives general information on watering wisely.

Pruning

To supplement the basic pruning information in Part Two, specific pruning needs of particular plants are noted here and diagrams are supplied where necessary. Pruning is a complicated subject; for pruning most of the major fruit trees I urge you to use one of the books on the subject listed in the bibliography.

Pests and Diseases

Specific pests affecting particular plants as well as suggested solutions, if not included in Part Two, are covered here. Drawings of the common pests, along with suggestions for their control, are provided in Part Two.

Harvesting

This subject is self-explanatory. Where possible, estimated yield ranges for mature standard-size trees or shrubs are given.

How to Purchase

Edible plants can be purchased as seeds, in containers, as bare-root plants, or balled and burlapped. Under the subheading "Forms and Sources" I have listed the most common form for each entry as well as sources where the plant is available. The sources noted here—indicated by a boldface number—are usually mail-order houses, whose full names and addresses are listed in Appendix B. In the "How to Purchase" section, the source number usually appears by the plant name or the plant description under the subheading "Varieties." Certain sources sell only one edible mentioned in this book.

Whenever possible, buy your edible plants locally. Your local nurseries know what grows best in your area. When mail-ordering fruit trees it is particularly important that you choose a source as close as possible to where you live. Fruit trees are bred and grafted onto rootstocks that are appropriate for certain soil types, weather, and disease and pest resistance. Only if you cannot find what you want from a local source should you consider ordering from distant sources. Do your homework well.

Before ordering plants from a mail-order nursery or the recommended sources, read the information these places supply on how to order, what they promise from their materials, their shipping dates, and their guarantees. These specifications are discussed further in Appendix B.

Pollinators

To bear fruits, many plants must be cross-pollinated (see glossary). Other plants will bear only a small crop unless they are cross-pollinated. And some plants need no cross-pollination at all. The latter are referred to as self-pollinating, self-fertile, or self-fruitful. When fruit is not involved, as when the leaves or the stalk are the edible parts, pollination is not a factor.

"Pollinators" falls within the "How to Purchase" section because at the time of purchase you need to know the pollination limitations. Where cross-pollination is required, you'll want to purchase a companion pollinating tree or shrub along with your original selection. In entries where pollination is not required, it usually is not mentioned.

Occasionally you will be fortunate enough to find a pollinator in a neighbor's yard. As a general rule, it is safe to assume that if you can see this pollinator from the proposed location of your new tree or shrub, it is close enough for effective pollination to occur.

Preserving and Preparing

In all encyclopedia entries, methods of preservation are recommended and described, with special emphasis on edibles that yield plentiful harvests. Basically, these are ways to put away some summer sun for winter pleasure.

Food drying in particular is a preserving method that should be practiced more. The APRICOT entry contains basic information on food drying. In the KIWI entry you'll find information on how to make jelly without added pectin. And the BASIL entry describes how to dry herbs.

One of the problems with growing edibles is that you often wind up with an overabundance of one particular food. Preserving is one answer, but other solutions exist as well. One of the best is instituting a barter system among friends and neighbors. I use this system extensively. In fact, I once had a marvelous mailman who streamlined the process and acted as an efficient distributor. While he completed his route he kept an eye on what was available. After work he would gather and redistribute the bounty. One day it would be young tomato plants, another day guava jelly or pears. Bartering works well and can be very enjoyable. Another solution for large harvests is creative cooking. In some encyclopedia entries I have included my favorite recipes for large harvests.

Beyond the Encyclopedia

The plants detailed in the encyclopedia are, of course, not the only edible plants that can be used in a landscape. Appendix A is a list of more than two hundred edible plants. Some of those listed can be used in a landscape, though others are best grown in a vegetable garden. This comprehensive list includes, where applicable, zones, sources, and part eaten, and briefly notes the plant's landscaping value, if any. To aid you in selecting plants for your yard, the items in the encyclopedia are included in Appendix A, marked with asterisks.

Almond

Prunus dulcis var. *dulcis*

Effort Scale

NO. 2
Vulnerable to some pests, including squirrels and jays
Large harvest on standard-size trees

E.3. *Almond tree in bloom. A floating deck has been constructed around the base to use for relaxation.*

Zones

6-9

Thumbnail Sketch

Deciduous tree
Standard, 20—30 ft. tall; semi-dwarf varieties, 8—20 ft. tall; dwarf variety to 8 ft. tall
Propagated by grafting or budding
Needs full sun
Leaves are bright green, narrow, to 3 in. long
Blooms in early spring
Flowers are profuse, white or pink
Nuts are edible; harvested in summer
Used as street tree, accent plant, interest plant, screen, patio tree; dwarf variety used in containers and as large shrub

How to Use
In the Kitchen

The almond is a versatile nut, popular with most people. It's delicious for eating out of hand, roasted or raw. Roasted almonds, either slivered or chopped, make a great addition to casseroles, vegetables, and meats, and almonds in many forms give flavor and texture to candies and pastries. *Amandine* is haute cuisine!

In the Landscape

This deciduous tree is 20—30 feet tall, and its spread can be as wide. The dwarf and semi-dwarf varieties are 8—20 feet tall. The almond's bloom is white or pink, 1/2 inches wide, grows in large clusters, and appears before the narrow, shiny, bright-green leaves develop. The tree has many uses in the landscape. An almond tree in bloom is one of the showiest flowering trees for early spring and makes an excellent accent or interest plant. One variety, 'Hall's Hardy', has fragrant pink blossoms and comes in both a standard and a dwarf size. The almond tree in leaf has a lacy appearance since the narrow leaves do not form a solid mass. Mature trees can be used as street trees, small shade trees, or patio trees. They line a driveway handsomely and of course can always be used in a backyard orchard. The dwarf varieties do well in containers and can be used as shrubs. See PEACH AND NECTARINE for more information on genetic dwarf trees.

How to Grow

Climate

Most varieties grow best where there are no spring frosts in March or April. The trees are quite hardy, but their blossoms come early and thus can be nipped by a frost. Almonds do not like cool summers or high humidity. 'Hall's Hardy' is as hardy as most peaches.

Exposure

Almond trees need full sun.

Soil

Trees will tolerate a variety of soils if they are well drained.

Fertilizing

Almonds respond well to compost mulches added annually. See Part Two for information on fertilizing common fruit and nut trees.

Watering

Trees are drought resistant once they are established. In rainy climates they need no extra watering. In arid climates they respond well to an occasional deep watering.

Pruning

Prune only enough to shape and remove dead wood.

Pests and Diseases

Almonds are susceptible to some of the problems that affect peaches, but not as often or as seriously (see PEACH AND NECTARINE). Spider mites are the most serious problem in the West, but squirrels and jays are the biggest pests nationwide.

Harvesting

Beat the squirrels! Harvest the nuts off the tree when the shells split. A mature standard-size tree will yield about 20—30 pounds of nuts annually.

How to Purchase

Forms and Sources

Named varieties are available at local nurseries and from many mail-order firms in bare-root form in late winter or early spring and often in 5-gallon containers in summer.

Pollinators

Most standard almond trees need cross-pollination. Plant more than one variety, and be careful to choose those that pollinate each other well. If space is too limited for two full-size trees planted separately, plant more than one variety in the same hole, choose a self-fertile variety, use a dwarf variety for the pollinator, or plant dwarf trees.

Varieties

'All-in-One'—sweet nut; very large, showy white flowers; self-fertile; semi-dwarf; quite hardy; will pollinate 'Texas' and 'Nonpareil'. (52,61)

'Garden Prince'—medium-sized nut, showy pink flowers; self-fertile; genetic dwarf to 8 ft.; new variety, so pollinating capabilities not yet known. (25,61)

'Hall's Hardy'—hard-shell nut; pink flowers; blooms late; partially self-fertile, better yield with 'Texas'. 'Hall's' is the hardiest almond variety (Readily Available). Dwarf 'Hall's Hardy' occasionally available.

'Ne Plus Ultra'—large nuts; white flowers; needs pollinator, is often planted as pollinator for 'Nonpareil' and is pollinated by 'Nonpareil'. (Readily Available)

'Nonpareil'—best nut available; widely grown; white flowers; needs pollinator, usually 'Ne Plus Ultra', 'Jordanolo' will also do. (Readily Available)

'Texas' ('Mission')—small nut; white flowers; good for cold winter areas; needs a pollinator: 'Nonpareil' or 'Hall's'. (6,17)

Preserving and Preparing

Almonds, like pistachios, filberts, and other nuts, have both a fleshy outside hull and an inside shell that contains the kernel. Nuts piled together with the hulls on tend to rot, so when you do the primary drying, spread the nuts out in a single layer. Dry almonds in hulls for a day or two, then after removing the hulls, dry in the sun for another week. Store in a dry, cool-place.

Praline Dip
   1/2 cup sugar
   2 tablespoons water
   1/2 teaspoon almond extract
   1/2 cup toasted almonds

   Caramelize the sugar with the water and almond extract. Boil until the mixture is deep brown, approximately 3 or 4 minutes. When sugar is caramelized, add 1/2 cup toasted almonds and bring mixture back to boil. Remove from heat and pour onto an oiled cookie sheet. When cold, break into pieces and pulverize in the blender.
   This exciting confection can be used as a dip for home-grown fruits, as a lining for ice cream and pudding molds, and as a topping for cakes and cookies.

ALPINE STRAWBERRY. See Strawberry.
AMERICAN ELDERBERRY. See Elderberry
AMERICAN GOOSEBERRY. See Currant and
   Gooseberry.
AMERICAN GRAPE. See Grape.

Apple and *Crabapple*
Malus species

Effort Scale
   No. 4 for most varieties
   Pests and diseases are major problems, particularly
      in wet-summer areas (some varieties are more
      resistant than others)
   Fertilizing and mulching necessary
   Picking up fruits necessary

E.4. *'Gravenstein' apples, a popular variety for cooking.*

   Standard-size tree yields large harvest
   No. 3 for disease-resistant varieties and dwarf varieties of apple

Zones
   3—9

Thumbnail Sketch
   Deciduous tree
   Standard, 20—30 ft. tall; semi-dwarf varieties, 12—
      18 ft. tall; dwarf varieties, 6—12 ft. tall
   Propagated by grafting, budding, or from cuttings
   Needs full sun
   Leaves are soft green, 2—3 in. long; new growth is
      woolly
   Blooms in spring
   Flowers are white or pink
   Fruits are edible; harvest in summer or fall
   Used as interest tree, patio tree, small shade tree,
      espalier, hedge; dwarf varieties used in containers

E.5. *Dwarf and semi-dwarf apple trees will grow well in large containers.*

How to Use
In the Kitchen
   The familiar apple is a fruit to eat out of hand in lunches or as that famous snack that keeps the doctor away.
   Cooked apples can become a sauce that, when canned, provides a touch of freshness in winter. Baked apples with hard sauce (butter, sugar and brandy) are sublime treats to the initiated, and dried apples are

popular among campers and backpackers. The many varieties of apple butter make delicious spreads, and a layer of clear, subtly colored apple jelly is equally delectable on bread. Fermented cider kept our fore-bears happy, and, of course, apple pie is the great American dish. The apple is one of our true blessings.

The crabapple is used less as a raw fruit, although its tangy flavor is appealing, and it makes an even more beautiful jelly than the apple. When the whole fruit is pickled it becomes an attractive garnish for any plate. Crabapples and apples are often used as a pectin source.

Note: Not all crabapples produce usable fruits. Be sure you have chosen a tasty variety such as 'Transcendent'.

E.6. Like many fruit trees, apples can be pruned to create a hedge.

In the Landscape

The apple, a deciduous tree, is not only productive but also provides a dazzling show in the spring. The profuse pink buds develop into white flowers up to 1 1/2 inches wide. Two varieties, 'Stark Red Bouquet Delicious' and 'Pink Pearl', have pink blossoms. The leaves of most apples are a soft medium green, and a gray fuzz on the back side of the leaves gives the new growth a gray tone. As the apples develop they become a decorative asset, whether they stay green or turn yellow or red.

Crabapples are even showier in the spring. Their buds are pinker than those of apples, their blossoms rosier, and their fruits are usually more colorful. In other respects crabapple trees are similar to apples.

Apple trees come in more different sizes than any other fruit tree. Standard trees grow as high as 30 feet, whereas dwarf or semi-dwarf varieties reach 6-18 feet. The smaller forms are usable in decorative containers, as espaliers, and as fruitful hedges.

Full-size crabapple trees are usually shorter than apples but standard-size trees are excellent shade trees. Both species form stately yet informal lines along a driveway, and because of their consistent beauty they are useful as interest plants. As with other fruit trees, neither type should be planted in a lawn, because both will compete for the lawn nutrients and water. Also, mowers are likely to nick trees so placed, giving problem diseases and insects a foothold. Finally, in the arid West, lawns stay moist near the crowns of trees, enabling the fungus causing crown rot to develop.

Note: Do not use apple trees near windows if apple scab and codling moth are severe problems. The sprays for controlling these conditions are usually difficult to clean off the glass.

How to Grow

Climate

Apples and crabapples are the hardiest of our popular fruits. A few varieties survive —40F, but most are not that stouthearted.

Both trees grow throughout most of the country except in areas with the warmest winters, where there is little or no winter frost. All varieties have some chilling requirements; that is, they require a certain number of hours under 45°F before dormancy is broken and good fruit can be produced. In mild-winter areas choose varieties with low chilling requirements.

Exposure

To grow the sweetest fruit and to prevent diseases both trees should be planted in full sun.

Soil

Both apple and crabapple trees grow best in well-drained garden loam supplemented with an organic mulch.

Fertilizing

Nutrients need to be renewed annually. See Part Two for details. Both trees benefit from annual applications of compost or manure.

Watering

In climates that have summer rain, well-established trees do not need watering. In dry-summer areas, deep watering is generally needed.

Pruning

For young trees, see Part Two, PRUNING. An established apple or crabapple tree needs only light pruning. Both species fruit on long-lived fruiting spurs. Prune when dormant to cut out weak growth and dead or crossing branches and to control the height

for easy fruit picking. If you are having a mildew problem, thin out some of the branches to improve air circulation. Drooping branches on older trees should be
cut back to prevent them from shading too much of
the lower foliage.

Pests and Diseases

Apples and crabapples are prone to many pests
and diseases. The most serious are codling moth,
apple maggot, San Jose scale, apple scab, mildew, and
fire blight. Dormant spraying is needed in most parts
of the country. See Part Two.

Harvesting

Pick apples and crabapples carefully to prevent
bruising. The fruits of a few winter-storage types
should be picked slightly underripe, but all other varieties should be harvested when fruits are fully ripe.
Quality of ripe fruits left on the tree declines quickly.

A mature standard apple tree yields about 15-20
bushels; a mature dwarf tree yields about 1-2 bushels.

How to Purchase

Forms and Sources

Purchase trees bare root or in containers from local
nurseries and mail-order houses. Some nurseries have
large selections of unusual, "antique," or new apple
varieties. You may want to send to the following for
catalogues: (3,30,60).

If you are curious about the taste of some of the
old-time apples, sample some through a mail-order
fruit company called Applesource. The address is:
Applesource, Route 1, Chapin, IL 62628.

Pollinators

Most varieties of apples need a pollinator; most
crabapples are self-pollinating. Self-pollinating types
bear more heavily if other varieties are around.

Varieties

Only a few varieties of crabapples are grown for
fruit, but hundreds of types of apples exist, all of them
long-lived. Choosing one kind is often like playing
roulette. There are apples suitable for severe or warm
winters, apples that fruit early or ripen late, and apples
resistant to some of the major diseases. Dwarf, middle,
and full-size trees are available. Hybridizers have made
many improvements to help the orchardist. Home
growers can take advantage of these improvements in
seeking the perfect tree for local conditions.

Before making your choice, gather as much information as possible. Consult your local university
extension service and do research at your library.
Organizations exist that are interested in sharing their
fruit-growing experiences, particularly when it comes

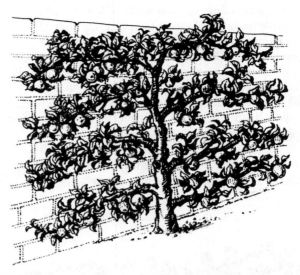

E.7. Apple trees can be espaliered in many different forms.

to apples. Often these groups also can provide budwood for some of the "antique" apple varieties.
Members of such organizations are interested in preserving living wood of hundreds of old-time varieties
whose valuable genes would otherwise be lost.
Examples of these organizations are the North
American Fruit Explorers, the Home Orchard Society,
and the Worcester County Horticultural Society.

BEST APPLE VARIETIES

The trees in this list have been selected because the
quality of their fruit and the strength of their disease
resistance are high and because they are available in
different sizes. Varieties are included that will grow in
each of the geographical areas.

'Anna' superior apple for low-chill parts of California
 and Florida; light green, crisp, and sweet; needs a
 pollinizer. (27,61)
'Fuji'—red fruits; older variety; short harvest season;
 good winter keeper; one of the varieties most resistant to apple scab and fire blight. (17,25)
'Gala'—crisp, arotmtic and delicious fruit; keeps well
 and tastes good fresh; ripens early.
 (6,10,17,30,35,46)
'Garden Delicious'—gold fruits with red blush;
 genetic dwarf 4-6 feet tall; late-summer fruiting;
 new variety. (27,70)
'Golden Delicious'—yellow fruits; great eating and
 cooking; self-fruitful in many areas; good pollinator; very adaptable; fall fruiting; somewhat resistant
 to apple scab. (Readily Available)
'Granny Smith'—yellow and green fruits; low chilling
 requirement; for southern California and Florida.

What Size Fruit Tree?

Just think of the glories of growing dwarf and semi-dwarf fruit trees in your yard. First, you'll have the sheer beauty of the blossoms to enjoy in the spring. Then, in summer and fall, you'll have the fullsize, tree-ripened, easy-to-pick fruits. You might have a dwarf apricot, a dwarf peach, and a dwarf apple in place of one standardsize tree. The three would make for good and varied eating over a long period.

The harvest of most dwarf or semi-dwarf trees is plentiful but not overwhelming. You would have fruit for preserving, but not in such a quantity that you would be forced to give over much time to canning, freezing, or drying, as with the yield of a standard-size tree. Furthermore, dwarf or semi-dwarf trees are easier to spray, prune, and harvest than standard trees, and on the average they bear fruit two to three years earlier. Finally, their size makes them feasible for even the smallest yards.

The practice of dwarfing fruit trees has been going on for a long time, but it wasn't until 1900 that two horticultural research stations in England, in Malling and Merton, put some order into the process. Apple-tree rootstock was sorted, identified, and classified at these stations, and a Malling/Merton (M or MM) number came to have a definite meaning. For example, an M #9 is a tree that grows to 6-9 feet; an M #7 is a semi-dwarf that grows to 12-15 feet. The M or MM number is still part of the name on many of these small apple trees. (There is no correlation between the M number and height.) Other dwarf fruit trees use different rootstocks. Pear is sometimes grafted onto quince rootstock. Peaches, plums, and apricots are usually grafted onto other species such as Prunus Besseyi, P. cerasifera, or P. armeniaca.

Using dwarfing rootstock simply makes the tree smaller; the fruits will be the same as on a standard-size tree. If there is a disadvantage to dwarf trees it is that they are reputed to be somewhat shorter-lived than the standard trees. Also, the M #9 and #26 rootstocks, both in common use, have shallow root systems, so the trees should be staked.

Genetic dwarf fruit trees are different from regular dwarf trees. They are naturally dwarfed but are still grafted for propagation purposes. See PEACH AND NECTARINE for more information on genetic dwarf trees.

E.8. Four sizes of apple trees. From left to right: an 8-foot tree on M#9 rootstock; a 12-foot on M#26; a 15-foot tree on M#7; and a if grown standard-size apple tree, 25 feet tall.

(Readily Available)
'Gravenstein'—green to yellow or light green and red striped fruits; very vigorous tree; widely grown; summer fruiting; world's best applesauce and pie. (Readily Available)
'Honey Crisp'—red fruits; good flavor; late fall fruiting; stores well; grows in coldest Midwest areas. (16,44,60)
'Jonafree'—red apple with characteristic knobs at base; many offspring; midseason fruiting; disease resistant. (24,35,61)
'Liberty'—red fruits; sweet; one of the most disease-resistant apples available; resists apple scab, fire blight, and mildew. (Readily Available)
'Empire'—red and green fruits; snappy flavor; tender flesh; stores poorly; late summer fruiting; quite susceptible to apple scab; has many improved offspring; grows well on East Coast and in cold areas. (10,30,35,44,60,61)
'Newtown Pippin'—green fruits; good eating; excellent cooking; late-season fruiting; grows over wide range. (Readily Available) 'Northern Spy'—red fruits; good for pies; slow to bear; quite susceptible to apple scab but resistant to fire blight; short har-

vest season; favorite on East Coast in cold areas. (Readily Available)

'Pink Pearl'—cream-colored fruits; excellent for eating fresh and for cooking; pink blossoms and flesh. (3,25,46)

'Dayton'—red and yellow fruits; good eating and cooking; mildew and fire-blight resistant and scab immune; new variety. (6,52)

'Red Free Mutsu'—red and yellow fruits; dessert type; good pollinator for 'Prima'; new variety; scab and fire-blight resistant. (17,61)

BEST CRABAPPLE VARIETIES

'Dolgo'—red, tart fruits; delicious for spiced jelly; extremely hardy to zone 3 and disease resistant; beautiful white flowers; good pollinator for apples; heavy bearer. (3,16,24,44,46,52,60,61)

'Transcendent'—yellow fruits with red cheeks; good for most areas. (17,70)

Preserving

Apple varieties differ as to ripening time. The summer apples do not usually store well and must be dried or made into applesauce. Some varieties are just for eating raw and are not good when preserved.

An old New England method is to wrap apples individually in newspaper, pack in barrels, and store in a cool place. Use only varieties designated as "winter apples" or good 'keepers' for this purpose; late fall varieties are usually the best. The so-called winter apples are picked when not quite ripe and are allowed to ripen slowly in a dark, cool place.

Apples can be canned, frozen, dried, made into apple butter, cider, hard cider, vinegar, chutney, apple leather, or apple jelly.

Apricot

Prunus Armeniaca

Effort Scale

No. 4
Mulching necessary
Susceptible to diseases and pests
Soft fruit ripens all at once
Large harvest
Pruning necessary

Zones

5—9 for most varieties

Thumbnail Sketch

Deciduous tree

E.9. With age, apricot trees often take on gnarled shapes. A mulch is used to keep the roots cool in summer.

Standard, 20—25 ft. tall; semi-dwarf varieties, 12—15 ft. tall; dwarf varieties, 4—8 ft. tall
Propagated by grafting, budding, or from cuttings
Needs full sun
Leaves are rich green, oval, 2—3 in. long; new growth is bronzy
Blooms in early spring
Flowers are white or pink, 1 in. across
Fruits are edible; usually harvested in July
Used as interest tree, small shade tree, espalier; dwarf varieties used as foundation shrub, and in containers

How to Use

In the Kitchen

Apricots are 2- to 3-inch-long peachlike fruits, though they are smaller and smoother than peaches and have their own glorious, yellow-orange color, often tinged with red. Tree-ripened apricots are delicious raw, stewed, canned, dried, in preserves and jams, or made into nectar.

In the Landscape

This small- to medium-size deciduous tree can grow as wide as it is tall, 20-25 feet. Most varieties have popcorn-white blossoms which contrast sharply with its almost black bark, making it an excellent interest plant. As they develop, the leaves are bronzy; as they mature they become deep green, and in the fall most varieties turn brilliant yellow. The fruits themselves are decorative. The apricot tree is, indeed, interesting in all seasons. Older trees tend to develop gnarled shapes, and even without foliage or flowers make a definite impact on the landscape.

To produce the best fruit, the tree must be heavily pruned. Unpruned trees produce many blossoms and numerous very small fruits. Many of the flowers are removed in such pruning; thus, one of the ornamental qualities of the tree is sacrificed for good production. Hand-thinning fruits reduces the need for severe pruning.

Full-size apricot trees are useful as small shade trees and are handsome when espaliered. Resist the temptation to plant them in a lawn. Like most fruit trees, they never live up to their potential in a lawn. Dwarf varieties are excellent in containers, as hedges, and as foundation plants. See PEACH AND NECTARINE for more information on genetic dwarf trees. The hardy pink-flowered Manchurian varieties (3,24,29) make useful shrubs in the coldest climates.

The luscious fruits are an extra bonus when you consider the beauty of the tree itself, but fruit dropping can be a nuisance over a patio or near a sidewalk. Therefore it is best to plant full-size apricot trees away from those areas.

How to Grow

Climate

Apricots are as hardy as peaches, but they bloom early so they do not fruit well where there are late frosts. New varieties that bloom later are being introduced. These would be worth a try in protected parts of zone 4; also a possibility in those regions is the hardy Manchurian apricot. Also in zones 4 and 5 try the dwarf varieties in movable containers, sheltering them during the coldest part of the winter and during late frosts. All apricots have a chilling requirement, but those with low chilling requirements are suitable in mild-winter areas. No apricots grow in the warmest winter areas.

Exposure

Apricot trees require full sun.

Soil

Apricots tolerate a variety of soils as long as they are well drained.

Fertilizing

Compost is beneficial in the spring and fall. Avoid overfeeding; it causes weak growth susceptible to splitting and diseases.

Watering

Occasional deep watering is needed in dry summer areas. Be particularly careful not to overwater on heavy soils.

Pruning

Apricots bear on fruiting spurs that live for three or four years. Annual pruning is needed to force new growth. The genetic dwarf apricots need less severe pruning. Follow the same procedure as with peaches, but prune less radically. Thin fruit if the fruit-set is very heavy.

Pests and Diseases

Apricot trees are susceptible to many pests and diseases. A dormant spray of oil or Bordeaux in spring is usually necessary to prevent scale, brown rot, and bacterial leaf spot. Good fall sanitation is a must. Destroy all old fruit and leaves in which disease organisms winter over. See Part Two for details.

Harvesting

Mature standard trees yield about 3—4 bushels annually; dwarf varieties about 1—2 bushels. Fruit is ready to be picked when slightly soft and fully colored. Try not to leave town during the short harvest season or you will return to find 50 pounds of fruit rotting on the ground!

How to Purchase

Forms and Sources

Apricots are purchased bare root in late winter or early spring or in containers through summer. They are readily available from mail-order firms and local nurseries in favorable climates.

Pollinators

Most varieties bear heaviest with cross-pollination.

Varieties

Taste differs less among apricot varieties than with most fruits. The major differences lie in levels of hardiness, blooming time, and winter chilling requirements.

New varieties are being tested for resistance to brown rot and bacterial leaf spot but are not readily available. 'Harcot' and 'Harogem' are two possibilities from the New York State Fruit Testing Station. Research is being done continually to improve the genetic dwarfs, so keep an eye out for the newest introductions. Check with your local university extension service to see which varieties grow best in your area.

The following varieties are recommended:

'Blenheim' ('Royal')—most popular variety on the West Coast. (Readily Available)
'Flora Gold'—consistent bearer of large crops; early harvest; good fresh or dry. (48)
'Goldcot' dwarf or standard; quite hardy. (Readily Available)

'Moongold'—one of the hardiest; should be planted with 'Sungold' for pollination. (Readily Available)

'Moorpark'—well suited for the West Coast; one of the most successful varieties for the Southeast. (Readily Available)

'Stark Sweetheart'—the only variety with edible kernels; all other varieties have poisonous kernels. (61)

'Sungold'—one of the hardiest; should be planted with 'Moongold' for pollination; has pink blossoms. (3,16,24,70)

Drying Fruit

The easiest, and the most environmentally sound, way to preserve fruits is to dry them. Drying uses much less fossil fuel than does canning or freezing; it's a solar method. The sun is there and it's free, so let's use it. Other advantages of drying over alternative methods are its relative cheapness and the comparatively small storage space required by the finished product. I suggest preparing small packets of dried fruits. These can be flattened out for storage and can serve as a single meal's offering. Once large packets are opened, air and moisture can enter, causing fruits to become moldy. Small packets are excellent for schoolchildren, backpackers, campers, and bicyclists, since the dried fruit is lightweight, rich in vitamins, and full of goodness.

If you live in a damp, cool climate where hot sun is not readily or consistently available, a food dehydrator is a good investment. It uses less energy than an oven, is compact, and can be used for all your food-drying needs, not just for fruits. You can dry fruits in an oven, but not in a microwave oven. The latter takes

E.10. When drying apricots, place them close together with the cup side up to preserve the juices.

too long and is too small for any kind of decent-size harvest.

The drying instructions below apply to apricots as well as most other fruit—apples, nectarines, peaches, and pears. Apricots don't need peeling, but apples, peaches, and pears usually do. Remember that apples and pears are usually picked when they are underripe and allowed to ripen in the house.

All the fruits mentioned turn brown when exposed to the air. If the discoloration doesn't bother you, it is a simple matter to dry the fruits after sectioning, pitting, or coring. However, if you prefer orange apricots, nectarines, and peaches and white apples and pears, methods exist for maintaining fresh-fruit color: blanching fruits for 3 minutes in boiling water; soaking fruit in a sodium metabisulfite solution for 1 minute; or sulfuring the fruit with sulfur smoke. The last two methods preserve more of the color and more of the vitamins than the first. They also kill any insects that might still be on the fruit. Ultimately, the choice of method is a personal one. Despite my prejudices against most chemicals, I find that fruits treated with sulfur taste and look better than blanched or untreated, so I offer these methods as alternatives.

Sodium metabisulfite is available in crystalline form at some local canning and supply stores. Directions for drying come with the crystals. The process involves making a solution and dipping the fruits.

To sulfur apricots, place them cup side up in trays made from plywood or recycle the 17 x 13-inch size fruit lugs. You may also use small, wooden, nursery flats. Elevate one tray with stacked bricks so it is 10 inches above the ground, then stack two or three trays on top, with blocks between them so there is good air circulation. Place a cup of sulfur (available from a drugstore or a nursery supply house) in a tin pie plate under the bottom tray. The 10-inch space will keep it from catching fire. Light the sulfur with a rolled-up paper wick. Cover the trays with a large cardboard box, at least 2 x 3 feet, and let the apricots sulfur for at least four hours or overnight.

Caution: Sulfur fumes are poisonous! Do the sulfering a safe distance from the house, and keep children away.

After at least four hours, remove the trays and place them in the sun. Drying takes between six and ten days, depending on the weather. If rain is imminent, take the trays inside. Sulfured fruits may also be dried in a food dryer.

Store thoroughly dried fruits in an airtight container. I use plastic bags with self-closing tops. Squeeze out all the air before closing.

When you are ready to use the dried apricots, pour boiling water over them. This washes them and plumps them up so they are ready to used in cookies, pies, and meat stuffings—money in the cupboard, again.

Preserving and Preparing

My home is situated in what was once a magnificent apricot orchard, and three venerable trees are left in my yard. My friends and neighbors know this versatile fruit intimately and have collected many wonderful ways to use it.

If you have an apricot tree, I highly recommend the booklet *A Harvest of Apricot Recipes*, obtainable from The Los Altos Quota Club, P.O. Box 731, Los Altos, CA 94023. Include $2.25 for tax and handling. The booklet contains 130 apricot recipes for nectar, cookies, cakes, candy, pies, and instructions for drying, canning, and freezing apricots.

Apricot Brandy

1 1/4 pounds rock candy
1 1/4 pounds dried apricots
1/2 gallon inexpensive vodka

Place all ingredients in a glass gallon jar (obtainable from a local restaurant; maraschino cherries and mayonnaise come in this type of jar). Close lid tightly; if the lid is metal, place plastic wrap on top of the jar before closing to prevent metal from coming in contact with the brandy. Brandy will keep well for a year.

Wait at least two months before using, though three months would be better. Decant brandy into bottles with lids. Remove candy strings from the mixture.

Store the brandied apricots in a wide-mouth jar. Seal well.

Use these brandied apricots for fruitcake, nut bread, or in the following recipe.

Maureens Apricot Trifle

1/2 cup stewed brandied apricots, cut into pieces
1 envelope boiled-custard mix such as Bird's Dessert
  Powder (or 1 recipe of boiled custard)
2 tablespoons sugar
1 3-ounce package of ladyfingers
1/2 cup apricot brandy
1/2 pint heavy cream
1 tablespoon sugar
1 teaspoon vanilla

Cover brandied apricots with boiling water. Add the 2 tablespoons of sugar and stew until soft.

Make custard according to directions.

Sprinkle ladyfingers with the apricot brandy and place half of them in the bottom of them in the bottom of a trifle bowl or clear glass 2-quart bowl. Cover with half the apricot mixture and half of the custard. Make a second layer of ladyfingers; cover with the rest of the apricots and custard mixture. Put plastic wrap on the surface to prevent a skin from forming. Refrigerate.

Before serving, whip the cream with 1 tablespoon of vanilla until stiff. Cover the top of the trifle with the cream and serve.

Serves 8 to 10.

Artichoke

Globe artichoke, *Cynara Scolymus*

Effort Scale

NO. 3
Spent fronds need cutting
Plant needs renewing every three or four years
Must be kept constantly moist
Mulching and fertilizing needed
Occasional pests
Winter protection required in some areas

Zones

8—9, more, if given winter protection

Thumbnail Sketch

Herbaceous perennial sometimes planted as annual
  3—5 feet tall
Propagated by seed, from offshoots, or from divisions
  Needs full sun; tolerates partial shade in hot climates.

E.11 Artichokes can line a fence beautifully. Allow a few of the chokes to bloom; the flowers are magnificent.

Leaves are gray-green fronds, 4 ft. long blooming
   time varies
Flowers are lavender thistles, 4—6 in. across
Flower buds are edible; harvest season variable
Used in herbaceous borders, as interest plants, in
   containers

How to Use
In the Kitchen
The artichoke is a giant thistle whose flower buds,
when cooked, are deliciously—and expensively, for
those who must buy them—edible. The bud is served
whole as a vegetable, or, with the "choke" removed, as
an edible serving dish for seafood and chicken. When
eating a whole artichoke you pull off the outside
leaves and use your teeth to scrape the flesh off the
bottom of the leaf. Tender young hearts of artichokes
are canned, marinated or not. The hearts are used as
an hors d'oeuvre or as an addition to salads or
casseroles.

In the Landscape
Artichokes have a dramatic, sculptured look when
placed in the back of a herbaceous border. Their
handsome, silvery-gray, deeply lobed leaves are quite
different from anything else in the garden.

The artichoke is fountain-shaped. Under average
conditions they grow to about 4 feet and spread as
wide. Six to eight plants should be ample for the average family and allow you to let some of the buds
flower. When not picked for eating, they develop into
massive blue-purple thistles that are extremely showy
and fragrant. They make spectacular dried flowers.
Artichokes can be used as shrubs, in containers on a
roof garden or patio, as interest plants, or as accent
plants to line a walk or driveway in the summer. In
areas with warm, arid summers, artichokes tend to die
back in the summer. Try interplanting them with a
few large pink and white cosmos. The cosmos grow
up and hide the thinning foliage. The delightful cosmos reseed themselves yearly after providing cutting
flowers all summer and shading the tender new artichoke fronds.

How to Grow
Climate
Artichoke plants need cool, moist summers and
mild winters. In cold winters they need protection, for
example, by way of an overturned basket filled with
leaves or straw and placed above the roots. In coldest
winter areas they are usually not successful unless the
roots are brought inside during the winter and kept
moist and cool. In hot, early summers the artichoke
buds open too soon and are tough.

Artichokes need to be dug up and thinned out

every three or four years or they will slowly decline
from overcrowding.

Exposure
Artichokes prefer full sun in cool summer areas
and partial shade in hot summer areas.

Soil
Artichokes require rich, well-drained soil with
plenty of organic matter. They respond well to deep
mulches.

Fertilizing
Compost and manure are beneficial. Extra nitrogen
should be added halfway through the growing season
and after harvest.

Watering
Keep these moisture-loving plants well watered;
deep mulches help.

Pests and Diseases
Aphids and snails are sometimes a problem. To
knock aphids off, use a strong jet of water. Hand-pick
snails.

Botrytis, a fungus disease, is serious but not common. It forms gray mold on leaves in warm, muggy
summers. Since there is no known cure, affected
plants must be destroyed. Send them to the dump or
burn them.

Harvesting
Pick the young artichoke buds before they start to
open. The younger the bud, the more tender it is and
the more of it is edible.

How to Purchase
Forms and Sources
Rooted cuttings are sometimes available at nurseries. Seeds are available from the following mail-order
firms: (7,15,20,45,49,53,54).

Varieties
Only one variety of artichoke is usually available,
'Green Globe', but there is a purple one available from
(20,53).

Preserving
Freeze or pickle artichoke hearts, or pickle whole
small artichokes less than 3 inches in diameter.

Asparagus

Asparagus officinalis

Effort Scale

No. 3
Initial soil preparation is heavy work
Vulnerable to some pests
Weeding necessary
Constant mulching necessary

Zones

4—11

Thumbnail Sketch

Herbaceous perennial 3—5 ft. tall
Propagated from seeds
Needs full sun
Leaves are tiny and fernlike
Blooms in summer
Flowers are white to green, insignificant
Female plant has red berries
Young shoots are edible; harvested in spring
Used as a background for a herbaceous border, or to
  line a walk

How to Use

In the Kitchen

Asparagus means spring to most of us. Despite the cost, those first bunches in the market are irresistible to asparagus lovers. Think of the pleasures you could have every spring from a bed of your own. Young, tender shoots are delicious raw in salads or served with flavorful dips. Most aficionados favor the simple approach to cooking asparagus; they like the stalks steamed or boiled until just tender and served with salt, pepper, and a touch of butter. Leftovers can be served vinaigrette the next night. Asparagus can be frozen or canned successfully. These processes alter the taste, but they do bring green to the winter table.

In the Landscape

Asparagus is a herbaceous perennial, dormant in the winter, whose edible spears show themselves early, heralding an end to winter. The shoots that are not cut for eating develop into airy, ferny foliage plants 3—5 feet high that can line a walkway or a split-trail fence, or serve as a billowy background in a flower bed. A row of large red salvia in front of them makes a beautiful combination. An added feature of asparagus are the bright red berries that develop on the female plants. As the plants often bear for 15 years you must plan a permanent place for them in the yard.

How to Grow

Climate

Asparagus grows in most areas of the U S except for the very coldest sections. Much information states that asparagus does not do well in warm winter areas, but I talked to experienced gardeners in Hawaii and Florida whose testimony contradicts that information.

Exposure

Asparagus plants need full sun.

Planting

Start asparagus from seed or year-old rooted crowns (the base of the plant). The average family will need about 30—40 plants.

Because asparagus plants remain in one place for many years, the soil must be prepared very well. You will need about 200 square feet for two rows 20 feet long and 4—6 feet apart. Spade generous amounts of manure and compost into the top two feet of soil. In this spaded area dig two trenches 8—10 inches deep, 12 inches wide, and 20 feet long; then place the crowns in the bottom, about 12 inches apart, with their roots well spread out. Cover with 3—4 inches of soil As the shoots emerge, continue to fill the trench with soil. The trench dimensions above are for a standard vegetable bed. If you are lining a walk or planting in the back of a flower border, you would vary the length of the trenches according to your design.

Soil

Asparagus needs a deep organic soil with good drainage. The pH of the soil should be 6.0—8.0.

Fertilizing

Use organic mulches 4—6 inches deep to provide nutrients and to control weeds. Supplement with a balanced fertilizer in the spring.

Watering

Only moderate amounts of water are needed during the growing season. In the arid Southwest, do not irrigate in the winter.

Harvesting,

Do not harvest until the second year. The first harvest year should be very light; in subsequent years harvest until the spears begin to thin to less than 1/2 inch in diameter. Cut the spears carefully to avoid injuring the crowns. An asparagus knife is available just for this purpose.

Pruning

In mild climates cut down plants when they turn brown; in cold climates wait until spring.

E.12. *Asparagus foliage provides a soft, fernlike background to a perennial border.*

Pests and Diseases

Asparagus beetles are generally the most serious pest. Fall cleanup helps remove some of the breeding adults. Keeping all the spears cut in the spring for a few weeks seems to help also.

The chalcid wasp is the asparagus beetle's natural predator. If you see the wasps around and do not find beetles in great numbers, do nothing. If the beetles are taking over, knock them off into a bucket of soapy water. Spray the larvae with pyrethrum.

Snails and a fungus disease called asparagus rust are occasional problems. The latter is usually associated with very damp weather. Plant resistant varieties, such as 'Waltham Washington', where asparagus rust might be a problem.

Where gophers are numerous they can be a serious problem. Plant crowns in wire baskets for protection

How to Purchase

Forms and Sources

Asparagus is purchased as seeds or one-year-old rooted crowns. The plants are readily available bare root in early spring and occasionally through early summer in containers from local nurseries or mail-order firms.

Varieties

'Mary Washington'—fairly rust resistant.
'Waltham Washington'—fairly rust resistant.
'Jersey Jiant' a new, all male variety developed at Rutgers Univcersity. Produces only edible spears. Very good yield. (7,35,49,50)

Preserving

Asparagus may be frozen or canned.

Avocado
Persea americana

Effort Scale

No. 2 in California

Some watering and fertilizing needed
No. 3 in Florida and Hawaii
Watering and fertilizing needed
Susceptible to disease problems
Large harvest of perishable fruit

Zones

10-11

Thumbnail Sketch

Evergreen tree
Standard, 20—40 ft. tall; dwarf variety available, 8—10 ft. tall
Propagated by grafting or budding
Needs full sun
Leaves are dark green, 4—8 in. long; new growth is bronzy
Blooms at different times, depending on variety
Flowers are insignificant
Fruits are edible; harvest season varies
Used as shade tree and screen; dwarf variety used as large shrub, in containers, and in greenhouses

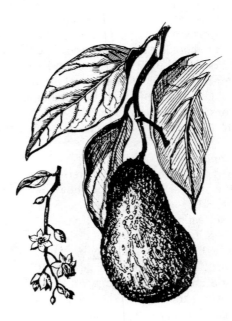

E.13. *A 'Hass' avocado, showing the pebbly skin characteristic of this variety.*

E.14. *Avocado trees form large, spreading canopies useful for shade.*

How to Use
In the Kitchen

Avocados are 3—6 inches long and pear shaped. For those who love them, their buttery, yellow-green flesh is one of the world's more toothsome pleasures. Others can get along without them very well. Avocados are usually eaten raw, combined in salads with citrus, tomatoes, and sweet onions. They make a marvelous dip, guacamole, and can be used in hot and cold soups. Halved avocados can be filled with jellied consomme.

In the Landscape

This large evergreen tree is 20—40 feet tall. Since its spread can grow as wide, the tree gives marvelous shade. In an area where it grows well it is a beautiful specimen. The flowers are not important, nor do the green or black fruits offer ornamental accents. The tree is the thing. It has big, lush, green leaves that are bronzy in new growth. The avocado tree can be controlled by judicious pruning, but it is better, if you have the space, to let it spread—you will have an enviable plant.

Leaf drop is constant, so the tree is a nuisance over a patio, though the shade might make frequent sweeping worthwhile. The fruit does not drop readily. It is usually harvested when mature but hard, and then ripened in a cool dark place.

The dwarf variety is handsome in a tub. It can also be grown as a large accent shrub or as a small screen.

How to Grow
Climate

The avocado is a semihardy tree. It freezes at 18—30°F depending on the variety. Winter flowers and small fruits are damaged by significant frost and the tree needs protection from wind. Avocados are limited to the warmest climates of California, Florida, and Hawaii.

Tubbed dwarf and young trees benefit from covering during the winter in borderline climates.

Exposure

This tree requires full sun.

Soil

Avocados need deep, rich, very well drained soil. Roots will rot where the water table is high. Avocados have a very low tolerance to salt in the soil.

Fertilizing

On most soils in California, the avocado needs only light amounts of fertilizer supplemented with chelated iron. In Florida fertilize avocados in a manner similar to citrus. Avocados should be thickly mulched with avocado leaves or compost. The avocado is very shallow rooted.

Watering

Keep soil moist but not wet for healthiest growth. Never let water sit around the base of the plant.

Pruning

Prune only to control size and shape. Be careful to protect any exposed branches from sunburn. Paint the trunk and any exposed branches with whitewash.

Pests and Diseases

In Florida the main pest nuisance is scale. Diseases of the plant there are cercospora fruit spot, avocado scab, and anthracnose. The trees should be given three or four sprayings with neutral copper. Ask local authorities about the proper timing.

Very few pests and diseases beset California avocados. However, southern California farmers are struggling with a root rot, *Pytophthora cinnamomi*, so in this region avoid planting avocados where they have been grown commercially.

Chlorosis can be a problem in avocados but can be treated with iron chelate. Salt burn can show up as a problem by stunted growth of the tree, or by brown edges of the leaves. If these symptoms appear, deep water the surrounding soil every third or fourth watering. Avoid manures and commercial fertilizers high in salts. If the problem continues, consult local authorities.

Varieties of Avocado

NAME	TYPE	CHARACTERISTICS OF FRUIT	FRUITING SEASON	FORM OF TREE	NOTE
'Bacon'	Mexican	Good; medium size; green	Winter	Upright growth	Consistent annual crop fairly hardy (8,17)
'Choquette'	Hybrid	Excellent; large size; green	Winter	Spreading	Freezes about 26°F; available in Florida
'Duke'	Mexican	Good; medium, size; green	Summer or fall	Moderately spreading	Freezes at about 20°F
'Fuerte'	Hybrid	Very good; medium size; green	Winter	Large	Grown primarily in California; (8,48)
'Hall'	Hybrid	Excellent; large; dark green	Winter	Spreading	Primarily grown in Florida; freezes about 29°F
'Hass'	Guatemalan	Excellent; medium to large size; black, pebbly skin	Spring and summer	Spreading	Grown primarily in California (8,48)
'Mexicola'	Mexican	Excellent; small size; black, smooth, thin skin	Summer or fall	Tall	One of the hardiest; to 18°F; often hard to find; (48)
'Whitsell'	Genetic dwarf	'Hass' type	Summer or fall	Very compact	Excellent dwarf avocado; will grow in container or greenhouse; (48)
'Gwen'	Genetic dwarf	'Hass' type	Summer or fall	Very compact	Excellent dwarf avocado; will grow in container or greenhouse; (48)

Many avocados, particularly the Guatemalan group, will bear heavily one year but poorly or not at all the next. This is the tree's pattern and has nothing to do with the health of the plant.

Harvesting

The fruits are harvested when they are mature but still hard. Fruits are ripe when they give slightly to pressure. Yields are generally higher in California than in Florida; for the varieties given in the accompanying table, a ten-year-old healthy tree will produce about 2—3 bushels of fruit in California, 1—2 bushels in Florida.

How to Purchase
Forms and Sources

Avocados are sold in containers from local nurseries and from a few mail-order sources.

Pollinators

Most avocado varieties are somewhat self-fruitful, but for most varieties growers recommend cross-pollination for heavier crops. 'Mexicola' seems to do well by itself.

Varieties

Three main types of avocados are grown in the

United States: Mexican, Guatemalan, and hybridized varieties. The Mexican varieties are the hardiest.

Preparing

Guacamole

Peel and mash 3 or 4 medium-size avocados. Add 1 diced tomato, 1/2 teaspoon garlic powder, 1 tablespoon lime juice, and Tabasco or taco sauce to taste. Mix well. Serve with corn chips or on sandwiches with cheese or bacon.

Guacamole can be frozen.

Basil

Bush Basil, *Ocimum minimum*
Sweet basil, *O. Basilicum*

Effort Scale

NO. 2
Must be planted annually
Watering and light fertilizing usually needed
Pinching and harvesting can be time-consuming

Zones

Annual

Thumbnail Sketch

Annual herb
1 1/2—2 ft. tall
Propagated from seeds
Needs full sun; will tolerate partial shade leaves are bright green or purple, 2—3 in. long
Blooms in summer
Flowers are white or pink, small
Leaves are edible; used for seasoning; harvested in summer
Used in flower beds, herb gardens, containers.

How to Use

In the Kitchen

The aromatic leaves are used fresh or dried in many dishes—soups, salads, stews, and spaghetti sauce, to name a few. To many people basil is best known as the base for pesto, an Italian herb sauce. To others it is the "only" accompaniment to fresh, ripe tomatoes. In any case, basil is an herb of many uses.

In the Landscape

This warm-season herbaceous annual can grow to 2 feet in height. The leaves of the common variety are 3 inches long and a glossy, bright green. They give a fresh touch to herb gardens, which often are mostly gray. Basil leaves also offer contrast in a mixed-flower bed and make a shining edge to a vegetable border. Planted among carrots basil adds solidity; planted among lettuces it often brings another shade of green. Basil combines well with dwarf marigolds and nasturtiums. The purple-leaved variety looks gorgeous with dwarf pink zinnias, or alyssum. All varieties of basil do well in containers.

How to Grow

Basil grows well in all areas of the country as long as it is planted in well-drained, fairly rich soil, receives full sun, and is watered regularly. Leaves stay large and succulent if the plants are fed once during the season with a fish-emulsion-type fertilizer. Pinch young plants to keep them bushy, and remove the flower spikes for better leaf production.

Pick as needed, for use as a fresh herb.

How to Purchase

Basil is obtained as seed or in small containers from nurseries. Sweet (sometimes called common) basil is the kind most widely available. In addition, there are many others with different tastes and growth habits. There is some confusion as to their names, and a number have two or three names. Nurseries that carry a large selection of different basils are (1,18,45,54,57,65). (18) carries 18 different kinds of basil.

Varieties

Particularly choice are cinnamon basil, which has a cinnamon taste and is decorative with pink-flower

E.15. *Basil is versatile in the kitchen, attractive and fragrant in the landscape.*

stalks; 'Dark Opal' basil with its distinctive purple foliage and pink flowers; lemon basil with its citrus flavor; and spicy Globe', a very compact and tasty green basil.

Preserving and Preparing

To preserve, follow the accompanying directions for drying herbs. Or make pesto, a wonderfully versatile sauce that freezes well.

Pesto

3 cloves of garlic
3 ounces freshly grated Parmesan cheese, or 2 ounces Parmesan and 1 ounce Romano
2 cups fresh basil leaves
1/4 cup pine nuts (or walnuts)
1 1/2 teaspoons salt
1/4 teaspoon pepper
1/2 to 1 cup olive oil

In a blender jar or food processor, combine the garlic, basil leaves, nuts, salt, pepper, and half the oil. Puree, slowly adding the remaining oil. Transfer to a bowl and add the grated cheese, mincing thoroughly. Use immediately or cover with plastic wrap, since pesto turns brown if exposed to air. If you're a garlic fan, increase the quantity to taste. Serve as a sauce for tagliarini or fettuccine noodles. Try combining cooked French-cut string beans with the noodles, or use pesto to flavor soups, spaghetti, grilled fish, or stews.

Pesto may be frozen and kept for four to six months. When freezing, leave the cheese out and add it before serving.

Drying Herbs

These directions may be followed for drying basil, borage, marjoram, mint, parsley, rosemary, sage, thyme, and other leafy herbs not included in the encyclopedia.

Pick the leaves in the driest part of the day. Wash quickly, if necessary, and pat dry. Place the leaves in a single layer on a screen. For quick drying, put the leaves in an oven at a very low temperature (104°F) for a few hours. If you have more time, place the screen in a warm, dry indoor place, such as a garage or attic, and dry for five to seven days. Stir the leaves once a day. When they are dry, store in airtight containers in a cool, dark place.

BAY. See Sweet Bay and California Bay.
BEACH PLUM. See Plum, Bush.

Beans

Bush bean, *Phaseolus vulgaris humilis*
Pole bean, *Phaseolus vulgaris*
Scarlet runner bean, *P. coccineus*

Effort Scale
NO. 3

Must be planted annually
Watering and light fertilizing needed
Vulnerable to some pests
Harvesting is time-consuming

Zones
Annual

E.16. Pole beans have tendrils and will climb a trellis or latticework fence. The flowers of some varieties attract hummingbirds.

Types of Beans

NAME	GROWTH	FLOWER	POD	NOTES
'Royal Burgundy'	Bush	Purple	Purple	Tolerates fairly cold soil; an Improved 'Royalty'; Readily Available
'Royalty' (bush)	Bush	Purple	Purple	Tolerates fairly cool soil; delicious; Readily Available
'Romano'	Bush	White	Green	Flat Italian sugar bean, very tasty: Readily
Scarlet runner	Vine	Red	Green	Perennial; lives through winter in mild winter areas pick beans when immature for tender string beans or eat fully mature as shelled beans; Readily Available
'Thomas' Famous White Dutch' runner bean	Vine	Large; white	Green	Perennial; lives through winter in mild winter areas; strong grower; attracts hummingbirds; pods and seeds delicious,sweet; pest and disease resistant; (1,55,57,71)
Wax beans	Vine or bush	White	Yellow	Many good varieties; look for disease-resistant types Readily Available

Thumbnail Sketch

Annuals or perennials treated as annuals
Vines, 6—8 ft. long; bushes, to 2 ft. tall
Propagated from seeds

Need full sun
Flower in summer
Flowers are white, purple, or red
Seeds and pods are edible; harvested in summer and fall
Bush types used in flower beds, raised beds, and in containers; vine types used to decorate arbors, trellises, and fences

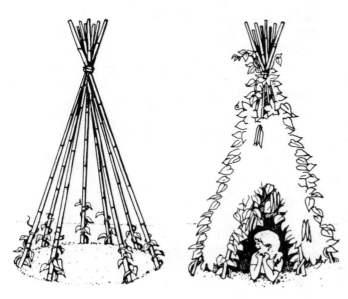

E.17. Bean teepees are a delightful addition tea play area. Wooden or bamboo poles can be used. The interior should be at least 4 feet in diameter. 'Royalty', pole or scarlet runner beans are a good choice; in cool conditions, 'Sugar Snap' peas also work well. Plant seeds outside the circle of poles, and use a deep mulch so that foot traffic does not compact the soil.

How to Use

In the Kitchen

Green beans, cooked until they are just tender, are one of life's better gustatory experiences. All they need is a little salt and pepper and a dab of butter; a touch of grated fresh ginger is nice. Marinated whole beans are an attractive addition to a relish tray. Beans can be dressed up with water chestnuts or cheese sauce for gala occasions.

Haricots verts, small and succulent, are the thin string beans preferred in France; the Italian 'Romano' beans or tender wax beans are meatier. 'Royalty' and 'Royal Burgundy' are purple string beans that turn green when they are cooked; children call them magic beans. Then there are all the different types of dried beans. Some, like kidney and pinto, are quite familiar, but there are numerous "heirloom" varieties such as 'Jacobs Cattle' and 'Lazy Wife' that are great in soups or served as baked beans.

In the Landscape

Whether bush or pole beans are grown as annuals, and they have not been considered particularly useful in landscaping. However, well-grown plants have attractive leaves and handsome, long pods and are not unattractive. Most varieties of beans do not have showy flowers. If you want color, try combining the bush types with nasturtiums or petunias. The pole varieties can be combined with morning glories. Some beans are attractive ornamentals in their own right. For example, the bush form of 'Royalty', with its deep-purple flowers, purple-tinged foliage, and purple beans, is a worthy background for a flower bed. The brilliant, red flowers of the scarlet runner bean, the large, white flowers of 'Thomas' Famous White Dutch' runner bean, and the purple flowers of 'Royal Burgundy' all look decorative on a trellis, arbor, or fence. Hummingbirds are attracted to the scarlet runner and 'Thomas' Dutch' vines.

Help remove the stigma from this family of ornamentals: remove overmature vines before they become yellow and shriveled, and save the hodgepodge of poles and wire cages for the vegetable garden.

How to Grow

Climate

Beans grow in most areas of the country. They are planted after all danger of frost is past; the purple varieties can tolerate colder soil than the standard green string bean. Sow seeds of bush beans 1 inch deep in rows 24 inches apart; thin seedlings to 6 inches apart. Pole beans need a fairly strong trellis or teepee to climb on. Plant the seeds 1 inch deep with the plants 6 inches apart. All beans need full sun and a good, loose garden loam with plenty of added humus. They are best watered deeply and infrequently at the base of the plants to prevent mildew from getting a start.

Beans have their share of pests—beanloopers, whiteflies, aphids, and cucumber beetles. Small numbers of these organisms are no problem. For large numbers, use water sprays to remove. See Part Two for a discussion of these pests.

Harvesting

Beans, whether you call them green, string, or snap, are most delicious when the seeds are still immature. To enjoy as many of them as possible, keep those immature pods picked. With most varieties, if too many pods are allowed to mature the plants will stop producing. I speak of this with some passion, because as a fledgling gardener I planted my pole beans on a fence. After a few good meals of delicious, tender beans, the plants stopped producing enough for a decent family serving. The vines had grown over the fence and produced beans I could not see; when all the pods on the other side became overripe, the plants stopped producing.

How to Purchase

Forms and Sources

Beans are grown from seeds, most of which are readily available in local nurseries and from mail-order sources. Most of the specific varieties mentioned in the accompanying table are usually available only by mail order. One nursery (71) specializes in beans and peas and has a large selection of both. Mail-order source number of European types of beans are (23,57). Nurseries that carry a large number of heirloom beans are (1,5,37,51,53,55). For sources of bean varieties, see the accompanying table.

Preserving

String-type beans can be frozen, dried in a food dryer, canned, and pickled.

Shelled beans can be blanched for 2 minutes and frozen, or blanched for 5 minutes (to prevent insect damage during storage) and dried. Store dried beans in airtight containers.

BEET. See Root Vegetables.
BELL PEPPER. See Peppers.

Bitter Melon
(FOO GWA, BALSAM PEAR, KARELI)
Momordica Charantia

Effort Scale
NO. 2
Must be planted annually in most climates
Large amounts of water and fertilizer necessary
Vines need training

Zones
5—11

Thumbnail Sketch
Perennial tropical vine; treated as an annual in zones 5—8
Tall, to 20 ft.
Propagated from seeds
Needs full sun
Leaves are palmate, 4—5 in. across
Blooms and fruits in summer and early fall
Flowers are yellow, 1 1/2 in. across
Immature fruits are edible; harvested in summer

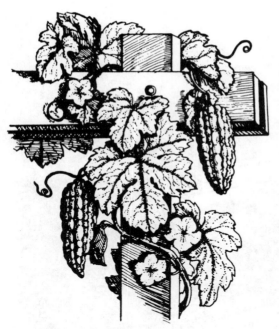

E.18. Bitter melon is a vigorous vine. The fruits are decorative, and the foliage is handsome throughout the summer.

Fruits are green when edible, 6—8 in. long
Used on arbors, trellises, pergolas, fences, and in
large containers

How to Use
In the Kitchen
Bitter melon is a classic Chinese and East Indian vegetable. It is rarely seen in grocery stores but can be grown beautifully in most yards. The melon is 6—8 inches long, green, pointed, and warty—most unusual looking. The flesh is soft when cooked, somewhat like that of summer squash, and has a definite bitter taste due to the presence of quinine. If you like quinine water or strong beer, you probably will like bitter melon and will enjoy eating it in many Chinese stir-fry or East Indian dishes. If you are inventive, you will also find ways to use it in American cooking— steamed, deep fried, sauteed with onions and spices, or stuffed and baked. It also does well as a substitute for zucchini or in omelets. The young leaves may be used as greens.

Caution: Do not eat the ripe seeds; they are reputed to be a purgative.

In the Landscape
Bitter melon has been widely planted as an ornamental in much of the world. Its lobed, deeply veined leaves and small, yellow flowers look striking cascading over a retaining wall or large oak barrel. Try combining the bitter melon with a black-eyed Susan vine, *Thunbergia alata*. The unusual-looking green fruit of the bitter melon is decorative and lightweight enough

be trained against a fence, or, in long, warm summer areas where it grows taller, on an arbor, trellis, or porch. Only the immature fruits are harvested, so if some get too ripe to eat, leave them to turn yellow and but open to reveal their scarlet-coated seeds. The burst fruit looks beautiful hanging down through the rafters of a patio cover.

How to Grow
Climate
Bitter melon is a perennial treated as an annual in most areas of the country. It will survive as a perennial only in the warmest winter areas. In some areas of the Southeast it has even gone wild.

Exposure
The plants need full sun.

Soil
Bitter melon requires a rich, well-drained soil.

Fertilizing
Large amounts of high-nitrogen fertilizer are needed throughout the growing season. Wood ashes have been recommended by some growers.

Watering
The soil around bitter melons should not be allowed to dry out for any length of time. Water frequently if the weather is hot or windy.

Pruning
The vines need to be trained and tied up, with the growth directed to where you want it on the fence or trellis. If you are growing bitter melon in a container, you can provide stakes, or let the runners cascade over the side.

Pests and Diseases
Bitter melon has few pests and diseases as a rule. Occasionally, though, it is bothered by the same problems as cucumbers.

Harvesting
The younger the melon the less bitter it is. Start harvesting before the fruits are fully grown, when the green fruits are 3—4 inches long. Try larger ones if you want more bitterness. Most people consider the fruits inedible once they start to turn yellow. Leave them on the vine for next year's seed and for ornamentation.

How to Purchase
Bitter melons are grown from seeds that can occasionally be obtained from a local nursery but usually

must be obtained through the following mail-order firms: (21,45,49,50,55,58,63). There are no named varieties.

Preserving and Preparing

Bitter melon may be sliced and dried or marinated with vinegar as a condiment. The following recipe may be frozen.

Bhadra's Fancy Bitter Melon

3 cups bitter melon, thinly sliced (as you would a cucumber
1 1/2 teaspoons salt
1 1/2 cups diced potatoes with skins
1/3 to 1/2 cup vegetable oil
4 teaspoons ground coriander seed
2 teaspoons ground cumin
1/3 to 1/2 teaspoon ground cayenne pepper, to taste
1 clove garlic, minced
1 tablespoon sugar
1 tablespoon raisins
2 tablespoons shredded coconut
2 tablespoons cashews
1 teaspoon lemon juice

Put sliced bitter melon in a dish. Sprinkle salt over it and let sit for 15—20 minutes. Squeeze the water out. (If you like your melon more bitter, leave some of the water in it.)

In a medium-size skillet, heat the oil over a medium flame. Add potatoes, and cook for about 5 minutes, stirring occasionally. Add the bitter melon and garlic, and cook until tender—about 10 minutes more. Add the coriander, cumin, and pepper, and stir for a few minutes. Just before removing from the heat, add the sugar, raisins, coconut, and cashews. Sprinkle lemon juice over the mixture just before serving.

For an authentic Indian meal, serve the bitter melon with split pea soup and Indian bread. (Tortillas, while less authentic, can be substituted.)

BLACKBERRY. See Brambleberries.
BLACK MULBERRY. See Mulberry.
BLACK WALNUT. See Walnut.

Blueberry

Highbush blueberry, *Vaccinium corymbosum*
Lowbush blueberry, *V. angustifolium*
Rabbiteye blueberry, *V. Ashei*

E.19. Blueberries are handsome in containers, and since they need acid soil, this is the only way you can grow them if your garden soil is alkaline.

Effort Scale
NO. 3 in acid soil
Constant mulching necessary
Must be kept moist
Susceptible to some diseases
Vulnerable to some pests, including birds
No. 4 in neutral soil
The same problems plus maintaining soil acidity

Zones
3—9

Thumbnail Sketch
Deciduous shrubs
1—18 ft. tall, depending on variety Propagated by seed or from cuttings
Need full sun; will tolerate partial shade in hot climates
Leaves are dark green in growing season and yellow or scarlet in fall, 3/4—3 in. long
Bloom in spring
Flowers are pinkish white, small, bell-like, grow in clusters

E.20. *Before pruning, a mature blueberry bush usually has too many old, weak, or crossing branches. To prune a mature bush, remove about a quarter of the oldest and weakest growth. If fruits have been small, remove some to the top growth.*

Fruits are edible; harvested in summer
Used for hedges, screens, interest plants, ground
  cover, in shrub borders, and in containers

How to Use

In the Kitchen

Blueberries are soft, blue berries that are wonderful fresh, with or without cream. Cereal topped with blueberries or pancakes with blueberry syrup make breakfast a banquet. Blueberry muffins right out of the oven are irresistible, and blueberry pie or cobbler (especially à la mode) is food for the gods.

In the Landscape

The three species named have many assets in com-

mon. They are deciduous shrubs with dark-green leaves in spring and summer, often turning brilliant yellow or red in the fall. Early spring growth, which is bronze in color, is quickly followed by clusters of pinkish-white flowers resembling lily of the valley (blueberries are all members of the heath family, Ericaceae). As summer progresses, the flowers become berries that change from green to red to the typically gray-blue fruit we enjoy. At all times the plants are decorative. In winter some even have red twigs that contrast beautifully with the snow.

Because they differ in size, these plants have varying uses in your garden. Highbush usually grow to 5—6 feet tall, and rabbiteye plants can grow 15 to 18 feet, and make excellent hedges and screens. A variation on the highbush is the half-high, a group of cultivars that range from 2 to 4 feet high. All of these can be combined with other acid lovers, such as mountain laurel, and sun azaleas, to form mixed shrub borders. The lowbush blueberries are not commonly cultivated but grow at the edge of woods or in wild gardens. Occasionally they are used as a ground cover or to line a woodland walk. All the cultivated blueberries make good container subjects because their appearance varies continuously.

How to Grow

Climate

The cultivated varieties commonly grown in the northern parts of this country are the improved offspring of the native highbush blueberry. They grow best in zones 5—8 and selected parts of zone 9. Some varieties are hardy to —20°F.

Lowbush blueberries, which are usually wild, are hardier and are grown in the northern parts of New England, Minnesota, and parts of Canada.

Rabbiteye blueberries are adapted to the southeastern United States. They are less hardy and more tolerant of warm weather than the other two species, and need less winter chill to produce good fruit. Blueberries generally prefer cool, moist conditions.

Exposure

Highbush and rabbiteye plants require full sun in most climates, though they take some shade in very hot climates.

Lowbush plants take full sun or some shade. Most blueberry authorities recommend growing lowbush plants in full sun only, but I remember as a child, on eastern Long Island, New York, picking lowbush blueberries in the dappled shade of an oak woods.

Soil

The most important considerations for blueberry culture are a light, well-draining soil and high soil acidity. Blueberries must grow in a very acid soil, pH

4.0—5.2. (See pH in the glossary.) This factor limits growth in many areas of the country. If azalea mountain laurel, and rhododendron grow in your yard, blueberries probably will too.

If in doubt test the soil. If your soil is neutral or only slightly acid, you can try to incorporate large amounts of acidic organic matter into the soil and apply constant acid mulches, sulfur, and fertilizers to maintain the high acidity. Acidic organic materials include pine needles, peat moss, composted oak leaves, and cottonseed meal. However, the added acidity will be constantly threatened by the surrounding soil, so it must be vigilantly maintained.

Planting blueberries in almost pure peat moss, in a large container, is a satisfactory solution if your soil is strongly alkaline. Do not let the peat moss dry out, as it is difficult to remoisten. Rabbiteye berries can tolerate a less acidic soil than the other types of blueberries.

If drainage is questionable, plant blueberries in raised beds or in containers. Blueberries are shallow rooted. Do not disturb the roots with deep cultivation.

Fertilizing

Adding compost and cottonseed meal to the mulches is beneficial, as are light applications of azalea and blueberry fertilizer available in some areas. On soils with a high pH, chelated iron and magnesium are often needed to alleviate chlorosis.

Watering

Blueberries should be kept slightly moist at all times. Rabbiteye berries do not require as much water as the other species. For all the blueberries, mulches help to keep the moisture in.

Pruning

Blueberries should not be pruned, except to remove broken or weak branches, until the bushes are four years old. Then prune lightly, thinning out some of the oldest branches and spindly, weak growth each year. (See Figure E.20.) Prune in late fall or early spring. If your fruit is undersized, cut back the tips of the canes so only four or five flower buds are left on each twig. That way the plant will not set as much fruit, and the remaining fruit will be larger. Most authorities recommend that you remove all the flowers the first year so that the plant will put its energy into vigorous growth.

Pests and Diseases

Birds are the biggest blueberry pest. Netting is often needed to keep your crop. The blueberry fruit fly, or maggot, can also be a problem. Dormant sprays help control scale if that is a problem in your area.

The major disease problem is a nutritional one. If acidity cannot be maintained, the plants are unable to take up enough nourishment and become chlorotic. The solution is to keep the acidity level below a pH of 5.2 by using acid mulches and fertilizers constantly. Chelated iron will help, too. Another disease is mummy berry, which causes berries to rot. Control this condition by removing rotten berries and destroying them. Canker can sometimes be a problem; plant resistant varieties.

Harvesting

To become completely ripe, blueberries usually need to stay on the plant for a week after they turn blue. Berries are ripe when they will fall off easily into your hand and they are sweet. Taste one to be sure. Most mature plants will yield about 5—6 pints of fruit annually.

How to Purchase

Forms and Sources

Blueberries are available bare root and in containers from local nurseries or from mail-order firms (see individual varieties below). One nursery (3) specializes in cultivated highbush blueberries.

Pollinators

For good crops blueberries need cross-pollination from at least one other variety.

Three or even more will usually give still better pollination.

Varieties

'Berkeley'—large berries; ripens midseason; tall, spreading plants; for northern California, the Northwest, and the Northeast into Maine. (Readily Available)

'Bluebelle'—large berries; grown in Florida and the Gulf Coast. (70)

'Bluecrop'-excellent flavor; erect, tall attractive plant; hardier and more drought resistant than most. (4,13,17,24,25,44,46,52,61)

'Blueray'—large, flavorful berries; ripens midseason; upright, spreading, attractive plant; for New England and the West Coast. (Readily Available)

'Collins'—large, excellent berries; ripens midseason; erect, attractive plants; good for Northwest. (4,30,44)

'Coville'—large berries; ripens late season; tall, open, attractive shrub; very large leaves; for the Northwest. (Readily Available)

'Earliblue'—earliest large berries; tall, upright growth; large leaves; readily available in the Northwest, Michigan, and Northeast. (25,30,61)

'Florablue'—for Florida and Gulf Coast. (Locally
Available)

'Jersey'—mediocre berries; ripens late season; erect,
tall plant; yellow fall color; widely grown in blueberry areas. (Readily Available)

'Northland'—early, medium-size berries with good
flavor; half-high, to 4 ft., spreading; for coldest
berry areas, even northern Michigan.
(3,13,16,35,60)

'Northsky'—superior berries; half-high, to 2 ft.; fall
color is flaming red. (16,46,52,60)

'Southland'-medium-size rabbiteye berries; ripens
late; compact bush; good companion for 'Tifblue'
in Southeast. (13,70)

'Tifblue'—excellent rabbiteye-type berries; ripens
late; upright growth for the Southeast.
(13,61,70)

'Tophat'—excellent berries; new, miniature bonsai-
type shrub, particularly good for containers; for
Michigan. (16)

For more information on varieties for your area,
contact your local university extension service or nursery concerning your particular climate.

Preserving and Preparing

To freeze, wash and pat dry 4 or 5 pounds of
berries, then mix together with 1 pound of sugar.
Place in airtight containers. Use for jam and syrup.

To dry, use firm but not overripe berries. Wash
and pat dry. Carefully spread the berries on a plastic
screen stapled to a wood frame. Place in a warm, dry
place but not in direct sun. If you are drying berries
outside, make sure the birds do not get a feast! Stir
occasionally to ensure even drying. Berries should be
dry in four to five days unless the weather is damp.
Dry berries rattle when stirred and exude no moisture
when squeezed.

To reconstitute dried berries, cover the berries with
water and refrigerate for several hours. Use in pies,
pancakes, corn bread, or any recipe that calls for
canned berries. My favorite use of frozen or reconsti-
tuted dried blueberries is in corn bread. Blueberry
corn bread makes a pleasant morning coffee cake.
Make up your best corn bread recipe and add 1 cup of
blueberries. Sprinkle the top with 1 1/2 tablespoons
of sugar. Bake a few minutes longer than usual.

For a dozen good blueberry recipes (and many
others) I recommend the *Blueberry Hill Cook Book* by
Elsie Masterton (New York: Thomas Y. Crowell Co.,
1959).

Borage
Borago officinalis

Effort Scale
No. 2
Easy to grow
Needs to be planted each year

Zones
Annual

Thumbnail Sketch
Annual herb
1 1/2—2 ft. tall
Propagated from seeds
Needs full sun, will tolerate light shade
Leaves are gray-green and woolly, 3—6 in. long
Blooms in summer
Flowers are cobalt-blue shooting stars, small, grow
in clusters
Leaves and flowers are edible; harvested in summer
Used in flower beds, herb gardens, containers

How to Use
In the Kitchen

Both the leaves and flowers of borage are edible.
The leaves, which taste something like cucumber, can
be used raw to season salads, iced drinks, and wine.
Claret cup, for example, is made with borage leaves.

E.21. *Borage is a perennial plant with gray-green foliage and
stunning cobalt-blue flowers.*

The raw leaves are hairy (the name borage is presumed to come from the Latin *barra*, meaning hairy garment). When cooked like spinach, the leaves lose this characteristic.

The raw flowers are added to salads. They can also be candied for eating or for use as decorations on pastries.

In the Landscape

Borage is a herbaceous annual that grows to 1 1/2—2 feet. Its gray-green, hairy leaves are 3—6 inches long. The flowers are a stunning electric blue, small but growing in hanging clusters. They are a great favorite of bees, which are good to attract to the garden because of their generous pollinating activities. Borage plants are a valuable addition to any bed, be it flower, herb, or vegetable. They make an admirable container plant, and form an eye-catching array when grown with eggplant and purple alyssum.

How to Grow, Purchase, and Preserve

Borage is readily available in seed from local and mail-order sources in all parts of the country. Plant when the soil warms up in the spring. It will grow in any soil but prefers soil that is somewhat dry. It withstands some shade. On occasion it will reseed itself.

Pull leaves off before flowers form so they will be young, tender, and flavorful. Pick the flowers just as they are opening.

The leaves may be dried according to the directions found under BASIL or frozen for use as a vegetable.

Use flowers candied or as a flavor-enhancing addition to a salad, lemonade, or white wine.

BOSTON LETTUCE. See Lettuce.
BOYSENBERRY. See Brambleberries.

Brambleberries

Black raspberry, *Rubus occidentalis;* Boysenberry, *R. ursinus* var. *loganobaccus;* Red raspberry, *R. idaeus;* Thornless blackberry, *R. ulmifolius;* Hybrids

Effort Scale
No. 4
Heavy pruning necessary
Mulching necessary
Vulnerable to diseases, and some pests, including birds
Most types need vine training
Harvesting is time-consuming
Provide winter protection in the coldest areas

E.22. *Raspberries don't necessarily need to be trained on wires and relegated to the back of the vegetable garden. Try training the compact types on a attractive lattice fence.*

Zones
3—9 for raspberry
5—8 for blackberry
8—9 for boysenberry, loganberry

Thumbnail Sketch
Deciduous, bushy plants with biennial canes
5—26 ft. tall, depending on species
Propagated by cuttings, from suckers, or by layering
Need full sun; will tolerate light shade
Leaves are compound, dark green; stems are prickly
Flowers are white or pinkish, 1 inch across
Fruits are edible; harvested in summer and fall
Used as barrier plants, hedges, and some types on
  trellises and arbors

How to Use
In the Kitchen

Red or black raspberries heaped on cereal, crushed and spooned over ice cream and meringues, or dripped over peaches in peach Melba—what elegant fare! Just as superb are boysenberries sun-warm and straight off the vine, in jam, or in hand-cranked ice cream on the Fourth of July. Aficionados can never get enough berries, but at today's prices, who can afford to have them often? Grow a hedge of these berries, and you will have enough for jam, wine, and pie, as well as your cereal bowl.

In the Landscape

Life has few guarantees, but you can be sure that no neighborhood children or dogs will push their way through your brambleberry hedge. A few thornless varieties do exist, but most of these hedges can be used to form impenetrable barriers.

Most types of brambleberries have deep-green leaves with light-colored undersides. They have prickly stems; open, five-petaled white flowers that grow in clusters; and red or black berries. Varieties with yellow and white fruit exist.

Brambleberry plants come in two different forms—erect, shrubby types and trailing, vinelike types. The former can be used as hedges or along fence rows. The latter must be trained on wires or trellises. To use brambleberries in a landscape successfully, you must keep them properly pruned and trained. Laxity will create a nightmare of sprawling, rampant vines.

A particularly attractive variety of brambleberry is the 'Thornless Evergreen' blackberry. It has beautiful, unusual foliage that turns purple in the fall.

How to Grow

The two major types of brambleberries are raspberries and blackberries. The raspberry-type fruits come off the vine without the core, while blackberry types come off core and all. Confusingly, both types of berries can be either red or black. Red raspberries are the most hardy of the brambleberries, and grow on upright canes—narrow woody stems that arise from the ground—or on somewhat trailing vines. Both black raspberries and most blackberries are slightly more tender than the red raspberries and grow either on upright canes or on trailing vines. Some of the trailing blackberries such as boysenberries are quite tender and grow only in zones 8 and 9. Most of the upright blackberries only do well in the Midwest and in the East. Red raspberries and most of the upright blackberries are propagated by suckers, shoots from the base of the plant. Most black raspberries are propagated by tip layering.

Climate

Red raspberries are very hardy. Some varieties are able to survive in milder sections of zone 3. Most black raspberries are hardy only to zone 5. Neither do well in hot summer areas, and only a few varieties are grown south of the Mason-Dixon line or in the Southwest.

Blackberries have a wide range of climate. There is a kind for most climates except the coldest winter areas, the Deep South, and desert areas.

To provide winter protection, in coldest areas mulch canes before the weather gets severe with 6—8 inches of straw. Where mice are a problem, or where canes are long, trench the soil and bury canes in 3—4 inches of soil, uncovering the canes as soon as possible in the spring.

Exposure

Brambleberries require full sun; in hot-summer areas they take light shade.

Planting

Prepare the Planting bed with generous amounts of manure. For hedges, Plant red raspberries 2—3 feet apart, black raspberries 3—4 feet apart. Plant erect types of blackberries 2—3 feet apart and trailing types

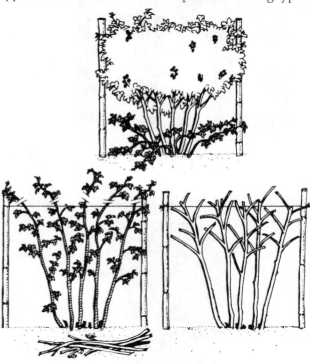

E.23. This sequence illustrates how to prune single-crop raspberries, black raspberries, and upright blackberries. Left: Two-year-old bearing canes are tied to the wire. (New shoots—identified with stripes—are shown emerging from the ground.) Center: Second-year canes that are finished bearing are cut off; 5 or 6 robust new canes are selected and tied to the wire. Right: In spring, the two-year-old canes are tip pruned.

4—6 feet apart. Large, vigorous types such as 'Thornless Evergreen' should be planted no closer together than 10 feet apart.

Soil

All brambleberries prefer soil with considerable organic matter and good drainage.

Fertilizing

Too much fertilizer on brambleberries gives lush growth and few berries. Fertilize with manure in the spring. Keep the plants well mulched with compost or leaves.

Watering

Brambleberries need to be kept fairly moist, but not wet. Do not let them dry out.

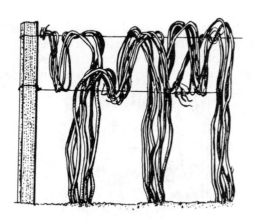

E.24. Trailing types of brambleberries can be woven along a wire trellis.

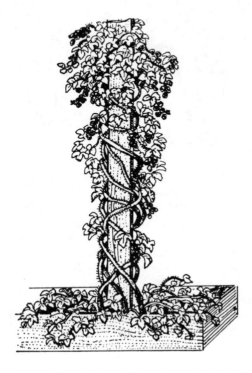

E.25. Long, trailing-type brambleberries can be trained on posts. (Note next years canes at the bottom.)

Pruning

Some varieties of brambleberries are upright or can be pruned short enough to stand erect by themselves. Most brambleberries, however, are easier to control if they are trained and tied to a wire or fence.

Most brambleberries bear fruit on biennial canes. The canes emerge from the ground and produce foliage the first year, go dormant in winter, and flower and fruit the next summer. The canes then die. Depending on the variety, brambleberries may also sucker or root at the tips of branches, and if not pruned back will create impenetrable thickets. All these factors determine the pruning methods.

Single-crop raspberries, black raspberries, and upright blackberries can be pruned in the following way. Figure E.23 shows the bush as it will appear the first year it bears fruit, with the two-year-old fruit-bearing canes tied to the wire. Next year's fruiting canes (identified by the striping) sprawl on the ground below.

After the fruit is harvested in summer, cut the two-year-old canes down to the ground. (See Figure E.23.) Select five or six of the healthiest new canes and tie them to the wire. To encourage new lateral growth along the wire, cut them back to within a few inches of the height of the wire, and cut the rest of the canes off at ground level. In winter prune the canes back to 4 or 5 feet high and Prune the lateral branches back to about 18 inches long. All through the year remove all suckers that come up away from the crown of the plant.

With everbearing red raspberries, pruning is slightly different. The canes bear twice: in fall and again in the spring. After the fall crop, remove the tops of the canes that have borne fruit. The lower part of the cane will have lateral branches that will bear in the spring. Remove these canes completely after they have fruited in spring.

Trailing blackberries, boysenberries, and loganberries are rampant growers and have trailing vines that need support.

Train on wires as shown in Figure E.24 or on a trellis or post as in Figure E.25. Like raspberries, these trailing berries bear on biennial canes. The training is similar to that described for one-crop raspberries, but the canes are longer. After the summer harvest cut old canes down completely. Select five or six vigorous canes from those that have been growing along the ground and cut them to 4 feet long. Train them as shown along the wire or tie to a post.

Pests and Diseases

Brambleberries are not usually bothered by insects. Mites are an occasional problem and can be controlled by dormant sprays. Wilting foliage means borers may have invaded the canes. Where borers are a problem, cut the cane off below the damage. Examine the canes for borers to confirm your diagnosis. If no borers are found, look for disease symptoms described below.

Diseases, rather than pests, are the most serious problem for brambleberries. You can avoid many troublesome conditions by buying only plants that are certified to be virus-free. Furthermore, choose resistant varieties, and when you detect symptoms—such as wilted, mottled, stunted, or deformed-looking growth—remove the plants. Virus diseases are common with black raspberries, and verticillium wilt is a serious problem with red raspberries. Blackberries are prone to more diseases in general than other species and have a particular problem with orange rust, which shows up as red-orange spores on the undersides of the leaves. None of the diseases mentioned has a cure. Remove the diseased plants as soon as you diagnose the problem. Do not compost the plants; burn them or take them to the dump.

Harvesting
Harvest brambleberries when they are fully colored and sweet. You will need to pick them every two or three days. Handle them very gently, as they are easily bruised. The large, trailing plants will yield about 1 quart of berries per foot of row; the erect, shrubby types about 1 quart per 2 feet of row.

How to Purchase
Forms and Sources
Purchase brambleberries bare root in early spring or in containers through early summer. Planting occurs in late fall in milder areas of the country. Buy your plants only from nurseries that carry certified virus-free plants. Combine early-, mid-, and late-season varieties to lengthen the harvesting season. Local nurseries and mail-order firms carry brambleberries. One mail-order nursery (4) specializes in berries.

Pollinators
Most brambleberries are self-fertile.

Varieties
RED RASPBERRIES
'Citadel'—large berries; ripens midseason; vigorous and resistant to leaf spot. (14)
'Heritage'—medium-size red berries; everbearing type, bears July and September; bush is erect and quite hardy. (Readily Available)
'Newburgh'—large red berries; ripens midseason; tolerates heavy soil fairly well; short plants need little support; resistant to mosaic virus. (Readily Available)

'Oregon 10-30' — Everbearing upright plant to 3 feet. Adapted to warm climates. (14)
'Southland'—medium-size berries with an early spring and late summer crop; disease resistant; best for southernmost berry gardens. (61,70)

BLACK RASPBERRIES
'Cumberland'—large berries, big crops; ripens midseason. (Readily Available)
'Logan'-medium- to large-sized berries; drought resistant; resists mosaic virus and many other diseases. (16,46,52)

ERECT AND HARDY BLACKBERRIES
'Darrow'—large berries; long harvest season; erect plants; one of the hardier blackberries. (Readily Available)
'Ebony King'—purplish berries; early season; resists orange rust; hardy to -20°F. (24,70)
'Thornfree'-medium-size berries; ripens midseason; semiupright growth; does not sucker. (Readily Available)

TENDER TRAILING BLACKBERRIES
'Boysen', or 'Thornless Boysen'—large wine-red berry; fairly hardy; long canes. (Readily Available)
'Olallie'—shiny, black berries; one of the best for California. (17,25,46)

Preserving
Blackberries can be frozen, canned, dried, and made into wine or jam.

BUSH BASIL. See Basil.
BUSH BEAN. See Beans.
BUSH CHERRY. See Plum, Bush.
BUSH PLUM. See Plum, Bush.
BUTTER LETTUCE. See Lettuce.
BUTTERNUT. See Walnut.

Cabbage
Brassica oleracea, Capitata Group

Effort Scale
NO. 4
Must be planted annually
Constant moisture and fertilizing needed
Susceptible to many pests and diseases

Zones
Annual

Thumbnail Sketch
Annual or biennial planted as annual

E.26. *Try combining different colored cabbages in one pot, here a soy tub.*

12—18 in. tall
Propagated from seeds
Needs full sun; prefers light shade in hot climates
Leaves are ornamental, curled, ruffled, green, blue-green, red, purple, or blue
Blooms in warm weather
Flowers are yellow, usually not seen
Leaves are edible; harvested in spring, summer, and fall
Used in herbaceous borders, flower beds, containers

How to Use

In the Kitchen

Cabbage is a succulent vegetable used in salads, soups, and such main dishes as New England boiled dinner, corned beef and cabbage, and stuffed cabbage. It is a great favorite served pickled, as sauerkraut or kimchee (Korean pickled cabbage). In fact, nearly every country in the temperate zone has a favorite cabbage recipe. Red cabbage and flowering cabbage are both colorful and tasty in salads. The cabbage is a truly versatile vegetable.

In the Landscape

The puckery Savoy cabbage or the flowering cabbages, which look like giant peonies, are spectacular in raised beds, containers, and flower borders. The foliage of the flowering type, fringed or crinkled, comes in shades of pink, lavender, purple, blue, white, or marbled cream. Together all varieties form a kaleidoscope of color and texture.

I like to plant the round-headed red variety up to its ruffled collar in a soy tub; it makes an elegant composition in color, texture, and form. All the cabbages perform beautifully in containers.

How to Grow

Climate

Cabbage is grown as a cool-season annual; it will bolt and go to seed in hot weather. In cold climates cabbage is grown in early spring or late summer; in the South and warm winter parts of the West, it is grown in fall, winter, and spring. The colorful flowering cabbages must have a frost to turn deep red or purple.

Exposure

Cabbage takes full sun, though in hot climates it takes light shade.

Soil

Cabbages need moist, rich soil.

Fertilizing

Fertilize with extra nitrogen.
Keep well mulched.

Watering

Keep plants well watered.

Pests and Diseases

The biggest problem in growing cabbage is keeping ahead of the pests. The white cabbage butterfly has flitted her way across the entire country, and her cabbage-worm offspring happily chew on cabbage all season long. I have never grown cabbage without a cabbage worm. If you get a severe infestation, the pesticide *Bacillus thuringiensis* controls the worm very effectively at very little cost to the environment. I usually control cabbage worms by picking the eggs off the undersides of the foliage where the butterfly deposits them every few days. These eggs are cream colored and about the size of a large pinhead.

Cabbage root fly is another pest that bothers cabbage. You can prevent the larvae from entering the soil by placing a 12-inch square of tar paper or black plastic directly over the roots of the plant. To do this, cut a slit about 6 inches long directly to the middle of the square and slip it around the plant.

Cutworms often attack young cabbage plants. A good preventive measure is to place a collar of cardboard around each seedling.

Aphids sometimes are a problem too. Try a heavy spray of water or consult Part Two.

Clubroot is a serious fungus disease of the cabbage family. Good plant hygiene is your best preventive here. Buy disease-free plants and do not accept plants from friends who have had the problem. Rotate members of the cabbage family with other vegetable families to discourage the fungus. And pull up all cabbage-family weeds: mustard and shepherd's purse are the most common.

Harvesting

Harvest head cabbages any time after they have started to head up well and before they become so large they split. Mature cabbages can take temperatures as low as 20°F, so do not rush to harvest all of them before a frost. The Savoy types are the most hardy. If a hard freeze is expected, harvest all the cabbages and store them in a cool place, stacking them in straw if possible.

Most cabbages will yield about 3 pounds per 1 1/2 feet of row.

How to Purchase

There are many different types of cabbages: red-leafed ones, Savoy types with their crinkly leaves, miniature ones for small areas, and the multicolored flowering cabbages. Some types are better for winter storage; some grow better in different times of the year; others are resistant to some of the cabbage diseases. Consult seed catalogs and packages to choose the varieties best suited to your needs and conditions.

Cabbage seed is readily available from local nurseries and many mail-order sources. Flowering cabbages are available from: (11,26,39,45,49,66). Large selections of Chinese cabbage are available from: (1,11,37,39,49,58,66).

Preserving and Preparing

The best way to preserve large amounts of cabbage is to make sauerkraut or kimchee.

Spicy Stuffed Cabbage

I created this recipe as a way to use an oversupply of wild-boar sausage. I am aware that not too many people have this problem, but the recipe works equally well with any good sausage. It also makes a good filling for peppers.

1 large cabbage
1 pound sausage meat
1 cup chopped onion
1 clove of garlic, mashed
2 cups of cooked rice
1/4 cup raisins
1/4 cup pistachio nuts or pine nuts
1/4 teaspoon allspice
1/4 teaspoon cinnamon
1/4 teaspoon black pepper
salt to taste

1 cup beef bouillon
1 cup tomato sauce

Prepare the cabbage for stuffing by pulling off the tough outer leaves and washing and coring the head. To separate the leaves, boil the cabbage head in a very large pot of water for about 5 minutes. Check after a few minutes to see if the outer leaves are getting soft and will pull away from the core easily. I usually end up taking the cabbage out and removing half the outside leaves and then boiling the remaining head for a few minutes more until the last of the leaves loosen.

Score the inside midribs of the very large leaves to allow for easy folding.

Brown and then crumble the sausage meat. Drain off all but 3 tablespoons of the fat, and cook the onions and garlic until translucent.

In a large bowl, combine the sausage, onions, garlic, rice, raisins, nuts, and spices.

Mix well. Stuff each cabbage leaf with 1—2 tablespoons of the meat mixture, depending on the size of the leaf. Fold the leaf around the mixture and place packets, folded side down, in a large roasting pan. If you have extra leaves, lay them over the top of the stuffed leaves before you add the sauce. (If you have extra filling, freeze it and use it for stuffing peppers.)

Combine the bouillon and tomato sauce, and pour over the stuffed cabbage leaves.

Cover the pan, and bake for one hour at 350°F. Add more sauce if necessary.

CALAMOMDIN. See Citrus Fruits.
CALIFORNIA BAY. See Sweet Bay and California Bay.
CALIFORNIA BLACK WALNUT. See Walnut.

Chamomile

Garden (or Roman) chamomile, *Chamaemelum nobile* [*Anthemis nobilis*]
Sweet false (or German) chamomile, *Matricaria recutita* [*M. chamomilla*]

Effort Scale

NO. 2
Perennial (garden) chamomile needs trimming and
    some weeding
Sweet false chamomile must be planted annually

Zones

4—10 for the perennial
All for annual

E.27. *Sweet false chamomile provides an informal background for garden areas. Garden chamomile (in the foreground) forms a matlike ground cover in rock gardens and between stepping stones.*

Thumbnail Sketch
Garden Chamomile

Perennial herb
3—12 in. tall
Propagate from seed or divisions
Needs sun; will tolerate partial shade
Leaves are small, bright green, fernlike
Blooms in spring and summer
Flowers are usually small, white, daisylike; some
   forms have yellow, buttonlike flowers
Flowers are edible; used as tea; harvested in summer
Used as walk-on ground cover and in herb gardens,
   herbal tea gardens, rock gardens, and between
   stepping stones

Sweet False Chamomile

Summer annual
2—2 1/2 ft. tall
Propagated from seed
Needs full sun, will tolerate partial shade
Leaves are small, bright green, fernlike
Blooms in spring and summer
Flowers are usually white, daisylike: some forms
   have yellow, bottonlike flowers
Flowers are edible; used as tea; harvested in summer
Used as walk-on ground cover and in herb gardens,
   herbal tea gardens, rock gardens, and between
   stepping stones

How to Use
In the Kitchen

The flower heads of these plants, dried and steeped, make a lovely, refreshing drink, and, as all readers of *Peter Rabbit* know, chamomile tea has soothing qualities. The flavor of the garden chamomile is stronger and more medicinal than that of the sweet false. The latter has a slight flavor of pineapple. Either plant offers refreshing, noncaffeinated beverages.

In the Landscape

Garden chamomile is an evergreen perennial. It forms a carpet of fine, ferny foliage that can be mowed. It can be used as a lawn substitute if it does not get too much foot traffic, and it stays lush if mowed a few times during the summer. It is also useful as a filler between stepping stones and as a specimen in rock gardens. The most commonly grown variety has flowers that are usually yellow, rounded buttons.

Sweet false chamomile is an annual, and has small ferny leaves. It grows taller than garden chamomile, and is used in flower borders, herb gardens, and containers. The flowers of this plant resemble tiny Shasta daisies. It is delightful combined with small yellow marigolds, black-eyed Susans, and 'Dutch Treat' peppers.

How to Grow, Purchase, and Preserve

Both plants thrive in most areas. They prefer full sun but will grow in light shade.

They have no particular soil or pollination requirements, nor do they need to be fertilized.

The part of chamomile used for brewing tea is the flowerhead. To pick the flowers, wait until the yellow center is conelike and the petals bend downward.

Garden chamomile can be bought in nurseries as small plants, usually in flats of 48 or 81 plants, or it can be grown from seed. Sweet false chamomile is usually planted from seed that is readily available from nurseries and seed catalogs.

Place the flowers on a cookie sheet in a very low oven or a very warm place until they are completely dry. Store them in an airtight container.

For a good cup of tea, you need 1—1 1/2 teaspoons dried flowers to 1 cup boiling water.

Let the mixture steep for 5—10 minutes, depending on the strength that pleases you.

CHARD. See Greens.

Cherry

Sweet Cherry, *Prunus avium*
Sour cherry, *P. Cerasus*

E.28. *The silvery, textured bark of cherry trees is a year-round decorative bonus. Their serrated, dark green foliage and bright red fruits complete the tree's visual appeal.*

Effort Scale

No. 3
Vulnerable to some pests, particularly birds
Harvesting is time-consuming

Zones

4—9

Thumbnail Sketch

Deciduous trees
Sweet cherry, standard, 25—35 ft. tall; semidwarf
  varieties, 10—15 ft. tall; dwarf varieties, 6—8 ft. tall
Sour cherry, 15—20 ft. tall; genetic dwarf, 8—10 ft.
  tall
Propagated by grafting and budding
Need full sun
Leaves are deep green, serrated, 2—6 in. long
Bloom in early spring
Flowers are white in large clusters, showy
Fruits are edible; harvested in summer
Used as shade tree, interest plant, large screen; dwarf
  used as hedge and foundation shrub, and in con-
  tainers

How to Use

In the Kitchen

Cherries, glorious cherries! If you have ever lived near a cherry tree, you know the pleasure of picking and eating your fill, and beyond. The luscious red, yellow, or black globes of the sweet cherry tree can be canned, used in jams, in a chilled cherry soup, and of course flamed in cherries jubilee.

Sour cherries are eaten raw too, but their main use is in that great American favorite, cherry pie. Many people prefer the tartness of sour cherry jam to jam made from sweet cherries.

In the Landscape

The cherry is among the most beautiful of trees. Even without its fruit it is a handsome addition to a yard. In the winter the dark, rich, reddish-brown or silver dotted bark lends color and texture, and in the spring both species of this deciduous tree burst forth with masses of showy white flowers. Later, the colorful fruits themselves are decorative among the rich-green, serrated leaves. The leaves are plentiful, and, since the standard-size trees can grow to 35 feet, they make excellent shade trees and tall screens. However, if cherry trees are used to shade a house, a screen should cover the gutters, because fruit that collects there will ferment and smell rank. Also, a tree that needs a lot of spraying is best not planted near a window.

Sour cherry trees are the smaller of the two, growing to only 20 feet. They look fine along a driveway, make an excellent specimen tree that can be admired up close, and are useful as a medium-high screen. Recently, semidwarf and dwarf cherry trees have been developed; these grow to only 8—15 feet in height. They can be grown in containers, as informal hedges or screens, and as small accent plants. The fruits on these small varieties are more easily accessible. See PEACH AND NECTARINE for more information on genetic dwarf trees.

How to Grow

Climate

Both sweet and sour cherries require winter chilling and cannot tolerate hot summers. Heavy rains just before harvest cause the fruit to split. Sweet cherries require about the same climatic conditions as peaches. The most successful sweet cherries are grown in the Hudson River Valley in New York, around the Great Lakes, and on the West Coast. Because they are more hardy, bloom later, and can tolerate more heat, sour cherries have a much broader range. They are grown along the Atlantic coast, in the colder sections of the West Coast, in the Mississippi Valley, and commercially in Wisconsin, Michigan, and New York.

Exposure

Sweet and sour cherries need full sun.

Soil

Cherries prefer light, well-drained, sandy soil. Some varieties of sour cherries can take a heavier soil. All cherries respond well to mulches of compost or manure.

Fertilizing

If the soil is fertile the trees may not need any fertilizer. Light amounts of a nitrogen-type fertilizer should be used if the foliage is pale. But beware: too much nitrogen increases the trees' susceptibility to disease.

Watering

Cherry trees have shallow root systems and thus need to be kept fairly moist. Sour cherry trees are more drought tolerant.

Pruning

Cherries bear on long-lived fruiting spurs. Except for routine maintenance, regular pruning of sweet cherries is not necessary; however, as sour cherries grow older their branches need to be thinned occasionally. Young trees of both types should be trained to have wide crotches, since in untrained trees the crotches are often too narrow, and therefore too weak. Young sweet cherry trees are usually trained to a leader system; sour cherries are generally pruned to a modified leader system.

Pests and Diseases

The specific name for sweet cherries is *avium*, which means, loosely, "for the birds." Birds are the biggest problem. Covering the tree with netting provides protection, and of course the dwarf varieties are easier to net. Growing a fruiting mulberry tree also is some protection, because the birds prefer the mulberries to the cherries, but mulberries do have a very messy fruit drop. During the very wet years, brown rot and cracking fruit are the worst problems affecting cherries. Cherries are prone to most of the diseases that plums get (see Part Two).

Tent caterpillars, black aphids, curculio, and cherry maggots are sometimes troublesome.

Harvesting

Pick cherries with their stems on to delay deterioration of the fruits. Be sure to leave the fruit spurs on the tree when you pull the cherries off, since the spurs bear the next year's fruits. Most mature trees yield about 1—2 bushels of fruit annually.

How to Purchase
Forms and Sources

Buy sweet and sour cherry trees bare root in late winter or in containers through summer from your local nurseries and mail-order houses. (For availability of specific varieties, see below.)

Pollinators

Most varieties of sweet cherries need a pollinator. Be careful to choose the right varieties; not all varieties pollinate all other varieties.

Sour cherries are not reliable pollinators of sweet cherries except in California. Most varieties of sour cherries are self-pollinating.

Varieties
SWEET CHERRIES
'Bing'—the most popular sweet cherry; dark-red fruits, prone to cracking in wet climates; excellent flavor; ripens midseason; needs a pollinator, usually 'Van', 'Sam', or 'Black Tartarian'; spreading tree and heavy bearer. (Standard, Readily Available; semidwarf, 24,30)
'Black Tartarian'—medium-size black cherry; excellent fruits; one of the earliest bearers; a good pollinator for 'Bing'; tree very erect. (Readily Available)
'Emperor Francis'—red, medium-size cherry; ripens late; easier to grow than many sweet cherries; more tolerant of soil type and good disease-resister. (Standard, 44)
'Rainier'—excellent yellow cherry; ripens early to midseason; quite hardy; trees spread more than most. (6,24,44,46)
'Royal Anne' ('Napoleon')—an old favorite; prone to cracking; red-blush yellow; ripens midseason; good fresh or canned; tree large and somewhat spreading; not very hardy. (Readily Available)
'Stella'—The only self-fertile sweet cherry; ripens midseason; a good pollinator for other varieties; a shorter, more compact 'Stella'—a genetic dwarf—recently introduced. (Readily Available)
'Van'—dark fruit; quite hardy; good in borderline areas; bears as a fairly young tree; pollinators, most cherries including 'Bing' and 'Royal Anne'. (Readily Available)
'Windsor'—dark cherry; ripens late; quite hardy and disease resistant. (30)

SOUR CHERRIES
'English Morello'—dark-red fruits; ripens late; good for cooking and preserving. (44)
'Meteor'—red fruits; extra-hardy dwarf; very good for northern gardens. (Readily Available)
'Montmorency'—red fruits; most popular sour cherry; medium- to large-size spreading tree. (Readily

Available)
'North Star'—red fruits; genetic dwarf 8—10 ft.; attractive and hardy; resistant to brown rot. (Readily Available)

Preserving

Sweet-cherry jam is good. Sweet cherries can be frozen or canned for use in cherries jubilee. Sour cherries can be made into excellent jams and jellies, canned, frozen, dried, or used to make wine. To dry cherries, wash fruits, remove stems and pits, and drain on paper towels for an hour. Use a food dryer, following the manufacturer's directions, or use your oven, placing fruits on cookie sheets and baking cherries at a very low heat until they are not sticky anymore. Start drying at 120°F; then raise temperature to 150°F until the cherries are dry. Dried cherries can be used in fruitcakes, cookies, and in any recipe calling for raisins.

Chestnut

Chinese chestnut, *Castanea mollissima*

Effort Scale

NO. 2
Raking is often needed
Occasional pest problems
Easy to grow
Harvesting large yields is time-consuming

Zones

5—9

Thumbnail Sketch

Deciduous tree
60 ft. tall, 40 ft. spread
Propagated from seed or by grafting
Needs full sun
Leaves are deep green, coarsely toothed, 3—7 in. long
Blooms in summer
Flowers are small and white on large catkins, showy
Nuts are edible; harvested in fall
Used as shade trees, street trees, large interest trees

How to Use

In the Kitchen

Roasted chestnuts are a cold-winter treat. City people associate them with street vendors, picturesquely warming their hands over the hot coals on which they roast their wares. Other images are traditionally American: "chestnuts roasting on an open fire," and

that luscious holiday specialty, chestnut turkey stuffing. These savory memories are associated with the native American *C. dentata* or imported European chestnut *C. sativa*, tragically decimated by blight early in this century. Happily, its Oriental cousin, *C. mollissima*, which is relatively blight resistant, is being introduced in many places.

Chestnuts are among the sweetest of the nuts and are delightful both by themselves and used in cooked vegetable dishes. They lend their sweetness to red cabbage, mushrooms, onions, carrots, and sweet potatoes. Chestnuts are at their best as stuffing for or accompaniment to roast turkey, goose, venison, or pheasant. And, of course, with a supply of *marrons glacés* (glazed chestnuts) in your pantry, you will be prepared for the most honored guest. Even an instant pudding becomes an elegant presentation when topped with this delicacy.

Chestnuts are very expensive to buy in the store. Thus, it is only when you are fortunate enough to have your own tree that you can relish them with abandon.

In the Landscape

Chestnuts are magnificent spreading trees that lend stature to any spacious yard. A large chestnut tree cannot help but inspire the thought, "Now, there's a *real* tree!" Chestnut trees are what trees are all about—stateliness, grace, and permanence.

Chestnut trees can shade a hot south house wall and, with their long sweeping branches, make a

E.29. *The serrated leaves of the chestnut are attractive, and the burrs guard the nuts from squirrels and jays.*

E.30. *Mature chestnut trees are magnificent giants that need plenty of room to spread.*

dramatic addition to a yard. They are not only a decorative asset, but, with their edible nuts, a practical one as well. In the eastern part of the country, chestnuts grow well on lawns, unlike most fruit-producing trees. And, wherever these trees grow, their sturdy trunks and branching structures provide firm support for the most ambitious of tree houses.

How to Grow
Climate
With a tolerance to temperatures from −20 to −15F, chestnut trees are slightly more hardy than peach trees and have the added advantage of blooming in early summer, which means their flowers escape damage from late frosts. However, these trees do not grow well in humid, tropical conditions, such as Florida and Hawaii.

Exposure
Chestnut trees require full sun. Young trees are susceptible to sunburn, so keep the trunk covered with whitewash or white latex paint.

Soil
Chestnuts do well in average soils and can tolerate gravelly soils, but they must have good drainage. They grow best in somewhat sandy soils that are slightly acid. Better soils result in bigger nuts and a larger harvest. These trees are intolerant of alkaline soil conditions.

Fertilizer
Chestnuts benefit from annual applications of manure and compost as well as leaf mulches. The roots of chestnuts are sensitive to burning from commercial fertilizers.

Watering
In areas with rainy summers, supplemental watering is unnecessary. In arid summer areas, occasional deep watering is needed.

Pruning
For pruning young trees, see HICKORY. Mature trees need pruning only to shape the tree and to remove dead or crossing branches.

Pests and Diseases
Chinese chestnuts are quite resistant to the blight fungus *Endothia parasitica*, which killed the American chestnut tree in the early 1900s.

Most of the pests and diseases that bother chestnuts are troublesome in the eastern part of the country. Oak wilt causes the leaves to wilt and then to look waterlogged. There is no control, and infected trees die.

The major pest is the chestnut weevil, an insect whose length varies according to the species from 1/4 to 1/2 inch long. The weevils are brown, have long snouts, and lay their eggs in the nuts. When they hatch, the larvae feast on the meat. To control, place a bedsheet under the tree and shake the tree. The adults will fall into the sheet. Destroy them. Also, pick nuts up off the ground daily and keep them in airtight containers to prevent the weevils from escaping and reinfecting next years crop. For moderate infestations, diatomaceous earth dusted on the foliage is effective.

Harvesting
Chestnuts are ripe just as they fall and the burrs start to open. Pick the nuts off the tree or collect nuts from under the tree every few days. This way you will beat the squirrels, who must wait for the burrs to open more widely before they can get to the nuts. Nuts that are left in the sun too long quickly dry out and deteriorate.

A mature tree will yield about 50—75 pounds of nuts annually.

Weevil-affected nuts might still be edible if the larvae are killed in the egg stage before the harvest is stored. To kill the eggs, soak the nuts in 122°F water for 45 minutes. Dry and store.

How to Purchase

Forms and Sources

Buy chestnuts bare root or in containers from local nurseries or from these mail-order sources: (3,9,27,46,49,52,61).

Pollinators

Chestnut trees need cross-pollination. Plant more than one. If space is limited, plant two or three in one hole to form a multistemmed tree.

Varieties

Most nurseries carry selected seedlings. The most common named variety is 'Colossal', available from: (3,6,46,52).

Preserving and Preparing

Chestnuts have a high water content and must not be allowed to dry out. They are best stored in the refrigerator, in a sealed plastic bag containing some peat moss; optimum temperature is 32—40°F

Chestnuts can be roasted in an oven. Before roasting, pierce each nut with a sharp knife; a criss-cross pattern works well. Place nuts in a shallow pan with a small amount of oil. Roast at 450°F for 10—15 minutes.

Peeled chestnuts may be braised for use as a vegetable. Place chestnuts in a heavy casserole and cover with beef broth. Bake covered at 325F until tender, about 1 hour.

CHINESE CHESTNUT. See Chestnut.
CHINESE CHIVE. See Chives.
CHINESE GOOSEBERRY. See Kiwi.
CHINESE PEA POD. See Peas and Snow Peas.

Chives

Chinese or garlic chives, *Allium tuberosum* [odorum]
Garden chives, *A. Schoenoprasum*

Effort Scale

NO. 1
Dead foliage and flowers must be trimmed off in the fall

Zones

All; grow as annual in very coldest areas

Thumbnail Sketch

Chinese Chives
Perennial herb
16—20 in. tall
Propagated from seed or divisions
Needs full sun
Leaves are grayish green, flat, and grasslike, to 12 in. tall
Blooms in spring and summer
Flowers are white, flat-headed cluster, 1 1 1/2—2 in. across, fragrant
Leaves and flowers are edible; used as seasoning; harvested throughout the growing season
Used in flower beds, rock gardens, herb gardens, containers

Garden Chives

Perennial herb
1—2 ft. tall
Propagated from seed or divisions
Needs full sun
Leaves are blue-green, tubular, grasslike, to 9 in. tall
Blooms in spring and summer
Flowers are lavender to purple, cloverlike
Leaves are edible; used as seasoning; harvested throughout growing season
Used in flower beds, rock gardens, herb gardens, containers

E.31. Chives are a natural for containers. You can stretch the fresh-chive season by growing some on a windowsill.

How to Use

In the Kitchen

These herbs have a mild onion or garlic flavor. They are used to flavor and garnish salads, cottage cheese, and cream sauce. A sprinkling of either one on a soup or a stew adds a fresh fillip. Pots of chives are a decorative asset to a sunny kitchen windowsill in winter; garden chives are preferable for this purpose, as Chinese chives go dormant.

In the Landscape

These herbaceous perennials are delightful in herb gardens, rock gardens, flower gardens, or containers. The plants are attractive enough to be used as a border and add variety to any bed, herb or flower. Both species are similar in height but there their similarity ends. Garden chives have bright, blue-green tubular leaves (the specific name comes from *schoinos*, "reed-like"). Their purple cloverlike blossoms come in the early spring, often blooming off and on again all summer.

Chinese or garlic chives have grayish, straplike leaves with white flowers in flat clusters in the summer. Some people think the flowers smell like roses; others, like violets—take your pick. Both chives combine well with frothy pink alyssum or ageratum, variegated sage, and thyme.

How to Grow, Purchase, and Preserve

Both kinds of chives are successful in all parts of the United States. They both prefer full sun, fairly rich soil, and moisture throughout the growing season. The old flowerheads and dead leaves should be removed from both species, and both plants should be divided and replanted every two or three years. Harvest chives as needed, cutting off the tops with scissors.

Garden chives are readily available as seeds or bedding plants. They are also available from friends who are dividing their plants. Chinese chive seed is readily available; plants from (18,35,45,54). Garlic chive seed (57)

To preserve, freeze harvested chives or bring a growing plant of garden chives indoors for winter use.

Citrus Fruits

Calamondin, Citrus *reticulata* x *Fortunella* sp. *mitis*
Grapefruit, *Citrus paradisi*
Kumquat, *Fortunella margarita*
Lemon, *Citrus Limon*
Lime, *C. aurantiifolia*
Limequat, *C. aurantiifolia* 'Eustis' x *Fortunella margarita*
Mandarin (tangerine), *C. reticulata*
Orange, *C. sinensis*
Pomelo (shaddock), *C. maxima*
Tangelo, *C. paradisi* x *C. reticulata*

Effort Scale

NO. 3
Fertilizer and mineral supplements usually needed
Deep watering required, particularly in arid climates
Susceptible to some pests and diseases, particularly in humid climates
Mulching necessary
Some pruning needed

Zones

9—11

Thumbnail Sketch

Evergreen trees or shrubs
4—30 ft. tall, depending on type
Propagated by budding or grafting
Need full sun; some species tolerate light shade
Leaves are bright green, 2—7 1/2 in. long
Bloom at different times of the year, depending on type
Flowers are small, white, fragrant, not showy
Fruits are edible; harvest season varies with type
Used as interest tree or shrub, screen, formal or informal hedge, foundation plant, espalier, and in containers

How to Use

In the Kitchen

For breakfast, you might squeeze lime juice on melon and spread lemon marmalade on toast.

E.32. *Citrus fruits are versatile landscape plants. Dwarf varieties planted around the front of this house include from left to right: lemon, kumquat (in front), orange, limequat, lime, calamondin, a second kumquat, and orange. The large tree is a full-size tangerine.*

Oranges, sliced and arranged with thin onion rings, might be your luncheon salad, and half a grapefruit, broiled with a little sherry, could serve as dessert for your evening meal. Such might be your citrus scenario for one day. On another day you might use these same fruits and flavors in a cream or chiffon pie or in mixed-fruit salads, or blend their juices into various sauces and dressings.

The less common citrus types lend an exotic touch. Calamondin makes magnificent marmalade. Small kumquats and limequats, their sweet rind and sour pulp eaten together, make a definite taste sensation, though whether or not a pleasant one is a personal matter. Both these small citrus preserved make handsome garnishes for meats. Mandarin oranges and tangerines are enjoyable just as they come from the tree owing to their ease of peeling. Canned, they make a delectable addition to fruit compotes and custards. Pomelos, one of the parents of the grapefruit, resemble their offspring but are larger. They are eaten raw and in sections as grapefruits are, but each section has to be peeled of its heavy membrane.

In the Landscape

Citrus fruit trees are as useful in the landscape as they are in the kitchen. These evergreens, whose foliage is bright green and very dense, can be either trees or shrubs. In both forms they are usually rounded, although kumquats and mandarins have a more upright growth than the others. The fragrance of numerous small, waxy, white citrus flowers is famous, and their orange, yellow, or green fruits are decorative in the winter, when few other plants have color.

The fresh foliage, the pleasing shape, the fragrance, the color—all these features make citrus plants a fine addition to any yard in a suitable climate. l rarely design a yard that does not include at least one citrus fruit tree. They fit in with any design and, with prices rising apace, the growers efforts are soon repaid.

Hybridizers have created a citrus for every niche, large and small. Most citrus trees come in standard and dwarf forms. The taller plants—lemon, orange, grapefruit, and tangerine—can shade a hot south wall. They can line a driveway or be used as single specimens, formal or informal depending on how they are pruned.

Take advantage of the famous citrus fragrance by planting a citrus fruit tree or shrub near your front entry—it will welcome your guests most pleasantly. And for your family's enjoyment, plant one on a patio or near a bedroom window, where the heavenly scent can waft inside.

The taller citrus trees can be espaliered against warm, two-story walls, while the smaller and dwarf kinds are useful as espaliers on low walls and fences. The dwarfs are also used as clipped or unclipped hedges, screens, as large shrubs in a border, and in foundation planting. The thorny kinds make excellent barrier plants. All the dwarfs are good in containers that can be moved to a protected corner on frosty nights.

The dwarf calamondins, kumquats, and mandarins lend themselves to pruning that leads to a gnarled and sculptured shape. The result is an exotic, semibonsai effect that is effective on patios and apartment balconies.

Citrus will not grow well in a lawn. They require a considerable amount of water that should go deep into the root zone, about 4 feet. At the same time, air must circulate all around their roots. These needs are not met with the frequent shallow watering that lawns receive. The constant wetness of lawns makes an ideal environment for the development of the fungus that causes root rot, though in sandy soils the problem is

E.33. Citrus fruits, counterclockwise from the top of the basket: pomelo, navel orange, lime, grapefruit lemon, calamondin, tangerine, and kumquat.

not as severe as in other soils. Finally, since lawns and citrus trees are both heavy feeders and compete for the soil's nutrients, neither will do well in conjunction with the other.

How to Grow

Space doesn't permit a more detailed discussion of citrus growing, so I recommend two books: *Florida Fruit*, by Albert Will, Eric Golby, and Lewis Maxwell, for residents of that state (listed in the bibliography); and a definitive book on citrus primarily for western- ers but of interest to all citrus growers: *Citrus—How to Select, Grow, and Enjoy*, by Richard Ray and Lance Walheim (also listed in the bibliography).

Climate

The best climate for citrus is determined by two factors: the amount of possible frost and the amount of heat available. For example, San Francisco is frost- free enough for most citrus to grow and develop fruit but does not have enough heat to sweeten oranges and grapefruit, though limes and lemons do well there. In any case, a citrus climate is a mild climate, so the use of this particular ornamental edible is limited to those parts of the country where the temperature does not fall below 20°F—the mild winter areas of Arizona, California, Florida, Hawaii, and Texas, and the warmest areas of the Gulf Coast. In borderline areas, some dwarf citrus do well if they are moved to a sunporch or a greenhouse as long as the humidity can be kept high. The following list will help you decide which citrus trees, if any, are appropriate for your cli- mate.

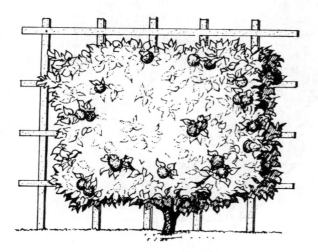

E.34. *Most types of citrus, such as this orange, make beautiful espalier plants. This is a particularly effective way to grow them in borderline climate areas because they can be nestled up against a south wall for extra warmth.*

The following plants accept some frost. They are listed from most to least cold-hardy.

Kumquat
Calamondin
'Meyer' lemon
Rangpur lime
Mandarin
Sweet orange
Tangelo
Pomelo
Grapefruit
Lemon

The following plants need long periods of high heat:

Most sweet oranges
Grapefruit
Mandarin orange

The following need moderate heat:

Lemon
Lime
Calamondin
Kumquat

Exposure

Except in the hottest climates, all citrus prefer full sun. Lemons, kumquats, and Mandarin oranges will take some shade, if they have sufficient heat.

Soil

All citrus require well-drained loam. The plants all tolerate a pH of 5.5—8.0, and respond well to organic matter added to the soil before planting. Mulching with this same material throughout the year is a good practice.

Fertilizing

Citrus need high amounts of nitrogen as well as enough of the trace minerals iron, zinc, manganese, and magnesium. Use a citrus fertilizer, and keep well mulched with compost. To increase cold tolerance, do not apply nitrogen after midsummer.

Watering

Citrus need moist but not soggy soil. Do not let citrus dry out. After trees are three or four years old and well established, they usually need watering every two or three weeks in dry summer areas, more often if the soil is light or the weather windy or very hot. Container plants always need regular watering.

Pruning

Shape trees and remove dead or crossing branches. Keep suckers removed. Espaliered citrus must be pruned regularly to maintain shape. In extremely hot areas, a citrus trunk that has been exposed by pruning should be painted with whitewash or a light-brown water-based paint to prevent bark sunburn.

Pests and Diseases

Citrus is prone to a number of diseases. Consult your local university extension service or nursery to familiarize yourself with diseases that might be a problem in your area. Poor drainage and too much water will lead to root rot.

Some pests can be a nuisance. Aphids, scale, mealy bugs, and spider mites are not foreign to citrus plants. To control these pests, try a water spray first; if that is not effective, try a light oil spray formulated for evergreens. Do not use oil spray if the weather is very hot or if freezing temperatures are expected.

Harvesting

Use clippers to cut fruit off the trees. Handle fruit carefully so it does not bruise.

How to Purchase

Forms and Sources

It's best to buy citrus locally where possible, as the plants are grafted onto rootstocks that are adapted to specific areas. Citrus plants are available in containers from local nurseries, and your nursery can special order from the following wholesale growers

Exotica Rare Fruit Nursery
POB 160
Vista, CA 92085

Pacific Tree Farms
4301 Lynwood Drive
Chula vista, CA 92010

The following mail-order sources also supply citrus; varieties are limited: (2, 8, 46,48).

Pollinators

Most citrus plants are self-pollinating.

Kinds and Varieties

CALAMONDIN

Very small, sour fruit; hardiest of the citrus; handsome upright plant; no varieties.

GRAPEFRUIT

All varieties—large yellow fruits; sweet if given enough heat; handsome, full, large tree or dense shrub.

'Marsh'—seedless, white-fleshed fruits; fruits take 12—18 months to ripen; handsome tree; good in desert heat, the West, Hawaii, and Florida.
'Red Seedless'—red-fleshed fruits; ripens in winter; for Florida.
'Ruby'—red-fleshed fruits; good in desert, for the West.
'Thompson Pink'—pink-fleshed, nearly seedless fruits; for Florida.

POMELO (SHADDOCK)

Relative of grapefruit; very large yellow-fleshed, tender fruits; needs less heat than grapefruit; not eaten like grapefruit, individual sections must be peeled because of heavy membrane.
'Kao'—the variety commonly available.

KUMQUAT

All varieties—fruits have very sweet rind and very sour flesh, are eaten all in one bite; handsome plant does very well in containers, can be trained in interesting shapes; full-size plant varies in size from 6 to 25 ft.; dwarf grows to 4 ft.
'Meiwa' Kumquat—grown mostly in Florida.
'Nagami' Kumquat—grown in the West and Florida; quite hardy.

LEMON

All varieties—yellow fruits; oval-shaped, medium-size tree to 20 ft. tall; when grown on dwarfing rootstock, small tree or large shrub.
'Eureka'—the grocery-store lemon; attractive shrub; few thorns; new growth purplish; grown commercially in California.
'Improved Meyer'—hardiest lemon; very perfumy taste (try one before deciding on it); grown in the West, Hawaii, and Florida.
'Lisbon'—full-size, handsome, small, thorny tree; can take more high heat and more cold than 'Eureka'; grown in Arizona and California.
'Villa Franca'—similar to 'Eureka' but larger and thorny; popular in Arizona, Hawaii, and Florida.

LIME

All varieties—small, 15—20 ft.; 'Bearss'—seedless juicy fruit; hardiest lime; tree quite thorny; grown in California.
Key Lime (Mexican)—fruits small, lemon-yellow color; grown extensively in southern Florida and southern California; seedling limes whose name refers to place of origin.
'Rangpur Lime'—Not a true lime, but a sour Mandarin orange; much hardier than limes; has red-orange flesh.
'Tahiti'—tender; grown in Hawaii and Florida.

LIMEQUAT

All varieties—cross between a lime and kumquat; tree shrublike, quite angular, and open; dwarf variety available.

'Eustis'—quite tender; tree shrublike and open; grown in West.

'Lakeland'—a little more hardy than lime; available in Florida.dense, rounded tree at maturity; some varieties quite thorny; dwarf limes available.

MANDARIN ORANGE AND TANGERINE

All varieties—beautiful, upright-branching, small tree; handsome structure; dwarf available.

'Clementine'—must have a pollinator; 'Dancy' tangerine, 'Orlando' tangelo, or 'Valencia' orange will do; semi-open spreading growth; very ornamental tree; needs less heat then other tangerines to produce sweet fruits.

'Dancy'—fruits peel easily; seedy; upright tree, grown in Florida and the West.

'Kara'—seedy fruits; spreading tree; standard commercial fruit.

'King Mandarin'—seedy fruits peel easily; grown in Florida.

'Owari' (satsuma)—small tree; quite spreading; hardy plant grown to 20°F in Florida, the Gulf Coast, and the West.

SWEET ORANGE

All varieties—large, round formal-looking tree; dense dark-green foliage; large shrub on dwarfing rootstock.

Arizona Sweet—a group of varieties grown successfully in Arizona, comprises 'Diller', 'Hamlin', 'Marrs', and 'Pineapple'.

'Hamlin'—fruit nearly seedless; fall bearing; popular in Florida.

'Robertson' navel—winter and spring fruiting, two to three weeks earlier than 'Washington'; grows in the West.

'Tarocco'—blood orange with red pulp; excellent flavor; lower heating requirement than many oranges; late-spring fruiting; willowy branches and open growth make interesting landscaping tree; dwarf variety makes a very good espalier.

'Temple'—fruits deep reddish-orange color, strong flavor; winter bearing; popular Florida variety; not actually an orange but a cross between a sweet orange and a Mandarin, called a tangor.

'Valencia'—most commonly grown juice orange in California and Florida; not good in Arizona; can be harvested over a long period.

'Washington' navel—most commonly grown variety in the West, eating orange; winter, spring fruiting.

TANGELO

All varieties—cross between grapefruit and tangerine; trees similar to grapefruit but smaller.

'Minneola'—fruits bright orange, tangerine flavor, few seeds; ripens in spring; grown in Florida and the West; for highest fruit production, provide cross-pollination.

'Orlando'—fruits medium-size, flattened, peels easily; tree similar to 'Minneola' but leaves are cupped; grown in Florida and the West; for highest fruit production, provide cross-pollination.

Preserving and Preparing

Most varieties of citrus are self-preserving for a long time; that is, they remain good to eat when left hanging on the tree. In the event of a heavy frost warning, however, the whole crop should be picked or well protected with plastic.

All citrus fruits make good marmalade. The rinds of all types can be candied, and mandarins and kumquats can be canned. Orange, lemon, lime, and grapefruit juices are easily frozen. Put the juice of lemons into ice cube trays. When they are frozen transfer them to plastic bags for frozen storage until needed. Two cubes, water, and sugar to taste, yield a lemonade that anyone can make.

Mandarin Almond Float

1 envelope unflavored gelatin
1/3 cup cold water
3/4 cup boiling water
1/4 cup sugar
1 cup milk
1 teaspoon almond extract
1/4 cup chopped or pulverized almonds (optional)
1 pint jar of home-canned Mandarin oranges (commercially canned fruit may be used)
1 kiwi, sliced

In an 8—inch cake pan, dissolve gelatin in cold water. Add the boiling water and sugar, and stir until mixture is completely dissolved. Add the milk and almond extract. Mix well. Refrigerate until hard.

Cut the gelatin mixture into 1-inch cubes, and combine with the fruit and its juice in small bowls.

Sprinkle almonds on top for a garnish.

Yields six to eight servings.

COMMON PEAR. See Pear.
COMMON SAGE. See Sage.
COMMON THYME. See Thyme.
CORSICAN MINT. See Mint.
CRABAPPLE. See Apple and Crabapple.

Cucumber, Squash, and Melon

Cucumber, *Cucumis sativus*
Melon, *C. melo*
Summer squash, *Cucurbita Pepo* var. *melopepo*
Watermelon, *Citrullus lanatus*

Effort Scale

NO. 3
Annual planting
Vulnerable to some pests
Occasional watering necessary
Some weeding necessary
Training of vining types necessary
Fertilizing and mulches necessary

Zones

Annuals

Thumbnail Sketch

Annuals
Bush types, 2—3 ft. tall; vining types, to 6 ft. long
Propagated from seed
Need full sun
Leaves are light to dark green, large, vary with
  species
Flowers are bright yellow, 1—4 in. across
Fruits are edible; harvested summer and fall
Used in herbaceous borders, raised beds, containers

How to Use

In the Kitchen

Cucumbers, summer squashes, and melons,
including watermelons, are all members of the
Cucurbitaceae family, and are sometimes referred to as
the cucurbits. These succulent fruits are associated
with meals on warm summer days. Crispy cucumbers
served with yogurt dressing are cooling and delicious;
and as crispy dill pickles they are a classic. Try melons
with ham slices, melons filled with vanilla ice cream or
cottage cheese, or melons served in fruit salad—all
great treats that aren't even fattening! Zucchini
sauteed with garlic, basil, onions, and green pepper is
a summer staple in some homes. The cucurbits are a
truly versatile family.

In the Landscape

Most of the cucurbits have large, hairy, rough, ivy
like leaves. Some, like the Armenian cucumber, are
2—3 inches across and light green; others, like the
zucchini, have 2-foot-wide dark-green leaves. All have
yellow, cup-shaped flowers. The flowers of cucumbers

E.35. Bush cucumbers such as 'Spacemaster' have attractive
foliage and can produce a respectable number of cucumbers in a
small area.

and melons are small, and those of many of the
squashes are large and showy.

The bush-type cucumbers, squashes, and melons
are useful in herbaceous beds near a patio or walk.
They all do well in large containers on balconies,
porches, or patios. The vining types can be used on
low trellises, fences, over embankments, or spilling
over the sides of a large hanging basket.

I do not include the long, running squashes and
pumpkins as a choice for landscaping because I feel
they belong in a vegetable garden. These vines get
very large, up to 12 feet long, and unruly. Often the
leaves at the base of the plant get brown, mildewed,
and unattractive before the fruits are ripe.

How to Grow

Cucumbers, melons, and summer squash are all
warm-season annuals. In short-summer areas, seeds
must be started indoors. These plants are usually
grown in hills with two or three plants to a mound. In
containers, they are planted singly. This group of
plants needs rich humus soil and ample water during
the growing season. Do not let the plants dry out.
Keep young plants well weeded. Mature plants can
usually crowd any weeds out.

Young plants in this family are susceptible to cutworms and snails. For cutworms, apply protective

cardboard collars around the main stems. For snails, use traps or bait.

Striped or spotted cucumber beetles are sometimes a problem. Their larvae attack the roots of corn, and the adults attack cucurbit vines. As yet there are no biological controls for large numbers of cucumber beetles. See Part Two for control suggestions.

Mildew is sometimes a problem on the cucurbits, particularly late in the season.

Mildew-resistant varieties are available, and you should choose from them if mildew is a problem in your area. I find that the mildew begins to show up just as the plants have almost finished producing, so I just pull the plants out.

Other diseases affect the cucurbits, the most serious of which are mosaic virus on cucumbers and anthracnose on melons. The symptoms of mosaic disease area mottling or shriveling of the leaves. Anthracnose symptoms are brown patches on the leaves and moldy fruit. Pull affected plants up, as no cure is known for either condition. Plant resistant varieties and rotate your crops to prevent the problem from recurring.

Dwarf bush cucumbers yield about 3—4 fruits per plant; the larger vining types, 8—12 per plant. Most types of melons produce about 2—4 melons per vine. Zucchinis produce about 1 fruit every day or two; the crookneck and pattypan types, about 1 every two or three days.

How to Purchase

The cucurbits and melons are sold in seed form by most local and mail-order nurseries.

Types and Varieties
CUCUMBERS

There are many different types of cucumbers: round, yellow 'Lemon' cucumbers; long, light-green Armenian cucumbers; 'Burpless'; and pickling types. All of the above types are grown on long vines, and are attractive grown in large hanging baskets or tall planter boxes. In a landscape situation, these vines are more attractive trellised or grown against a fence or decorative support rather than on bean poles. A number of dwarf bush cucumbers are available; these are valuable for small areas and for herbaceous borders.

Cucumbers chosen for cooler areas should be resistant to mosaic virus and scab; in warm, humid areas, varieties should be resistant to mildew and anthracnose. Check the list that follows. Cucumbers are picked when they are immature. Do not let them ripen (turn yellow) on the vine, or the vine will stop producing.

The following varieties of cucumbers are recommended.

'Amira'— delicious small fruit, thin sweet skin. One of the best slicing cucumbers available. (45,58,66))

'Armenian'—delicious, long, grooved, light-green cucumbers, edible by those who cannot digest standard cucumbers; vines are long and need support. (Readily Available)

'Burpee's M & M'—standard long, green cucumbers; vines are resistant to mosaic and mildew. (7)

'Bush Whopper'—standard cucumbers on compact bush; suitable for small gardens. (49)

'Euroamerican'— large fruit, thin sweet skin, very productive and delicious. One of the best tasting cucumbers available. (49,66)

'Liberty'—All America winner; dark-green pickling cucumbers resistant to most cucumber diseases. (Readily Available)

'Marketmore'—standard cucumbers; resistant to mosaic and scab. (Readily Available).

'Patio Pik'—standard cucumbers; can be picked young and used for pickling; disease resistant; small compact plants suitable for containers and hanging baskets. (Readily Available)

E.36. 'Gold Rush' zucchini has beautiful golden fruits and decorative split leaves. (Illustration by Hoppner, courtesy of All America Selections.)

'Pot Luck'—full-size 6-in. cucumbers on a very small 18-in. plant. (Readily Available)

'Spacemaster'—standard cucumbers on bush-type plant; mosaic resistant. (Readily Available)

'Sweet Success'— more productive than 'Euroamerican' and very good eating. (66)

MELONS

Numerous types of melons exist. Varieties of muskmelons (also known as cantaloupe in this country) and honeydew are available on compact, bushy plants used in a number of ways in the landscape. Most melons, however, grow on long vines suitable for growing on a fence or over an embankment.

To produce sweet fruit, melon plants need a long, hot growing season. If you plant them in a cool-summer climate, you can increase the heat around the plant by letting the vines run on concrete or by spreading black plastic under the vines in the vegetable garden. If you let the vines cascade over a rocky embankment, the rocks will hold the heat at night and achieve the same effect.

The following varieties of melons are recommended.

'Ambrosia'—standard-size fruit; one of the best eating cantaloupes; long vines, mildew resistant. (49,50)

'Bushwhopper'—cantaloupe, compact plant 2 1/2 ft. wide. (27)

'Minnesota Midget'—small, sweet cantaloupe; ripens in 60 days; good in places with short growing season; 3—ft. vines, good for small planting areas. (24)

'Oval Chaca Hybrid'—cantaloupe; large vines, resistant to fusarium wilt and powdery mildew. (45,50)

'Short and Sweet'—cantaloupe; small plant with bushy growth, resistant to heat, drought, and powdery mildew. (49)

'Oliver's Pearl Cluster'—honeydew; 4—8 in. diameter, compact plant 2 ft. across, needs 110 days to ripen. (49)

SQUASHES

A number of squashes grow on bush plants. The large, deep-green leaves of the bushes are often up to 4 feet across. These plants are particularly attractive in large containers. One or two zucchini plants are usually sufficient for the average family, as this type is such a heavy producer, but three or four plants may be necessary for the yellow crookneck or pattypan types.

Choose from a large selection of zucchini, yellow summer squash, and pattypan types. All are bush-type squashes. The new All America hybrid 'Gold Rush' was particularly bred for small gardens and has a beautiful cut leaf and upright shape. The old standard 'Hybrid Zucchini' has been a prolific producer for years.

WATERMELON

Watermelon is a vining, hot-weather annual. The culture is similar to the other melons mentioned. The watermelon grows on very large vines with particularly beautiful crinkled leaves similar in shape to ivy leaves. Most varieties grow too rampantly to be used easily in a landscape situation, but a few small bush and vine varieties exist. Cucumber beetles can be a problem.

The following varieties of watermelon are recommended.

WATERMELON

'Burpee's Sugar Bush'—6—8 pound melons, bush-type growth covers 6 square feet. (7,12,39)

'Golden Midget's'—small yellow melons, small vines. (24)

'Kengarden'—10—12-pound melons, bush-type growth, for small areas. (24)

'Sugar Baby'—6—pound melons, good vines for short-summer areas; ripens in 70 days. (Readily Available)

Preserving and Preparing

Cucumbers, summer squash, underripe cantaloupe, and watermelon rind can all be pickled or made into relish. Cucumbers and squashes can be dried. Melon balls can be frozen, but they tend to be quite mushy when defrosted. I have successfully used the following recipe (adapted from *The Better Homes and Gardens Home Canning Cookbook*) with both zucchini and Armenian cucumbers.

Bread and Butter Pickles

4 quarts unpeeled Armenian cucumbers, zucchini, or pickling cucumbers, sliced

6 medium-sized onions, sliced

2 green or red peppers, sliced

3-4 cloves of garlic

1/3 cup pickling salt

5 cups sugar

3 cups cider vinegar

2 tablespoons mustard seed

1 1/2 teaspoons celery seed

1 1/2 teaspoons turmeric cracked ice

Combine the first 5 items, place in a large pot, and cover with cracked ice. Stir mixture well and let sit for at least 3 hours. Drain completely. Mix together the remaining ingredients and pour them over the cucumber mixture. Bring to a boil and pack immediately in hot, sterilized jars (1/2-pint or 1-pint), leaving 1/2 inch of headspace. Adjust the lids. Process in a canner in boiling water for 10 minutes. Makes 8 pints.

Currant and Gooseberry

Red currant, *Ribes sativum*
American gooseberry, *R. hirtellum*
European gooseberry, *R. uva-crispa*

Effort Scale
NO. 3
Some pruning necessary
Control of occasional pests and diseases necessary
Harvesting is time-consuming
Mulching helpful

Zones
3—8

Thumbnail Sketch
Deciduous shrubs
3—5 ft. tall

E.37. *Some varieties of gooseberries, such as the plant on the left, have a graceful, draping form. On the right is an upright-growing currant.*

Propagated from cuttings or by layering
Need full sun in cloudy-summer areas; grow well in filtered shade in hot-summer areas
Leaves are medium green, small to 3 in., palmate, decorative
Bloom in spring
Flowers are small, green to violet, not showy
Fruit is edible; harvested in summer
Used as foundation plants, interest plants, to cascade over retaining wall, and in shady borders and containers

How to Use
In the Kitchen
Currants are famous as a jelly. The color of currant jelly looks like something from a cathedral window, and the taste, to keep the imagery consistent, is heavenly. Currant jelly is superb on French toast or scones, or as a glaze to line a tart shell heaped with crème chantilly. Fully ripe currants are a real treat. Eaten out of hand, they are tartly sweet and juicy; in cooking they are used in sauces and sherbets and make an unusual spiced garnish.

To some, gooseberry pie is among life's greatest pleasures. Some people crave it to such an extent that they are driven to rush out in the middle of the night to buy a piece. I have a dear friend who has made this midnight run on numerous occasions. To be honest, gooseberry lovers baffle me, but I accept the fact that when it comes to gooseberries, to each his own.

The small green or pink berries of the gooseberry plant are extremely tart, tasting somewhat like juicy rhubarb. A few varieties are sweet enough to be eaten fresh, but these are generally European varieties that do poorly on the North American continent. The gooseberries grown here are usually served cooked. Some varieties of gooseberries have fruits with small spines.

Gooseberry lovers rave not only about gooseberry pie and gooseberry pie a la mode, but about gooseberry cobbler, gooseberry tarts, and gooseberry "fool," a traditional Scottish dish. Other favorites are gooseberry jams and jellies and spiced gooseberries.

In the Landscape
These medium-size deciduous shrubs fill a void in edible landscaping. Few plants will produce food without full sun, but these bushes do very well in partial shade. In addition, their size makes them ideal for foundation plants or for growing under spreading trees. Try alternating gooseberry bushes and plum trees down a driveway, planting the plums back far enough from the concrete to prevent dropping fruit

E.38. *Currants have interesting leaves, and most varieties have decorative red fruits.*

E.39. *Some varieties of gooseberries are quite thorny. This one is an unusual white gooseberry.*

from making a dangerous mess. Some of the gooseberry bushes are weeping in shape and cascade nicely over a retaining wall or down an embankment. Many varieties of gooseberries are quite thorny and can be effective barrier planting; currants are thornless.

Both currants and gooseberries do well in large containers. The bright red clusters of currant fruits are a nice addition to a patio landscape.

How to Grow

Climate

Currants and gooseberries are extremely hardy; most varieties can be grown well up into Canada. Both plants prefer cool, humid summers and do poorly in hot, dry climates.

Exposure

These berries can take more shade than any of the other commonly grown fruitbearing plants. Some varieties even do well on the north side of the house. In hot climates they are grown with only three or four hours of morning sun or under highbranching trees with filtered sun. In cloudy, cool summers they do better with full sun.

Soil

Currants and gooseberries prefer good garden loam but can take heavy or sandy soil quite well. A soil pH of 5.0—7.0 is optimum. Good drainage is necessary.

Fertilizing

These plants require mulching with generous amounts of manure or compost. Nitrogen should be kept to a minimum, as it stimulates succulent growth susceptible to mildew.

Watering

Only moderate watering is needed in arid climates; usually none is required in areas with rainy summers.

Pruning

Currants and gooseberries need annual pruning. The fruit is borne on new wood and on spurs—short twigs specialized for fruiting—of two- and three-year-old wood.

Thin out the canes—woody stems arising from the base of the plant—in early spring, keeping a balance between one-, two-, and three-year-old canes. Eight to ten canes are usually optimum on an established plant.

If you forget to prune for a year or two or move to a place where old bushes are growing, remove a third of the branches each spring, and in a few years the bushes will be back to full production.

Pests and Diseases

Currants and gooseberries are hosts to a serious disease known as white pine blister rust. This disease is fatal to pine trees but leaves the currant and goose-berries unscathed. Because the disease must live on both pine trees and currants or gooseberries to complete its life cycle, the fruits are banned in a number of states that protect white pines. Before you order bushes, check with your local university extension service to be sure these plants are allowed in your area.

Currants and gooseberries are generally quite healthy, but occasionally a disease takes hold. The most serious disease affecting these plants is powdery mildew. The problem is particularly serious with regard to European varieties and is the main reason why they have not been widely grown in this country. If you have a problem with mildew, make sure the plant has good air circulation by pruning so that the middle is open.

Anthracnose is sometimes a problem. 'Welcome' is a gooseberry that is quite resistant to this disease.

Some unusual virus diseases affect currants and gooseberries, but you can avoid these by buying from a reputable nursery and by examining carefully any gift plants from friends.

Occasional pests affecting both plants are aphids, scale, saw flies, and fruit flies. Generally these pests are no problem, but if infestations get out of hand, try pyrethrum. Dormant sprays help too.

Harvesting

Pick currants by the cluster. Choose underripe clusters for the best jams and jellies. Fully ripe berries are best eaten out of hand.

Pick gooseberries carefully one by one; they have thorns. Some varieties are more prickly than others.

The less ripe the gooseberry, the more sour it is. Some varieties become quite sweet and turn pink or light purple, a sign that they are fully ripe.

Currants yield about 2—3 quarts of fruit per plant annually; gooseberries, about 3—4 quarts.

How to Purchase

Forms and Sources

Currants and gooseberries are available bare root in the spring and in containers throughout the growing season from local nurseries and is readliy available from mail-order nurseries.

If you are interested in growing European gooseberries, which are superior in flavor and more versatile but harder to grow, contact (59). This source has the largest selection of gooseberries (nearly a dozen varieties) in the country.

Pollinators

Currants and gooseberries are self-pollinating.

Varieties

Be careful to choose varieties that produce good edible fruits. Some varieties are grown for their flowers only. The following are the most commonly available.

CURRANTS
  'Red Lake'—red, medium to large berries; adaptable to all currant climates; late season. (Readily Available)
  'White Imperial'—white berries, an improved 'White Grape'. (52)
  'Wilder'—large; red currants; very productive; ripen midseason. (3)

GOOSEBERRIES
  'Pixwell'—large, green berries, easy to pick because the fruit hangs away from the thorns. (Readily Available)
  'Poorman'—red berries, high quality; shrub vigorous and productive. (3,6,44,46,52)
  'Welcome'—pink to red berries, makes red jam; bush almost thornless; somewhat resistant to anthracnose. (13,16)

Preserving and Preparing

Currants and gooseberries can be made into jams, jellies, and sauces. They also can be preserved by canning, freezing, or pickling.

Fresh Gooseberry Fool

2 cups fresh gooseberries (or other berries)
sugar to taste, starting with 1/3 cup
1 recipe of boiled-custard mix (or 1 cup whipping cream and 1/4 cup sugar)

Cook gooseberries with 1/4 cup water and 1/3 cup sugar until tender. Puree gooseberries by forcing them through a sieve or blending in a blender. Chill. Make custard with custard mix, or whip cream and sugar. Just before serving, fold the gooseberry puree into the custard or whipped cream.

DAMSON PLUM. See Plum.
DWARF NASTURTIUM. See Nasturtium.

Eggplant (AUBERGINE)

Solanum Melongena var. *esculentum*

Effort Scale
  NO. 2
  Must be planted annually
  Watering and fertilizing necessary

Zones
Annual; 10-11

Thumbnail Sketch
Herbaceous perennial cultivated as an annual
2—3 ft. tall
Propagated from seeds
Needs full sun
Leaves are gray and velvety, 4—5 in. long
Blooms in summer
Flowers are purple with yellow stamens, 1—2 in. across
Fruits are purple or white; edible; harvested in summer
Used in flower beds, herb gardens, raised beds, containers

How to Use
In the Kitchen
Ratatouille, moussaka, parmigiana—the names of eggplant dishes indicate the area of origin of this versatile plant. Although eggplant, a member of the potato family, is often used in combination with meats or other vegetables, it has a distinct life of its own when flavored with olive oil and garlic, soy sauce, or mixed herbs and broiled. Eggplant caviar, in all its varieties, is a conversation piece when served with dark bread in a colorful pottery bowl or a shell made from a hollowed-out eggplant.

In the Landscape
Eggplant is a tender, herbaceous perennial that is usually grown as an annual in the United States. It grows to 3 feet, and because it is beautiful in all phases of its growth is an addition to any part of the garden. Its leaves are large and lobed, and have a definite purple overtone. The gracefully drooping blossoms are purple with contrasting yellow stamens. The dark-purple, shining fruits are either large and round or oval or, in the Japanese type, smaller and more slender. Some white, yellow, and striped eggplants exist too. All the fruits are decorative, usable in a border or alone in a decorative container. For a spectacle, try planting eggplants against a background of cleome and surrounding them with blue ageratum, purple basil, chives, and thyme.

How to Grow
The eggplant's climate requirements are similar to that of its relative, the tomato. Eggplants are susceptible to freezing, so start seeds 6—8 weeks before the date of your last frost. Plant the seeds 1/4 inch deep, in its or flats. When the soil has warmed up, place the plants 18 inches apart and water well. Eggplants grow best in a well-drained garden loam that is fertilized with blood meal and manure or fish emulsion about three times, during the growing season. They need moderate watering and should never be allowed to dry out.

Flea beetles, spider mites, and whiteflies can be a nuisance, and mildew will develop in too humid climates. Treat flea beetles with rotenone. Verticillium wilt can be a problem. Choose resistant varieties if it is a problem in your area. If verticillium wilt or flea beetles disfigure your plants, grow them in the vegetable garden, not in the flower border.

How to Purchase
Many varieties of eggplant are available, and all are beautiful. 'Black Beauty' is a common standard-size fruit, 'Japanese' is a fruit of smaller size, and 'White Beauty' produces an unusual and decorative white-skinned fruit. 'Burpee Hybrid' is more resistant to drought and disease than other varieties. Eggplant seed is readily available from the major vegetable-seed catalog firms. Many unusual European varieties are available from (57), Oriental varieties from (21), and heirloom varieties from (55).

E.40. All eggplants grow well in containers. This variety is 'Black Beauty'.

The fruit is ready to pick when it is full colored but before it begins to lose any of its sheen, 60—80 days depending on the variety. To help prevent fruits from deteriorating, they should be cut rather than pulled from the plant. Plants will produce more if fruits are picked regularly. Average annual yields are 6—8 fruits per plant.

Preserving and Preparing

Except when prepared as a luxury item such as pickled baby eggplant, this vegetable is used fresh.

Eggplant Caviar

1 large eggplant (about 1 1/2 pounds)
1/2 cup large eggplant (about 1 1/2 pounds)
1/2 cup scallions including some green top, chopped fine
3 tablespoons lemon juice
1 tablespoon catsup
1 teaspoon salt
dash of coarse ground pepper
1 tablespoon olive oil

Prick skin of eggplant. Bake whole on cookie sheet in 400°F oven until soft, about 45 minutes. Remove from oven and cool until eggplant can be handled. Cut in half and scoop out flesh. Discard skin. Mash flesh and beat smooth. Add other ingredients, mixing well. Let mixture stand overnight. Serve with black bread. The caviar can be garnished with black olives, fresh dill, parsley, or chives.

To make an eggplant serving dish, slice a thin piece lengthwise from a raw eggplant.

Scoop out the pulp, leaving about a 2-inch rim. Brush the rim and the inside of the shell with lemon juice. Fill with eggplant caviar.

Elderberry

American or sweet elderberry, *Sambucus canadensis*

Effort Scale

NO. 3
Suckers must be removed on some varieties
Pruning necessary in early spring
Protection from birds necessary
Harvesting and processing are time-consuming

Zones

2—9

E.41. *Elderberries have handsome cut leaves that partially hide clusters of deep-purple berries.*

Thumbnail Sketch

Deciduous shrub or tree
6—10 ft. tall
Propagated from seeds, cuttings, or suckers
Needs full sun, will tolerate some shade
Leaves are divided into leaflets, usually seven to a leaf; medium green; 6 in. long
Blooms in spring
Flowers are large, white, grow in clusters, fragrant, 6—10 in. across
Fruits and flowers are edible; harvested in summer
Used for informal hedges, screens, shrub borders

How to Use

In the Kitchen

The, small blue or purplish-black fruits of the elderberry are an excellent source of vitamin C. These berries are a great favorite of birds; humans usually enjoy them cooked in pies and jellies or fermented in wine. The dried berries are used to make a fruity, flavorful tea much sought after by herb-tea aficionados. In some households the flat-topped flower clusters are combined with pancake batter to make elder-blow fritters, described as a springtime treat by those who have eaten them.

Caution: The fruits of most red elderberries are not edible.

In the Landscape

Many types of elderberries grow wild in many areas of the country. Some species grow very tall, to 50 ft. These wild elderberries are usually rampant and sprawling, and are best reserved for wild gardens and backlot areas. Hybridizers have developed a number of varieties that are less unruly and make handsome additions to the yard.

These hybrids of the American elderberry are hardy deciduous shrubs that can grow to 6—10 ft. and can be pruned to a clumping, somewhat fountain-shaped shrub.

Elderberries have magnificent clusters of white, fragrant flowers, decorative berries, and long compound leaves made up of leaflets up to 6 in. long. This combination of features makes them useful in many landscapes. Use them as you would spirea, lilacs, or other large deciduous shrubs. Elderberries are excellent as informal hedges, screens, and in shrub borders.

How to Grow

Climate

Elderberries are extremely hardy. Wild varieties grow from Florida to Nova Scotia and as far west as California. However, the new hybrid varieties are seldom grown except in cold winter climates. The new varieties are experimental in the colder parts of the West, but star in the Midwest and Northeast.

Exposure

They require full sun, but will tolerate some shade.

E.42. Cultivated elderberries have a graceful, informal shape and produce clusters of white flowers.

Soil

To fruit well, elderberries require a moist, fertile soil. Wet conditions are tolerated with good drainage.

Fertilizing

These plants respond well to compost once a year.

Watering

They need average water but will accept much if drainage is good

Pruning

In early spring, bushes should be cut back by one-half to encourage fruiting wood and to keep the size and shape under control. Prune off suckers extending more than 2 feet from the crown of the plant to keep the shrub under control.

Pests and Diseases

Birds are the chief pests. Pick berries as soon as they ripen. Net the bushes if possible. The birds can strip the bushes overnight.

Harvesting

Berries are ripe when they are slightly soft and deep colored. The birds will be your guide.

How to Purchase

Forms and Sources

Elderberries are available bare root or in containers from local nurseries and the following mail-order sources: (3,6,13,44,60,64).

Pollinators

Cross-pollination is needed. Plant more than one variety unless wild ones are nearby.

Varieties

All of the following are hybrids and grow best in cold winter regions.

'Adams'—most often planted; large plant with large berries and clusters; early fruiting; good for early frost areas. (3,13,35,44,60)

'Johns Improved'—large berries; plant 5-6 ft. tall. (44,60)

'Nova'—large bush; heavy bearer; sweet, early ripening fruits. (3,13)

'York'—large bush known for its large berries; ripens late. (3,35,52,60)

Preserving and Preparing

Elderberries can be frozen, canned, dried, or made into jellies, jams, or wine.

Elderberry Jelly

    3 pounds fully ripe elderberries
    1/4 cup lemon juice
    4 1/2 cups sugar
    1 3/4-ounce package powdered pectin

Wash, stem, and crush berries. In a heavy pot, cook gently until juice starts flowing; then simmer for 15 minutes. Strain berries in a jelly bag or through cheesecloth. Combine 3 cups of berry juice with lemon juice in a large cook pot. Follow the standard procedure for making jelly with powdered pectin.

ENDIVE. See Greens.
ENGLISH WALNUT. See Walnut.
ESCAROLE. See Greens.
EUROPEAN FILBERT. See Filbert.
EUROPEAN GOOSEBERRY. See Currant and Gooseberry.
EUROPEAN GRAPE. See Grape.
EUROPEAN PEAR. See Pear.
EUROPEAN PLUM. See Plum.

Fig

Ficus carica

Effort Scale
    NO. 2

E.43. 'Black Mission' figs hang from the branch, protected by dramatic palmate leaves.

Raking of spoiled fruits and dead leaves necessary
Sizable harvest

Zones
    8—11

Thumbnail Sketch
Deciduous tree
Standard, 15—30 ft. tall; dwarf varieties, to 10 ft.
Propagated by grafting, air layering, or from cuttings
Needs full sun
Leaves are large, deeply lobed, palmate; 4—9 in. long
Usually "blooms" in summer
Flowers are insignificant
Fruits are edible; harvested in summer and fall
Used as shade tree, interest tree, espalier, large
    shrub, screen, and in containers

E.44. Fig trees grown in western climates become large, spreading shade trees. In cold climates, they occasionally freeze back and regrow as large shrubs.

How to Use
In the Kitchen

A ripe, plump, soft fig—black, brown, or green—is a real sweetmeat. Its sweetness makes it useful in pastry and cookie fillings. Fig newtons are almost a standard part of growing up, and dried figs are among everyone's favorite dried fruits.

The so-called "fruits" of the fig are not true fruits, but actually fleshy receptacles for the tiny flowers that grow inside.

In the Landscape

The fig tree is a beauty the year round. Its smooth gray bark, reminiscent of an elephant's hide, is dramatic against a sodden winter sky. In the spring and

Fig 67

summer this bark contrasts sharply with the tree's rich-green, deeply lobed leaves. In fall, in most climates, the leaves turn bright yellow. The trunk can become gnarled with age.

Although the fig tree can grow to 30 feet, it can be kept pruned to 15 feet. As a large tree the fig offers dense shade. As a small tree or shrub, in or out of a container, it makes a superb accent plant. Its interesting bark and sturdy branches lend themselves to training as a handsome espalier.

The softness of figs makes fruit drop a nuisance if the tree is planted too near a patio or deck, but the close-up beauty of the plant makes watchful picking worthwhile.

How to Grow

Climate

The mature fig tree is semihardy to about 15°F. In colder areas figs should be planted near a south or west wall and given extra protection or planted in tubs. The tubs should be moved to a protected area during the coldest periods and watered once a month. The harvest from container plants will be limited but worth the effort. In zone 8, where it often freezes, and in much of the Southeast, the fig is usually grown as a large shrub.

Exposure

Figs require full sun. The more heat they receive the sweeter the fruits become.

Soil

Figs fruit best in medium to poor soil but need good drainage. Sometimes they are planted in containers if the soil is too rich; this restrains their roots, forcing them to bear well. Add lime in acid areas.

Fertilizing

Use organic matter for fertilizer. Avoid adding nitrogen, however, because it leads to foliage rather than fruit production. Do not apply nitrogen fertilizers unless the tree is producing less than 1 foot of new growth a year.

Watering

Figs are drought tolerant once established, but optimum fruit production in arid climates will result from an occasional deep watering. Do not water once fruit has started to enlarge or the figs will split. In the Southeast, sandy soils and nematode problems often make regular supplemental watering necessary.

Pruning

Train young trees to branch 2—3 feet off the ground and to have three or four main branches. For mature trees, prune while dormant. Remove dead or crossed branches. To encourage fuller growth, cut back some of the end growth slightly.

In temperate climates many varieties of figs, such as 'Mission', 'Osborn', and 'Kadota', bear two crops of figs a year. The first crop is called breba. Breba-crop figs are borne on the ends of the previous year's growth. Therefore, when pruning these varieties, make sure you do not cut off all the end growth.

Different varieties are pruned in different ways, so it's advisable to consult local authorities about the optimum method for your particular plant.

Pests and Diseases

Figs are susceptible to very few pests and diseases. Mites are sometimes a problem.

Do not plant where cotton has grown, since fig trees can contract cotton root rot. In Florida, fig rust can be a problem, requiring a spray of neutral copper when the leaves are half mature. Where nematodes might be a problem, try to find plants grafted onto resistant rootstock.

In some parts of the South the dry fruit beetle can enter the "eye" of the fig fruit and spoil it. Plant varieties such as 'Conadria', 'Celeste', and 'Texas Everbearing' that have closed eyes.

Harvesting

Pick fruits when they are soft and fall easily into your hand. If they exude white sap they are not ripe enough. If you plan to dry them in arid climates you can let them wither on the tree and then pick them. A mature tree will yield about 25—35 pounds of fruit per year.

How to Purchase

Forms and Sources

Fig trees are available bare root in early spring from local nurseries and some mail-order firms, or in containers from nurseries and the following mail-order firms during the summer: (6,27,31,46,52,61). One nursery specializes in figs: The Fig Tree Nursery, Box 124, Gulf Hammock, FL 32639.

Pollinators

Figs commonly used in the home garden are self-pollinating.

Varieties

'Black Mission' ('Mission')—black fruit; large tree; popular in California; resistant to oak-root fungus. (Readily Available)

'Brown Turkey' ('Black Spanish')—brownish purple fruit, good for eating fresh; small tree; can be pruned back readily; grown in many areas. (Readily Available)

'Celeste' ('Blue Celeste', 'Sugar')—bronze colored
   fruit; quite hardy; popular in Southeast. (13,27,70)
'Conadria'—white fruit, excellent flavor; large vigorous tree; fruit resistant to decay, small eye.
   (6,8,13,27,70)
'Magnolia' ('Brunswick', 'Madonna')—yellow fruit;
   one of the hardiest; good for borderline fig areas.
   (6,9,13,70)
'Texas Everbearing' ('Dwarf Everbearing', 'Eastern
   Brown Turkey')—dark-brown fruit; quite hardy;
   good in containers. (6,13,70)

Preserving and Preparing

Figs can be dried, canned, pickled, frozen, candied,
or made into jam.

Fig Filling for Cookies and Coffee Cake

Place 2 pounds fresh figs and sugar to taste (start
with 1/4 cup) in a saucepan. Cook on low heat, stirring occasionally, until thick. Freeze in containers.
Makes approximately 1 1/2 cups filling.

Fig Needhams
   1 cup butter
   1 cup brown sugar
   2 egg yolks
   3 tablespoons milk
   2 teaspoons vanilla
   2 1/2 cups unbleached flour
   2 teaspoons cream of tartar
   1 teaspoon soda
   1/2 teaspoon salt
   1/2 cup fig filling (recipe above)

Cream butter and sugar. Add egg yolks, milk, and
vanilla, and beat well. stir together the dry ingredients
and add to mixture. Chill dough for 1 hour.

On a well-floured board, roll out the dough to 1/8
inch thick. Cut with round cookie cutter. Place 1/2
teaspoon fig filling on half the round surfaces. Cut
small holes in center of other rounds and place these
on top of the rounds holding the filling. Press edges
together with a fork. Bake on ungreased sheet at
350°F for 10—12 minutes.

Filbert (HAZELNUT)
European filbert, *Corylus Avellana*

Effort Scale
NO. 3

E.45. Filbert leaves are showy, and the nuts are encased in decorative coverings.

Moderate amount of pruning needed
Mulching beneficial
Some raking required
Harvest must be processed
Vulnerable to some pests, including birds and
   squirrels

Zones
4—8

Thumbnail Sketch
Deciduous tree or shrub
Standard, 15—25 ft. tall; dwarf variety, 4 ft. tall
Propagated by layering and grafting
Needs full sun
Leaves are dark green, woolly underneath, 4 in. long
Blooms in winter or spring
Female flowers are inconspicuous; male flowers are
   catkins
Nuts are edible; harvested in fall
Used as large shrub, hedge, screen, small multistem
   tree, interest tree, screen, patio tree

How to Use
In the Kitchen

European filberts are tasty, round, hazel-colored
nuts, closely related to the American hazelnut. They
are a delectable and nutritious snack when roasted
and salted, and are marvelous in stuffings for poultry,
or as an addition to vegetable dishes. Filberts can also

E.46. Filbert trees can be grown as large shrubs or trained as multistemmed trees like this one near an entryway.

contribute to memorable desserts, as in filbert pie, filbert meringues, and fudge and brownies with filberts added. How decadent can you get!

In the Landscape

Filberts have large, dramatic leaves that stand out from each other clearly. The trunk is usually multistemmed and can be trained to sculptured shapes. Trained filberts look nice near a patio or entryway. The nut coverings add another ornamentation to this already beautiful tree. They are fringed and frilly, usually green, and sometimes have pink edges. The nuts grow in clusters of three to seven. In the winter the bare branches are decorated by the interesting male catkins, which hang on until spring.

Try using filbert trees as decorative screens or accent plants. In shrub form they serve admirably as informal hedges or screens.

How to Grow

Climate

European filberts are quite hardy, but they flower in late winter or early in the spring, exposing the delicate catkins to frosts. This factor limits nut production and consequently affects the tree's distribution. Filberts do poorly in areas with high summer heat, another limiting factor. They are grown most success-

fully in the inland areas of the Northwest; 95 percent of all filberts grown in this country come from Oregon and Washington. Scattered attempts at growing European filberts in the East have met with varying degrees of success. If you want to try them, choose a northern, cold exposure so a warm winter day will not inspire them to bloom prematurely.

Exposure

Filberts need full sun.

Soil

Filberts bear well in good, deep, well-drained garden loam mulched with 3 or 4 inches of organic matter.

Fertilizing

Organic mulches provide most of the nutrition filberts need. However, if the leaves are getting small or pale, apply nitrogen in moderate amounts. In cold winter areas too much nitrogen will produce succulent growth susceptible to winterkill.

Watering

Filberts need an occasional deep watering in arid summer areas. In the Northwest, where they are grown commercially, mature trees seldom need watering.

Pruning

Prune a young plant to a single trunk with four to six main branches if it is to be grown as a standard tree, or to three main trunks if grown as a multistemmed tree.

Filberts bear on last year's wood, and need to be lightly thinned out every year to encourage new growth. Prune at the end of the blooming season. If you are growing filberts in a tree form, remove suckers throughout the year.

Pests and Diseases

The most serious problem for filberts is eastern filbert blight, a disease common in filberts grown on the East Coast. There is no cure, and affected plants eventually die.

Common pests of filberts are jays, crows, and squirrels.

Aphids and mites are sometimes a problem, though usually easily controlled. Try dormant sprays.

Harvesting

Gather nuts after they have fallen and before the birds discover them. A mature tree can yield 25 pounds of nuts to a crop. Filberts usually bear their crops in alternate years. This is normal.

How to Purchase

Forms and Sources

Buy filberts bare root from local and mail-order nurseries in spring, or in containers from nurseries and the following mail-order firms into the fall: (3,6,17,46,52).

Pollinators

Filberts need cross-pollination. Choose the varieties carefully, as all filbert varieties do not pollinate all others.

Varieties

Be careful when choosing filbert varieties, since some are grown only as ornamentals and bear few or inferior nuts.

'Barcelona'—most popular filbert; commercial variety; large nuts of excellent quality; very susceptible to eastern filbert blight but high bud-mite resistance; 'Royal' is a good pollinator. (Readily Available)

'Du Chilly'—large nut; slow growing to 15 ft. (17)

Preserving and Preparing

Filberts stored at room temperature will soon become rancid. Store them in an outside building, such as a garage, where temperatures are in the fifties and the humidity is fairly high.

The foolproof way to preserve filberts is to shell and freeze them.

To toast filberts, place shelled nuts in a shallow pan and bake in a 350°F oven until light golden brown, about 15 minutes. Watch carefully, as they can easily overbake.

Nutty Meringues

3 egg whites
1/4 teaspoon cream of tartar
1/4 teaspoon salt
1 teaspoon vanilla
3/4 cup sugar
1 1/4 cups filberts (or almonds),chopped fine

Preheat oven to 250°F. Make sure all the utensils are grease free. Place egg whites, cream of tartar, and salt in a clean bowl. Beat until soft peaks form. Add the vanilla, and gradually add the sugar, beating constantly, until peaks become very stiff. Fold in the chopped nuts. Cover a baking sheet with heavy brown paper. Drop meringue in 12 dollops onto the paper. Using the back of a large spoon or a rubber spatula, make a hollow in the center of each mound. Bake for 1 hour at 250°F. Turn off heat and allow meringues to set in oven for 1 1/2 hours. Serve meringues filled with ice cream or chocolate mousse (recipe below).

Chocolate Mousse

Make 1 small package of chocolate pudding (not the instant type), using 1/2 cup less milk than directions call for. Chill mixture for at least 3 hours. Remove from refrigerator and beat with a wire whip until creamy. Make whipped cream from 1 cup heavy cream, 1/2 teaspoon vanilla, and 2 tablespoons sugar. Fold whipped cream into pudding. Fill each meringue with a large spoonful of the chocolate mixture. Garnish with filberts.

FLOWERING KALE. See Greens.
FOO GWA. See Bitter Melon.
FRENCH SORREL. See Sorrel.
GARDEN CHAMOMILE. See Chamomile.
GARDEN CHIVES. See Chives.
GARDEN NASTURTIUM. See Nasturtium.
GARDEN RHUBARB. See Rhubarb.
GARDEN SORREL. See Sorrel.
GARDEN STRAWBERRY. See Strawberry.
GARLIC CHIVES. See Chives.

Grape

American (fox) grape, *Vitis Labrusca*
European (wine) grape, *V. vinifera*
Muscadine grape, *V. rotundifolia*
Hybrids

Effort Scale

NO. 3
Susceptible to some pests and diseases
Yearly pruning needed
Harvesting and preserving are time-consuming

Zones

4—10

Thumbnail Sketch

Deciduous climbing, woody vines
Can reach 50—100 ft.; usually kept at 12—20 ft.
Propagated from seeds and cuttings, and by layering, grafting, budding
Need full sun
Leaves are medium- or blue-green, palmately lobed, 4—8 in. long
Bloom in spring
Flowers grow in clusters, are insignificant
Fruits and leaves are edible; fruits are harvested in

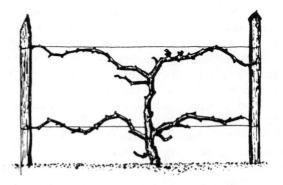

E.47. Grape arbors are a landscaping tradition.

early fall, leaves in summer
Used on pergolas, fences, arbors, patio covers; can
  be trained as a small weeping tree

How to Use
In the Kitchen

Grapes, wonderful grapes! These fruits are luscious
and juicy when fresh. Just to have a bunch of, say,
'Concord' or 'Niagara' grapes in your hand can make
you feel refreshed. A platter piled high with different
kinds of grapes makes a lovely centerpiece—and an
elegant dessert, along with cheese. Some grapes, such
as the 'Concord', though eaten fresh are mainly used
to make purple grape jelly. Grape juice is a nice
change from other juices, grape leather is a favorite
with youngsters, and of course wine grapes have a
story all their own. The latter are not particularly
palatable fresh, but where wine is concerned, the
proof of the vintage is in the drinking, not the eating.

Table grapes can be frosted with egg whites and
sugar for an unusual garnish; blue grapes make an
excellent pie; white grapes add texture and flavor to
chicken or meat salads; and all the grapes that do well
out of hand belong in a seasonal fruit cup.

The fruit of the vine is not the grape's only gift. A
supply of brined grape leaves in your pantry is like
money in the bank when unexpected company
arrives. You can simply fill the leaves with a meat or
vegetable and rice mixture and roll them into dolmas,
a Middle Eastern delicacy served hot or cold.

*E.48. American grapes and most wine grapes can be trained on
wires in what is called the four-arm Kniffen system. Before pruning (top), there is much extra growth. After pruning (bottom),
only the four "arms," each bearing 8-12 buds, remain.*

In the Landscape

Grapes grow on gnarled, woody, climbing vines
with peeling bark. Grape leaves are palmately lobed,
usually medium-green to blue-green, lush, and dramatic, turning yellow in the fall.

The plants can be trained to climb on or cling to
many different structures. They are beautiful on pergolas or pool houses, and the grapes themselves are eye-
catching when they hang down through the lattice of a
patio roof. (In the latter case, pick the grapes conscientiously as they ripen; otherwise fallen grapes will
make the patio slippery.) Where grapes are espaliered
against a wall, wires strung along the wall help to support the vine. The espalier treatment is particularly
beautiful and advantageous in cool summer areas; if
the wall faces south it absorbs extra heat to sweeten
the grapes.

Many varieties of grapes can also be trained to be
small weeping trees. See the box above for details.
Use weeping grape trees for a focal point near a patio
or as beautiful accent plants. Lining a walk or
arranged geometrically on the edges of an herb garden, they can supply grapes for the enthusiastic wine-
maker.

Grape arbors are traditional trysting places, and for children they are magical hideaways. To sit under an arbor and smell the ripening grapes, to reach up and pluck a few ripe ones, or to just lean back and enjoy a glass of homemade wine—that's fine living.

How to Grow

Four major classes of grapes are grown in the United States: the American grape, the European grape, the muscadine, and hybrids of the three named. All the members of this family differ somewhat in taste, use, climate adaptability, pruning requirements, and disease susceptibility.

American grapes—sometimes referred to as Fox or 'Concord' type grapes—are native to the Northeast and are grown in bunches, have skins that slip off easily, and are generally eaten fresh or made into jelly, juice, and occasionally wine.

European grapes have tight skins and a typically winey flavor. They separate into three main categories: those used for wine, the dessert grapes, and the raisin grapes.

Muscadine grapes, best characterized by the 'Scuppernong', are native to the Southeast. They grow in loose clusters, have a slightly musky flavor, and are eaten fresh or made into jelly and occasionally into a fruity wine.

Many hybrids have been developed which combine many of the characteristics of the American, European, and muscadine grapes.

Climate

One or more types of grapes can be grown in almost every part of the country except for the high desert and the very coldest parts of the Midwest. All grapes are heat lovers. They grow strong and produce sweet fruits in the sun. Without heat grapes are sour and vines are prone to diseases. The American 'Concord' type is the hardiest and will grow in colder climates than its European relatives. It is the principal grape grown in the area east of the Rocky Mountains and north of Delaware. European grapes are less hardy, usually tolerating cold only to 5°F, and they require many hours of heat to produce good grapes. These grapes are grown in milder sections of the East and Midwest but are best suited to California, Arizona, and Oregon. In the Southeast, muscadine grapes thrive. They take much heat and humidity, are fairly tender, and are seldom grown north of Delaware.

Many hybrids have been developed for specific areas of the country. Consult local authorities if you cannot find specific information about the climate adaptability of the variety you are interested in. It is very important to choose varieties suitable for your area.

Exposure

All grapes require full sun. In coldest grape areas, plant grapes on south walls and give them extra shelter during the coldest nights.

Soil

Grapes need deep, well-drained soil. They are not as fussy as most fruits about fertility but will produce more and better fruit on fertile soil.

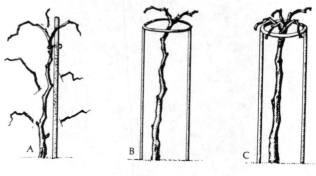

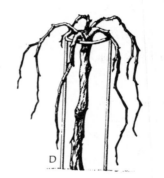

E.49. How to prune a weeping grape. A. Second-year dormant pruning. Cut off all lateral growth and remove the central shoot, or leader, leaving only two or three lateral branches. B. Build a support of 2-inch metal or wooden posts. Attach a metal hoop 18-24 inches in diameter to the top. C. The third year, prune off all but two or three cane-producing spurs. D. The fourth year, you will have a permanent framework of five to seven main branches that will look like this before pruning. E. After pruning, only five to seven spurs, each bearing two buds, will remain. (The buds have been exaggerated for clarity.) F. The final product of your training–a graceful weeping grapevine.

Fertilizing

If your vines need fertilizer, apply compost, manure, and moderate amounts of a nitrogen-type fertilizer at the beginning of the growing season. Too much nitrogen at the end of the season produces lush foliage but few grapes. A nitrogen deficiency is characterized by pale foliage. In coldest areas, stop applying nitrogen fertilizer by midsummer so that vines can harden off before a heavy frost.

Muscadine grapes need more fertilizer than other species, since they are usually grown on sandy soils.

Watering

In arid climates, encourage grapevines to grow deep roots by occasional deep watering. The water should penetrate the soil to 3 feet. Apply water to the base of the plants, since many of the grapes grown in arid climates will develop fungus problems if watered from above. Grapes grown on sandy soils in the Southeast respond well to drip irrigation. Stop watering after August to allow the vines to harden off for winter.

Pruning

All grapes require heavy pruning for these reasons: (1) to maintain the vine at a manageable size, since an unpruned vine can reach 100 feet in length; (2) to encourage the continuous growth of new wood and fruiting buds, since grapes bear their fruit on the current year's growth; (3) to remove unproductive old canes (excess growth from the preceding or earlier seasons); and (4) to provide for the next year's growth by favoring one-year-old wood that will be ready to take over the next year (the best fruiting wood for a current year is produced from the buds of the preceding year's wood).

Grapevines have branches only in what is called the renewal area, and all the branches in this area must be pruned every year. The renewal area can be 7—8 feet high up on an arbor, spread out on four arms such as shown in Figure E.48, or 5—6 feet off the ground as shown in the diagrams accompanying the weeping grape.

It's important to know that different types of grapes are pruned in different ways. American grapes will not bear fruit on buds near the main stem, so leave longer canes when pruning them than you would for other types. Leave at least 10—12 buds on each vine cane. European wine-type grapes will bear too heavily if you leave that many buds; during the dormant period they should be cut back to two or three buds—to what is called a spur. Most of the previous year's growth is pruned off, and only these few spurs are left near the main trunk.

Muscadine grapes bear on spurs that produce for three or four years. They are extremely vigorous and need severe pruning to keep their canes from crowding each other out, as well as for aesthetic reasons. Muscadine grapes are generally trained on a single wire 5 feet off the ground or on arbors. They are cut back annually to spurs with 3 buds.

When purchasing grapevines, ask the nursery to point out the buds. Once you see the plant, this explanation will seem less confusing. But if you still need reassurance, many good books on pruning are available (see the bibliography).

Grapes that are to be trained up against a fence or on wires can be arranged in what is called the four-arm Kniffen system. In this system, four canes, two in each direction, are trained along parallel wires or on arbors and trellises (see Figure E.48). The support should be made of sturdy material, because grapevines are heavy and long-lived. This training system is the one most commonly used for most varieties of both spur- and cane-pruned grapes, and much information is available about it. The weeping-grape method is less usual.

Pests and Diseases

Grapevines are often bothered, especially in humid climates, by fungal diseases, mildew (powdery white fungus on leaves and fruit), anthracnose (blotches of brown spots on leaves and fruits), and black rot (which turns fruit black and rotten). Selecting varieties of American or muscadine type, where appropriate, helps because they are more resistant to diseases than those of European-type grapes. Good pruning that provides good air circulation also helps. Choosing the right grape for a particular climate and avoiding susceptible varieties are the best solutions. Some varieties can be grown only with an aggressive fungicide program. However, in wet weather even these measures do not seem to help. In arid climates do not plant grapes near lawns that get overhead watering.

Japanese beetles are sometimes a problem. To control, hand-pick, use milky-spore disease (see Part Two), and use bug traps. The larvae of the grape-berry moth are sometimes a problem; they can chew their way through your grapes. See Part Two for information on *Bacillus thuringiensis*.

Pierce's disease is a serious problem on grapes in the Southeast. There is no cure. In affected areas, plant muscadine grapes, or one of the few varieties of European grapes that are immune. Choose from 'Blue Lake', 'Lake Emerald', 'Norris', or 'Stover'.

Birds are sometimes a problem—cover plants with netting.

How to Train a Weeping Grape

The weeping grape, a beautiful and fruitful interest and accent plant, is best developed from spur-pruned rather than cane-pruned grapes. Most European and California wine grapes, as well as the cultivars 'Muscat', 'Tokay', 'Perlette', and 'Black Monukka', can be trained to be a weeping grape.

During the first year, do not prune the plant at all, but during the second year be prepared to be ruthless—though with a definite plan. Your guiding principle is to create a clean trunk. Select a central stem to be trained as the central leader or trunk. Stake this stem. This will become the permanent structure or trunk of the vine.

Establish the height of the weeping grape—5–6 feet is recommended—by heading back; that is, taking the top off of the central leader, leaving only two or three lateral branches at the top. Cut all other lateral branches off to bring out the tree form (Figure E.49A). Next, build a supporting structure with brown- or black-painted metal pipes or 2-inch wooden posts. On top of this structure attach a hoop of metal tubing 18–24 inches in diameter, or a recycled tricycle wheel (Figure E.49B).

When pruning the third year, create two or three more main branches (Figure E.49C) and cut off the rest of the previous year's growth. If any flower buds appear in the spring, remove them. Fruiting diverts energy from the developing vines.

By the fourth year you will have a permanent renewal area at the top of the trunk. Before being pruned it will look like Figure E.49D; after pruning it will look like Figure E.49E (the size of the buds has been exaggerated for clarity). Every succeeding winter you will prune off all the long canes and leave the permanent four or five branches, each with two buds. Figure E.49 F shows the final form of the weeping grape.

Harvesting

Cut off bunches of grapes when they are fully colored and sweet. Ripe grapes will come off easily in your hand, and their seeds are brown. Grapes will not ripen further once they are picked.

How to Purchase

Forms and Sources

Buy bare-root plants in late winter or plants in containers throughout the year. Both are readily available from local or mail-order nurseries.

Pollinators

Except for muscadine grapes, the great majority of varieties are self-pollinating. Muscadine grapes come in two types—those that are perfect-flowered, that is, self-pollinating, and those that are female only and need a pollinator. The perfect-flower type not only will pollinate themselves but will also pollinate other varieties that are female only. Check carefully when you order to make sure that you have a suitable pollinator.

Varieties

Hundreds of varieties of grapes exist. The following have been chosen for their disease resistance, availability, and quality of fruit. Among them you should find ones suitable for your growing conditions.

AMERICAN GRAPES

American grapes are adaptable to the East, Midwest, and Northwest. These grapes are readily available from local nurseries and mail-order firms. They are usually pruned to the cane method.

'Alden'—reddish, purple-black large grapes; excellent quality; strong and vigorous vines. (44)

'Beta'—blue grapes; heavy producer as hardy as the wild grapes; good for coldest climates. (16,60)

'Concord'—the standard to which all other American grapes are compared; excellent blue, slip-skin grapes; widely adaptable; will tolerate cool summers; 'Concord Seedless' also available. (Readily Available)

'Delaware'—standard of excellence for its type; pale red grapes with sweet flavor, good for eating fresh or as wine; one of the most ornamental vines but susceptible to mildew. Do not plant in areas where this is a problem. (59)

'Fredonia'—one of the best black grapes; hardy vines; early ripening. (Readily Available)

'Himrod'—American hybrid; best of the white seedless for the East; very hardy. (Readily Available)

'New York Muscat'—reddish-black grapes; dessert fruit; not very vigorous vines. (44)

'Niagara'—very old variety; white grapes; very vigorous vines; heavy bearer; moderately hardy. (Readily Available)

'Steuben'—blue-black grapes; hardy vine; disease resistant. (Readily Available)

EUROPEAN TABLE GRAPES

These table grapes are mostly for warmer parts of the East and West. They are readily available from local nurseries or mail-order firms.

'Black Monukka'—reddish-black seedless grapes; one of the hardiest European grapes; prune to cane or spur. (8,17,25)

'Muscat of Alexandria'—green to pink grapes; well known for its musky sweet taste; used for wine and raisins; spur-type pruning. (17,48)

'Olivette Blanche' ('Ladyfinger')—deep-green grape; prune to cane. (8,17)

EUROPEAN WINE GRAPES

These varieties are generally limited to the wine-growing areas of California, Washington, and Oregon. Good sources for many of these grapes are (3,8,13,17).

'Cabernet Sauvignon'—red wine grapes for cool climates; needs a long growing season. (3,8,27,44)

'French Colombard'—white-wine grapes; very vigorous and productive; needs a long hot growing season. (8)

'Grenache'—red-wine grapes; for moderately cool to hot climates. (8)

'White Riesling'—white-wine grapes; for cool areas; one of the hardiest of the wine grapes; can produce good wine as far north as Geneva, New York. (3,8,44,46)

'Zinfandel'—red-wine grapes; makes good jelly; for areas with mild winters and cool summers. (8,17)

MUSCADINE GRAPES

The muscadine grapes are for the Southeast. Perfect grapes, identified as such below, do not need a pollinator. Good sources are: (13,27,70).

'Carlos'—medium-size grapes, gold with a pink blush; very vigorous; quite hardy; disease resistant; perfect. (70)

'Fry'—very large, bronze grapes with good flavor; high yield; particularly good in Florida; female plant needs a pollinator (a good one is 'Southland'). (27,70)

'Hunt'—black grapes with very good flavor; good for wine or juice; highly recommended; highly disease resistant; female plant needs a pollinator. (70)

'Jumbo'—very large, black grapes; good eaten fresh; single grapes, not clusters; disease resistant; female plant needs a pollinator. (27,70)

'Magoon'—medium-size reddish-black grapes; excellent flavor; highly disease resistant; for northern Florida; perfect. (27)

'Scuppernong'—oldest grape variety in the United States; many imitations exist, so make sure you get the real one; this muscadine is *the* muscadine; used as a benchmark, all the others are compared to it; bronze fruits with distinctive flavor and aroma; excellent fresh or for juice or wine; female plant needs a pollinator. (27,61,70)

'Southland'—black grapes; good eaten fresh or as jelly; for southeastern part of Gulf Coast; probably the best grape for Florida; perfect. (27,70)

HYBRIDS

The following American-European hybrids are all wine grapes suitable for colder regions. Good sources of many of these grapes are (30,31,44,59,60).

'Aurora' (Seibel 5279)—white grapes; ripens early; needs sandy soil; resistant to downy mildew, but somewhat susceptible to powdery mildew. (Readily Available)

'Baco #1' ('Baco Noir')—black grapes; very vigorous; resistant to mildew. (27,31,44)

'Catawba'—purple or bronze-red grapes; a leading wine and juice grape; not for coldest climates. (Readily Available)

'De Chaunac' (Seibel 9549)—blue grapes; vines vigorous and productive; among the best for home wines. (44)

'Missouri Kiesling'—American wine grapes; produces semidry wine; very hardy; for protected areas of zone 4; the wine grape most resistant to mildew. (Locally Available)

'Seibel' 9110 ('Verdelet S-9110')—yellow, tender-skinned grapes; produces superior wine; vines need protection in coldest areas. (30,44)

'Seyve-Villard' 12-375 ('Villard Blanc')—yellow grape; somewhat hardy; resistant to mildews. (13,30)

Preserving

Grapes can be canned whole or as juice. They can be frozen whole or dried to make raisins; seedless grapes are best for these uses. Grapes are also preserved as jelly, jam, and conserves. Finally, they can be pickled or made into vinegar. (For jam directions, see KIWI.)

The most famous way of preserving grapes, of course, is to make them into wine. Choose your varieties carefully if you plan to put your grapes to this use. Home winemaking is becoming a popular hobby; supplies and kits, as well as books on the subject, are available.

Greens

Endive and escarole, *Cichorium Endivia*

Kale and flowering kale, *Brassica oleracea*, Acephala Group

Mustard (India mustard) and spinach mustard, *B juncea*

New Zealand spinach, *Tetragonia tetragonioides*

Spinach, *Spinacia oleracea*

Swiss chard, *Beta vulgaris* var. *cicla*

Effort Scale

NO. 2
Must be planted annually
Watering, mulching, and fertilizing usually needed
Some weeding necessary

Zones

Annual

Thumbnail Sketch

Annuals, biennials, or perennials planted as annuals
6—24 in. tall
Propagated from seeds
Need full sun or partial shade in hot weather
Leaves vary with species
Flowers are not seen
Leaves are edible; most harvested in cool part of the
   year
Used in flower borders, herb gardens, raised beds,
   hanging baskets, containers

How to Use

In the Kitchen

What would we do without greens? All species are
good steamed, and a pot of fresh greens flavored with
butter or pork drippings is a springtime delight.
Spinach and New Zealand spinach make savory cream
soups. For entrees, spinach soufflé, spinach omelet,
and my favorite, spinach or chard feta strudel, are rich
and nutritious. All of the greens named here add variety to a tossed green salad, and a spinach salad with
raw mushrooms and artichoke hearts is a meal in
itself.

In the Landscape

Playing with the varied textures, forms, and colors
this plant group offers can be great fun. All shades of
green are represented—the light yellow-green of
endive, the bright green of mustard, the darker bright
green of Swiss chard, the deeper green of spinach, and
the more sombre gray-green of New Zealand spinach.
The spectrum of color is matched by a variety of leaf
shapes—cut and frothy, curly and ruffled, and smooth.
It is possible to create a picture by combining curly
blue-green kale or curly lettuce-green mustard with
the smooth-leaved 'Bibb' lettuce. All three take the
same growing conditions. Another colorful scene
might be composed of tall ruby-colored chard, with its
bright red stalks, standing upright next to a bed of
lush, trailing New Zealand spinach. The possibilities
are endless for creating your own patterns, geometric
or free form. Try the ornamental kale, which grows
into frilly, amethyst-colored bouquets and is also edible, in pots on your patio.

How to Grow and Purchase

Chard, endive, kale, mustard, and spinach are all
cool-season crops. New Zealand spinach, while it
prefers cool weather, does quite well in the hot summer. During warm weather, these leafy vegetables
need partial shade. All greens should be started from
seed in early spring and planted in rich fertile loam,
and all should be kept fairly moist. To become tender
and succulent, greens should grow quickly and vigorously. To encourage such, growth, give supplemental
organic matter and an extra source of nitrogen during
the growing season.

With the exception of kale, the greens mentioned
here are vulnerable to very few pests or diseases,
though aphids, flea beetles, and snails are occasional
problems. Kale is a member of the cabbage family and
is often plagued by the pests that bother head cabbage
(see CABBAGE).

These greens can all be enjoyed a few leaves at a
time as required. The entire plant need not be harvested, as in commercial production. New Zealand
spinach in particular will bear over a very long season,
so it is wise to pick the new shoots as they appear.

E.50. All greens can be grown in containers. Pictured from left to
right are, top row: mustard, chard; second row: ornamental
flowering kale, New Zealand spinach; bottom row curly endive,
spinach.

Wash all greens well to remove grit and dirt before using.

Nurseries with large selections of greens are: (11,32,37,45,55,57)

Endive, Curly Endive, and Escarole

Leafy, green endive and its close relatives are popular in fresh salads or cooked as "greens." (Do not confuse this type with the Belgian or French endive, known as witloof chicory, which is actually the blanched sprouts of another species, *Cichorium Intybus*.)

In hot weather endive and escarole become bitter and often go to seed. Plant in early spring or late summer. Before eating, blanch the leaves by shading them from the light for a week after harvesting. Bring them into a garage or cellar in containers, and cover them with a paper bag. Or leave them on the plant, tying outer leaves up around the inner ones, and keep the plant watered.

There are many varieties of endive. Some have smooth leaves and look like lettuces; others, usually called escarole, have finely cut fringy leaves that contrast dramatically with smooth-leaved plants such as basil, chard, and butter lettuce.

Many kinds are readily available.

Kale and Flowering Kale

Curly, blue-green kale is beautiful as well as tasty, but its show-off cousin, flowering kale, puts most flowers to shame. Both can be enjoyed in the early spring or fall, and neither do well in warm weather. Flowering kale will not produce its brilliant red or purple foliage unless it has some frost, and the flavor of both plants is improved by frost.

These kales are usually eaten cooked, but the tender new growth is good raw in salads too. Unlike endive, kale is never bitter. The flowering types add color to a green salad in winter, 'when your only color choice is often the bland, nearly pink store-bought tomatoes.

Many different kinds of kale are readily available.

Mustard (India Mustard) and Spinach Mustard

These stouthearted members of the cabbage family are spicy and crisp when eaten raw and superb when cooked with salt pork. All mustards need sufficient water or they will become too hot to eat. The younger the leaf, the less bite it has.

'Ostrich Plume' and 'Fordhook Fancy', with their curled and frilly edges, are among the most beautiful of the mustard greens. 'Tendergreen' (sometimes called mustard spinach) is a smooth-leaved variety. Its flavor is usually not as 'hot' as that of the others, and it is easier to clean.

Many mustard varieties are readily available.

Note; The mustard used on hot dogs comes from the ground-up seeds of plants in this family. The best condiment mustards are made from white mustard, *Brassica alba*, or black mustard, *B. nigra*. Seeds for these kinds of mustards are available from: (36). The young leaves of these plants can be used as potherbs. To make condiment mustard, allow these plants to go to seed. Harvest the seeds when the pods turn yellow. Put the seeds in a blender with wine vinegar, black pepper, allspice, salt, and water if needed.

New Zealand Spinach

New Zealand spinach is a trailing plant with succulent, triangular leaves. It is not related to spinach but tastes similar to it and can be used in any recipe calling for spinach, raw or cooked. Standard spinach cannot tolerate heat and quickly goes to seed after a few warm days, but New Zealand spinach can tolerate great amounts of heat without going to seed. It tastes better in cool weather but if shaded in summer will bear "spinach" for three to four months. Keep harvesting the new growth to stimulate new young shoots. Old leaves are tough and bitter.

New Zealand spinach makes a marvelous temporary ground cover, is good in hanging baskets, and will cascade over the sides of planter boxes. Grow it on the patio soil will be close at hand to add to your morning scrambled eggs along with dill and cheese.

This plant can be damaged by frost but can take oceanside conditions. I have seen it growing wild along the Pacific Ocean on cliffs above the water.

New Zealand spinach is somewhat drought tolerant, but the leaves will taste their best if the plant is kept well watered.

New Zealand spinach seems to have few pest or disease problems. (Readily Available)

Spinach

Just think of spinach soup or spinach souffle to measure the value of this noble vegetable.

If the weather is cool and the soil rich and filled with humus, spinach is easy to grow. It has few pests and diseases, and the deep-green, smooth leaves contrast nicely with the oak leaf lettuces, nasturtiums, carrots, or blue-green kale. Spinach seed is readily available.

Swiss Chard

Chard grows upright and straight. Its strong supporting midribs are either white or cherry red, and its deep-green leaves are usually ruffled and rich looking. The red chards, often called rhubarb or ruby chards, look handsome when planted with the other greens. Chard's colors and forms are fun to design with. Try ruby chard with red nasturtiums and carrots in a large oak barrel or with strawberries in a flower border around the patio. Chard seed is readily available.

Preserving and Preparing
Greens may be canned or frozen.

Sweet-Sour Sauce for Greens
    6 slices bacon, cut into small pieces
    1/2 cup onion, chopped
    3 teaspoons sugar
    1/2 teaspoon salt
    2 teaspoons flour
    1/2 cup vinegar
    1/3 cup water

Brown bacon lightly and remove from pan. Fry onion in drippings until golden brown, and blend in the dry ingredients. Add vinegar and water, stirring and cooking until thickened and bubbly. Remove from heat, add bacon bits, and pour sauce over your choice of raw spinach, New Zealand spinach, or chard.

GROUNDNUT. See Peanut.
GUAVA. See Pineapple Guava.
GUMBO. See Okra.
HAZELNUT. See Filbert.
HEAD LETTUCE. See Lettuce.

Hickory

Shagbark hickory, *Carya ovata*
Shellbark hickory (king nut), *C. laciniosa*

Effort Scale
    NO. 3
    Vulnerable to some pests and diseases
    Nuts are hard to shell
    Some raking necessary
    Fertilizing and mulching necessary
    Harvest is time-consuming

Zones
    4—9

Thumbnail Sketch
    Deciduous trees
    100—120 ft. tall
    Propagated by budding, grafting, or from seeds
    Need full sun
    Leaves are compound with 5 or 7 leaflets, 6—9 in.
      long

E.51. *Hickories are tall, handsome shade trees. When planted near a south wall they can protect a two-story house from summer sun.*

    Bloom in spring
    Flowers are green catkins
    Nuts are edible; harvested in fall
    Used as a shade tree, street tree, interest tree

How to Use
In the Kitchen
    The rich, white hickory nuts have a sweet, distinctive taste and are savored in pies, cakes, breads, and cookies. They can be munched as appetizers with cheese or nibbled alone. The nuts are hard to shell but well worth the effort.
    Some people smoke their meat over a fire of hickory prunings to give it a hickory-smoked flavor.

In the Landscape
    These dignified trees add a note of grandeur to the landscape. They have an upright pyramid form. With age, both species develop an attractive shaggy bark and a strong branching structure. A hickory can shade a simmering south wall, but the tree's stately form is shown to best advantage as a street tree or in a row lining a driveway, where the outstanding shaggy bark plates can be appreciated at close range.

How to Grow

Climate

The shagbark hickory is one of the hardiest nut trees. Its range extends from southern Quebec south to northern Florida and Texas, and from the East Coast west to Minnesota. The natural range of the shellbark hickory is from southern Ontario, south into Louisiana, and west to Oklahoma from the East Coast. Hickory trees are not being grown in the West at the present time.

Exposure

These trees need full sun.

Planting

Like most nut trees, hickory trees are sometimes difficult to establish if their long taproot has been injured in transplanting or en route from the grower to the planting site. If possible, check the root structure carefully before you buy. To plant your tree, dig a hole deep enough to accommodate the entire length of the taproot. Carefully place the root in the hole without bending it, and just as carefully place the soil around the root. Water the tree well and keep it mulched with organic matter. Staking may be necessary.

Soil

Hickory trees need deep, well-drained soil.

E.52. Shagbark hickory has strikingly textured bark.

Fertilizing

Hickories respond well to fertilizer and organic mulches.

Watering

The young trees should be kept fairly moist, but usually once the tree is established no supplemental water is needed.

Pruning

New trees should be pruned carefully to establish a strong branching structure. They should be trained to a strong central leader (see Part Two), and the branches, where they meet the main trunk, should have wide crotches, with an angle of no less than 45 degrees. Do not allow major branches to come off the main trunk opposite each other. Once the tree is shaped and established, it will not need regular pruning to produce nuts. Annual shaping and removal of dead growth is sufficient, and will keep you supplied with wood for hickory-smoking meat.

Pests and Diseases

A number of pests—weevils, moth larvae, scale, and aphids—bother the hickories. Also, these trees are susceptible to a number of diseases, namely, scab, anthracnose, leaf blotch, and crown gall. As a rule, these problems do not endanger the life of the tree. Since the trees are grown in their native habitat, the pests are usually in balance with the predators in the areas. But if things seem to be getting out of hand, consult with your local university extension service.

Most hickory trees bear nuts on alternate years. This is normal.

Harvesting

Hickory nuts fall from their husks and are harvested off the ground. Collect the nuts often to prevent the squirrels from getting too many.

How to Purchase

Forms and Sources

Buy grafted hickory trees or seeds from local nurseries or the following mail-order sources: (3,6,60,61).

Pollinators

Most authorities recommend at least two trees for cross-pollination. If native trees are close by, they will be sufficient.

Varieties

Much work is being done on the hybridizing of hickory trees. The new varieties have thinner shells and larger nutmeats, both of which make hickory nuts easier to enjoy. Check the mail-order sources and your local nurseries for the latest varieties; new improved varieties are continually being introduced. You will have the most success if you plant varieties that have been developed in your geographical area.

Varieties of shagbark that are often available are 'Davis', 'Fox', 'Glover', 'Neilson', 'Porter', 'Weschcke', and 'Wilcox'. Shellbark varieties are 'Bradley', 'Ross', 'Scholl', and 'Lindauer'.

Preserving

Hickory nuts can be stored in their shells in a cool, dark place or shelled and frozen. The shells are very hard. To make shelling easier, soak the nuts in very hot water for 10—15 minutes.

HIGHBUSH BLUEBERRY. See Blueberry.

Jerusalem Artichoke

(SUN CHOKE)
Helianthus tuberosus

Effort Scale
NO. 1
Stalks must be cut down
Mulching required in coldest climates

Zones
2—9

Thumbnail Sketch
Herbaceous perennial
6—10 ft. tall
Propagated from tubers
Needs full sun
Leaves are dark green, oval, 6—8 in. long
Blooms in early fall
Flowers are medium size, sunflower like, 3—5 in.
  across
Tubers are edible; harvest in fall after first frost
Used as a quick-growing screen and in the back of
  flower borders

How to Use
In the Kitchen
The crunchiness of Jerusalem artichokes—which neither come from Jerusalem nor taste much like artichokes—makes them a natural addition to a raw-vegetable platter served with a tasty dip. They add an unusual texture to mixed salads, can be served cooked as a vegetable by themselves, or as a substitute for

potatoes in stews and soups. Their carbohydrate is in the form of inulin rather than starch, which means it is an acceptable carbohydrate in diabetic diets.

In the Landscape
This rangy, stiff, herbaceous perennial, a native to North America, has only a few landscaping uses. Though the sunflowerlike blooms are showy, they are overshadowed by the ranginess of the plant itself. To use Jerusalem artichokes effectively, screen them with a low fence, tall flowers, or shrubs. They grow to a height of 6—10 feet, so they can be used when a quick-growing screen or hedge is needed, and as a tall background to a flower bed. Whether planted with flowers or vegetables, their height should be considered so they do not shade other plants.

How to Grow and Purchase
Jerusalem artichokes are easy to grow in most parts of the country. They require little care and no fertilizer and thrive in both light and heavy soil. Their only pests are gophers. They do equally well with summer rains or with occasional irrigation in arid summers, springing back quickly if wilted. The fact is, these plants are so easy to grow that you should plant them only where you want them to stay. Otherwise, if you decide to move them, one little tuber or even part of one left behind will grow into a plant the next summer, thus becoming a weed. For the same reason, avoid throwing peeling's or discarded chokes into the

E.53. Jerusalem artichokes are fast-growing perennials that die down every winter. They make good screens.

compost pile, or you may be surprised when new Jerusalem artichoke plants appear among your zinnias. Plant chokes 6 inches deep and 18 inches apart in spring. Keep well mulched.

Jerusalem artichokes can be harvested in the fall, but most people wait until after the first frost because the frost seems to improve the flavor. The artichokes can be harvested all at once and stored. they can also be left in the cold ground if it is heavily mulched and dug up as needed.

Chokes can be purchased from the grocery store or from a few mail-order sources: (Readily Available). There is a new variety 'Stampede' Jerusalem artichoke. It has larger tubers, is shorter (to 6 feet) than the old type, and blooms in July for six to eight weeks. 'Stampede' is obtainable from (37).

Preserving and Preparing

Store tubers in plastic bags in the refrigerator or root cellar.

Creamed Jerusalem Artichokes

approximately 1 pound Jerusalem artichokes
3 tablespoons butter
2 tablespoons flour
dash of salt, pepper, and nutmeg
1/4 cup chopped onions
1 1/2 cups milk
Tabasco sauce to taste

Wash, peel, and slice the Jerusalem artichokes. Place them in a saucepan with a small amount of salted water and simmer covered until tender, 10—15 minutes. Lightly brown the onions in 1 tablespoon of the butter.

To make a cream sauce, melt remaining butter in a saucepan and blend in the flour and seasonings. Stir mixture over low heat and cook until frothy, about 2 minutes.

While stirring, bring milk to a boil in another pan. Remove the flour mixture from heat, and quickly stir in the boiling milk. Cook until thickened. Add the browned onions and Tabasco sauce.

Pour sauce over the cooked Jerusalem artichokes; reheat if necessary. Garnish with chopped parsley.

Jujube (CHINESE DATE)

Ziziphus Jujuba

Effort Scale
NO. 1

E.54. *Jujube fruits grow in a zigzag pattern on the branch. The leaves are shiny with three prominent veins.*

E.55. *Many varieties of jujube have a weeping shape.*

Easy to grow and harvest
Suckers are sometimes a problem
Plants are hard to find

Zones
6—10

Thumbnail Sketch
Deciduous tree
15—30 ft. tall
Propagated from seeds or by grafting
Needs full sun
Leaves are shiny, rich, green, yellow in fall, 2—3 in. long

Blooms in summer
Flowers are insignificant
Fruits are edible; harvested in fall
Used as interest tree, lawn and shade tree, espalier

How to Use
In the Kitchen
The small, round or oval fruits of the jujube tree are reddish-brown with a crisp flesh. They have an applelike flavor when barely ripe but become spongy and very sweet when fully ripe. They can be eaten fresh or dried. Dried, they are something like dates. Jujubes are a favored sweet in Asia.

In the Landscape
This handsome, deciduous tree grows to heights of 15—30 feet. It has a graceful, weeping shape and a zigzag branching pattern that makes it dramatic in winter. In the summer it is covered with shiny green, strongly veined leaves, and thus makes a comforting shade tree, which will grow in a lawn. In fall the leaves turn a rich yellow.

The year-round attractiveness of the jujube makes it an unusual accent plant, whether grown to its full size or, by judicious pruning, kept to a size suitable for container growing. It is another tree that can be espaliered against a hot south or west wall.

Note: The one disadvantage of jujubes is that they tend to send out invasive suckers.

Deep, infrequent watering helps overcome this tendency. Root pruning or concrete barriers may be necessary to keep the roots from heaving the nearby sidewalks, coming up through asphalt, or coming up in unwanted areas.

How to Grow
Climate
Jujubes are hardy; they tolerate temperatures down to −20°F. But they only fruit well where summers are long, hot, and dry. They dislike humidity.

Exposure
Jujubes require full sun.

Soil
Jujubes are tolerant of heavy clays, alkalinity, and poor drainage, but they prefer good, well-drained garden soil.

Fertilizing
Jujubes grown in average soil seldom need fertilizing. If foliage turns pale, feed with nitrogen.

Watering
These trees need occasional deep watering to reduce suckering and to keep the roots from coming to the surface.

Pruning
Prune only to shape and encourage weeping outline, and to remove dead branches.

Pests and Diseases
Jujubes are free of most pests and disease problems except in desert areas, where Texas root rot can be a problem.

Harvesting
Most people prefer jujubes fresh and crisp, just as they are turning from green to brown. For candying and drying, the fruits must be fully ripe.

How to Purchase
Forms and Sources
Jujubes are hard to find. Purchase them bare root or in containers from local nurseries catering to Oriental clientele, or from mail-order firms. Trees are available at; seed is (36) available at (2,6,13,31).

Pollinators
Jujubes need cross-pollination. Plant more than one variety.

Varieties
'Lang' and 'Li' are the only two varieties generally available. Both are the weeping, pendulous forms. (13,14,46,70)

KALE. See Greens.
KARELI. See Bitter Melon.

Kiwi (CHINESE GOOSEBERRY KIWIFRUIT)
Common kiwi, *Actinidia chinensis*
Hardy kiwi, *A. arguta*

Effort Scale
NO. 2
Some pruning and tying required
Fertilizing and watering necessary

Zones
5—10

E.56. *Kiwi fruits are brown and fuzzy. The cream-colored flowers are large and showy.*

Thumbnail Sketch

Deciduous perennials
Vines to 30 ft. long
Propagated by budding or cuttings
Need full sun, or light shade in hot climates
Leaves are deep green, 6—8 in. long; new growth is
  bronzy
Bloom in spring
Flowers are cream colored, 1—1 1/2 in. across
Fruits are edible; harvested in fall
Used on trellises, arbors, pergolas, fences

How to Use

In the Kitchen

The kiwi's brown fruits are egg-shaped, fuzzy objects 3 inches long. To some people they look as if they ought to be stepped on. However, one taste of the bright-green, almost transparent flesh beneath the rough exterior quickly alters that opinion. The flavor is sharp but sweet, with overtones of strawberry, melon, and pineapple. It has to be tasted to be believed.

The hardy kiwi is a close relative of the more familiar kiwi. Its fruits are about the size of a large cherry and they are green with a smooth skin. The fruit is eaten all at once like a seedless grape. The flavor is great, very similar to a common kiwi.

Kiwis are eaten out of hand or in fruit compotes and salads. They make a beautiful garnish for salads and desserts—in Australia, they often top the national dessert, a meringue-like cake called Pavlova. The juice serves as a tenderizing marinade for meats and also makes a bright and zesty jelly.

In the Landscape

Both types of kiwis are strong, twining, deciduous vines that need a firm and sturdy support. When the vines can be properly attached, they are extremely useful for covering arbors, pergolas, fences, and even walls. All elements of the plant contribute to the overall effect: the new growth of the common kiwi is covered by a warm, bronzy fuzz; the leaves are big, round, and dark green on top with a lighter underside; and the branches are gnarly, slightly hairy, and light brown. The cream-colored flowers, 1—1 1/2 inches across, bloom in May, and are followed by clusters of the brown fruit, which contrast in color and texture with the foliage. Hardy kiwis are large vines with glossy green foliage and red leaf stalks. Because the fruit of both varieties is firm, it is not a problem over a patio or deck.

How to Grow

Climate

Common kiwis are semihardy. The ripening fruits are not able to withstand the frosts of late October. These plants need approximately 235 days without

E.57. *Kiwi vines make handsome arbor plants.*

frost, and protection from wind. They are not good in the desert, and they are still experimental in Florida. A new low-chill variety, 'Vincent', needs less than 100 hours of chilling and is carried by (48). The hardy kiwi is hardy to −25°F and has been grown as far north as New Hampshire.

Exposure

In most areas kiwis prefer full sun but can tolerate some shade. In hottest areas give them some afternoon shade.

Soil

Kiwis must have good garden loam and excellent drainage.

Fertilizing

These vines require a thick, organic mulch and regular feeding during the growing season.

Watering

Kiwis need constant watering during the growing season in arid climates. They should not be allowed to dry out.

Pruning

The common kiwi requires pruning twice a year. In the dormant season heavy pruning is done to cut down excessive "bleeding" and to stimulate fruiting, which occurs on the first 3—6 buds of the current year's growth. The pruning of kiwis is very similar to the pruning of grapes. Since kiwis are rampant growers, a light summer pruning is necessary to control and shape. Opinion is divided as to whether the hardy kiwi needs pruning.

Pests and Diseases

Pests and diseases are not generally a problem.

Harvesting

Kiwis are usually picked just before they are fully ripe and start to soften. If you pick them when they are not ripe enough, they will shrivel and will taste too tart. Determining the right time to pick them takes some experience. When kiwis are fully ripe they will give slightly, like peaches, to a little pressure of your fingers. You will have to experiment by picking and ripening a few to become familiar with the best time of harvesting for your use.

How to Purchase

Forms and Sources

Buy kiwis in containers from local nurseries or from mail-order firms. Both the common and the able from the following mail-order sources:

hardy kiwis are now readily available from mail order nurseries.

Pollinators

Cross-pollination between a male and female plant is necessary.

Varieties

'Chico' and 'Hayward' are the two fruiting female varieties of the common kiwi usually available. (They may be the same variety.) 'Meader' (female or male) and 'Issai' (self-fertile) are the most common varieties of hardy kiwi.

Note: For more information, write Actinidia Enthusiasts Newsletter, P. O. Box 1064, Tonasket, WA 98855. There is a nominal fee for a subscription.

Preserving and Preparing

Slightly underripe kiwis can be stored in a refrigerator and brought out a few at a time to ripen.

To freeze kiwis, peel and cut into thick slices. Place in plastic containers, pouring sugar syrup (3 cups sugar to 4 cups water) over them.

To can kiwis, peel and leave whole or cut in small slices. Cover with a light sugar syrup (2 cups sugar to 4 cups water). Leave 1/2 inch of space between the mixture and container cover. Seal and process in boiling water—pints for 20 minutes, quarts for 25 minutes.

Kiwi Jam

    2 pounds kiwis
    1 cup water
    1 lemon
    3 cups sugar

Peel fruits or cut in half and scoop out the pulp. Put in a large saucepan with the water and lemon juice. Bring the mixture to a boil and simmer for 10 minutes. Crush the fruit pulp well and add sugar. Boil, stirring frequently, to the jelly stage.

To determine that your mixture is at the jelly stage, dip a cold spoon into the mixture and hold the spoon over the pan, but out of the steam. Let the mixture drip off the spoon. If it has reached the jelly stage, two streams will flow together, or "sheet," as they fall off the spoon. Take the jam off the stove, pour into hot, sterilized jars, and seal.

These directions may be followed for any fruit recommended for jam or jelly. Proportions of ingredients differ, but the process is the same. The product is called jam when it includes any solid part of the fruits; jelly is made from the juice alone, which is strained through a jelly bag before combining with other ingredients.

KUMQUAT. See Citrus Fruits.
LEAF LETTUCE. See Lettuce.
LEMON. See Citrus Fruits.
LEMON THYME. See Thyme.
LETTUCE. 151

Lettuce (HEAD, ROMAINE, AND LEAF LETTUCE)
Lactuca sativa

E.58. *Lettuce comes in many shapes. From left to right: romaine, iceberg, red lettuce, and 'Salad Bowl' are grouped under a young 'Weeping Santa Rosa' plum tree.*

Effort Scale
NO. 2
Continuous planting needed
Some weeding, watering, and fertilizing required

Zones
Annual

Thumbnail Sketch
Annual
6—12 in. tall
Propagated by seed
Needs sun or partial shade
Leaves fight to medium green or red, 4—12 in. long
Flowers are not seen
Leaves are edible; harvest season varies
Used in flower beds, herbaceous borders, raised
  beds, containers

How to Use
In the Kitchen
The leaves of the lettuce are a standard salad item—in fact, they are almost indispensable for America's great love affair with salads. Where they are not part of a salad itself, the leaves are often used as serving shells for a salad. In some less common recipes, lettuce is braised or stuffed like cabbage.

E.59. *More assorted lettuces. In the background, from left to right: 'Ruby' lettuce, romaine, and spiky 'Oak Leaf'. In the foreground: 'Buttercrunch' and some young seedlings of Bibb and 'Oak Leaf'.*

In the Landscape
Lettuce comes in a wide variety of forms: firm, round, light-green head lettuce; soft, crinkle-leafed, darker-green Boston lettuce; rosette-shaped leaf lettuce in a spectrum of colors and differing leaf shapes; and tall, upright romaine lettuce. All types make formal edges to flower borders. They can be planted near herb gardens, where their form and color will contrast with the smaller-leaved herbs. A container planted with Boston lettuce is like a bouquet of green roses. And in a mixed flower bed, these herbaceous annuals are effective in combination with violas, nasturtiums, fibrous begonias, spinach, purple basil, and Alpine strawberries.

How to Grow, Purchase, and Preserve
Lettuce is a cool-season annual crop that can be grown in most areas of the country. It will go to seed rapidly when hot weather comes, although leaf lettuce will take more heat than the heading types. Lettuce will grow in considerable shade, and in mildwinter areas can be grown year round. Lettuce is easy to grow when its requirements are met. Its needs are a slightly alkaline, rich loam with humus added; regular

moisture; and light feedings of a fish-emulsion-type fertilizer to keep it growing vigorously. Sow seed in early spring either in flats or directly in the ground. Barely cover the seeds as they need light to germinate. Thin the seedlings between 4—12 inches apart, depending on the variety and also on the size you prefer for harvesting.

Seeds for all kinds of lettuce are readily available, and nurseries offer seedlings. Whether homegrown or nursery-grown, seedlings can be transplanted into empty spaces left by harvested plants. Another advantage of leaf lettuce is that the outer leaves rather than the whole plant can be picked as needed, so harvesting does not leave gaps in your garden.

The succulent young lettuce leaves are ambrosia to slugs, snails, aphids, and cutworms, so protect your seedlings until they lose some of their succulence. 'Oakleaf' seems to have some snail resistance.

Superior varieties of Bibb or butterhead lettuce are 'Capitane', 'Mantilia', 'Merveille de Quatre Saison', and 'Tom Thumb'. For romaine or cos lettuce try 'Romance' and 'Erthel' ('Crisp Mint'). Wonderful leaf lettuces are 'Green Ice', 'Oak Leaf', 'Salad Bowl', and 'Red Salad Bowl'. Mail-order nurseries that carry a large number of lettuce varieties are (11,19,23,26,32,37,55,57,62,66). More than 50 varieties are carried by (11,23).

There is no way to preserve lettuce.

LIME. See Citrus Fruits.
LIMEQUAT. See Citrus Fruits.
LOGANBERRY. See Brambleberries.

Loquat

Eriobotrya japonica

Effort Scale
NO. 3
Susceptible to some diseases
Needs moderate fertilizing and mulching
Occasional raking of large leaves needed
Large harvest

Zones
8—10

Thumbnail Sketch
Evergreen tree
15—25 ft. tall
Propagated from seeds and by grafting
Needs full sun; will tolerate partial shade

E.60. Loquats grow in clusters surrounded by dramatically large leaves.

Leaves are dark green, woolly underneath, 6—10 in. long; new growth is bronzy
Blooms in late winter
Flowers are cream colored, grow in clusters, fragrant, 1/2 in. across
Fruits are edible; harvested in spring
Used as interest plant, shade tree, screen, large espalier, and in large containers

How to Use
In the Kitchen
Loquats are round, yellow-orange fruits 1—2 inches in length. Their sweet and juicy globes ripen earlier in the spring than other fruits; thus, since they break the winter-long fruit fast, we can overlook their big seeds. Loquats are eaten fresh, made into jelly, and canned. You may have eaten them in commercial cherry pies without knowing it. Before passage of the truth-in-labeling laws, it is reputed that they were sometimes colored and used as cherries.

In the Landscape
This handsome, dramatic evergreen tree grows to 15—25 feet, and its spread can match its height. The tree's botanical name reflects its main characteristic—woolliness—for the *erio* of *eriobotrya* comes from the Greek *erion*, meaning wool. The loquat's huge deeply veined, dark-green leaves are woolly and light-colored on the underside. Its new growth is bronzy and woolly,

its branches are woolly, and its clusters of white, fragrant flowers are woolly. The fruits, which also grow in clusters, contrast nicely with the rich foliage. Thus, the loquat tree is one of those plants that have everything: color, texture, fragrance, and edible fruit.

If the fruits are important to you, try to get a grafted name variety. Ungrafted seedlings are ornamental but their fruits are not guaranteed high quality. You might have to do some searching, since most nurseries only carry seedling loquats.

The loquat tree can be pruned to either a dense, round shape or an open, sculptured appearance. Either way it can make a stunning accent. It looks well as a formal tree near an entrance if kept clear of walks, an espalier on a large wall, or a container plant for close-up enjoyment. Fruit drop can be a problem over patios or decks.

How to Grow

Climate
Loquat trees are semihardy, tolerating temperatures of 15°—20°F. The flowers and fruits that form early in spring are damaged by freezing weather. This limits their fruiting range. The trees do well near the ocean, and they are often used in beach plantings. In borderline areas, they should be grown on a warm south wall.

Exposure
Loquats prefer full sun but will tolerate partial shade.

Soil
These trees prefer a well-drained garden loam but will tolerate fairly sandy or clay soils. They need a soil pH of 5.5—7.5.

Fertilizing
Loquats respond well and produce better fruits when organic mulches and annual fertilizers are applied.

Watering
The trees are quite drought tolerant once established, though fruit size is sometimes reduced by meager watering.

Pruning
Prune to shape and remove dead or crossing branches. Fruits will be sweeter if the inner leaves are exposed to the sun. Thin fruits to increase their size.

Pests and Diseases
Fire blight is a common problem, particularly in Florida. If leaves and stems turn black at the end of

E.61. Loquat trees make stunning interest plants. This one is trained to a multistemmed form to avoid a "lollipop" look.

branches—a symptom of fire blight—prune back at least 12 inches into healthy wood. Sterilize pruning shears with a 10 percent bleach solution between cuts and burn diseased prunings.

Harvesting
Fruits are ready when slightly soft and fully colored.

How to Purchase

Forms and Sources
In areas where loquats grow readily you can buy grafted loquat plants in containers from local nurseries and from (6,48). Seeds are available from (2).

Pollinators
Loquats are self-pollinating.

Varieties
'Champagne'—excellent, tart fruits, 1 1/2 in. across with white flesh and yellow skin; April fruiting; best tree for warmest areas. (48)

'Gold Nugget'—good fruits, 1 1/2 in. across, orange; fruits early, often in March; vigorous ornamental tree; widely available. (48,70)

'Premier'—excellent, sweet fruit, 1 in. across, pale yellow; fruits early; slow-growing tree. (Locally Available)

Preserving and Preparing
Loquats are good for canning or making jelly. (See ELDERBERRY or KIWI.)

Loquats in Ginger Syrup
1/2 cup sugar
1 cup sugar
1 cup water

3 thin slices fresh ginger
1/2 teaspoon vanilla
3 tablespoons lemon Juice
2 kiwis, peeled and sliced
2 oranges, peeled and sectioned
3 cups fresh loquats (or 1 cup canned, drained),
sliced

In a saucepan, combine sugar, water, and ginger, and bring to a boil. Stir until sugar dissolves; then boil for 5 minutes more. Remove from heat and stir in lemon juice and vanilla. Cool. Remove ginger and add fruit. Chill well for at least 3 hours or overnight. Serve fruit covered with the syrup in small bowls. Serves eight.

Marjoram

Sweet marjoram, *Origanum Majorana*

Effort Scale
NO. 1
Easy to grow
Must be taken indoors or planted annually in coldest areas

Zones
All; as an annual in 1—7

Thumbnail Sketch
Herbaceous perennial
1—2 ft. tall
Propagated from seeds or division
Needs full sun
Leaves are gray-green, small
Blooms in summer
Flowers are small, white or lavender, grow in spikes
Leaves are edible; used as seasoning; harvest season varies
Used in herb gardens, flower beds, rock gardens, containers

How to Use
In the Kitchen
The aromatic leaves of marjoram are used, fresh or dried, as a seasoning in soups, stews, omelets, and vinegars. They are a necessary ingredient in spaghetti sauce and herb stuffing for poultry. A pinch improves many vegetables and adds interest to fish and meats.

In the Landscape
This small-leaved, gray-green, herbaceous perennial grows to 2 feet in height. Therefore, it can be used in the middle of a mixed-flower border and is ideal as well in herb and rock gardens. Marjoram's white or light lavender flower spikes and gray foliage combine well with chives, dittany of Crete, lavender, or 'Silver Mound' artemesia.

E.62. Marjoram, like many herbs, flourishes in containers. Keep it close to the kitchen on a porch or patio so it is handy for cooking.

How to Grow, Purchase, and Preserve
Marjoram grows almost anywhere. It needs medium-rich, well-drained soil, plenty of moisture, and full sun. In harsh-winter areas, plants brought into the house will thrive on a sunny windowsill. But wherever they are grown, marjoram plants should be kept pruned back so they will not become woody.

Pick leaves anytime for use fresh, but for drying harvest them before the plant has started to flower to ensure a good texture and rich flavor.

Marjoram seed or young plants are readily available.

To dry leaves, see the section on drying herbs under BASIL.

MELON. See Cucumber, Squash, and Melon.

Mint

Peppermint, spearmint, orange bergamot mint, pineapple mint, Corsican mint, *Mentha* species

Effort Scale
NO. 2
Vulnerable to some pests
Pruning needed to keep plant trim and bushy

Zones
4—10 for most species

Thumbnail Sketch
Perennial herb
1/2—3 ft. tall
Propagated from seeds, cuttings, or divisions
Needs partial shade
Leaves vary from deep green or variegated to light
  green, 1/4—2 in. long
Blooms in summer
Flowers are lavender, purple, or white, grow in
  spikes, small
Leaves are edible; used as flavorings; harvest season
  varies
Used as ground cover, in herb gardens, rock gar-
  dens, containers

How to Use
In the Kitchen
The aromatic leaves of all types of mint are eaten
fresh as a seasoning in salads, drinks, and jelly. Dried,
mint is used in teas.

In the Landscape
These fresh-smelling plants deserve a place in our
gardens just so we can pick an occasional leaf and

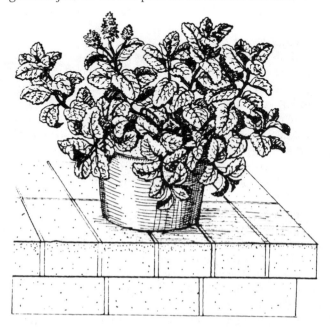

E.63. *Spearmint is best grown in a container to control its invasive roots.*

enjoy its pungency. Most types have one common
flaw: their underground roots spread—invasively—and
therefore must be controlled in containers or by deep
header boards.

All but Corsican mint can grow as high as 2—3
feet. All mints have crinkly leaves, but color varies
with type. Spearmint and peppermint are dark green,
pineapple mint is lighter and somewhat variegated,
and orange bergamot mint has purple-edged leaves.
All look well together and all combine beautifully with
impatiens and begonias. Corsican mint is a tiny-leaved
miniature, 1 inch tall, which can be grown between
stepping stones in mild climates. It is not as invasive
as the other mints.

How to Grow, Purchase, and Preserve
Except for Corsican mint, all the mints are hardy
and easily obtainable as seeds or plants from nurseries, seed catalogs, or friends. A large selection of
mints are available from: (54). They all grow best in
rich, moist soil, and prefer shade but will grow almost
anywhere if they get enough water. Prune the large
mints often to keep them bushy. Mint is attractive to
whiteflies.

Fresh mint can be picked anytime. The leaves have
a better flavor if the flowers are kept picked off.

Pick leaves for drying during a dry spell. They do
not dry as easily if they are too succulent. See BASIL
for drying information.

Mulberry (BLACK MULBERRY)
Morus nigra

Effort Scale
NO. 2
Vulnerable to some diseases and pests, including
  birds
Harvesting is time-consuming

Zones
5—10

Thumbnail Sketch
Deciduous tree
15—30 ft., depending on variety
Propagated by seed, budding, or from cuttings
Needs full sun
Leaves are medium green, heart-shaped, 6—8 in.
  across
Blooms in spring or summer
Flowers are insignificant
Fruits are black or red; edible; harvested in summer

E.64. *Mulberries are a favorite fruit of birds.*

Used as background plant, screen, espalier; weeping
variety used as interest plant

How to Use
In the Kitchen
The mulberry looks like a small blackberry and is
juicy and quite seedy. The flavor varies with variety.
The best is delicious and relatively seedless; poorer
quality berries are best described as insipid. Fruit is
commonly eaten off the tree, but it is also used for
jams, jellies, and syrup. It is occasionally dried for later
use.

In the Landscape
These deciduous trees can attain a height of 15–
30 feet and they develop a spreading crown. Their
leaves are large, medium green, and heart-shaped.

The weeping mulberry 'Pendula', the variety most
commonly sold as an ornamental, has variable fruits.
Someday, when edible ornamentals have become
more popular, a true weeping mulberry with superior
fruit will probably be available. As it is, you take a
chance when you plant one that the quality of the
fruits will be poor.

The standard, more readily available mulberry tree
is less decorative than the semipendulous and weeping forms. However, it can provide a good background
to shrub borders. Several planted close together make
a dense screen or hedge. They grow well in a lawn and
as shade trees, but at fruiting time sitting under them
is hazardous. The fruit drop makes these trees unde-
sirable near patios and sidewalks. The fruit on the
ground becomes slippery, and it stains.

Both the standard tree and the semipendulous
form can be used as a handsome, fan-shaped espalier

on a warm wall, and the trees can also be kept to container size. Mulberry trees are often planted in a yard
with cherry trees; birds seem to prefer the mulberries
to the cherries.

Note: When buying a mulberry tree for fruit, make
sure you do not get one of the most commonly planted, fruitless mulberries.

How to Grow
Climate
Black mulberries are semihardy. They grow as far
north as Virginia on the East Coast, and Seattle on the
West Coast. They prefer a hot and dry climate in the
summer.

Exposure
Mulberry trees need full sun.

Soil
These trees are fairly tolerant of most soils. They
prefer good garden loam but will grow on rocky or
gravelly soils.

Fertilizing
Mulberries usually do not need fertilizing though
they benefit from an organic mulch.

Watering
The trees are somewhat drought tolerant once
established.

Pruning
Prune only to shape and to remove dead branches.

Pests and Diseases
Mulberries are usually free from pests and diseases;
however, spruce budworms and tent caterpillars are
an occasional problem. Try to remove the colonies by
hand. A bacteria-caused canker is sometimes a problem. Cut into the diseased branch at least a foot below
the cankerous tissue. Sterilize the pruning instrument
with a 10 percent solution of bleach between cuts.

Birds are the chief pests. Cover trees with netting
during harvest season to protect the fruit.

Harvesting
The easiest way to harvest mulberries is to spread a
clean, white cloth or a piece of plastic under the tree
when most of the fruit is ripe—black and soft—and
to shake the tree gently. The berries should be gath-
ered as they fall. Red, not-quite-ripe berries can be
picked and are tart and good for jellies and pies.

Note: If you are going to pick mulberries by hand,
invest in a package of see-through plastic gloves to
protect your hands from staining. They are available

E.65. *Mulberries are among the few berries that grow on trees.*

from beauty-supply houses, are inexpensive, and one package will last for years.

How to Purchase
Forms and Sources

Mulberry trees are available bare root or in containers from local nurseries and from the following mail-order firms: (Readily Available).

Pollinators

Mulberries are self-pollinating.

Varieties

There are a number of varieties of mulberries offered by mail-order nurseries: some are black, some are red, and others are white. The most often preferred berries are the black ones. 'Black Satin', 'Black Giant', 'Hicks', 'Downing', and Persian mulberries are varieties to look for. Occasionally local nurseries carry weeping mulberries. Sometimes these have tasty fruits, but generally they are insipid. Try to taste the fruits before you buy this type of mulberry.

Preserving

Dry mulberries outdoors by laying them out in a warm, dry place, out of the sun, in a single layer on a screen for four to five days. Protect them from birds. Alternatively, use a food dryer.

To freeze, lay the fruits on a cookie sheet and place it in the freezer. Gather fruits when frozen and put them in freezer bags. Or combine 1 cup sugar with 5

cups fruit. Mix together, put in a container that seals well, and freeze.

MUSCADINE GRAPE. See Grape.
MUSTARD. See Greens.
NANKING CHERRY. See Plum, Bush.

Nasturtium
Dwarf nasturtium, *Tropaeolum minus*
Garden nasturtium, *T. majus*

Effort Scale
NO. 2
Annual planting required
Fairly frequent watering needed

Zones
Annual

Thumbnail Sketch
Herbaceous perennials; grown as annuals in most climates
Vine, to 10 ft.; dwarf varieties, to 1 ft. tall
Propagated from seeds or cuttings
Needs full sun; in hottest areas, prefers partial shade
Leaves are lily-pad shaped, bright to blue-green, 2—3 in. across
Blooms in spring, summer, and fall
Flowers are red, mahogany, yellow, orange, or cream colored, 2—3 in. across
Flower buds and leaves are edible; harvested in spring, summer, and fall
Used in flower beds, herb gardens, containers; vining types used on trellises, over retaining walls, in hanging baskets

How to Use
In the Kitchen

Nasturtium buds or young seed pods are often pickled and used as a substitute for capers. Tender, young leaves add a peppery flavor to salad, and the flowers can brighten a salad as well.

In the Landscape

These succulent plants are grown as popular annuals in cold climates and as perennials in mild climates. Their large, lily-pad-shaped, bright-green leaves form a good backdrop for the large brilliant flowers, which can be red, orange, yellow, mahogany, or cream colored. The flowers are gently but spicily fragrant. Some nasturtium varieties have double flowers.

The compact dwarf plants, about 1 foot high, are used in herb gardens and flower borders. Try inter

E.66. Nasturtiums make a colorful hanging basket.

planting them with lettuce, carrots, spinach, chard, or alpine strawberries. The vining kinds, which can trail to 10 feet, are lovely in containers or hanging baskets, flowing over a rock wall, interplanted with vining peas or cucumbers, or climbing up a fence or a post. They are always a bright spot to lift the spirit.

How to Grow, Purchase, and Preserve

Nasturtiums grow so easily that every garden can have some. They grow in any well-drained soil, want moisture but not sogginess, and get along without extra feeding. Aphids are an occasional problem. Nasturtiums often reseed themselves. They are generous in their blooming habits, so you can have bouquets over along period.

The leaves are delicious as long as you harvest them when they are young. To use the buds as capers, pick them just before they open or use half-grown seed pods.

The flavor of the many varieties of nasturtium is very similar. The landscaping uses, however, are more varied. Local nurseries carry a few varieties but for more choice, order from mail-order nurseries. Nurseries with the largest selection are (11,23,45).

Varieties

'Alaska'—flowers yellow, orange, and red shades; foliage is variegated green and white; plants compact to 12 in. (11,23,45,55,57,62)

Climbing Mixed—flowers in orange, red, and yellow; vines to 8 ft. (Readily Available)

'Empress of India'—deep-red flowers; gray-green foliage on 2-ft. vines; great for hanging baskets. (11,45,55,57,62)

'Jewel Mix'—yellow, red, orange, pink, and bicolored flowers; compact plants to 12 in. (1,11,12,35,37,39,45,55,58,62)

'Whirlybird'—mahogany, orange, red, gold, and rose flowers; blooms are large and upward facing; spurless flowers; compact plants to 12 in. (11,12,23,26,35,57,62,64)

Nasturtium Seed Capers

1 pint nasturtium seed pods
3/4 cup cider vinegar
1/4 cup water
1/4 cup brown sugar
1 teaspoon salt
1 teaspoon mustard seed
1/2 clove garlic, crushed (optional)

Gather the half-grown seed clusters, wash, and pack into sterilized small (1/2-pint) canning jars. In a stainless steel or enamel saucepan, combine the other ingredients and boil for 10 minutes. Pour over nasturtium seed pods. Seal the jars tightly. Store in a cold place. Do not use for two weeks.

Natal Plum
Carissa grandiflora

Effort Scale
NO. 2
Easy to grow
Some pruning needed
Fruits are usually processed

Zones
10-11

Thumbnail Sketch
Evergreen shrub
2—18 ft. tall, depending on variety
Propagated from seeds and cuttings
Needs full sun in coastal areas, partial shade inland
Leaves are round, glossy, deep green, 3 in. long
Blooms in spring, summer, and often all year
Flowers are white, fragrant five-petaled stars, 2 in. across
Fruits are edible; harvested in spring and summer
Used as interest plant, hedge, espalier, foundation plant, barrier plant, ground cover, in containers

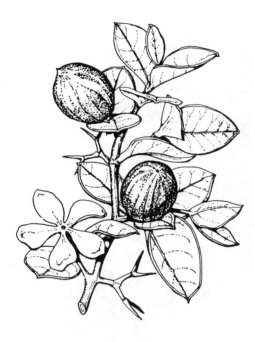

E.67. *Its starlike fragrant flowers and brilliant red fruits make the natal plum an especially ornamental plant.*

How to Use

In the Kitchen

The beautiful, red fruits of the natal plum plant are 1—2 inches long and are often used for jelly, sauces, and pies. With their combination of sweet and tart flavors, they are delicious fresh in fruit salads or eaten plain as well.

In the Landscape

This handsome evergreen shrub comes in many sizes and shapes and can therefore be used in many situations. Its deep-green, leathery leaves, fragrant, white, jasminelike flowers, and green or red fruits, which are sometimes on the plant simultaneously with the flowers, are all decorative. A low-growing carissa makes a good ground or bank cover. A tall variety can be trained as a small multistemmed tree that goes well near a doorway or entrance, where its fragrance can be enjoyed. This plant also can be kept small enough for container growing. Most varieties have thorns which make them useful as barriers. Try combining them with citrus, loquats, avocados, and guavas.

How to Grow

Climate

The one disadvantage of this plant for all seasons is that it is hardy only to 24°F. Still, because of its

beauty it is often used in cooler climates in containers, to be moved to protected areas when the weather turns cold; or planted in zone 9 on a protected south wall and covered when frost threatens. A big advantage of this plant is its tolerance of seacoast conditions; that is, it withstands salt spray. The natal plum grows best in the southern part of California, Hawaii, in Florida, and along the Gulf Coast.

E.68. *Low-growing varieties of natal plum are suitable for containers.*

Exposure

The natal plum requires full sun in foggy coastal areas but some shade in hot, desert areas.

Soil

This plant is not fussy about soil type except that it must be well drained.

Fertilizing

Minimal fertilization is required.

Watering

In sandy soil and in hot climates, natal plum should be watered occasionally. Almost no watering is needed under cool seacoast conditions.

Pruning

It is necessary to shape this plant and to cut out dead or crossing branches. It can be sheared as a hedge but it will not produce as much fruit that way.

Pests and Diseases
The plant has few pests and diseases.

Harvesting
Pick fruits carefully when they become fully colored. Most varieties have thorns at the base of the fruit.

How to Purchase

Forms and Sources
Natal plum plants are available in containers from local nurseries. Seeds are available from (2,20,54).

Pollinators
To ensure pollinating, plant more than one natal plum.

Varieties
'Fancy'—the best producer of excellent fruits; upright, growth to 6 ft., very thorny; considered self-fertile.
'Tuttle'—fruits are not as good as on 'Fancy'; 2—3 ft. tall with a 3—5 ft. spread; used as a tall ground cover.

Preserving

Natal Plum Jelly
4 cups natal plums
2 cups water
sugar as needed

Wash fruits and slice or crush them. Pour fruit pieces or pulp and water into a kettle. Bring mixture to a boil, and simmer for 20 minutes.

Extract juice by straining it through a jelly bag; measure it, and mix it with an equal quantity of sugar. In a pot, boil mixture until it reaches the jelly stage. Pour the jelly into hot, sterilized glasses and seal. Each cup of juice yields approximately one 8-ounce glass of jelly. See KIWI for detailed jelly directions.

NECTARINE. See Peach and Nectarine.
NEW ZEALAND SPINACH. See Greens.

Okra (GUMBO)
Abelmoschus esculentus [Hibiscus esculentus]

Effort Scale
NO. 2
Annual planting required
Vulnerable to a few minor pests

E.69. *Most okra plants grow to 4-5 feet. 'Dwarf Green Long Pod', shown here, grows to about 2 1/2 feet.*

Zones
Annual

Thumbnail Sketch
Herbaceous annual
Standard, 4—6 ft. tall; dwarf variety, 2—4 ft. tall
Propagated from seeds
Needs full sun
Leaves are lobed, 6—10 in. across
Blooms in summer
Flowers are hibiscuslike, yellow or red and yellow, 2—3 in. across
Seed pods are edible; harvested in summer and fall
Used in the back of flower beds, or containers

How to Use

In the Kitchen
Okra, like the olive, is usually an acquired taste. Its best-known use is in seafood or chicken gumbo; the pods are also served as a hot, boiled vegetable or chilled and served vinaigrette as a salad. It can also be fried and is often used in lamb dishes.

In the Landscape
These herbaceous summer annuals are in the same family as hollyhocks and hibiscus. The family resem-

blance is expressed in their large, creamy yellow blossoms, which usually have red throats. The tall types are 4—6 feet tall and belong in the back of a large flower bed, perhaps in front of your still-taller Jerusalem artichokes. The dwarf varieties, which grow to 2—4 feet tall, can be used in the midst of a flower border or in a container.

The large leaves, 6—10 inches across, the showy flowers, and the green pods that follow give the plant summer-long appeal. One variety, 'Red Okra', has deep-red stems, yellow and red flowers, and red pods—a real eye-catcher. Try combining it with peppers and large red salvia.

How to Grow

Okra likes heat and will not tolerate cloudy, cool summers. Where corn grows well, okra will usually thrive. Besides heat, it requires well-drained soil that includes plenty of humus. Too much nitrogen fertilizer will make it go to leaf instead of pods. It does not take much water, and it has few pest problems. If caterpillars show up, hand-picking is often sufficient since you probably will not be growing very many okra plants (a dozen are usually enough for all but the most ardent okra lovers). *Bacillus thuringiensis* can be used for a serious caterpillar infestation.

Okra pods are best picked before they are 3 inches long. If they are allowed to mature much beyond that, the plant will stop pod production.

How to Purchase

Okra seed is readily available from nurseries and mail-order sources.

Varieties

'Clemson Spineless'—pods green; good for thickening soup; plant grows 4-4 1/2 ft. (Readily Available)

'Dwarf Green Long Pod'—pods green and ribbed; bears early (55 days); plant grows to 2 1/2-3 1/2 ft. (Readily Available)

'Emerald'—medium green pods; leaves somewhat grayish; plant tall, 6-9 ft. (27)

'Park's Candelabra Branching'—green thick pods; bears 4-6 spikes per plant; high yield. (49)

'Red Okra'—red tender tasty pods; ornamental plant; tall, to 5 ft., with red stems and leaf veins; flowers yellow with red. (1,12,20,27,55)

'White Velvet'—light-green, tender pods; plants grow to 3 1/2 ft. (12,27)

Preserving

Okra can be canned, frozen, or dried.

Olive
Olea europaea

Effort Scale

NO. 4
Very easy to grow
Some pruning needed
Harvesting and preserving are time-consuming

Zones

9—10

Thumbnail Sketch

Evergreen tree or shrub 25—30 ft. tall
Propagated from cuttings and by grafting and budding
Needs full sun
Leaves are gray-green with whitish undersides, narrow, 1—3 in. long
Blooms in spring
Flowers are fragrant but insignificant
Fruits are edible if processed; harvested in fall or winter
Used as multistemmed tree, interest plant, screen, large shrub, to line a driveway, near an herb garden

E.70. The olive's glossy fruits are set off by its subtle gray foliage.

E.71. *Older olive trees take on gnarled shapes and should be pruned to accent this feature.*

How to Use

In the Kitchen

Salad Niçoise, pot roast Provençale, Italian poultry stuffing, Greek olives, Spanish olives—the recipes alone indicate that the Mediterranean area is olive country. The fruits of the olive tree are versatile and add great richness to many dishes. They also are a favorite garnish for salad plates and sandwiches. However, I cannot with good conscience urge you to try preserving olives yourself. The standard procedure for removing the bitterness from the fruits requires that they be soaked in a lye solution. Not only is lye a caustic substance, and so difficult to work with, but also the risk of botulism developing in a nonacid home-canned product is great. All things considered, it is best to purchase canned olives.

However, pickled olives and olive oil are less hazardous to produce. Olive presses are available for making olive oil at home. The flavorful oil of olives improves salads and adds a distinctive flavor to browned meats and poultry, so it is worth preparing fresh and keeping as a staple. Although admittedly olive oil is a chore to produce, the superior product and the resulting money savings for heavy users make the effort worthwhile.

In the Landscape

Olive trees are extremely beautiful—in fact, they are among the loveliest of the edible ornamentals. Their gnarled trunks, graceful branching structures, and soft, gray-green foliage give them the appearance of living sculptures. Nevertheless, these trees are often cursed as a nuisance, since their food crop is exceedingly messy, but they are so beautiful that people put up with the inconvenience to use them as ornamentals. Olive trees are effective in a Spanish- or mission-style landscape; their sculptural qualities are shown to their best advantage against white stucco walls.

Olive trees should never be planted near patios, sidewalks, or driveways. Their oil, although tasty in salads, is slippery and staining on hard surfaces. Nor should they be planted in a lawn. The ideal location is with ground covers or a mulch.

Note: If your yard is small, I do not recommend that you use up your growing space for edibles with an olive tree. The trees are numerous but very few people process their olives. Whenever I have asked neighbors if I might have some of their olives, naturally expecting to share the resulting olive oil with them, they have readily assented, delighted to know that their olives would be used. If olives have been made available to you, be sure to find out if the trees have been sprayed with pesticides or if herbicides have been applied. Avoid olives that have been so treated.

How to Grow

Climate

Olives need high heat and some winter chill to fruit properly. They are hardy to 13°F. The fruits, which ripen late in fall, need a very long summer to mature. The fruits are injured by temperatures below 27°F.

High humidity inhibits pollination, so these magnificent trees are limited to the warmer parts of the Southwest for fruit production.

Exposure

Olive trees need full sun.

Soil

Olive trees adapt to a wide variety of soils but must have good drainage.

Fertilizer

Occasional applications of nitrogen fertilizer increase fruit production, but trees on normal soils generally produce plenty of fruits without being fed.

Watering

Olive trees are extremely drought tolerant, but deep watering in arid climates once or twice a summer increases fruit production.

Pruning

Prune these trees to shape them. Enjoy accenting their graceful lines. Extreme pruning cuts down on fruit production, but moderate pruning to shape and thin creates a beautiful tree. If you want very large olives, thin the fruits. Olives tend to bear fruits on alternate years. By pruning moderately and thinning the fruits, you can modify this tendency.

Pests and Diseases

Olives are usually unaffected by pests and diseases. You might have some problems with scale or a disease that produces galls (a swelling of plant tissue) on the twigs or branches. Cut those out, and sterilize your tools between cuts.

Do not plant olives where verticillium wilt is a problem, since these trees are quite susceptible. It is not a good idea to plant strawberries as a ground cover under olive trees, as strawberries sometimes carry this disease.

Harvesting

Pick olives green for curing, or green or black for olive oil. To get a very high quality oil, use green olives. You will trade off on amount, however, since fully ripe and black olives produce more oil.

Olives must be processed to remove the bitterness before they are edible.

How to Purchase

Forms and Sources

Buy olive plants in containers at your local nursery.

Pollinators

Most olives are self-pollinating.

Varieties

Make sure you choose a fruiting variety. The "fruit-less" varieties usually do produce some fruits, but their crops are poor. The following varieties have good productivity.

'Manzanillo'—large fruits; low growth habit. (8)
'Mission'—small fruits with good flavor and high oil content; the most readily available variety. (Locally Available)

Preserving

For information about olive curing, order: "Home Pickling of Olives," Bulletin Number 2758; price $1.25. It is available from: Publications, Division of Agriculture and Natural Resources, University of California, 6701 San Pablo Ave., Oakland, CA 94608-1239.

Making Olive Oil

Pick the olives when they are still green. Dry them on racks for a week or ten days in a warm place out of the sun, turning the olives a few times a day to ensure even drying. Alternately, use a food dryer and follow the directions.

Press the dried olives in an olive press or a cider press. During pressing, do not squeeze hard enough to crush the pits (the pits contain oil but it is inferior for eating and is used to make soap). Collect the juice as it comes out.

Strain the juice through cheesecloth into glass jars and allow it to separate from remaining solids. Siphon the oil off, using plastic tubing. Now the two- to three-month process of clarifying begins. During that time, as sediment builds up on the bottom of the jar siphon off the oil again, leaving the sediment on the bottom and again straining the oil through multiple layers of cheesecloth. This can be done every two weeks for as many as five times. When the oil is clear, pour it into sterilized jars and seal. Once the oil is opened, refrigerate it, since it becomes rancid at room temperature.

For more information on making olive oil, send for leaflet Number 2789 from: Publications, Division of Agriculture and Natural Resources, University of California (address above).

ONION. See Root Vegetables.
ORANGE. See Citrus Fruits.
ORANGE BERGAMOT MINT. See Mint.

Oregano (WILD MARJORAM)

Origanum vulgare

Effort Scale

NO. 1
Very easy to grow
Annual planting required in coldest zones

Zones

All

Thumbnail Sketch

Perennial herb, grown as an annual in cold climates
2—2 1/2 ft. tall
Propagated from seeds, divisions, and cuttings
Needs full sun
Leaves are dull gray-green, small
Blooms in summer
Flowers are pale pink, white, or lavender, grow in spikes, small

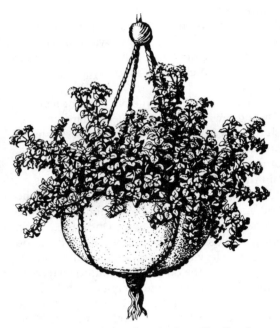

E. 72. Oregano's sprawling form lends itself well to hanging containers.

Leaves are edible, used as seasoning, harvested year round

Used in herb gardens, to sprawl over a rock wall, in hanging baskets, containers

How to Use

In the Kitchen

Oregano leaves are aromatic and are used as a seasoning in pizza, spaghetti sauce, soups, stews, and salads. So-called Greek oregano is the strong version preferred by many cooks when a hearty oregano taste is wanted, such as in pizza or in classic tomato sauce. Common oregano is milder and is pleasant in soups or delicate sauces.

In the Landscape

These herbaceous perennials grow to a height of 2 1/2 feet. They are inclined to be rangy, but their dark gray-green leaves and pale-pink flowers make them a colorful addition to a flower border. You can keep oregano cut back to stay bushy, or you can use the plant's ranginess to advantage, letting it spill over a rock wall. Oregano combines well with the pinks and lavenders of alyssum, garlic chives, ivy geraniums, and marjoram. It is especially showy when planted with any of these in a container. Every herb garden should contain oregano.

How to Grow, Purchase, and Preserve

Oregano can be grown from seed or cuttings and is simple to grow. It needs well-drained, medium-rich soil, plenty of sun, and moderate amounts of water. In winter in the coldest climates, this herb should be brought inside or a new one planted in the spring.

Oregano can be harvested any time during the year for fresh use. However, if you are planning to dry it for the winter, you should harvest the leaves before the plant has started to flower to ensure good texture and rich flavor.

For drying information, see BASIL.

Purchase seed or young plants from local or mail-order nurseries. Greek oregano is available from: (1,2,11,12,18,19,23,37,54,66).

ORIENTAL PEAR. See Pear.

Parsley Petroselinum crispum

Italian parsley, *P. c. neapolitanum*

Effort Scale

NO. 2
Annual planting required
Flower heads must be removed
Must be kept fairly moist

Zones

All

Thumbnail Sketch

Biennial herbs, usually planted as annuals
6 in.—3 ft. tall, depending on variety
Propagated from seeds
Need partial shade; full sun in cloudy, cool climates
Leaves are curled, tufted, dark green
Flowers greenish-yellow in umbels; not usually seen
Leaves are edible; used as seasoning; harvested year round
Used in herb gardens, flower borders, raised beds, containers

How to Use

In the Kitchen

Both species have aromatic leaves that are used fresh as a garnish and a seasoning and dried as a seasoning in salad dressings, soups, stews, and sauces. The Italian species has a stronger flavor than common parsley.

In the Landscape

These herbaceous biennials are grown as annuals. Common parsley is a small, curly-leaved herb. The dark-green, stiff, segmented leaves are 6—8 inches

Common parsley does not retain as much of its flavor as most herbs when it is dried, though it is still satisfactory. Italian parsley dries very well. For drying information, see BASIL.

Pawpaw

Asimina triloba

Effort Scale
NO. 4
Finding good varieties difficult
Establishing plant difficult
Hand-pollination needed occasionally
Pruning and removing suckers usually needed
Fertilizing and mulching necessary

Zones
5—9

Thumbnail Sketch
Deciduous tree or shrub 20—25 ft. tall
Propagated from seeds, by cuttings, and by layering
Needs full sun or light shade
Leaves are oblong, light green, large, 8—12 in. long
Blooms in spring
Flowers are maroon, cup-shaped, 1—2 in. across
Fruits are edible; harvested in fall

E. 73. *The clear green of parsley makes a bright spot in any landscape.*

long. Italian parsley, with its cut but only slightly curly leaves, grows to 3 feet. The flowers of both species resemble miniature Queen Anne's lace, but they should not be considered landscape material, since they must be picked before opening to stimulate leaf production.

The dark-green of both these plants makes them usable as borders in herb or flower beds. Italian parsley, being taller, can also be grown in the middle of a flower border. I like to combine them in containers with orange violas and alpine strawberries.

How to Grow, Purchase, and Preserve
Parsley is easy to grow and thrives in all areas of the country. In the spring it can be started from seed or from seedlings, available from local nurseries. The seeds take a long time to germinate, so growers are often advised to soak them for twenty-four hours before planting. If you do not follow this advice be patient; the seeds may not sprout for several weeks. The old herbals claimed that parsley seeds had to go to the devil and back seven times before they could sprout.

Parsley prefers partial shade; well-drained, rich, fairly moist soil; and a frost-free climate. In cold-winter areas, plants may be dug up during the winter and brought indoors to a warm windowsill.

Harvest the leaves before the plant has started to flower. The leaves will have a better texture and usually more flavor.

To use parsley fresh, pick leaves as needed.

E.74. *Pawpaw fruits, leaves, and flowers.*

Used as interest plant, small tree, in a lawn; as a
shrub, may be used as accent, screen, or hedge

How to Use
In the Kitchen
The custardlike, yellow-orange flesh of the pawpaw
tastes something like that of the banana. Although
they are usually eaten fresh, the fruits can be used in
custard pies, plum-type puddings, and preserves.

Pawpaw leather is made from the dried fruits. The
pawpaw is the American relative of the delicious custard apple, or cherimoya, of Peru and Ecuador.

Note: Some pawpaws have white flesh. These fruits
are usually bitter and unpleasant tasting. Always look
for the darker-fleshed fruits.

In the Landscape
The pawpaw is native to the United States as far
west as Texas, north to Michigan, and south to northern Florida. It is a large deciduous shrub that will
grow, slowly, to 25 feet in height. The gracefully
drooping, light-green, foot-long, oval leaves help to
make this plant useful as a screen or an informal
hedge. When trained as a pyramid-shaped tree, the
pawpaw contrasts nicely with rounder shapes in the
shrub border. Conversely, it can highlight similarly
shaped evergreens. The pawpaw grows well in a lawn,
and is handsome and dramatic enough to be used as
an accent plant. The maroon, cup-shaped flowers and
the 5-inch fruits, which turn from green to yellow to
brown, are not showy but add interest to the tree.

How to Grow
Note: Despite the fact that pawpaw trees are
indigenous, they are sometimes difficult to establish
and seem to vary in their need for cross-pollination.

Climate
Pawpaws are hardy to −30°F. They require some
winter chilling and hot summers..They star in the
Midwest.

Exposure
They need full sun or light shade.

Planting
Pawpaw trees are sometimes temperamental about
being transplanted. There is a difference of opinion.
Some research has indicated that filling the planting
hole with a mixture of half soil, half vermiculite helps
the plant to adapt. Other researchers suggest that
pawpaws need a symbiotic soil fungus to grow properly, and that soil from around the base of another,
successfully growing tree should be added to the

E.75. *Pawpaws are generally grown as shrubs, but the plant can
be pruned to a single trunk. Most trees will grow into a pyramid
shape.*

planting hole. You are on your own on this one.
Consult the *1974 California Rare Fruit Growers
Yearbook* for more details (see Appendix C).
Transplanted pawpaws should be handled with care.
Get as much of the root system as you can. Do not let
the roots dry out. Keep the young trees well watered
the first year. Cut the main trunk back to a foot above
the graft line at the time of transplanting.

Soil
These trees prefer well-drained, rich garden loam.

Fertilizing
Where pawpaws are not planted in rich bottom
land, they respond well to an organic mulch and moderate amounts of fertilizing.

Watering
Pawpaws have high water requirements. They grow
best in areas that get at least 30 inches of rain a year.
They will grow with irrigation in the arid West.

Pruning
Pawpaws naturally sucker and will form a thicket if
not controlled. For a screen or group planting of pawpaws, allow suckers to come up only where you want
them; remove all others. To train as a tree, or to main-

tain the integrity of a grafted plant, remove all suckers as they appear. The plant will sucker less as it ages.

Pests and Diseases

Pawpaws have very few pests and diseases.

Harvesting

Pawpaws are ready to be picked when they are fully colored and slightly soft. Bring them inside to fully ripen.

How to Purchase

Forms and Sources

Pawpaws are available as seeds and as seedlings or grafted varieties in containers.

Some nurseries carry them.

Note: Pawpaw is referred to as America's Cinderella fruit. The fruit does not ship well and has therefore received relatively little scientific and commercial attention. But a small group of home gardeners has kept up interest in the plant, and a few mail-order nurseries carry pawpaws for the home grower: (6,15,24,27,31,46,61,70). Seeds are available from (2,14). Corwin Davis Nursery, 20865 Junction Rd., Bellevue, MI 49021 is particularly knowledgeable about pawpaws, and puts out a pawpaw bulletin; send $3.00 when ordering the bulletin.

Pollinators

Usually more than one tree seems to be needed for pollination. For most varieties, hand-pollination can help fruit production but is not always necessary.

Varieties

Some grafted named varieties have been produced, but most of the plants available are ungrafted seedlings with variable fruit.

The most readily available varieties of pawpaw are 'Sunflower', 'Taylor', and 'Taytwo'.

Preserving

Pawpaws can be dried, frozen, and baked into breads.

To freeze, wash, peel, and seed the fruits. Pack the pulp in rigid plastic containers and freeze. The frozen pulp can be stored for four to six months. When thawed, the fruit will be very soft. Eat it promptly.

Peach and Nectarine

Peach, *Prunus Persica*
Nectarine, *P. P.* var. *nucipersica*

E.76. *Few pleasures approach the taste of sun-ripened peaches right from the tree.*

Effort Scale

Standard Peach and Nectarine
NO. 5
Vulnerable to many diseases and pests, including birds
Heavy pruning necessary
Fertilizing and mulching usually necessary
Large yield must be harvested quickly
Cleanup of fruit mandatory

Genetic Dwarf Peach and Nectarine
NO. 3
Vulnerable to many pests and diseases
Very little pruning needed
Harvest is pressing but manageable

Zones
5—9

Thumbnail Sketch
Standard Peach and Nectarine
Deciduous trees 15—20 ft. tall
Propagated by budding or from cuttings
Need full sun

Leaves are narrow, 3—6 in. long
Bloom in spring
Flowers are pink, showy in some varieties; 1—2 in.
  across
Fruits are edible; harvested in summer
Used as interest trees, espalier, screens

Genetic Dwarf Peach and Nectarine
Deciduous small trees or shrubs
4—10 ft. tall
Propagated by budding
Need full sun
Leaves are medium green, 6—8 in. long
Bloom in spring
Fruits are edible; harvested in summer
Used as interest plant, hedge, espalier, flowering
  shrub, foundation plant, and in containers

How to Use
In the Kitchen

Fresh peaches and nectarines are lusciously juicy
and sweet. They bring a real note of midsummer to
our menus. Whether served as a salad, a simple desert
consisting of a perfect specimen, sliced and sweetened
as a topping for ice cream and shortcake, or as the
fruit base in fresh ice cream, the special flavor and
color of these fruits enhance our dining pleasure.
When cooked or canned, the flavor of both fruits
changes but is as delicious and adaptable as that of
the fresh fruits. Peach Melba, for example, combines
the flavor of cooked peaches with jelly made from currants or raspberries, both of which might originate in
your yard. Peach upside-down-cake mixes the flavor
of peaches with brown sugar. And who can resist a
piece of nectarine pie? Even an unadorned dish of
home-canned peaches or nectarines makes a nice end
to a meal, and brandied peaches constitute a more
dramatic dessert. Both peaches and nectarines result
in delicious jams and marmalades, and are excellent
as fruit leather.

In the Landscape

Standard peach and nectarine trees are of only limited use in the landscape. If you choose a variety with
showy flowers and good form and maintain it with
care, the tree will serve as an interest plant or a small
tree near a driveway, as long as you plant it back far
enough to prevent the fruit from dropping on the concrete. Planting it near the street is tempting fate—and
passersby, who might help themselves.

Genetic dwarf peaches and nectarines are far more
versatile and attractive in the landscape. All varieties
have beautiful foliage—long, narrow, rich-green leaves
that grow in graceful, hanging clusters—and showy,
deep-pink flowers.

E.77. *Nectarines make good door-yard trees, but make sure they
are not too near windows or paths.*

These graceful plants can be used as informal
hedges, foundation plants, or interest plants in a
shrub border, in geometric patterns in an herb garden,
along paths, in raised beds, and in large containers.

Note: Do not plant peach or nectarine trees near
windows because the trees will need to be sprayed.

How to Grow
Climate

Probably no fruit tree elicits more wishful thinking
than the peach tree. Everyone wants a peach tree. But
no matter what you wish, neither peaches nor their
close cousins, nectarines, survive in very cold or very
warm winters—period.

Some very hardy peach varieties, such as 'Reliance',
are beginning to widen that range, hut for all practical
purposes, no peaches or nectarines are successful in
the coldest sections of New England or the Northern
Plains. In borderline areas, try growing genetic dwarf
peaches and nectarines in containers so you can bring
them inside for the coldest part of the winter. Cold-
weather considerations are discussed in more detail in

the subsection headed "Genetic Dwarf Peaches and Nectarines," under "Varieties," below.

Peaches and nectarines do poorly in areas with very warm winters too, since, like most temperate-zone fruit trees, they have a chilling requirement.

Some varieties of peaches and nectarines that have a very low chilling requirement grow in the warmest areas of Florida and the warm deserts, but their fruit is disappointing compared to the real thing.

Exposure

It is extremely important that peaches and nectarines receive full sun.

Soil

Both peaches and nectarines are fussy about soil; they will not grow well in heavy soils and must have good drainage. They prefer well-drained sandy loam.

Fertilizing

A difference of opinion prevails regarding the fertilizing of peaches and nectarines. Some authorities favor feeding them high amounts of nitrogen, and other say that large amounts of nitrogen produce lush, weak growth susceptible to disease and frost.

It is my educated guess that large amounts of nitrogen are called for in commercial growing in fairly warm climates where trees are treated heavily with insecticides and fungicides, and the highest fruit production at whatever cost is the objective. But for growers trying to maintain their landscapes with as few chemicals as possible, I recommend feeding peaches and nectarines in the spring with moderate amounts of nitrogen and keeping the trees mulched with compost or manure during the growing season. The symptoms of nitrogen deficiency are lack of vigor and a pale, light-green or slightly yellow leaf color. On trees showing this characteristic, use a supplemental nitrogen fertilizer in early summer. If you live in a cold-winter area, it is critical that this feeding be administered by July 1.

Pruning

Genetic dwarf peach and nectarine trees need pruning only to shape and to remove dead or crossing branches.

Standard and semidwarf trees, however, need heavy pruning to produce good fruit in most climates. Consult local authorities for pruning information if you live in the coldest peach climates. Prune in early spring just as growth is starting so that pruning wounds heal quickly and thus are less apt to become diseased.

Peaches bear on one-year-old wood only. Therefore, new wood must be continually produced to permit fruiting in the following year. To prune standard, semidwarf, and regular dwarf trees, thin out a number of branches, particularly in the middle of the tree, to allow sunlight to enter and good air circulation to occur. Prune heavily, removing one third to one half the new growth. Remove any weak growth or crossing branches. Pruning time is a good time to check the crown of the tree for borers.

The crops peaches and nectarines set are usually too heavy and fruit must be thinned when the fruits are about an inch across. Leave 6—8 inches between fruits on the early types of peaches and nectarines, 4—5 inches between late-season fruits. If you do not thin your fruits, the tree can be weakened, the peaches will be small, and the branches may break from the weight. Also, the next year's peach crop will probably be small.

Pests and Diseases

It is nearly impossible to grow any size or variety of peach and nectarine without some sort of chemical help. These trees are the weaklings of the fruit world. They are susceptible to many pests and diseases, and must be dormant sprayed in the winter.

Diseases are best controlled by planting resistant varieties when possible, choosing proper exposure with good air circulation, keeping the trees well mulched and pruned, and scrupulous hygiene.

A Bordeaux mixture or lime-sulfur should be applied in late fall and again just before flower buds start to swell in spring to help control peach leaf curl, brown rot, and scale. With peach leaf curl the foliage develops bumpy, red, swollen areas. This condition slowly defoliates the tree and weakens it.

Brown rot is a common problem for the growers of these trees, particularly nectarines. It makes the fruits turn brown and mushy just before ripening. Clean up all affected fruit and destroy it. If the problem is severe, check with your local Extension agent for control measures.

Powdery mildew is a severe problem in damp climates. On affected trees the leaves, twigs, or fruits become covered with a white, powdery substance.

Peach tree borers are deadly to both peach and nectarine trees. One or two can kill a young tree by girdling the trunk.

San Jose scale and plum curculio are sometimes a problem. Dormant sprays help somewhat on scale. Good hygiene helps also.

See Part Two for more information on these pests and diseases.

Peaches and nectarines are short-lived trees; their life expectancy is eight to twenty years. Neglecting them or allowing the diseases that affect them to go uncontrolled will shorten their lives even more. Peach trees are questionable choice for purely organic gardeners or for those who want maintenance-free gardens.

Harvesting

Peaches and nectarines ripen over a fairly short period of time, usually two or three weeks. Try to plan to be at home for the harvest, not off camping, since, once ripe, the fruits won't wait.

Peaches and nectarines are ripe when they are fully colored, come off the tree easily in your hand, and give slightly to the touch. You can expect to harvest 2—3 bushels yearly from a mature tree.

How to Purchase

Forms and Sources

Peaches are available bare root from local and mail-order nurseries in late winter to early spring, and in containers throughout the growing season. Nurseries with a particularly good selection are (17,27,46,61).

Pollinators

The great majority of peaches and nectarines are self-fruitful. The most commonly grown peaches that need a pollinator are 'J. H. Hale' and 'Indian Free'.

Varieties

Most of the varieties of peaches and nectarines listed have showy flowers, but not all varieties do. Also, most of the varieties listed have some resistance to disease. Peaches and nectarines come either with a loose pit—freestone—or clingstone, that is, with the pit attached to the flesh. Usually the freestone are easier both to work with in the kitchen and to eat fresh.

STANDARD PEACHES
  'Alberta Red Haven'— (27)
  'Elberta'— (61)
  'Encore'— (61)
  'Harrow Beauty'—large, freestone fruits; good for freezing and canning. (44)
  'Madison'—medium-size, freestone fruits; very tolerant to frost during blooming. (13,44,61)
  'Crest Haven'—medium-size, freestone fruits; flowers showy; tree hardy. (44)
  'Reliance'—large, freestone fruits; probably the hardiest of all the peach varieties, good to -20°F; flowers showy. (13,24)
  'Rio Oso Gem'—large, freestone fruits; good peach for freezing; large, showy, light pink blossoms. (Readily Available)

STANDARD NECTARINES
  Some nectarine varieties with showy flowers are 'Cherokee', 'Double Delight', 'Flavortop', 'Garden

E.78. Genetic dwarf peaches and nectarines have showy flowers, a beautiful shape, and graceful leaves.

State', 'Lafayette', 'Nectacrest', 'Redbud', and 'Sun Grand'. 'Fantasia'-large-size, mid- to late-season freestone fruits; flowers showy; low chilling requirement. (8)
'Independence'—medium-size, early-season freestone fruits; flowers showy; will take warm winters. (8)
'Red Chief'—medium-size, late-season, freestone, white-fleshed fruits; flowers showy; highly resistant to brown rot. (8)

GENETIC DWARF PEACHES AND NECTARINES
Over the last decade much effort has been put into developing a new type of dwarf fruit tree—the genetic dwarf. Genetic dwarfs differ from regular dwarf fruit trees in that they are naturally small rather than grafted onto dwarfing rootstock; they are themselves grafted for propagation purposes and for strong root systems. In the case of peaches and nectarines, the genetic dwarf varieties have many qualities, some good, some bad, that the standards do not. Advantages of genetic dwarf peaches and nectarines are:

1. Genetic dwarf peaches and nectarines are more attractive and have more landscaping uses in the home garden than standard trees.
2. Most varieties need less chilling.
3. They are easier to spray for disease control.

4. Their size makes them easier to use in small yards.

5. Harvesting is easier.

6. Their harvest is smaller. Standard-size peaches and nectarines produce large amounts of very perishable fruits, the processing of which requires large banks of time. Their harvest season is short, meaning that you can only enjoy freshly ripened peaches for a brief period. But three or four mature genetic dwarf trees yield a more manageable harvest of 30 to 40 full-size fruits at one time. Furthermore, if you stagger the harvest time by planting different varieties, you can enjoy fresh-ripened peaches for as long as six to eight weeks instead of two or three.

7. Genetic dwarf peaches and nectarines need very little pruning.

8. These miniature trees are not as hardy as some of the standard trees but they can be planted in colder climates because they take readily to container planting, and during the coldest part of the year they can be moved into a garage or a sheltered place. If you have to take this measure while the trees are in bloom, you might have to hand-pollinate them with a pencil eraser—a racy endeavor—since the bees are often not out when the weather is cold.

Disadvantages of the genetic dwarf peaches and nectarines are:

1. None of the varieties yet developed have the same eating quality as the best standards. They are improving every year, but the definitive genetic dwarf peach or nectarine is yet to be found.

2. Because of their compact growth habit, they are actually prone to more disease problems than the standards. Thin out some of the inside vegetation to improve air circulation.

Many other fruit and nut trees have genetic dwarf varieties available. They include: almonds, apricots, apples, cherries, plums, and pears. Most of these have the same advantages and disadvantages as mentioned above. In addition, most are self-pollinating.

Many varieties of genetic dwarf peaches and nectarines exist and, because of the increasing demand, many more are being hybridized each year. The following list contains the best currently available, but it is wise to stay informed about new introductions. The flavor of these fruits is generally good, and some of the new introductions are excellent. Except where noted, the trees have a characteristic short, squat form and long leaves.

‘Bonanza II’—an improved variety of the best-known genetic dwarf peach; medium quality, early-season, freestone, yellow-fleshed fruits; needs moderate amounts of winter chilling to fruit; flowers pink, semidouble, and showy. (Readily Available)

‘Compact Redhaven’—peach of a different breeding stock than other genetic dwarfs; a mutation of the full-size ‘Redhaven’; taller than other dwarfs, to 10 feet, with form and leaf similar to standard peaches; one of the best early peaches; yellow flesh; good for freezing. (Readily Available)

‘Stark’s Sensation’—very good quality freestone peach; needs 850 hours of chilling. (61)

THE ‘GARDEN’ SERIES (ZAIGER GENETIC DWARFS)

Floyd Zaiger is a plant breeder of much accomplishment who has produced a number of superior genetic dwarf trees for the home garden. Among them are the following varieties:

‘Garden Beauty’—clingstone nectarine; ripens midseason; striking dark-pink double flowers. (48)

‘Garden Delight’—clingstone nectarine; ripens midseason. (48)

‘Honey Babe’—freestone peach; ripens early midseason; best-tasting of the Zaiger series. (48,52)

THE ‘SOUTHERN’ SERIES

Another group of genetic dwarf fruit trees is carried by the wholesale grower L. E. Cooke and Co. The company distributes its trees through local nurseries and a few mail-order sources. These varieties are:

‘Southern Belle’—freestone nectarine; ripens late. (48)

‘Southern Flame’—freestone peach; ripens midseason. (25)

‘Southern Rose’-freestone peach; ripens midseason. (25)

‘Southern Sweet’—freestone peach, ripens early midseason. (48)

Preserving

Peaches and nectarines can be canned, spiced, pickled, brandied, and made into jams, jellies, fruit leather, chutneys, nectar, and brandy. The fruits can also be frozen.

Peanut (GOOBER, GROUNDNUT)
Arachis hypogaea

Effort Scale
NO. 3
Annual planting necessary

Good soil preparation necessary
Some weeding necessary
Watering usually necessary
Vulnerable to some pests
Harvesting and curing time-consuming

Zones
Annual

Thumbnail Sketch
Herbaceous annual
1—2 ft. tall Propagated from seeds
Needs full sun
Leaves are bright green, somewhat cloverlike,
1 1/2—2 1/2 in. long
Blooms in summer
Flowers are yellow, small, leguminous
Seeds are edible; harvested in fall
Used in flower borders, raised beds, temporary
  ground covers, containers

How to Use
In the Kitchen
Eating goober peas, what fun! If only I could stop!
Peanut butter toast with pomegranate jelly, peanut
brittle, chocolate-covered peanuts, and peanut butter
brownies or fudge all make delicious use of the
peanut. And then there are "tin roof" sundaes (made
with vanilla ice cream, chocolate sauce, and Spanish
peanuts) and, of course, peanut butter cookies. All
that pleasure, and protein too!

In the Landscape
These annual, perky, green providers are beautiful
in flower borders combined with yellow petunias flowing over a sandy bank or planted in a decorative container. They make good temporary ground covers
between newly planted trees and shrubs. their growth
habit—developing a "peg" (shootlike structure) from
the pollinated flower that enters the soil where the
peanut will grow—makes them a good subject for
close-up observation near an outdoor living area.

How to Grow
Climate
Peanuts need hot summers at least four months
long. They can tolerate no frost.

Exposure
These plants need full sun.

Planting
Carefully shell peanuts—do not scratch the surface
or remove the papery skin. Plant shelled peanut seeds
4 inches deep in warm areas of the South and 2 inches deep in the North. Plant them 4 inches apart, and
thin to 1 foot apart once they are growing well.

Soil
Peanuts produce their "nuts" (peanuts are actually
seeds rather than nuts) on long pegs that descend
from the flower. These pegs need to be able to penetrate soft earth before they can produce their peanuts,
so the soil must be extremely loose. This quality is
achieved by adding large amounts of organic matter or
sharp sand.
The seeds will rot if the soil is not well drained.
Peanuts prefer a slightly acid soil, with a pH of 5.0—
6.0.

Fertilizing
Peanuts are leguminous, which means that nitro-
gen-fixation bacteria attached to their roots provide
them with their own source of nitrogen. But peanuts
do need substantial amounts of potassium and calcium. Average garden loam with added humus usually
is sufficient, but if your nuts do not fill out their pods
well, before planting next year add calcium in the
form of gypsum or add as an extra measure eggshells
in the compost you work into the soil, and increase
potassium by working in extra compost, manure,
granite dust, or green sand.

Watering
Keep peanuts well watered during the growing season, particularly when first planted and while they are
flowering. Do not water near harvest time or you may
stimulate the peanuts to sprout.

Pests and Diseases
Weeds are usually the major pest problem affecting
peanuts in home gardens. If you have a long growing
season, you will probably have the luxury of preparing
your seed bed early and stimulating the weeds to grow
with a little extra water. Let the weeds germinate and
then chop them out before you plant your crop. Heavy
mulches, at least 3—4 inches deep, help considerably;
they also keep the soil soft for the pegs and minimize
water loss.
Many pests bother commercially grown peanuts,
but as a rule homegrown peanuts are relatively pest
free. The most common pests are thrips, cutworms,
corn earworms, spider mites and various caterpillars.
Try hand-picking, or for severe infestation of caterpillars and corn earworm, use Bacillus thuringiensis.
Peanuts are susceptible to a few diseases. Leaf spot
causes spotting on lower foliage. Southern blight
symptoms include dying plant tops and white mold
on stems at the soil line. Both can usually be controlled by good plant hygiene and crop rotation.

E.79. *Peanut flowers develop "pegs" that burrow into the ground and become the peanuts. Harvesting them is like a treasure hunt.*

Harvesting

Digging up peanuts is like going on a treasure hunt. What will the next forkful uncover?

Start testing for ripeness when the foliage starts to turn yellow. Pull up a few plants to see what you have. Do not be too eager to pull all the plants up, as the peanuts still get some food from the dying stems. The peanuts are ripe when they look well formed and the insides of the pods begin to develop dark-colored veins.

In northern gardens, before the yellow-leaf stage, check for mature nuts under the central, main part of the plant. This will be your main crop, as the peanuts on the outer pegs probably won't have time to fully ripen. By harvesting when the majority of the central peanuts are ripe you will take no chance of losing your main crop. Cure the nuts for a few weeks in a warm, dry place before eating them. See cautionary note under "Preserving and Preparing" below.

How to Purchase

Form and Sources

Peanut seed is readily available from southern local nurseries and the following mail-order sources: (7,12,24,49,53,58).

Varieties

'Jumbo Virginia'—large peanuts; plant is vine type; growth to 3 1/2 ft. across; for southern areas. (7)
'Spanish'— mall Spanish-type nuts; plant matures in 100-110 days and will produce mature nuts well into Canada if given light, sandy soil and a southern exposure; must be planted by end of May. (Readily Available)
'Tennessee Reds' ('Valencia')—Spanish peanut; small nuts, red skins, two or three nuts per pod; will grow as far north as New York; matures in 120 days; must be planted by end of May. (12,49,53)
'Virginia Jumbo'—large nuts; plant upright; matures in 120 days; for southern areas. (12,49)

Preserving and Preparing

Cure harvested peanuts by leaving the plants in the warm sun for a few weeks. If it looks like rain, bring them inside. To ensure quality if you wish to cure large amounts, you may want to send for a free brochure: *Peanut Harvesting and Drying*, ANR-118, available from Alabama Cooperative Extension Service, Auburn, AL 36830.

An alternative method, usually needed in cold climates, is to hang entire plant from the rafters of the garage or attic. Make sure the room is warm and dry; do not use a basement or cellar floor where the peanuts might stay damp. It is very important to keep the nuts dry, and to allow the moisture in the nuts to evaporate.

Curing and storing peanuts correctly is very important for two reasons. The first is flavor; peanuts have a high oil content and easily become rancid. The second reason is much more important to your health. Moist nuts get moldy. One mold that commonly attacks peanuts produces Aflatoxin, a substance dangerous to humans. Aflatoxin is not removed by heat.

Caution: Do not eat moldy peanuts. Throw them away!

To store peanuts for a short period of time, shell them, place them raw in airtight containers, and refrigerate. For longer periods of storage, freeze them.

Pear

Common (European) pear, *Pyrus communis*
Oriental pear (sand or pear apple), *P. pyrifolia*

Effort Scale

NO. 3
Vulnerable to many pests and diseases
Large harvest is time-consuming

Zones

4—9 for common
5—9 for Oriental

Thumbnail Sketch

Deciduous trees

Standard, 30—40 ft. tall; semidwarf, 15—20 ft. tall;
  dwarf varieties, to 15 ft. tall

Propagated by budding or grafting

Needs full sun

Leaves are deep green, 1—2 1/2 in. long

Blooms in spring

Flowers are white, grow in clusters, showy, 1—1 1/2
  in. across

Fruits are edible; harvested in summer or fall

Used as interest tree, small street tree, espalier, patio
  tree; dwarf types are good for informal hedges,
  shrub borders, and in containers

How to Use

In the Kitchen

An exquisitely ripe European pear, whether it be a
late-summer 'Bartlett', a fall 'Comice' or 'Anjou', or a
winter 'Bosc', is a delight. Served with Camembert or
Brie cheese, it becomes a dessert course that is acceptable in the haughtiest cuisine. The Oriental types offer
a different experience. They are smaller and crisper
than common pears, and sometimes a little gritty but
sweet and juicy. These slightly more exotic types have
a flavor all their own and are certainly worth growing.

Pears of all kinds can be canned or used in jams
and preserves. As desserts they can be poached

E.80. Pear trees characteristically have an upright growth habit.

and served with flavorful sauces that make use of
liqueurs, raspberries, or cranberries. Cooked pears are
inclined to blandness; my preference is for fresh ones.
Most pears store very well. To my way of thinking,
stocking up on several different kinds, properly
picked and stored, is much preferable for winter pear
eating to making do with cooked ones.

In the Landscape

The shape of most pear trees is strongly vertical,
almost like that of a candelabrum. The leaves, medi-
um-dark green, 1—2 inches long, and glossy, follow a
big show of white flower clusters. An advantage of the
pear is that the fruit is produced on long-lived spurs,
so the flower show does not have to be pruned off.
Except for pears such as 'Max-Red Bartlett' and
'Starkrimson', the fruits are not particularly showy,
except insofar as any fruit on any tree is an example of
nature's skill. The Oriental pear varieties are vigorous
trees with shiny, slightly larger deep-green leaves that
turn purplish red. The fruits are round and applelike.

Full-size pear trees can be used for shade. They do
better than most fruit trees in a lawn, and since with
most varieties their fruits are picked before they fall,
these trees do not cause a fruit-drop problem. Lawn
use while never optimum is limited to the East and
Midwest, however, because crown rot is a major problem in arid-summer areas. Any size pear tree can be
used to line a driveway, can be planted near a patio,
and can serve as an entrance accent or a small street
tree. Dwarf varieties can be used in containers, as a
handsome hedge, and espaliered wherever small trees
are needed. The standard tree can be trained into
interesting, gnarled shapes. See PEACH AND NECTARINE
for more information on genetic dwarf trees. Do not
plant disease-prone trees near windows, because they
usually need to be sprayed.

How to Grow

Climate

Pear trees are hardy but bloom fairly early. They
are more fussy regarding climate than apples, and you
must select the variety carefully if you live in a late-
frost area or a region where winters are warm. Pears
need winter chilling, but the amount required varies
from variety to variety. Most varieties of pears flourish
in cool-summer areas.

Exposure

These trees need full sun.

Soil

Pears need good garden loam that is on the heavy
side. While they prefer good drainage, they can tolerate heavy soil and poor drainage better than other

popular fruits. (This is not true of pears grafted on quince rootstock, however.)

Fertilizing

Pears respond well to a thick organic mulch. Avoid large amounts of nitrogen, because it encourages succulent new growth susceptible to fire blight.

Watering

Pears require moderate amounts of water. In arid summers, deep watering once a month, depending on the soil, is usually sufficient. In rainy-summer areas, supplemental watering is usually unnecessary for mature trees.

Pruning

Train young trees to three or four main branches. Like apples, pears bear fruit on long-lived fruiting spurs and need little regular pruning, except to shape and to remove dead or weak growth. Oriental pears need slightly more pruning than common pears. With established trees; thin about 10 percent of the branches and of the fruiting spurs annually. Thin fruit of both species if the tree sets too large a crop.

Pests and Diseases

Pears are plagued with some of the same pests and diseases that bother apples, namely codling moth, San Jose scale, scab, and fire blight. Fire blight is the most serious disease affecting pears. Plant resistant varieties in areas of the country where this condition is a problem.

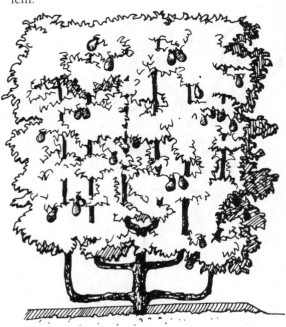

E.81. An espaliered pear

Follow the dormant-spray schedule recommended in Part Two for fruit trees to control scab, scale, and two particularly troublesome pests affecting pears: pear slugs and pear psylla.

Harvesting

Common pears are harvested before they fully ripen. Have you ever eaten a grainy, sawdusty pear that had a brown center? It was probably picked when ripe. Common pears are picked green and firm, at the point when a small tug will separate the stem from the branch. Allow them to ripen at room temperature or store them for later use. Oriental pears are allowed to ripen on the tree, like apples. Standard pear trees produce 3—5 bushels annually when mature. Dwarfs produce 1/2—1 bushel yearly.

How to Purchase

Forms and Sources

Common pears are readily available bare root or in containers from local nurseries and mail-order sources. (See individual varieties below.) Oriental pears are available in some local nurseries and from mail-order sources. One source (17) has a large selection of these pears.

Pollinators

Nearly all varieties need pollinators. Most varieties will cross-pollinate; notable exceptions are 'Seckel' and 'Bartlett', which will not pollinate each other reliably.

Some Oriental varieties will not readily cross-pollinate with common pears. Check with local nursery before purchasing your Oriental pear trees.

Varieties

COMMON PEARS

'Anjou'—buttery-green to yellow, great-tasting, late-ripening fruits; strong grower; somewhat susceptible to fire blight; needs mild weather; for Northwest. (Readily Available)

'Bartlett' ('Williams')—most widely known commercially; yellow fruits; ornamental qualities below average; usually sets more fruit with a pollinator other than 'Seckel'; susceptible to fire blight; the following improved varieties are more disease resistant: 'Winter Bartlett', 'Sure Crop', 'Improved Bartlett'. (17,24,44,61)

'Clapp's Favorite'—large, excellent, early-ripening fruits; hardy but susceptible to fire blight; best in late-spring areas. (Readily Available)

'Comice'—best eating pear, rich and smooth; stores well; moderately susceptible to fire blight; for mild climate, best in Northwest. (Readily Available)

'Golden Spice'—good for pickling and canning; very

hardy variety. (60)

'Harrow Delight'—this Bartlett type pear, large fruit, white flesh, sweet and tender. Good fresh and for canning. (3,44)

'Honey Sweet'—seckle type is fireblight resistant and very good tasting. (61)

'Kieffer'—medium-quality, gritty fruits; Oriental pear hybrid, fire-blight resistant; for mild and coldest climates, low chilling requirement. (Readily Available)

'Moonglow'—yellow, good dessert or canning-type fruits; excellent, fire-blight-resistant tree; good for areas with severe fire-blight problems; wide climate tolerance. (Readily Available)

'Patten'—yellow fruits similar to 'Bartlett', good fresh but not recommended for cooking; tree particularly hardy; good where other pears cannot grow. (16,60)

'Seckel'—small, very tasty, brown fruits, good for canning; resistant to fire blight; a good pollinator but not for 'Bartlett'; good in mild areas; widely adaptable. (Readily Available)

ORIENTAL PEARS

These crisp pears do well in all pear climates except the very coldest. Sometimes they are listed in catalogs under the name pear apple or Nihon Nashi, which means Japanese pear. They are available from (3,6,17,25,46,48,59).

'Kikusui'—round green fruits, delicious eating; medium-size tree, spreading and somewhat drooping form; susceptible to fire blight. (3,46)

'Orient'—medium-size, reddish-brown, pear-shaped fruit, cans well; tree large and resistant to fire blight; low chilling requirement. (70)

'Shinseiki'—round yellow fruit, keeps well on tree 4—6 weeks; large tree; partially self-pollinating. (Readily Available)

'Twentieth Century' ('20th Century')—round crisp juicy fruit; needs a pollinator, either 'Bartlett' or 'Shinseiki' will do. (Readily Available)

Preserving

Store pears at a temperature as close to 32°F as possible until you want to use them. Do not let them freeze. Most varieties may be stored this way for four to five months, though they tend to deteriorate slowly in quality after the third month.

Pears can be dried, canned, or made into jam, butter, pickles, or chutney.

PEAR APPLE. See Pear.

Peas and Snow Peas
(SUGAR PEAS, CHINESE PEA PODS)

Peas, *Pisum sativum*
Snow peas, *Pisum sativum* var. *macrocarpon*

Effort Scale
NO. 3
Must be planted annually
Pests occasionally a problem
Harvesting is time-consuming

Zones
Annual

Thumbnail Sketch
Herbaceous annual vines
2—6 ft. tall
Propagated from seeds
Need full sun; tolerate some shade in hot climates
Leaves are blue-green, oval, 1—2 in. long
Bloom in spring or winter
Flowers are leguminous, white or purple, grow in clusters
Seeds or pods are edible; harvested in spring
Used in large, herbaceous borders, raised beds, containers, and cascading over retaining walls

E.82. 'Dwarf Gray Sugar' peas have lavender blossoms that contrast with their gray-green foliage.

E.83. 'Dwarf Gray Sugar' peas make a fast-growing, sprawling ground cover. They are superb for informal places, such as these railroad-tie steps, but must be replaced with other annuals ('Royalty' bush beans, for example) when the weather warms up.

How to Use

In the Kitchen

Few garden vegetables are as succulent or sweet as fresh garden peas. Steamed shelled peas are a luxury to be savored one spoonful at a time, or if the harvest is generous, to be squandered in soups, salads, and stews.

Used fresh, the sweet, crunchy, succulent pods of the snow pea dress up a salad or add sophistication to a raw-vegetable platter. They can be steamed briefly and served as a cooked vegetable and are often used in stir-fried Oriental dishes. Snow peas are extremely expensive in the market, adding to the pleasure of growing your own.

In the Landscape

The pea plant is a long climbing vine from 5 to 6 feet tall. It has bluish-green leaves 1—2 inches long, white legume-type flowers, and some tendrils. Most varieties of peas (and their close cousin, the snow pea) have attractive foliage and can be grown on a trellis or fence combined with a flowering vine such as nasturtium.

One variety of snow pea in particular, 'Dwarf Gray Sugar', is quite decorative by itself. 'Dwarf Gray Sugar' peas grow on short vines to 2 feet. This variety is somewhat sprawling and loose in habit and has purple-lavender flowers that bloom in beautiful clusters. The size and shape of the dwarf plants make them pleasant as part of a flower border; 24—36 plants are usually enough for the average family. Try them in a border in front of stock or pink and purple snapdragons. Or grow them in a large hanging basket with alyssum, or by themselves in large, decorative containers. Let your guests pick their own hors d'oeuvres.

Caution: Do not confuse or combine garden or snow peas with sweet peas. Sweet peas are poisonous.

How to Grow

Peas are annuals requiring full sun, high humidity, and cool weather. They can tolerate some frost and do poorly in hot weather. They are grown in the spring in cold climates, and in the winter and spring in mild winter areas.

The soil should be nonacidic and well drained. Peas need very little fertilizer but respond well to organic mulches.

Pests include the pea weevil. To deter these creatures, try lightly dusting wet or dew-covered foliage with lime. For pea moth, use Bacillus thuringiensis. For pea thrip, try a hard spray of water with a nozzle, or sponge foliage with a mild, soapy water solution. To prevent mildew, do not water plants from above in warm weather.

Because the harvest is fairly large and the pods small, harvesting is time-consuming. You can expect to pick 2—3 pounds from a 15-foot row over a one-week period. The harvest season lasts from 4 to 6 weeks. The plants should be pulled out after most of the pods are harvested or they will become scraggly and brown or mildewed.

How to Purchase

Varieties

One mail-order nursery (71) has a particularly large selection of peas. Semileafless dwarf varieties of shelling peas are a lacy addition to a flower border. Varieties are 'Lacy Lady' (16,71) and 'Novella' (11,19,24,35,49,58,64).

'Dwarf Gray Sugar'—small edible-podded peas; lavender flowers; good disease resistance; short bush vines, 2—2 1/2 ft. tall. (Readily Available)

'Sugar Snap'—a new vegetable, thick tender pods, eat pods whole or shell like peas. Pods grow on long vines and have white flowers. (Readily Available)

Preserving and Preparing

Shelled peas and snow pea pods can be frozen, but frozen pods lose some of their crispness.

Snow peas add color and texture to many Chinese stir-fry dishes, and are good in a raw-vegetable platter with dip.

Pecan

Carya illinoinensis

Effort Scale
NO. 4
Susceptible to many pests and diseases
Fertilizing necessary
Raking necessary
Large harvest is time-consuming

Zones
6—9

Thumbnail Sketch
Deciduous tree
75—100 ft. tall
Propagated from seeds, by grafting, and budding
Needs full sun
Leaves are compound, composed of 11—17 leaflets, medium green
Flowers are catkins, not showy
Nuts are edible; harvested in fall
Used as shade tree, street tree, screen in large yards

How to Use

In the Kitchen

When you have a pecan tree you are a rich person. The nuts, which might as well be flecked with gold in the marketplace, are so versatile that having them in your cupboard ensures good eating. Try them in a tea sandwich, finely chopped with mayonnaise and some tender, young nasturtium leaves, or add them to a mixture of hard-cooked eggs and green olives for a heartier sandwich. Pecans braised in soy sauce are a hot snack that will mark you as an A-1 cook.

E.84. The pecan is an excellent shade tree.

It is in desserts that pecans are most commonly used. But pecans also make innovative additions to breads made from bananas, persimmons, and zucchini. Pecan pie is one of the great high-calorie indulgences, of course. Make pralines—brown-sugar and pecan patties—for a truly special treat, and just try to limit the intake. To double the pleasure, crush pralines, blend them with butter creme, and spread the mixture between the layers of that sumptuous French pastry, genoise, or between any plain white or yellow cake. Or bake pecan drop cookies or bars and see how quickly they disappear.

In the Landscape

The pecan, like most nut trees, is large and stately. Its cut leaves and graceful, branching pattern provide good shade along with the tree's edible bonus. A few pecans planted in a large backyard can lower the temperature of that yard 5—10 degrees on a hot, sultry day. 'Cheyenne', a dwarfish variety for the West, is more suitable for small yards. Use pecan trees to line a driveway or street, block a view, or shade a hot south wall.

Pecan trees are large deciduous trees that lose many leaves at one time. This necessitates raking in manicured yards.

How to Grow

Climate

Pecans grow in the Eastern states west to Iowa and Texas, and from Illinois south to the Gulf of Mexico and into Arizona. Some plantings have been successful in the San Joaquin Valley of California. The southern varieties need 270—290 warm growing days, and the northern varieties can produce nuts with as few as 170—190 warm days. Much research is being done to produce hardier cultivars, and the northern range of pecan growing is being extended. At present, though, no pecan varieties exist for the Northeast or the Northwest. Pecans do not do quite as well in areas with high humidity, since their pollen production is inhibited when the relative humidity is 80 percent or more. Pecans are also prone to more diseases in humid conditions.

Exposure

Pecan trees need full sun.

Planting

See HICKORY.

Soil

Pecans need deep, well-drained, rich, alluvial soil. They prefer a soil pH of 5.8—7.0.

Fertilizing

Pecan trees respond well to large amounts of fertilizer, particularly nitrogen. A rule of thumb is that a mature, bearing tree should grow 7—15 inches a year. If growth is less than 6 inches, apply more fertilizer; if it is more than 20 inches, apply less. An annual application of a nitrogen fertilizer plus a mulch of compost or manure is usually sufficient in fairly rich soil. If your pecan tree is in a lawn, it is harder to keep well fertilized. Apply nitrogen fertilizer on the lawn and deep-water it in or, better yet, use a root feeder. Pecans suffer from zinc deficiency in some soils. This condition is indicated by chlorotic leaves and a "rosetting" on the shoots. Where these symptoms appear, application of a foliar spray (a method of fertilizing through the leaves by spraying) with a special-formula fertilizer containing zinc is called for. Follow the directions on the package.

Watering

In sandy soils or in hot climates, pecans usually need supplemental watering. A pecan tree growing in a lawn will require deep-watering beyond that given the lawn.

Pruning

See HICKORY.

Pests and Diseases

A number of diseases and pests may attack pecans. They vary with location. The most likely pests are pecan weevils, scale, shuckworm, webworm, and aphids. The most serious and common disease of pecans is scab, a fungus that attacks the leaves and nuts. Dormant spraying helps to control some of these pests and diseases. The average pecan tree needs to be sprayed three or four times during the year to produce high-quality nuts. Consult your university extension service for more information specific to your area.

Pecan trees tend to bear their nuts on alternate years. While this is normal, it is exacerbated by a diseased or weakened condition.

Harvesting

In order to beat the squirrels to your harvest, collect nuts off the ground as soon as they fall. Healthy pecan trees produce a large harvest. A ten-year-old tree bears around 10 pounds of nuts, and a mature tree can bear 100 pounds annually.

How to Purchase

Forms and Sources

Buy pecans bare root from local nurseries or mail-order firms in late winter or early spring, or buy in containers spring through fall.

Pollinators

Some varieties will bear a few nuts when planted singly but to ensure proper pollination plant more than one variety.

Varieties

It is important to choose a pecan variety suitable for your part of the country. In the list below, pecan varieties with a short growing season have been designated as Northern, those resistant to some of the major fungus diseases as Southeastern, and those with a tolerance for alkaline soils as Western.

The Northern Nut Growers Association is offering seed of hardy pecans to its members. If you are interested in growing nut trees, you should join this organization. One of the ways pecans are judged is by their cracking quality—that is, how easily the shell cracks and whether the nut comes out easily in one piece. The term "papershell" refers to nuts that crack easily, not to a specific variety.

NORTHERN VARIETIES
'Colby'—nuts have good flavor but poor cracking quality; tree retains foliage late into season; very hardy. (6,61,70)
'Giles'—high-quality nuts; best for southern part of northern zone. (70)
'Major'—good-size nuts with good cracking quality; one of the best for the North. (6,61,70)

SOUTHEASTERN VARIETIES
'Candy'—vigorous tree, scab resistant. (70)
'Cape Fear'—excellent nuts; disease resistant; pollinate with 'Stuart'. (61,70)
'Desirable'—not good for west Texas; scab resistant. (70)
'Stuart'—one of the old varieties; widely grown; quite disease prone. (24,61,70)

WESTERN VARIETIES
'Cheyenne'—excellent cracking quality; small tree, good for small yards. (61,70)
'Western-Schley'—most commonly grown; vigorous tree. (61,70)

Preserving

Shell pecans after harvesting and freeze.

Peppers

Capsicum species

Effort Scale
NO.3
Must be planted annually
Some watering and weeding necessary
Easy only within a fairly narrow temperature range

Zones
Annual; 10-11 as perennial

Thumbnail Sketch
Herbaceous perennial usually treated as an annual;
  grown as a perennial in zone 10
1 1/2—3 ft. tall
Propagated from seeds
Needs full sun, will tolerate some shade
Leaves are deep green, 2—4 in. long
Blooms in summer
Flowers are insignificant
Fruits are edible; harvested in summer

*E.85. All types of peppers are beautiful in containers. Pictured at
left is the sweet green bell pepper 'Yolo Wonder'; on the right is
the hot and colorful 'Holiday Cheer.'*

Used in flower borders, raised beds, herb gardens,
  containers

How to Use
In the Kitchen
The fruits of the pepper, whether from sweet,
green, or red bells or "hot" peppers, are a popular
source of seasoning for stews, salads, and casseroles.
Peppers find their way into the cuisines of many countries. Some recipes call for use of the whole fruit as
container for a stuffing. Chiles rellenos, using chili
peppers, is a very satisfying dish. Salsas are made from
peppers in all degrees of heat, and pickled peppers
vary too in accordance with the species. Peppers have
the further advantage of being a good source of vitamin C.

In the Landscape
These herbaceous perennials, which are grown as
annuals, are all handsome bushy, dark-green plants
with upright growth. Their leaves are 2—4 inches
long, somewhat glossy, and plentiful, so the plants are
quite lush looking. The flowers are white with yellow
stamens, attractive against the rich, green foliage but
insignificant. The fruits come in all sizes, shapes, and
colors: even the green ones are noticeable the plant.
Some varieties of peppers even display their yellow or
red fruits upright at the top of the plant.
Because these plants are so decorative they are at
home in a flower border, where they might be combined with dwarf zinnias, red verbena, or portulaca.
All pepper plants are striking in containers. They
look especially nice in a large, fashioned clay pot. The
colors seem meant for each other.

How to Grow
Peppers are a warm-weather crop. They cannot tolerate frost and they will no fruit unless the weather is
at least 65°F but does not exceed 80°F. They also
need a long growing season, 120 days, and are, therefore, impractical for some northern gardens. To grow
peppers, start them in flats or in peat pots 8—10
weeks before your last frost. After they are 6—8 inches
tall and all danger of frost is over, transplant them into
garden, placing them at least 18 inches apart in full
sun or part shade in rich deep soil.
Water regularly and fertilize before the flowers
have set. The fertilizer used should not be too high in
nitrogen, since that element encourages leaf development at the expense of fruit development.
Tender pepper plants are popular with snails,
slugs, aphids, and cutworms. Keep plants mulched
and weeds under control. Otherwise, the plants are
relatively pest free. They are occasionally prone to the
same diseases that afflict tomatoes.

Sweet peppers are picked at the green or red stage. The hot peppers should be allowed to ripen completely. Both types produce from 1 to 2 pounds per plant.

If you plant peppers that hold their fruits upright, be sure to provide some afternoon shade to protect them from sunburn.

How to Purchase

Plants and seed for peppers are available from local nurseries, but for a wide selection of varieties you will need to contact a mail-order firm. For a large selection of European varieties, contact (11,37,57,66); for a good selection of particularly ornamental varieties, such as 'Park's Pot', 'Tequila Sunrise', and 'Thai Hot', contact (2,12,57); Hot varieties are available from (57); and for a good selection of heirloom varieties, contact (55). Two nurseries that specialize in peppers are (33) and The Pepper Gal, Betty Payton, POB 23006, Ft. Lauderdale, FL 33307.

Varieties

The following peppers are attractive as well as tasty.

'Cherry' (hot)—bright red, round, hot pepper, good for pickling. (Readily Available)

'Golden Bell'—large, yellow, sweet fruits; compact plant. (26)

'Gypsy'—wedge-shaped, yellow, thin-walled, medium-size, sweet fruits; All America Selection; fruits tender and crunchy; plants 12-20 in. tall. (Readily Available)

'Jalapeno'—narrow medium-size, red, hot pepper, used in traditional Mexican food. (Readily Available)

'Sweet Banana'—long, tapered fruits with thin walls, pale green, very productive over a long season, great taste. (Readily Available)

Preserving and Preparing

Use peppers fresh or preserve them by hanging them up to dry in a warm place. Sweet peppers can be cut up and frozen in plastic bags. See the recipe under CABBAGE for a suggested stuffing for stuffed peppers.

PEPPERMINT. See Mint.
PERSIAN WALNUT. See Walnut.

Persimmon

American persimmon, *Diospyros virginiana*
Oriental persimmon, *D. kaki*

Effort Scale

NO. 2

E.86. *The fruit of the 'Hachiya' persimmon is large, 4-5 inches long, and usually seedless.*

Occasional pruning to shape necessary
Sucker growth must be removed in American species
Large harvest

Zones

5—9 for American persimmon
6—11 for Oriental persimmon

Thumbnail Sketch

American Persimmon

Deciduous tree or shrub
30—40 ft. tall
Propagated from seeds, cuttings, by grafting or budding
Needs full sun
Leaves are dark green, shiny, oval, 6 in. long
Blooms in spring
Flowers are greenish yellow, not showy 1/2—2 in. across
Fruits are edible; harvested in fall
Used as interest plant, shade tree, large shrub, screen

Oriental Persimmon

Deciduous tree
25—30 ft. tall
Propagated from cuttings, budding, and grafting
Needs full sun
Leaves are heart-shaped, glossy, dark green, red-orange in fall, 5—7 in. across
Blooms in spring
Flowers are yellowish white, not showy, 3/4—2 in. across

Fruits are edible; harvested in fall
Used as interest plant, patio tree (some varieties),
  screen, shade tree, espalier

How to Use
In the Kitchen

Both the American and Oriental persimmon are
beautiful orange fruits that can be eaten raw. Though a
few wonderful varieties can be eaten firm ripe, like an
apple, most varieties must be dead ripe and very soft
or they have a puckery, unpleasant quality. You have
only to taste an underripe persimmon once in your
life; you will never forget it. In contrast, a fully ripe
persimmon is velvety and sweet.

Both types are used in desserts. One fabulous pudding, similar to English plum pudding, has become a
Thanksgiving tradition at our house (see recipe under
"Preserving and Preparing"). You can also enjoy persimmons in cookies and breads. A seedless persimmon may be frozen whole and eaten out of its skin
like a kind of sherbet.

In the Landscape

The trees that bear this glorious fruit are deciduous. Both species are slow growing; they may reach 30
feet but can be kept smaller with pruning. The bark is
of an interesting checkered pattern that makes the
bare tree a handsome sight in the winter landscape. In
spring the big leaves, 5—7 inches in length, become
shiny and dark green, and in the fall most varieties
turn bright yellow-orange or red. As if that is not
enough, those orange, decorative fruits add their own
kind of beauty. The Oriental types are as big as 5 inches long and heart-shaped. The American types are
smaller and rounder. These fruits nestle among the
big leaves; when the leaves fall, the fruits stay on the
bare tree looking like Christmas tree ornaments.

The bark, handsome foliage, colorful fall leaves,
and fruits make the persimmon tree one of the finest
edible ornamentals. These trees are stunning accent
plants, small shade trees, and fine espaliers. They are
exceptionally well suited to Oriental gardens, and
their fall foliage color is breathtaking when backed by
pines or other conifers.

Note: Do not plant the trees near a street unless
you intend to harvest conscientiously when the fruits
are still firm. Fully ripe, juicy persimmons offer a
strong temptation to young passersby. The larger
ones, in particular, make a spectacular splat on the
pavement.

How to Grow
Climate

Oriental persimmons are hardy to about 0°F. They
are limited to areas below the Ohio River and as far

E.87. Graceful 'Fuyu' persimmon trees frame a formal entrance.
The 'Fuyu' tree is smaller than most persimmons, and its fruit
can be eaten crisp.

south as southern Florida, and are popular on the
West Coast. The American species is hardier, growing
as far north as Rhode Island and across to the Great
Lakes. Hybridizers are improving these hardier plants,
making their fruits less seedy, larger, and sweeter, so
they will become an item more to be considered in
colder climates.

Exposure

Both species require full sun.

Soil

Persimmons prefer a good garden loam, but they
will grow in less than optimum conditions. They must
have good drainage, and will grow where oak root
fungus is a problem.

Fertilizing

Light, organic mulch is beneficial. Avoid large
amounts of nitrogen around young trees; it causes the
fruit to drop.

Watering

Once established, the trees need very little watering. In arid climates infrequent deep-watering is desirable. Persimmons are quite drought resistant.

Pruning

Young trees should be trained to three to five main
limbs. Mature trees need to be pruned only for shape.
The American persimmon needs pruning to remove
suckers.

Pests and Diseases

The trees in the West have very few pests and diseases. In the deep South, trees are sometimes bothered by anthracnose and scale. Use dormant spray with copper oil. Flat-headed borer occasionally is a problem in the East; remove by hand.

Harvesting

Most varieties are not edible until dead ripe. Pick fruits when firm and fully colored and allow them to ripen indoors. Large-fruited types can be expected to produce 50—75 pounds of persimmons per year, while 'Fuyu' and the American types produce 25—30 pounds.

How to Purchase

Forms and Sources

Purchase persimmons bare root in the spring or in containers in the summer from local nurseries. They are also available from these mail-order firms: (3,24,25,27,31,49,61).

Pollinators

The Oriental varieties are self-fruitful in the West. Many varieties require a pollinator in the East. 'Gailey' is the usual pollinator for most varieties. Some American varieties need a male and female plant. Some of the newer named varieties are selfpollinating.

Varieties

AMERICAN PERSIMMONS

The American persimmons are most readily available as ungrafted seedlings, but for more consistently high fruit quality and fewer seeds, choose a grafted variety such as those listed below.
  'Early Golden'—very good flavor; ripens in September; most readily available. (3,46)
  'Meader'—almost seedless; excellent flavor; developed in New Hampshire. (Locally Available)
  'John Rick'—excellent flavor; ripens in September; superior variety. (3)

ORIENTAL PERSIMMONS
  'Chocolate'—brown-streaked fruits; large tree; available in the West. (17,27)
  'Fuyu' ('Fuyugaki')—tomato-shaped fruits, can be eaten firm; one of the best; small tree; finest fall color; needs a pollinator in the East; 'Gailey' is recommended; available in most areas. (17,46)
  'Gailey'—inferior red fruits; grown for pollination of other varieties; locally available in the East.
  'Hachiya'—large fruits; most shapely tree; heavy bearer; available in the West.
  (9,14,17,25,27,46,52,70)
  'Tanenashi'—large fruits; thick, pasty flesh; some

what weeping; heavy bearer; available in the South. (9,27,52,61)

Preserving and Preparing

Persimmons can be dried and frozen. Their pulp can be used as a substitute for applesauce in recipes.

To dry persimmons, thread them onto a string and hang them in the sun.

To freeze, put the pulp of the persimmons in containers. Force out the air at the top by placing plastic wrap directly onto the pulp. Fruit can be frozen for approximately six months.

Eleanor Witherspoon's Persimmon Pudding
  1 cup sugar
  1/2 cup melted butter
  1 teaspoon cinnamon
  2 teaspoons baking soda dissolved in 2 tablespoons water
  2 teaspoons vanilla
  1 cup seedless raisins
  1/2 cup ground pecans
  1 cup persimmon pulp
  1 cup flour, unbleached
  2 eggs
  1/4 teaspoon salt
  1 teaspoon lemon juice

Mix ingredients together in the above order and pour into a greased plum pudding mold (or substitute a 2-pound coffee can, and use aluminum foil as a cover).

Cover the mold (or coffee can), place in a large pan, and add boiling water until it reaches halfway up the mold. Cover the large pan and simmer on the top of the stove 2— hours. Do not let water level drop; add more if needed. Serves 6—8.

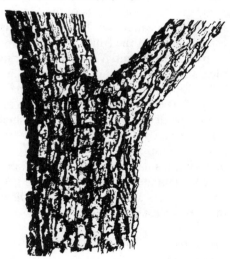

E.88. Persimmon trees have a checkered bark.

PIE PLANT. See Rhubarb.

Pineapple Guava
Feijoa Sellowiana

Effort Scale
NO. 1
Easy to grow
Fruit drop needs some attention

Zones
9—11

Thumbnail Sketch
Evergreen shrub or small tree
15—18 ft. tall
Propagated from seeds, cuttings, or by grafting
Needs full sun; will tolerate partial shade
Leaves are oblong, deep glossy-green above, light woolly gray-green below, 3 in. long
Blooms in spring and summer
Flowers have gray-green fleshy petals and bright dark-red stamens, are showy, 1 1/2 in. across
Fruits and flower petals are edible; fruit harvested in fall
Used as shrub for windbreaks, screens, espaliers, formal or informal hedges, as accent plant, in containers; as a small tree for patios, as accent, multi-stemmed tree, and in containers

How to Use
In the Kitchen
The gray-green, oblong fruits of the pineapple guava are delicious eaten raw. Their flesh is tangy and sweet, especially when the fruits are allowed to ripen fully-ripe fruits usually fall. A slightly underripe fruit is not unpleasant, but it does not have the full, rich flavor that develops with maturity. When served raw, pineapple guavas are usually cut in half like miniature melons, with the flesh spooned out of the shell. The fruits can be peeled and sliced as an exotic addition to a fruit salad or compote.

Because of the small size of these fruits, peeling them for jelly making is tedious work. The jelly that results, however, has a subtle and delicate flavor, and the color is the palest gold.

In the Landscape
Pineapple guavas are outstanding ornamentals. As small multistemmed trees they are effective near a

E.89. Pineapple guavas are gray-green fruits. The flowers have deep red stamens and the petals are tasty in salads.

patio. The bark is mottled and checked in interesting patterns and the leaves are ever-changing—deep green one minute and then almost white as the wind causes the undersides to show. In late spring or early summer the flowers are profuse and add a deep red to this color display. Feijoa is in the Myrtaceae family, and, as in the flowers of its relatives, bottlebrush, eucalyptus, and eugenia, the many stamens of these blossoms give them the appearance of little brushes. The fruits are egg-shaped, green, and dusted with a white powder, 2—3 in. long.

In its shrub form, pineapple guava is as useful as it is beautiful. It will serve as a windbreak, screen a poor view, accent a yard, or give privacy. If used as a clipped hedge some fruits and flower display will be lost because flowering and fruiting will be forced to the inside branches. It can be used in containers and raised beds, along walks, and as an espalier. This is a truly versatile edible ornamental.

How to Grow
Climate
Pineapple guavas are hardy to about 15—20°F, which limits their growth to the Deep South and warmer parts of the Southwest. The fruits are tastiest in cool-summer areas. They will not set fruit in the desert or in the southernmost part of Florida. In parts of Hawaii they grow so well that they can become a weed.

Exposure

These plants prefer full sun or partial shade.

Soil

They are adaptable to most soils but need good drainage. They prefer a soil pH of 5.5—7.0. They can tolerate salt fairly well.

Fertilizing

Pineapple guavas prefer a good organic mulch.

Watering

They are drought tolerant but can take a lot of water and can even be planted near a lawn provided the drainage is good.

Pruning

Pineapple guavas can take any amount of shearing, but severe pruning reduces fruit production. Light pruning is usually needed for shaping and removing dead branches. Prune in late spring.

Pests and Diseases

Few serious pests or diseases affect pineapple guava. Dispose of dropped and decaying fruit from under trees.

Harvesting

Pineapple guavas are rarely ripe until they fall from the tree.

How to Purchase

Forms and Sources

Pineapple guavas are available in containers from local nurseries and as seed from (14); plants are available from (6,24,46,49).

Pollinators

Some varieties need a pollinator, but those commonly grown are self-pollinating.

Varieties

Most pineapple guavas sold in local nurseries are seedlings grown for their ornamental qualities whose fruits are sometimes mediocre. To be sure, ask for a grafted name variety, such as 'Coolidge' and 'Pineapple Gem', both of which are self-pollinating.

Preserving

The pulp of the pineapple guava is preserved by freezing or in jelly and jam. See master jelly recipes under ELDERBERRY and KIWI.

PINEAPPLE MINT. See Mint.
PINEAPPLE SAGE. See Sage.

E.90. *The pineapple guava can make a graceful multistemmed tree. Prune carefully to accent its sculptured form.*

Pistachio
Pistacia vera

Effort Scale

NO. 3
Usually obtainable only by mail order
Some pruning necessary
Fertilizing and mulching necessary
Harvesting and shelling are time-consuming

Zones

7—9

Thumbnail Sketch

Deciduous tree
20—30 ft. tall; male plant may grow taller
Propagated from seeds, and by budding
Needs full sun
Leaves are medium green, yellow in fall, oval, grow in roundish clusters, 2—4 in. long
Flowers are insignificant

E.91. Pistachio nuts grow in custers at the ends of branches.

Nuts are edible; harvest in fall
Used as screen, informal hedge, street tree

How to Use
In the Kitchen
One has to work hard to shell a handful of delicious, rich pistachio nuts, but the reward is worth the effort. Pistachios can be eaten raw or roasted and salted. They are used in ice cream and as an exquisite garnish on other desserts. They are often sprinkled over liver patés as an elegant touch.

In the Landscape
The leaves of these deciduous trees are medium green and are made up of three to five round leaflets. The leaves tend to grow in clusters at the ends of bare branches, so tip pruning and training when the tree is young are necessary to overcome a somewhat scraggly, scarecrowlike appearance. These leaves turn a brilliant yellow in the fall. The flowers are insignificant, but the heavy clusters of yellowish or red fruits can be showy.

Both male and female trees are required for nut production. Male trees generally grow taller than females eventually. Both can be used in the background, as shade or street trees, as screens, or to line a driveway.

How to Grow
Climate
Pistachios can usually be grown where olives are grown. They dislike high humidity but need hot summers as well as some winter chilling; the ideal is 100 days of heat and 30 days of cold. They are not hardy below 10°F. They thrive and are becoming a commercial crop in the Sacramento Valley of California.

Exposure
These trees need full sun.

Soil
Pistachios prefer well-drained, alkaline soil.

Fertilizing
Pistachio trees respond well to an organic mulch and supplemental nitrogen.

Watering
Once the tree is established, it is drought resistant. However, for superior nut production, water as you would an apple tree.

Pruning
Encourage young trees to branch about four feet above the ground. Train to a modified leader with a framework of four or five main branches. For young trees pinch the tips of new growth to keep tree bushy and neat. Prune mature trees to remove dead wood and suckers, and shape and cut back rank growth.

Pests and Diseases
Pistachios are susceptible to verticillium wilt and to cankers on the shells. Neither condition has a known cure. Sometimes shells do not fill out, usually due to an overly cool summer or incomplete pollination. Pistachios tend to bear nuts in alternate years.

Harvesting
To beat the squirrels to your harvest, pick nuts off the tree. The nuts are ripe when the hulls have turned yellow or reddish, when they separate easily from the tree, and when the hull comes away from the inside shell easily if squeezed. Remove the hulls immediately or they will start to rot within hours. A mature tree (ten years old) should provide 10—20 pounds of nuts annually, older trees much more.

How to Purchase
Forms and Sources
Pistachio trees are not sold bare root. Buy them in containers from a limited number of local California nurseries. One nursery specializes in pistachios: Fiddyment Farms, 5010 Fiddyment Road, Roseville, CA 95678.

Pollinators

Pistachios must be cross-pollinated, with male and female trees being planted within 50 yards of each other. If space is limited, a piece of male branch can be grafted onto a female tree.

E.92. *At left is a large male pistachio tree; at right is the smaller female tree.*

Varieties

The only varieties available at this time are 'Kerman' (female), 'Peters' (male), and 'Red Aleppo' (female).

Preserving

Follow preserving methods under ALMOND.

Plum

Damson plum, *Prunus insititia*
European plum, *P. domestica*
Japanese plum. *P. salicina*
Purple-leaf plum (flowering plum), *P. cerasifera* 'Atropurpurea' [*P. pissardi*]

Effort Scale

NO. 3

Vulnerable to pests and diseases
Some pruning necessary
Fertilizing and mulching necessary
Large harvest needs immediate attention

Zones

4—10

Thumbnail Sketch

Deciduous trees
Standard, 20 ft. tall; dwarf varieties, 8—12 ft. tall
Propagated by budding or from cuttings
Need full sun
Leaves are medium green or in some varieties wine red above, slightly woolly below, 3—4 in. long
Bloom in spring
Flowers are white or pink, abundant, showy, to 1 in. across
Fruits are edible; harvested in summer
Used as interest tree, screen; dwarf kinds used as large shrub, in containers.

How to Use

In the Kitchen

Plums are a delightful fruit with varied uses in the kitchen. All types can be eaten fresh, canned, or made into fruit leather. Most can be used for jams or jellies.

In this encyclopedia entry, I will discuss four types of plums: Damson, European, Japanese, and a few varieties of the so-called "flowering plum," some of which bear small, cherry-type fruits. Another type, the American bush plums and their close relatives, will be covered in the next encyclopedia entry, PLUM, BUSH, which discusses these hardy fruiting bushes.

European plums can be small or large. The small types include Italian and French prune plums, which, with their high sugar content, are ideal for drying. They can also be stewed, used in prune whip, made into a delicious filling for Danish pastry, or combined with other fruits in a pork stuffing. In the cuisines of other countries, prunes are sometimes served as an accompaniment to meat dishes. They can also be eaten raw or, along with some of the jelly made from your currant bushes, can be used as a filling for a Belgian tart (see recipe under "Preserving and Preparing").

The large-fruited plums, both European and Japanese, are all excellent for eating out of hand or for canning. They make good sharp sauces to serve over tapioca or other bland puddings.

The small-fruited cherry-type plums that are a bonus on some varieties of flowering plums are sweet and tasty; they make wonderful eating, fresh or in jams or jellies.

E.93. *Plum trees are useful as front-yard accents.*

In the Landscape

Plum trees are small- to medium-size trees with a graceful vase-shaped form. Most varieties are covered with white blooms in early spring. A few types have pink flowers. Their leaves, which follow the blossoms, are 3—4 inches long and usually green, but they are wine red on a few types.

The trees look lovely along a driveway, but they must be far enough away from the pavement to keep fruit drop from being a problem. Plum trees make nice accents in a front or back yard. The dwarf varieties can be espaliered, used as hedges and screens, and grown in containers. One variety, 'Weeping Santa Rosa', is pendulous in form and is good for espalier. See PEACH AND NECTARINE for more information on genetic dwarf trees. Like most fruit trees, plums do not thrive in a lawn.

How to Grow

European plums are the most widely grown of all the plums since they are adapted to most parts of the country. This type, which includes the prune plum and its close relative the Damson, have solid flesh and a wide range of flavors. The fruits should be allowed to ripen on the tree. These trees need moderate amounts of pruning and fruit thinning. They are more resistant to brown rot than other kinds and are grown in zones 5—9.

Japanese plums are primarily grown in the milder plum climates, zones 6—10. The Japanese plum trees bear large, sweet, and juicy fruits, which can be picked when slightly underripe and taken indoors for further ripening. The trees are vigorous growers. They need annual pruning so they will not overbear and lose branches because of the weight. They are also more susceptible to fruit rot.

Climate

Different types of plums need different climatic conditions. For the coldest areas, plant the bush plums covered in the next encyclopedia entry. They are the hardiest. The Damson and European forms are the next hardiest group and can be grown in most of zones 5—9. However, they are primarily grown in the East. Most of the Japanese types are less hardy and are primarily grown on the West Coast.

Plums bloom from one to two weeks earlier than apples, so even in areas that are usually fine for plums, crops occasionally are lost to a late frost. If you can, plant plum trees on the side of a hill so that cold, frosty air will sink away from them.

Plums do poorly in the warmest winter areas because, like most stone fruits, they require some winter chilling. In the warmest parts of zones 9 and 10, be sure to order varieties with a low chilling requirement. Plums cannot be grown in the warmest parts of Florida and Hawaii.

Exposure

Plums need full sun.

Soil

To grow vigorously, plums need a rich soil high in organic matter. The European and Damson type plums grow best on clay or heavy loam; the Japanese types do better on lighter soils. They require good drainage and a pH of 6.0—8.0.

Fertilizing

Plum trees are heavy bearers for their size, so they need large amounts of an organic mulch and fertilizer added yearly to replenish the soil. If your plum tree is not growing consistently and vigorously, or if the leaves get pale in color, add nitrogen. Supplemental nitrogen is particularly beneficial to the Japanese types.

Watering

In the arid parts of the country, plums need occasional deep watering. If the tree has been dry for quite a while and the fruits have started to form, delay watering until after harvest or the fruits will split.

Pruning

The European types are usually trained to a central leader and when mature usually need only slight thinning and shaping annually. They bear only on long-lived spurs. The Japanese types are usually trained to a vase shape and when mature need fairly heavy pruning annually. They bear on both long-lived spurs and one-year-old wood, and they tend to bear too heavily if the branches are not thinned out and some of them shortened. The Japanese types set too much fruit, and the fruit usually has to be thinned in June so that the trees will not become exhausted and the branches will not break.

Pests and Diseases

In most areas of the country, plums need to be dormant sprayed to control scale, borers, mites, aphids, and brown rot. See Part Two.

Plum curculio is another pest that occasionally assails plums in the East. This small weevil attacks the fruits, making them rot. Pick up and destroy dropped fruits every day. Pyrethrum might be necessary for a severe infestation.

Harvesting

For cooking, plums are best harvested when somewhat underripe, before they become very soft but after they have developed a whitish "bloom." For juicy, fresh eating, pick plums that are warm from the sun and give slightly to pressure.

Mature standard-size trees will produce 1—2 bushels of plums annually. Dwarf varieties will produce 1/2—1 bushel.

How to Purchase

Forms and Sources

Plums can be purchased bare root in late winter and early spring and in containers throughout the year from local nurseries and mail-order firms. (See individual varieties, below, for sources.)

Pollinators

Few plums are self-pollinating, but even those that are usually bear more heavily with cross-pollination.

The different plum types rarely cross-pollinate each other. With a few exceptions, European plums pollinate only other European plums, Japanese plums only pollinate Japanese plums. However, many of the small American bush plums covered in the next entry will pollinate all kinds of plums. (See individual varieties, below, for pollinating information.)

Varieties

Scores of varieties of plums exist. Consult local nurseries and university extension services to determine which plums are best for your area. The following lists contain the most popular varieties of each type.

EUROPEAN AND DAMSON PLUMS

'Allred'—medium-size red fruits; striking red foliage and flowers; hardy to zone 4; needs a pollinator; 'Ozark Premier' will do. (13,34)

'Damson'—small blue fruits, great for cooking; improved varieties include 'French Damson' and 'Shropshire'; widely adaptable; self-pollinating. (Readily Available)

'French Prune'—small, deep purple, very sweet fruits, good for drying; widely grown in California; large tree; self-pollinating. (Readily Available)

'Green Gage'—old-timer, considered one of the best; greenish-yellow fruits, good for eating fresh and for cooking; widely adaptable; hardy to zone 4; self-fertile. (Readily Available)

'Stanley'—dark-blue fruits; prune plum; planted in most areas of the East and Midwest; best for zones 5—7; self-pollinating. (Readily Available)

JAPANESE PLUMS

'Cocheco'—small, reddish, tasty fruits; beautiful white flowers and red foliage; quite hardy; needs pollinator, any Japanese variety. (13)

'Mariposa'—maroon skin and flesh; needs little winter chill, good for southern California; needs 'Santa Rosa' for a pollinator. (Readily Available)

'Methley'—small reddish-purple fruits; low chill requirement; grown in warmer climates including Hawaii; self-pollinating. (6,27,52,70)

'Ozark Premier'—large, red, tasty fruits; resistant to brown rot, canker, and bacterial spot; good pollinator for Allred'; for zones 5—9; dwarf available; self-pollinating. (27,61,70)

'Redheart'—large fruits; newly introduced; resistant to brown rot and canker. (61)

'Santa Rosa'—crimson-skinned, high-quality fruit for eating fresh and cooking; widely grown; stars in the West; tree has upright growth, self-pollinating. (Readily Available)

'Satsuma'—wine-red skin and flesh; excellent fruits for eating, superb for jelly; great combined with 'Santa Rosa' as pollinator. (Readily Available)

'Weeping Santa Rosa'—small tree with graceful form; somewhat more suitable for cold climates than 'Santa Rosa' since it blooms a little later; self-pollinating. (46,48,52,70)

ORNAMENTAL FLOWERING AND FRUITING PLUMS

The following are the most popular of this type. Some of the plants sold as flowering plums in local nurseries bear excellent small cherry-type fruits.

Prunus cerasifera (cherry plum)green leaves, white flowers; fruits red, 1 in. across; tree 30 ft. tall.

P. c. 'Atropurpurea' [*P. pissardii*] (purple-leaf plum)—red leaves; white flowers, small red plums.

P. c. 'Hollywood'—leaves dark green above, red below; flowers white to light pink; plums red, 2—2 1/2 in. across.

Preserving and Preparing

Plums can be frozen, canned, or made into sauces, jams, and jellies. See master jelly recipes under ELDERBERRY and KIWI.

Prune plums are the best for drying.

To dry, pick ripe fruits. Wash and boil them for one to two minutes until the skins split; this procedure makes the plum skins porous and allows moisture to escape. Another way to do this is to prick the plums all over with a sharp object.

Spread the plums out to dry in a warm, dry place outside in the sun (cover with screening to protect fruit from birds and insects). Or dry them in your oven, spreading them on racks and starting the oven at 130°F. Over the course of twenty-four hours, slowly raise the temperature to 165°F, turning the plums often. If you raise the temperature too quickly, the' outside of the plum will dry too fast and moisture will be sealed in toward the pit causing the prune to eventually rot in storage. If your oven can't be set this low, buy an oven thermometer and turn the oven on for a few minutes every hour during the day to keep the temperature up.

Pack the prunes in airtight containers and refrigerate or freeze.

Belgian Plum Tart

1 1/2 pounds blue plums, cut in half lengthwise and pitted
1 tablespoon sugar
1/2 cup red currant jelly
3 tablespoons cold water
unbaked, 10-inch pastry shell

Preheat oven to 400°F. Arrange plums in circles, cut side up, in the pastry-lined pan.

Sprinkle them with sugar.

Bake the tart in lower part of the oven until pastry is lightly browned and plums are tender, 35 to 40 minutes. If crust browns too quickly, cover lightly with aluminum foil. Remove tart from oven.

When tart is cool, heat jelly and water in a small saucepan, stirring until the jelly melts. Cook for a few minutes until mixture is syrupy. Cool slightly and remove any scum. While the jelly mixture is still warm, brush it on the plums. Let the tart stand before serving.

Serve with whipped cream, if you wish. Serves 6—8.

Plum, Bush (BUSH CHERRY)

Beach plum, *Prunus maritima*
Nanking cherry, *P. tomentosa*
Western sand cherry, *P. Besseyi*
Bush plum hybrids

Effort Scale

NO. 2
Easy to grow
Processing takes time

Zones

5—7 for beach plum
3—5 for sand cherry, Nanking cherry, bush plum hybrids

Thumbnail Sketch

Bush Plums (Except Beach Plum)

Deciduous shrubs
4—8 ft. tall, depending on variety
Propagated by budding and from suckers
Need full sun
Leaves deep green, narrow, 1 1/2—3 in. long, some types woolly underneath
Bloom in spring
Flowers are white or pink, small, abundant, showy
Fruits are edible; harvested in summer
Used as foundation plants, hedges, interest plants, and in containers

Beach Plum

Deciduous shrub or small tree
6—10 ft. tall
Propagated from seeds and cuttings
Needs full sun
Leaves deep green, oval, woolly underneath, 1—2 1/2 in. long
Blooms in spring
Flowers are white, small, abundant, showy
Fruits are edible; harvested in summer
Used for beach planting, erosion control, interest plant, large shrub, screen, hedge

How to Use

In the Kitchen

The term bush plum covers a number of small fruits similar in taste to plums and cherries. The fruits are small, generally 1—2 inches in diameter, and are either red, yellow, or purplish black. They can usually be eaten fresh but are most often used in jams, jellies, sauces, pies, and canned.

Many bush plums are native plants and are remembered fondly by those of us who, as children, entertained Raggedy Ann at tea next to a fruiting bush plum hedge and served handfuls of these luscious small fruits.

In the Landscape

The bush type plums, such as the sand cherry, Nanking cherry, and bush plum hybrids, make beautiful hedgerows that in early spring are completely covered with white or pink blossoms. Often they are among the earliest flowering shrubs. The bushes can serve as flowering accents planted as freestanding shrubs, are pleasant near a patio, and are popular as a foundation plant. Some types of western sand cherries have silvery green foliage that turns red in the fall.

Beach plums can be used as medium to large shrubs and informal flowering hedges. These plants become even more attractive as their dark, shiny bark grows gnarled with age; in a seaside planting, windblown plants take on picturesque forms. Some plants are quite thorny and can be used for a barrier hedge.

How to Grow

Climate

Bush plums are a delicious substitute for cherries and plums in the coldest parts of the country. All varieties are quite hardy.

The native western sand cherry is a star performer in the Midwest, including Wyoming, Minnesota, Colorado, and up into Manitoba.

Beach plums are native to the shores of the East Coast from Maine to Virginia. They are not as cold hardy as the other bush plums, but have been grown inland successfully in milder areas of the Midwest, New England, and along the shores of the Great

E.95. *Beach plum trees get sculptured shapes when exposed to ocean winds.*

Lakes. They can also tolerate seacoast conditions. All bush plums need heavy winter chilling, and do poorly in mild-winter areas.

Exposure

Bush plums need full sun.

Soil

Bush plums thrive on a wide variety of soils. The small bush types can tolerate fairly poor drainage though they do not prefer it.

Beach plums will grow in poor, sandy soil but need good drainage.

Fertilizing

All bush plums benefit from an annual application of an organic mulch.

Watering

Bush plums are usually grown in areas that receive precipitation the year round, and need no extra watering once established.

Pruning

The sand cherry plums bear fruit along the entire length of their branches; consequently, they can be pruned to form a tailored hedge. Tailored bushes still bear fruit, but their yield is smaller than that of untrimmed plants. All the bush plums will bear fruit without regular pruning but look better with some care and shaping.

Pruning on most types is best done by August. Many of next year's flower buds will be lost if the plants are not pruned until fall.

E.94. *Dark-red bush plums grow in clusters.*

Beach plums and the taller bush plums can be trained to be small trees, but they need constant pruning to keep their shape. Their natural form is as a shrub, and they will continue to send up suckers unless pruned carefully.

Pests and Diseases

Bush plums have few pests and diseases, though birds can sometimes beat you to the goods. To ensure a sufficient harvest, plant extra bushes for the birds. Plum curculio, tent caterpillars, and brown rot are occasional problems.

Harvesting

Pick bush plums when they are fully colored and give slightly when pressed.

How to Purchase

Forms and Sources

Buy bush plums in containers from your local nursery or from these mail-order sources: (27,31,57).

Pollinators

Some types of bush plums are self-fruitful, but the majority will bear more heavily with cross-pollination, and most types require it.

Varieties

BEACH PLUM

All varieties—fruits are red-purple, usually eaten cooked; 6—10 ft. high and wide; plant becomes gnarled and windblown near the ocean; can be trained to be a small tree; needs a pollinator; varieties are 'Autumn', 'Squibnocket', 'North Neck'. (Available locally)

BUSH PLUM HYBRIDS

'Black Beauty'— superior, large, maroon-red fruits, 1 in. in diameter; eaten fresh or cooked. (29)

'Compass'—old varriety; red fruits eaten cooked or fresh; bush grows to 8 ft; a very good pollinator for other cherry plums; needs pollinator; (16)

'Golden Boy'—yellow fruits; otherwise similar to red cherry plums. (29)

'Red Diamond'—large maroon freestone fruits, 1 1/2 in. in diameter; eaten fresh or preserved; bush 6 ft. high; needs cross-pollination, any bush plum. (16,35)

'Sapa'—a widely available hybrid; dark purple-black fruits; sweet and almost freestone; can be pruned to be a small tree; needs pollinator, 'Compass' recommended. (Readily Available)

'Sapalta'—from Canada, this Sapa-type plum is very sweet, with small stones; needs pollinator, 'Compass' recommended. (Available 16)

NANKING CHERRIES

All varieties—very hardy, grow in the Great Plains from New Mexico to South Dakota, including high desert regions; many seedlings and improved varieties available; all have white flowers and woolly foliage underneath; excellent hedge plants; fruits bright red, good fresh or cooked; varieties, 'Fields Special Nanking', 'Nanking Cherry', 'Nanking Hybrid Cherry', 'Scarlet Gem', are available from (3,10,16,24,52).

WESTERN SAND CHERRIES

A hardy native of the midwest plains and Rocky Mountains; breeding stock for many improved hybrids; superior dark-red fruits eaten fresh or cooked; generally 4—6 ft. tall; bush can take extreme cold and heat; needs cross-pollination; best-known improved variety is 'Hansens'. (3,10,31,51,52)

Preserving

All bush plums can be canned or made into sauce or jams.

PLUM, NATAL. See Natal Plum.
POLE BEAN. See Beans.

Pomegranate

Punica granatum

Effort Scale

NO. 1
Very easy to grow
Occasional pruning to shape needed
Only occasional watering necessary
Fruit processing requires work but is not necessary

Zones

9—10

Thumbnail Sketch

Deciduous shrub or small tree 10—20 ft. tall
Propagated from seed, cuttings, or by layering
Needs full sun
Leaves are bright green, yellow in fall, 2—3 in. long; new growth is bronzy
Blooms in spring or summer
Flowers are bright red, showy, 1 1/2—2 in. across
Fruits are edible; harvested in fall
Used as small to medium-size multistemmed tree, patio tree, large shrub, screen, interest plant, hedge, espalier, and in containers

E.96. *Pomegranate plants bear brilliant red flowers and fruits—sometimes both at once.*

E.97. *In autumn pomegranate trees are usually covered with bright red fruits that hang on the tree for weeks.*

How to Use
In the Kitchen

The big, round, red fruits of the pomegranate are filled with seeds covered with a clear, ruby-red, juicy substance. It is this tart-flavored seed covering that gives pomegranates their special quality. The seeds themselves are used raw to decorate salads and desserts. The juice is extracted for use in drinks, for marinating meat and poultry, and as the base for grenadine syrup. The juice also makes good jelly.

In the Landscape

This deciduous, woody plant can be pruned into a large, fountain-shaped shrub or a small, somewhat pendulous tree. No matter how it is trained, this 10—20-foot plant will offer beauty over a long period. Its new growth is bronzy, and its long, narrow leaves are a light, bright green that in most climates turn clear yellow in the fall. The extremely showy, orange-red flowers are 1 1/2—2 inches across, many to a branch. The floral display can continue for as long as six weeks in summer. Occasionally one of those clusters contains a flower bud, a full-blown flower, a beginning fruit, and a more mature fruit all at once—a real show-and-tell affair. Some of the fruits remain after the leaves have dropped, looking decorative among the bare branches.

Its size and its continual interest make the pomegranate one of the most ornamental and versatile of the edible plants. It is particularly handsome combined with nandina in a shrub border or against a wall. It may be used as a small interest tree or shrub and as a hedge, a screen, or an espalier on a hot, south wall. This latter use is particularly suitable for colder climates. Pomegranate shrubs can be kept to a proper size for container growing. In this form, their various stages can be appreciated close up.

How to Grow
Climate

Pomegranates generally freeze at around 18—20°F. They prefer hot summers and low humidity. They do poorly on the California coast and in southern Florida. The fruits can tolerate very high summer temperatures. Pomegranates are a good desert plant.

The trees have been grown as far north as Puget Sound on the West Coast, and as far north as Virginia on the East Coast. In these northern zones, they must be grown on a hot south or west wall and given winter protection.

Exposure

Pomegranates need full sun.

Soil

They prefer good garden loam, pH 5.5—7.0, but can tolerate considerable amounts of alkalinity and sodium in the soil. They need good drainage.

Fertilizing

Use a humus mulch. If the foliage is pale apply iron chelate and supplemental nitrogen.

Watering

Pomegranates are drought resistant, but for superior fruits in arid climates or on very light soil, occasional deep-watering is usually necessary. Do not deep-water after along dry spell if fruits have formed, or they will split.

Pruning

Pomegranates fruit on new wood and will fruit whether they are pruned heavily or not at all. Young pomegranates can be trained as a bush, or as a single or multistemmed tree. If training as a tree, cut all growth to the ground except one strong branch that will become your trunk for a single tree or three strong branches if you want it to be multistemmed. To keep it in a tree form you will have to cut new sucker growth off for a number of years. In early spring, remove dead growth and shape shrub or tree.

Pests and Diseases

The leaf-footed plant bug is a pest in some desert areas. Pyrethrum in late spring may be needed for severe infestations. Leaf spot occurs in parts of the South. Try dormant oil sprays. Otherwise, few pests and diseases affect the pomegranate.

Harvesting

You can pick a pomegranate once the fruits have turned red. If you leave fully ripe pomegranates on the tree they will often split open.

How to Purchase

Forms and Sources

Pomegranates are available bare root in late winter or in containers from local nurseries. Mail-order sources for plants are (14,27,31,49,70). Seed is available at (2).

Pollinators

Pomegranates are self-pollinating.

Varieties

Many varieties of pomegranates only flower but do not set fruit. Be sure you get a fruiting variety. 'Wonderful' is the one most frequently grown. 'Spanish Ruby' is available in Florida.

Preserving and Preparing

If picked before full maturity, pomegranates can be stored for months in a cool, dry place.

Pomegranate juice stains and tends to splatter. The best way to keep clean while using pomegranates is to submerge the fruits in water as you work with them. When you separate the seeds from the pulp, they will sink to the bottom of your container and the waxy fiber and skin will float to the top.

To extract the juice, place seeds in a blender, two cups at a time, and puree for one minute. Put this juicy pulp in a cheesecloth bag and allow it to drip through. This liquid is the base for grenadine, jelly, marinade, and can also be used as is for drinking.

Pomegranate Jelly

3 1/2 cups pomegranate juice, fresh or frozen and thawed
1/4 cup lemon juice
1 package (2 ounces) powdered pectin
4 1/2 cups sugar
Follow the standard directions for making jelly that come with the powdered pectin.

Grenadine Syrup

Mix equal parts pomegranate juice and sugar. Let mixture stand for three days. Bring to a boil and simmer for three minutes. Strain the syrup and pour into sterilized jars. Use over ice cream, fruit salad, and cut grapefruit.

POMELO. See Citrus Fruits.
POTATO, SWEET. See Root Vegetables.
POTATO, WHITE. See Root Vegetables.

Prickly Pear (INDIAN FIG)
Opuntia species
Nopalea species

Effort Scale

NO. 2
Very easy to grow
Spines must be removed from most varieties before eating

Zones

5—11

E.98. Prickly pear fruits form at the base of the showy flowers.

Thumbnail Sketch

Cactus
  3—15 ft. tall
  Propagated from joints and seeds
  Needs full sun
  Leaves are padlike with thorns, green or gray-green
  Blooms in spring
  Flowers are orange or yellow, similar to large portulacas, 3—4 in. across
  Pads are edible, harvested in spring; fruits are edible, harvested in fall
  Used as interest plant, barrier plant, hedge, on slopes, and in containers

How to Use

In the Kitchen

The prickly pear is a double-barreled plant in the kitchen. The fruits are plumshaped, 1 1/2—3 inches long; they must be handled carefully and the bristly hairs removed before eating. Their lush red pulp looks like that of watermelon. Some species have orange or yellow flesh. This pulp is sweet, but also extremely seedy, so it has to be eaten with some care. Prickly pear is usually served as a fresh fruit, well chilled. In the Middle East, fruit vendors sell it from trays of shaved ice, and it makes a pleasant, cool treat on a hot day.

The young joints of this cactus, usually referred to as pads, are the other edible part. They also are covered with bristles that must be removed before eating. These pads are cut up, boiled, and served with salt, pepper, and butter. The taste most closely resembles that of string beans, but is unique. It must be experienced to be appreciated. The pads are not too often available in a produce market except those that have a Mexican or Spanish clientele. Nopales, as they are called, are more readily available canned, but the most delicious nopales are fresh and home grown.

In the Landscape

The flat, bristly pads of these evergreen, herbaceous, perennial cacti can be 4—6 inches long. The most commonly grown species will grow to 15 feet in height and are exceptionally dramatic as accent plants, especially with Spanish architecture. Most species have showy, yellow blossoms, similar to large portulaca blooms, and green or red fruit. Both the flower and the fruit are decorative against the green or gray-green pads. The plants add height to desert cacti groupings, can be used on rocky banks, and, because of their prickles, are effective barrier plants. They are dramatic planted against a white stucco wall or in large earthenware containers.

How to Grow

The propagation, planting, and cultivation of cacti are different from those for other kinds of plants. The Sunset book *Cactus and Succulents* is a useful reference. The following sections cover some of the basics.

Climate

Some species of prickly pear cacti are hardy to around 20°F. Most are much more tender but are easily grown in containers in colder climates where they can be brought indoors.

Exposure

The plants need full sun.

Planting

If you are able to get a pad from a friend's plant, let the cut portion heal and dry for a few days; then place it right side up in slightly damp sand. If you are using seeds, plant them one-quarter inch deep in good planting mix. Keep barely moist and out of the sun. The germination period is very long; it can last up to six months.

Soil

Prickly pears are not fussy about soil type but must have extremely good drainage.

Fertilizing

These cacti, if grown in the ground, usually do not need fertilizing.

Watering

Prickly pears grown in the ground take care of themselves after the first year, but before that should be watered once a month during the summer if it is dry. The plants are easily overwatered. If you are growing them in containers consult a book on cactus or local authorities.

Pests and Diseases

These cacti have few problems with pests and diseases.

Harvesting

Irritating bristles grow on the fruits and pads of most species. Harvest both with leather gloves. Rub the fruits and pads with rough canvas to remove the bristles and wash to remove the residue. Check carefully, as some bristles are hard to see.

How to Purchase

Forms and Sources

Prickly pear cactus is available as seed or plants from local nurseries and some mail-order sources. Grigsby Cactus Gardens, 2354 Bella Vista Drive, Vista, CA 92083 specializes in cactus. (catalog price: $1.50).

Varieties

Many edible *Opuntia* and *Nopalea* species are available. Few named varieties are available.

Nopalea cochenillifera—native of Mexico, often called the true 'Nopal'; fruits and pads are edible; flowers are pink to rose; plant grows to 15 ft.

N. dejecta—this cactus has a trunk; flowers and fruits are dark red; plant grows to 6 ft.; from South America.

Opuntia Ficus-indica (Indian fig)—most commonly planted and most commonly eaten; usually considered the best; yellow flowers; plant has variable growth habit, sometimes sprawling, sometimes upright, to 15 ft.; there is a spineless variety, bred by Luther Burbank, and a variety popular in the Middle East that is practically seedless.

O. humifusa (often sold as *O. Opuntia*)—many-branched plant, usually prostrate in habit; yellow flowers; the most hardy prickly pear; grown from Massachusetts to Montana, south to Florida, and east to Texas.

O. leucotricha—treelike; grows to 15 ft.; pads are 4—10 in. long; yellow flowers; from Mexico.

O. phaeacantha (often sold as *O. Engelmannii*)—low-growing, sprawling plant; pads are 4—16 in. long, eaten fried or steamed; yellow flowers; most of these cacti grow in Texas, California, Arizona, New Mexico, and are prized by native Indians and Mexicans.

Preserving and Preparing

The fruits of the prickly pear can be pickled or used to make jelly.

Prickly Pear Dessert

Peel and slice fruits into individual dishes. Sprinkle slices with lime juice and top with sweetened whipped cream to which a small amount of orange liqueur has been added.

Quince

Cydonia oblonga

Effort Scale

NO. 3
Vulnerable to some pests
Mulching helpful
Fruits must be processed

Zones

5—9

Thumbnail Sketch

Deciduous tree

E.99. A large prickly pear becomes a living sculpture near an adobe-style house.

E.100. *Quince fruits are usually yellow and quite decorative.*

10—20 ft. tall
Propagated from cuttings and by budding
Needs full sun
Leaves are oblong, deep green, woolly underneath,
  yellow in the fall, 4 in. long
Blooms in spring
Flowers are white or pale pink, showy, 2 in. across
Fruits are edible; harvested in fall
Used as interest tree or shrub, screen, patio tree,
  espalier, hedge

How to Use
In the Kitchen
The yellow, orange, or green, woolly, oblong fruit of the quince is too hard and astringent to be eaten raw. Combined with apples, it can be used for sauce or pie. The fruit can be baked like an apple and is often spiced and canned or used in chutney. The Spanish use it in a dessert called *dulce de membrillo*, a molded quince puree. Generally, though, we know quince as the source of an exquisitely colored and flavored jelly. Quince is a good source of pectin and is sometimes used in combination with less pectinous fruits for jelly. Or it can be made into a fruit paste and rolled in sugar.

In the Landscape
The gnarled and twisted form that develops in the quince with age brings an interesting shape to the landscape, whether the tree is used as an accent near a patio or as a container plant. Delicate white or pink flowers sit above the foliage in the spring and colorful fruits in the fall add visual interest, and the fragrance of the fruit enhances the observer's pleasure.

E.101. *The quince is an attractive small tree. This one is planted near a fence with a recycled spool gate.*

All these advantages make the quince a good espalier subject. As trees or as shrubs, quinces can line a garden walk. The shrubs make a solid screen or hedge.

How to Grow
Climate
Quinces can be grown over a wide area of the country. They are quite hardy but are subject to severe winter injury at −15°F. Since the flowers blossom late in the spring, however, they are not harmed by frost. Because the quince tree is susceptible to fire blight, it does not do well in the warmest, most humid areas of the country.

Exposure
Quinces require full sun.

Soil
Unlike most fruits, quinces will tolerate somewhat poor drainage, but they prefer well-drained, fairly heavy loam. They will not fruit well in very heavy or very light soils.

Fertilizing
Large amounts of nitrogen should be avoided. Nitrogen encourages succulent new growth, which is particularly susceptible to fire blight. When quince is grown on average soil, an occasional compost mulch or manure is generally all the fertilizer needed.

Watering

Quinces are somewhat drought tolerant, but they bear more reliably with good soil moisture.

Pruning

If you grow quince as a tree, you will have to remove suckers occasionally, since the plant generally grows as a shrub. Keep the tree pruned to shape. You can cut it back quite a bit if you want, because quinces bear on the tips of current growth and pruning will not remove much fruiting wood. Pruning is done in the winter. In areas where fire blight is severe, keep pruning to a minimum, as it encourages the highly susceptible, succulent new growth.

Pests and Diseases

Quinces are susceptible to many of the same problems as apple trees, but seem to be less often affected. Codling moth is the most common pest. Quince curculio, scale, and borers are sometimes problems. Fire blight is the most common disease. See Part Two. Leaf blight causes reddish spots on the leaves and occasionally on the fruits. Use lime sulfur for control. Consult local authorities for a spraying schedule.

Harvesting

Pick quinces when they have turned color and are fragrant. Handle them carefully. Quinces are hard, but the skin bruises easily.

How to Purchase

Forms and Sources

Quinces are available from local nurseries bare root in the late winter or early spring or in containers throughout the fall. They are also available from the following mail-order firms throughout the fall: (17,31,46).

Varieties

'Orange'—range-yellow flesh; matures late August. (70)
'Pineapple'—white flesh tastes somewhat like pineapple. (17,25,52,70)
'Smyrna'—oblong yellow fruits with a strong fragrance; considered the superior variety. (17,52,70)

Preserving and Preparing

Quinces make a delicious jelly (see below). They can also be used to make a sauce with apples that can be canned. Spicing and canning quinces is another storing technique; use a recipe for spiced pears if you cannot find one for spiced quince.

Quince Jelly

3 pounds fully ripe quinces

4 1/2 cups water
1/4 cup lemon juice
7 1/2 cups sugar
1/2 bottle liquid pectin

Wash the fruits, removing stem and blossom ends and cutting off bruises. Grind or chop very fine the remaining flesh, including skin and cores. Put pieces in a large saucepan, add water, and bring to a boil. Simmer for 15 minutes. Press through a jelly bag or a bag made from double layers of cheesecloth. Keep 4 cups of fruit and combine with the lemon juice and sugar. Follow the directions for making jelly that come with the liquid pectin. Pour into glass jars and seal.

RABBITEYE BLUEBERRY. See Blueberry.
RADISH. See Root Vegetables.
RASPBERRY. See Brambleberries.
RED CURRANT. See Currant and Gooseberry.
RED PEPPER. See Peppers.

Rhubarb (GARDEN RHUBARB, PIE PLANT)
Rheum Rhabarbarum

Effort Scale

NO. 1
Mulching necessary
Watering necessary in arid climates

Zones

1—9

Thumbnail Sketch

Perennial herb, treated as annual in high desert areas
  3—5 ft. tall
Propagated by divisions or from seeds
Needs full sun; partial shade in desert areas
Leaves are large, deep green, wavy, 1 1/2 ft. wide; stems are red or green
Blooms in summer
Flowers are greenish or reddish, in tall spikes
Stalks are edible; harvested in spring
Used as interest plant, in herbaceous borders, flower beds, containers

How to Use

In the Kitchen

In many parts of the country rhubarb is the first "fruit" of spring. The thick, fleshy leaf stalks of the handsome plant are used for sauce and pie. Both dish

E.102. *Rhubarb's large dramatic leaves look good in containers.*

es are great favorites of those who like them at all, but the world could probably be divided into those who care for rhubarb and those who truly dislike it. Many people make a wine out of the stalks.

Caution: Rhubarb leaves are poisonous.

In the Landscape

A rhubarb plant is a long-lived addition to a yard. It is a herbaceous perennial that can grow to 5 feet tall. Its 18-inch, crinkly, rich-green and red-veined leaves are dramatic atop their rosy-red stalks. (One variety, 'Victoria', has green stalks. It does not compare in beauty with the red-stalked varieties; nor does its sauce seem as appealing.) Rhubarb is so handsome that it fits into any herbaceous border or flower bed. It can be an accent in a container or it can fill a corner spot in a garden or yard. It is eye-catching when planted with red geraniums.

The flowers of rhubarb grow on tall stalks, but they should be cut off so the energy used in their development is diverted to the stalks and the leaves.

How to Grow

Rhubarb has some rather definite requirements. It needs cold winters and is not productive in areas with very hot summers, even though it prefers full sun. In the high desert areas it is planted in the fall as a winter annual and should be given partial shade for coolness.

Its soil requirements are not precise, but it does best in acidic, well-drained, loam rich in organic matter. Mulch annually with manure. If placed correctly and given a modest amount of attention, a plant will last a lifetime.

How to Purchase

Seed or rhizomes of rhubarb are available from local nurseries or mail-order firms. Alternatively, you can be around when your neighbor is dividing a plant.

Do not harvest rhubarb stalks the first year. After that, harvest by pulling the thickest, healthiest stalks off gently. Do not take more than half the stalks of any one plant. Three plants should be adequate for the average family.

Preserving and Preparing

Rhubarb can be made into jam or wine. Stewed rhubarb can be frozen or canned.

Stewed Rhubarb

Cut washed stems into 1—2 inch pieces and place in a saucepan with enough water to prevent sticking. Cover and cook over medium heat until soft. Add sugar to taste.

Root Vegetables

Beet, *Beta vulgaris*
Carrot, *Daucus Carota* var. *sativus*
Onion, *Allium Cepa*
Potato, *Solanun tuberosum*
Radish, *Raphanus sativus*
Sweet potato, *Ipomora Batatas*

Effort Scale

Beets, Carrots, Onions, Potatoes, Radishes
NO. 2
Must be planted annually
Thinning usually needed
Water, mulching, and fertilizing needed
Some weeding necessary
Sweet Potatoes
NO. 4
Must be started from slips
Special soil, fertilizer, and water requirements
Susceptible to many pests and diseases

Zones

Annual

Thumbnail Sketch

Annual, or biennials planted as annuals; 4 in.—3 ft.
  tall
Propagated from seeds, tubers, bulbs
Most need full sun but some need partial shade in
  hot weather
Leaves vary with species
Flowers are not usually seen
Roots, tubers, and bulbs eaten; some have edible
  leaves
Used in flower borders, raised beds, and containers

How to Use

In the Kitchen

Most of these root vegetables were mainstays of
our ancestors' diet; even today there is hardly a cook
who doesn't use these wonderfully versatile food
plants on a regular basis. What would soups be, for
example, without carrots, onions, and potatoes?
Imagine carrots with almonds in a pureed soup, or
yellow beets adding sweetness to your soups and stir-
fry's (without discoloring them as their red cousins
would do). Think of onion soup gratinée, deep-fried
onions covering a casserole, or super-sweet onions
eaten raw on a hamburger. Potatoes are such a staple
food that we almost ignore them; to give them fresh
emphasis, try the all-blue potatoes in a Fourth-of-July
potato salad. And the tangy radish, available in black,
red, pink, or white varieties, can be enjoyed in salads
and sandwiches, or just as a snack. Boiled or baked
sweet potatoes make a pleasant change from the more
routinely served white potatoes.

In the Landscape

The root vegetables are harder to manage in the
landscape than other vegetables because, when you
harvest them, they leave holes in the planting bed. A
number of solutions are available. If you plant them in
containers you can harvest the vegetables and then
move the containers out of sight. Another option is to
grow small seedlings of lettuces or other greens to be
transplanted into the holes as your root vegetables are
harvested. Still another solution can be borrowed from
the art of bulb culture. The foliage of many flowering
bulbs, such as tulips, daffodils, and hyacinths, turns
an unattractive yellow-brown after blooming and
lingers long after the beautiful flower is just a memory.
Growers of strictly ornamental gardens have dealt
with this problem for years by planting in the same
vicinity a fast-growing floriferous plant. Spreading
flowers such as violas or marigolds soon cover the
unsightly foliage (or fill in the bare spots if the bulbs
are removed after blooming). This technique works
equally well with root vegetables.

Another problem with some root vegetables, name

E.103. Beets, potatoes, and carrots are fast-growing annuals that
adapt well to container culture if they are given plenty of root
room and good drainage.

ly onions and potatoes, is that the tops must turn
brown and die back before they are harvested.
Therefore, these vegetables are best suited to large
containers that can be moved out of sight while the
plants cure.

Root vegetables are a varied lot and have different
uses in the landscape. Most beet varieties have red-
veined green foliage that contrasts attractively with
white varieties of flowers such as petunias, lobelia, and
candy tuft. Carrots have feathery light-green foliage
and are beautiful when used to edge a path or to outline the design of a bed; Onions have stiff, upright,
blue-green leaves and can look coarse by themselves,
but provide definition when combined with soft-look-
ing foliage such as that of lettuce or other greens.
Potatoes have dark-green coarse-looking foliage that is
best used as background or in containers. Radishes
have rather nondescript foliage and a very short life
span; for these reasons they are best interplanted with
flowers such as dwarf marigolds and nasturtiums.
Sweet potato vines will cascade gracefully over the
sides of a planter. If they bloom they have pink flowers, so they are nice planted as a ground cover in front
of low-growing pink zinnias or interplanted with pink
petunias.

How to Grow and Purchase

Most of the root vegetables prefer cool weather.
You can plant them in early spring, as soon as your
soil has warmed up, or as a fall crop. In cool summer
areas you can plant beets, carrots, radishes, and potatoes in the summer. While onions can also be grown
in the summer, they are daylength sensitive, so choose
varieties that are appropriate to your lattitude.

All of the root vegetables need loose and well-
drained soil.

Beets

Most are not heavy feeders and in good soils can get by with very little fertilizing. In dry climates keep these vegetables well watered. Most of them have very few pests and diseases and are fairly easy to grow once the seedlings are well on their way.

Sow seeds directly in rich, well-drained soil in early spring. Some people are convinced you get sweeter beets if the plants have some chilling. Beets can take some frost. Plant the seed 1/4-inch deep in wide rows. Beet seed is actually a cluster of seeds, so thinning is necessary to prevent crowding. Thin to 3 inches apart. Even watering is the key to succulent beets; do not let them dry out. In most parts of the country beets have few pest and disease problems; the occasional aphid or flea beetle can usually be controlled with water spray or Safer's soap. Harvest most varieties when root is 2—3 inches across. Most varieties are ready in 50—60 days.

One of the best red beets is 'Detroit Dark Red'; there is also a cylindrical red beet called 'Cylindra'. My favorite is the 'Golden Beet', which has the same flavor as red beets but can be used in soups, salads, and stir-frys without bleeding. One beet variety, 'Lutz', has been developed for its superior greens. Nurseries with a particularly large selection of beets are (5,7,16,19,24,37,45,49,55).

Carrots

Sow carrot seeds directly in rich, well-drained soil in early spring. If you have heavy clay soil, select some of the short, stubby varieties. The best soil preparation for carrots is well-aged compost (do not use manure, as it causes the carrots to fork). Cover the seed with a very light dressing of soil and keep the seed bed even

E.104. Onions, garlic, radishes, and parsnips are easy to grow and enrich your table fare.

ly moist; *never let the soil dry out.* In warm weather it helps to cover the seed bed with burlap or an old sheet to keep moisture in, but be sure to remove the cloth the instant the seedlings appear. As carrot seed is very short-lived, use fresh seed for the best germination. Once the seedlings are up, protect them from snails and slugs (and sometimes even birds). Thin to 1 1/2—2 inches apart—you can use the thinnings as baby carrots if you wait until they are an inch in diameter. Once sprouted, carrots are easy to grow in most parts of the country. However, a pest called the carrot fly is a problem in some areas. The maggots of this fly will infest the carrots, making them nearly inedible. The carrot fly can be partly controlled with crop rotation or by covering plants with floating row covers.

Carrots are generally considered to be most flavorful when grown in cool seasons, but acceptable carrots can be grown through most of the summer and fall, even in the winter in mild climates.

Harvest when the soil is moist or the carrot will break off in the ground. Harvest when roots are 1/2 inch or more across the top, but do not let them get too big or they will be woody and tough. Most varieties are ready in 70—80 days.

Superior varieties of carrots are "Amstel', a very tender and sweet carrot particularly when picked as baby carrots; 'Planet', a small round baby carrot that stays small even when mature; 'Nantes'; 'Royal Chantenay'; and, for variety, a white carrot, 'White Belgium'. Mail-order nurseries that carry a good selection of carrots are (5,16,19,37,45,49,50,58,62).

Onions

Onions are grown from seeds or from young bulbs called sets. It is important to select the right variety for your climate and the time of year because the bulbs are formed according to day length—there are long-day onions and short-day onions. Check catalogs to find the right variety for your garden. Sow seeds or put out sets in early spring, or in the fall in mild climates. The soil should be rich and well drained and kept evenly moist during the growing season. Grow onions in wide rows or interplant them in groups among flowers or vegetables in a border. You can thin onions and use them as scallions; thin to 4—5 inches apart. Keep them growing quickly for the best production by watering often and fertilizing if needed. Many pests affect onions; the most common are the onion maggot and thrips. Pyrethrum might be needed to control thrips; crop rotation and scattering onions among other plants help control the onion maggot.

To harvest onions, wait until the tops die down, then dig up the onions and let them stay on top of the soil to dry out. Most varieties are ready in 90—110 days. Store in a cool, dry place.

Most onion varieties are the long-day types. Try 'Torpedo', 'Yellow Spanish', 'Bermuda', and 'Walla Walla'. Mail-order nurseries with a particularly large selection are (7,16,37,41,55,62). One company (58) specializes in difficult-to find onions including multiplier, topset and shallots.

Potatoes

Potatoes are started by planting pieces of the tuber that contain an "eye." They should be set out as soon as the ground can be worked in the spring but after all danger of frost is past. They are best grown on well-drained, fertile, organic soils. For an easy and large harvest, plant potatoes in a 6-inch-deep trench, and once the plants are growing strongly, fill in the trench with organic matter. For highest production keep the plants fairly moist. If planted with plenty of organic matter they generally require little fertilizer.

Potatoes are bothered by a number of pests and diseases. The Colorado potato beetle, flea beetle, and aphids can attack the foliage, and wire worms and white grubs can damage tubers. The foliage pests can be fairly well controlled with Safer's soap or covering with floating row covers, and the tuber pests are best controlled by crop rotation and the addition of wood ashes into the soil. If your soil is highly alkaline, your potatoes may develop a disease called scab; make the soil acidic to correct this condition. Potatoes usually take around 100 days to develop tubers. Feel under the ground to see if they are large enough to harvest. You can extend your potato-eating season by harvesting a number of the small, early potatoes, which are delicious boiled and served very simply. The major harvesting is done after the foliage has died down and large potatoes can be dug up in clusters; "mining" for potatoes is one of the most enjoyable gardening adventures. Brush the dirt off the tubers and bring them inside to store in a cool place. Two major types of potatoes—baking and boiling—are grown in this country. The average local nursery will generally carry only one of each type, but there are a number of different varieties that you may want to try just for a change. One of the best is 'All Blue', carried by (19,24,49,55,57); other good varieties are 'All Red' and 'German Fingerling'. If you are interested in growing some of the more unusual varieties, contact Becker's Seed Potatoes, R.R. 1, Trout Creek, Ontario, Canada POH 2L0 or Ronniger's Seed Potatoes, Star Route, Moyie Springs, ID 83845. Ronniger's carries more than 100 varieties of potatoes. Be aware, however, that while many of the unusual varieties are extremely tasty as well as fun to use (think of blue fried potatoes), most of these old potato varieties are not as vigorous or as high-yielding as some of the newer hybrids.

Caution: Potato foliage and green tubers are poisonous.

Radishes

Radish seeds are very quick to sprout and certainly one of the easiest vegetables for children to grow. Sow seeds directly in the garden after the last frost, or sow them in fall in mild winter areas. Plant seed 1/2 inch deep, and thin to 2 inches apart. Soil should be light and well drained; generous amounts of compost will produce better radishes. It is critically important to keep the young radishes constantly moist. Most varieties of radishes are ready in 20—30 days, but some of the winter radishes, the Chinese types, take 60 days.

In some areas of the country radishes are bothered by root maggots. These pests are best controlled by crop rotation and by spotting groups of radishes around the garden instead of planting them in large concentrations; floating row covers give some control.

Harvest most varieties when they reach the size of a cherry or a little larger, though some large black and golden varieties will reach 2 inches across. In a class by themselves are the very large Chinese radishes that can grow to 2 feet long, including some that will weigh 4—5 pounds.

A great number of varieties are available. The most popular and consistent performer among small salad radishes is 'Cherry Bell'; others of this type are 'Easter Egg' and 'Champion'. Seed companies that carry a large selection of radishes are (7,24,49,55).

Sweet Potatoes

Sweet potatoes are the most heat-tolerant vegetable grown in the United States. They not only tolerate but must have great amounts of heat to produce a good crop. They need at least 140—150 hot summer days.

Sweet potatoes are planted in spring by slips, which are sprouts produced by the tubers. To start your own slips, place tubers in a hotbed (a wooden tray with heating coils in the bottom and filled with sand) about 6—8 weeks before the weather warms up. Cover the potatoes with damp sand and maintain a hotbed temperature of 75—85°. Pull, do not cut, the shoots off; they and their roots will pull off easily.

Dig and loosen the planting area very well. The soil should be sandy loam, not clay. Sweet potatoes grown in heavy clay become gnarled and stringy. In planter boxes and containers use a rich, light soil mix. At planting time, use a generous amount of a fertilizer high in potassium and phosphorus. Mix in well. Bury bottoms of slips 4 inches deep and 1 foot apart. Keep the vines fairly moist until they are well established. The plants require less moisture after they are growing vigorously.

E.105. *Sweet potatoes can be grown in containers filled with loose, rich soil. Tubers are shown here in cutaway view.*

A number of pests affect sweet potatoes. Check with your local extension service, since problems differ with region. Choose sweet potato varieties that are resistant to the diseases in your area.

Harvest potatoes in late fall before a frost or when the tops die back. Handle the tubers carefully, because they bruise easily.

Store sweet potatoes at temperatures above 50°F or they will rot. Under optimum conditions, they can be stored for four or five months. Sweet potatoes also can be canned or frozen.

Slips are available in spring from some local nurseries and mail-order houses. Two mail-order nurseries, Fred's Plant Farm, Dresden, TN 38225, and Steele Plant Farm, Box 807, Gleason, TN 38229, offer a large selection of varieties in spring.

Because sweet potatoes are susceptible to many diseases it is important to choose varieties that are resistant to diseases that affect your area. The following are recommended:

'Allgold'—moist, sweet potatoes; resist viral disease, internal cork, and stem rot; store well; good in the Midwest. (16)

'Bunch Porto Rico'—compact vines, grow to 18 - 24 in.; good for smaller areas and greenhouses. (16,27)

'Beauregard'—light purple skin with dark orange flesh; developed at the Louisiana State University. (35)

'Centennial'—bright copper skin; smooth deep orange fine-textured flesh; good yield; wilt-resistant. (16,27,49)

Preserving and Preparing

Most root vegetables store very well. Carrots, beets, and white potatoes keep the best. Harvest root vegetables before the ground freezes in the fall and store them in a place that is around 40°F For detailed information on preserving root vegetables, as well as recommended varieties that are good "keepers," consult *Root Cellering* by Mike and Nancy Bubel, published by the Rodale Press in 1979.

Golden Beets and Broccoli Stir-Fry

    3 tablespoons vegetable oil, using 1 tablespoon oil, if desired

    2 tablespoons minced ginger

    1 tablespoon minced fresh hot pepper, more or less to taste, or 1 teaspoon dried pepper (optional)

    1 cup 'Golden Beets' in 1/4-inch slices

    3 cups broccoli, stems peeled and cut in 1/4- x 1 1/2-inch slices, flowers separated to bite size

    2 cloves minced garlic

    1/2 onion, chopped

    1/2 cup toasted cashews

    2 tablespoons rice vinegar

    3 tablespoons sherry or sweet sake

    Soy sauce, oyster sauce, or hoisin sauce to taste

Heat oil in wok or skillet on medium to medium-high heat. Add beets, ginger, and hot pepper and cook 1 minute. Add garlic, onion, and broccoli stems; cook and stir about 3 minutes. Stir in broccoli flowers, cover for 1 minute, stir, and add vinegar and sherry. Cover for 2 minutes. When vegetables are done crisp-tender, stir in cashews and seasoning sauces and serve with rice. Serves four as a side dish. As a main course, add 1 cup diced firm tofu when you add the broccoli flowers, or add leftover diced chicken, shrimp, etc.

Patriotic Potato Salad

    Red peppers diced, or 'All Red' potatoes

    White potatoes

    'All Blue' potatoes

    Use your favorite potato salad recipe and substitute 1/4 to 1/3 of the white potatoes with the blue and red ones, or use just All Blue' and add red peppers. Cook the different colored potatoes separately. Be careful not to overcook them, and combine them carefully, so that the colors will stay separate.

Rosemary
Rosmarinus officinalis

Effort Scale
NO. 1
Almost grows by itself

Zones
All

Thumbnail Sketch
Evergreen, woody shrub grown as an annual in
  zones 1—6
2—4 ft. tall
Propagated from seeds or cuttings
Needs full sun
Leaves are needlelike, gray-green, 1/2—1 1/2 in.
  long
Blooms in spring
Flowers are blue, pink, or white, small, showy
Leaves are edible; used as seasoning; harvested year
  round
Used as ground and bank cover and in herb gar-
  dens, raised beds, containers

How to Use
In the Kitchen

The aromatic leaves of this herb yield a slight taste
of pine. They are commonly used to season lamb,
pork, veal, and poultry, as well as casseroles and egg
dishes. The leaves can be steeped and added to a fruit
punch. Boughs of rosemary can be added to barbecue
coals at the end of the cooking process to impart a
subtle flavor to roasted meats or poultry.

In the Landscape

This woody perennial ranges in height from 2 to 4
feet, depending on the variety. The tall, upright plants
make beautiful flowering hedges. Unpruned, they can
be used as shrubs or, with their interesting, gnarled
shapes, as container or accent plants. The prostrate,
trailing varieties are ideal as bank covers or cascading
over a retaining wall. Their strong root systems are
helpful in controlling erosion. All kinds can be used in
herb gardens, and in containers.

All rosemary plants have needlelike leaves with
gray undersides. These leaves set off the plentiful
blooms, whether they be light blue, lavender, or deep
violet-blue. Rosemary is attractive to bees.

How to Grow
Rosemary is semihardy from approximately 0°F to
5°F. It is drought tolerant, but in the desert it needs

*E.106. Rosemary comes in many forms. Shown here draped over
a retaining wall made of recycled railroad ties, from left to right:
common rosemary, upright 'Collingwood Ingram', and
'Prostratus'.*

watering three or four times a summer. Its soil requirements are few: alkaline soil and good drainage.

Rosemary can be harvested at any time of the year
for use fresh. However, if you are planning to dry it for
the winter, harvest the leaves before the plant has started to flower. The leaves will have a better texture and
will usually be richer in flavor.

How to Purchase
Forms and Sources

Common rosemary is easily obtained as seed or
plants from local nurseries or mailorder firms.
Nurseries with a large selection are: (18,23,45,54).

Varieties

The following varieties of rosemary are available as
plants from local herb specialists.
  'Collingwood Ingram'—shrub type, 2 1/2 ft. tall, 4-ft.
    spread; bright, deep-blue flowers. -
  'Lockwood de Forest'—trailing type;, bright-blue
    flowers.
  'Prostratus'—trailing type, lavender-blue flowers.

Preserving
See BASIL for drying information.

Saffron

Crocus sativus

Effort Scale
NO. 2,
Easy to grow
Harvesting is tedious

Zones
6—9

Thumbnail Sketch
Herbaceous corm
4 in. tall
Propigated from offsets (divisions of corms)
Needs full sun
Leaves are grasslike, 3—4 in. tall
Blooms in fall
Flowers are mauve; 2 in. tall
Flower stigmas are edible; used as seasoning; harvested in fall
Used in rock gardens, flower beds, containers

How to Use
In the Kitchen
Saffron is the most expensive of all herbs to buy. It is produced from the red-orange stigmas (threadlike female flower parts that receive pollen) of *C. sativus*, also called saffron crocus. Its vivid orange color and strong flavor make it effective in very small amounts. It is an important ingredient in paella, bouillabaisse, and Spanish rice. Saffron is also used in certain breads.

In the Landscape
Saffron is similar to the ordinary spring crocus, but it blooms in the fall. Its glasslike leaves are 3—4 inches tall and its flowers are mauve to purple, not as showy as those of the spring bulbs but lovely nevertheless and a pleasant surprise in the fall landscape. It is used the way spring crocuses are used in landscaping—in rock gardens, in large clusters under high, branching trees, and in containers.

Caution: Do not confuse saffron crocus with autumn crocus, *Colchicum autumnale*, which is poisonous.

How to Grow, Purchase, and Preserve
Like spring crocus, saffron crocus grows in zones 6—9. Plant the bulbs in August, 3—4 inches deep, in rich, well-drained garden loam.

To harvest, remove the stigmas with a tweezer and dry them in a warm place.

These plants are often difficult to obtain. They are sometimes available at local nurseries, and can be ordered from (45,54,55) and from P. de Jager and Sons, P.O. Box 100, Brewster, NY 10509.

You will not have enough to preserve; hundreds of stigmas are needed to make half an ounce. (This is why saffron is so expensive.)

E.107. Saffron crocuses can be grown in clusters.

Sage

Common sage, *Salvia officinalis*
Pineapple sage, *S. elegans* [*S. rutilans*]

Effort Scale
NO. 1
Very easy to grow
Common sage should be taken inside in coldest winter areas

Zones
All for common sage
9—10 for pineapple sage

Thumbnail Sketch
Common Sage
Evergreen, woody herb 1—2 ft tall

E.108. Sage is a small, versatile plant. The variegated type shown here looks pretty against a background of rocks.

Propagated from seeds or divisions
Needs full sun
Leaves are gray-green, purple, or variegated, 1—2 in. long
Blooms in summer
Flowers are small, blue or white, on spikes
Leaves are edible, used as seasoning, harvested year round
Used in herb gardens, flower beds, containers

Pineapple Sage
Evergreen woody herb; perennial, often planted as an annual 2—3 1/2 ft. tall
Propagated by cuttings
Needs full sun
Leaves deep green, 2—4 in. long, underside slightly woolly
Blooms in fall
Flowers are red on tall thin spikes
Leaves are edible; used as seasoning; harvest season varies
Used in herb gardens, back of flower beds, containers

How to Use
In the Kitchen
The aromatic leaves of common sage are used as a seasoning for poultry stuffing and homemade sausage. Sage adds a good flavor to soft, mild cheese that is spread on crackers and, because of its congeniality with the chicken flavor, is good in the dressing used on a chicken salad. Pineapple sage has a slight pineapple flavor and is used in jellies and fruit compotes.

In the Landscape
These woody perennials differ sharply from each other in appearance. Common sage grows to 2 feet high and has gray-green, woolly, crinkly leaves and blue or white, spiky flowers. It is used in herb gardens and in containers. The variety 'Tricolor' has purple, red, and white variegated leaves that make a striking accent alone and combines well with purple alyssum and johnny-jump-ups in the spring and with low, pink dianthus in the summer. It is particularly lovely in a small herb garden, planted in a strawberry jar (one with "pockets" on the outside) along with thyme, parsley, and purple basil.

Pineapple sage grows higher, is more open in appearance, and has deeper-green, softer-looking leaves than common sage. Its flowers are bright red and grow in slender spikes. Pineapple sage should not be confused with scarlet sage (*Salvia splendens*), the strictly ornamental sage. Pineapple sage is a nice addition to any flower bed, toward the back because of its height. Try it with Shasta daisies, green basil, ruby chard, and red zinnias.

How to Grow, Purchase, and Preserve
Garden sage grows in most areas of the country. In the coldest areas grow it as an annual. Pineapple sage is quite tender. Both sages need good drainage, ordinary garden soil, and full sun. Neither needs much watering.

Sage can be harvested at any time of the year for use fresh. However, when you are planning to dry it for the winter, harvest the leaves before the plant has started to flower to ensure good texture and maximum flavor.

Both seeds and plants of common sage are readily available. Pineapple sage plants are sold in small containers in specialty herb nurseries such as (18,45,54).

See BASIL for information on drying.

Sorrel
French sorrel (oseille), *Rumex scutatus*
Garden sorrel, *R. Acetosa*

Effort Scale
NO. 1
Occasional watering and weeding necessary
Occasional pest problems

Zones
5—9

E.109. *Sorrel has distinctive sword-shaped leaves.*

Thumbnail Sketch

Perennial herbs
18 in.—3 ft. tall
Propagated from seeds or divisions
Needs full sun, will tolerate partial shade
Blooms in summer
Flowers are green or brown, in thin spikes 2—3 ft.
  tall
Leaves are medium green, shield-shaped, 3—6 in.
  long
Leaves are edible; harvest time varies
Used in herb gardens, flower beds, woodland paths,
  raised beds, containers

How to Use

In the Kitchen

Soup lovers claim that cream of sorrel soup is without peer. The slightly sour taste of the leaves in combination with chicken broth, cream, and eggs is delicious and satisfying. The leaves are often used in sauces for salmon or shrimp, and a few can be added to a mixed salad. French sorrel is milder in flavor than the common sorrel. Try them both. Do not confuse garden sorrel with wood sorrel, *Oxalis acetosella*.

In the Landscape

Both species are herbaceous perennials whose rich green foliage differs from that of the more common herb garden plants, so they make a nice change. They are close relatives of dock, a weedy pest. The foliage of garden sorrel is long, to 2 feet, and shield-shaped. The French sorrel has much smaller leaves, to 6 inches long. Both plants drape their leaves and are somewhat sprawling. If not allowed to bloom, they give a soft graceful shape to a flower border. If allowed to bloom, the plants look more upright. Try combining the taller garden sorrel with zinnias or tall marigolds in the background. The shorter French sorrel looks well planted with Alpine strawberries, parsley, and white lobelia. The latter combination is lovely in containers and can be grown in partial shade.

The small green or brown flowers of the sorrel are borne on tall spikes; they are somewhat decorative and can be used fresh or dried in flower arrangements. As is often the case with leafy edibles, however, when you want to use the leaves of a plant you should not allow the flowers to develop.

How to Grow, Purchase, and Preserve

Garden sorrel is native to Europe and Eurasia but has gone wild in North America and can be found in most areas of the country. Its requirements are few, although it does like a moist soil. It will grow in full sun or partial shade. French sorrel is native to central Europe, likes a rather dry soil, and tolerates both full sun and partial shade. Neither species is bothered by cold or heat.

Both plants are prone to minor pest and disease problems, such as black aphids and shothole fungus. And, of course, those succulent, green leaves are attractive to snails and slugs.

You should divide sorrel every three years to keep the leaf production at a high level.

Harvesting sorrel is simply a matter of cutting the leaves as you need them. Always allow the plants to regrow and fill in to renew themselves after each harvesting.

Plants are available at local nurseries and some mail-order firms. Seeds are readily available mail-order and plants from (18,54). Also look to friends who might be dividing the crowns of their plants.

Sorrel can be frozen like greens, or as sorrel soup. If adding egg yolks or cream to your soup, leave them out when freezing and add them after the soup base is thawed.

SOUR CHERRY. See Cherry.
SPEARMINT. See Mint.
SPINACH. See Greens.
SQUASH. See Cucumber, Squash, and Melon.

Strawberry

Alpine strawberry (fraise des bois), *Fragaria alpina semperflorens*
Garden strawberry, *F.* x *Ananassa*

Effort Scale

Alpine Strawberry
NO. 2
Fertilizing and weeding are necessary
Watering needed in most areas
Picking fruits is time-consuming
Replanting necessary every three or four years
Winter protection needed in many areas

Garden Strawberry
NO. 4
Susceptible to some pests and diseases, including
   birds
Replanting necessary every three years
Runners must be controlled
Watering and fertilizing necessary
Weeding necessary
Harvesting the large, perishable yield is time-con-
   suming
Winter protection needed in many areas

Zones

3—10

Thumbnail Sketch

Herbaceous perennials 6—12 in. tall
Propagated from seeds or runners
Garden needs full sun; Alpine prefers partial shade
Leaves are compound; garden species, deep green;
   Alpine species, medium green
Blooms in spring and summer
Flowers are white, small
Fruits are edible; harvested in spring and summer
Used in flower beds, raised beds, to line a woodland
   path, rock gardens, hanging baskets, containers,
   and for ground covers

How to Use

In the Kitchen

A bowl of garden strawberries served with a little
powdered sugar and cream is my idea of the perfect
dessert. Close behind are strawberry pie, whether
plain, chiffon, or cream, strawberry Bavarian cream,
strawberry soufflé, meringues filled with strawberries,
and strawberry shortcake, all of which dress up strawberries without spoiling their flavor. Scandinavians use
the berries in a wonderful pudding and soup, and
Australians often top their meringuelike cake, Pavlova,

E.110. *Alpine strawberries lack runners; they bear their berries
on stalks that keep them off the ground.*

with fresh berries. If you dress whole, fresh berries
with a bit of curaçao about two hours before serving,
they will have a marvelous fresh look. The curaçao
does not draw the juices, but the amount should be
small—about 2 tablespoons for 48 berries—so the
berry flavor is not covered.

Strawberry jam is such an American tradition it
hardly needs mentioning. What a pleasure jam is
when it brings the taste and smell of summer to our
winter breakfast tables.

If you like garden strawberries, you will love Alpine
strawberries (the French call them *fraises des bois*).
They are strawberries with the flavor volume turned
up. I remember paying $8.00 for a bowl of small, fra-
grant Alpine berries in France; you can enjoy this delicacy for very little if you choose to grow them.

In the Landscape

Perky, red garden strawberries dangling from
hanging baskets or over the side of a strawberry jar are
treats for the eyes as well as the taste buds. These productive ornamentals lend themselves to a number of
uses. The deep-green leaves and the small, white flowers contrast nicely with the dark color of wooden tubs
or brick walks. The plants form a rich, green ground
cover that is nice next to walks or patios, where you
can bend down and help yourself to the choicest
berry. Strawberries are also good in raised beds or to
line flower borders. Ripe strawberries must be harvested daily to keep the fruits from rotting.

Alpine strawberries are star edible ornamentals.
These plants are even more graceful than the garden

strawberries. They have the further advantage of having no runners, so they remain neat-looking when planted near a lawn or a walk. The fruits are smaller and are not as pressing to harvest. They dry up and fall off instead of rotting, as the large garden strawberries do. The flowers and fruits sit above lightgreen foliage in a truly ornamental fashion. They look beautiful combined with sweet woodruff, mint, lettuce, dwarf nasturtiums, and begonias.

How to Grow

Climate

A strawberry variety exists for nearly every area of the United States and Canada. Alpine strawberries are quite hardy and can be grown well into zone 4. In areas with coldest winters, mulching with straw is necessary In fact, in cold climates all types of strawberries should be covered with a heavy mulch, preferably straw, when heavy frosts are expected, and the mulch should not be removed until hard freezes are over. Alternate freezing and thawing of the soil sometimes heaves the plants out of the soil; the mulch helps keep the soil from freezing.

In desert climates and regions that receive over 300 frost-free days, garden strawberries are usually treated as a winter annual. 'Sequoia' and 'Tioga' are varieties adapted to this method of growing.

Exposure

Plant garden strawberries in full sun. Alpine strawberries prefer morning sun or filtered shade from a high-branching tree. Do not plant Alpines in full sun or in hot, afternoon sun in warm-summer areas.

Planting

Garden strawberries should be grown for only three to four years in one place, because the mother plants stop producing and the runners get too crowded. Diseases are also more of a problem when strawberries are grown in the same place for many years. Plant strawberries in beds that have been well prepared with humus. Plant crowns of the plants at ground level. Strawberry plants that are planted too deep will rot; if they are planted too high they will dry out.

Alpine strawberries are usually started from seeds; follow package directions. For best production divide the plants every three or four years.

Keep the strawberry bed well weeded; mulches help considerably.

Soil

Both types of strawberries need fairly rich, well-drained soil that is high in organic matter. Keep strawberries well mulched. When good drainage cannot be

E.111. Hybrid strawberries can be grown in place of many ground covers.

assured, strawberries are often planted in hills. Strawberries prefer a slightly acidic soil pH of 5.0—6.0.

Fertilizing

Both types of strawberries should be kept well mulched with manure or compost.

Do not fertilize with large amounts of nitrogen, but watch for symptoms of nitrogen starvation—foliage turns light green or yellowish—and treat by applying small amounts of nitrogen.

Watering

Strawberry plants need to be kept moist. They have a low tolerance for salt, and in areas with high water salinity, as in some high-desert areas, strawberries are difficult to grow.

Pruning

For spring-bearing varieties of garden strawberries, prune off flowers the first year after planting to encourage strong growth. This means you will have no strawberries that year from these plants. Prune off the spring flowers on everbearing varieties, but allow fall flowers to fruit the first year. If you remove most of the runners on your plants you will get more and larger berries. Keep some of the runners intact to provide replacements for the older plants as they decline.

Alpine strawberries need no pruning.

Pests and Diseases

A number of pests bother strawberries but usually chemical controls are unnecessary. Snail and slug problems are an exception. Hand-picking. If slugs are a large problem, plant rows 3 feet apart. Remove all plant debris and don't mulch. Japanese beetles are sometimes a problem. To control these pests, hand-pick and use milky-spore disease. A preventive planning measure is to keep strawberry patches away from lawns, where the grubs overwinter. Where weevils are a problem, use spring-bearing berries. Pull up the plants after the second spring and plant something else in their place for the next few years to prevent the weevil population from building up. Aphids, another potential problem, can usually be controlled with a sharp blast of water from the hose nozzle. Nematodes and mites can be a problem in the Southeast. To control the first, use the soil solarization method discussed in Part Two before planting; mites require Safer's Mite Killer™ control.

The diseases that affect strawberries—verticillium wilt and red stele (root rot)—can be serious, but are not common with home-grown plants if they have been purchased from a nursery that carries certified disease-free plants. The most important control is crop rotation. Once plants have become diseased, remove them and do not plant strawberries again in the same bed for three or four years. Even if diseases have not affected your fruit, you should alternate strawberries with other plants in succession in the same garden spot.

Harvesting

Pick strawberries the day they become ripe—when they are fully colored and slightly soft. Pull them off carefully with the stem and cap still attached. Check the vines daily. Refrigerate berries, but use them quickly, as the quality declines rapidly.

A mature garden strawberry plant should produce about 1 pint of berries each season. Alpine strawberries produce a lighter harvest—plan to grow 4—5 dozen plants for a family of four.

How to Purchase

Forms and Sources

Buy garden strawberries bare root in early spring from local nurseries or mail-order sources, or in containers through the fall.

Varieties

GARDEN STRAWBERRIES

It is very important to choose strawberry varieties appropriate for your climate. The following varieties are disease resistant. Look for them in your local nurs-ery. Mail-order nurseries with a particularly large selection of varieties are (23,49,70).

'Ft. Laramie'—everbearing, large, aromatic berries; extremely hardy, good for Midwest as well as southern states; nice for hanging baskets. (24,35,54,64,70)

'Tri-Star'—day-neutral berry that is not affected by the length of sunlight per day and beary all summer long. (Readily Available)

'Ozark Beauty'—large berries; everbearing; very hardy and adaptable to many climates. (Readily Available)

'Redchief'—good dessert fruits; resistant to red stele and mildew; for Southeast. (58,61)

'Sequoia'—one of the best-tasting strawberries; resistant to many diseases and somewhat tolerant of soil alkalinity; for West Coast. (Readily Available)

'Shasta'—good flavor; ripens midseason; resistant to some virus diseases and mildew; for California. (Readily Available)

'Sunrise'—good flavor; ripens early season; resistant to red stele, mildew, and verticillium wilt; for Southeast. (70)

'Surecrop'—good-quality fruits; ripens early; resistant to most major strawberry diseases and drought; for East Coast. (Readily Available)

'Tennessee Beauty'—good-quality berries; ripens late season; resistant to a number of diseases; for Southeast. (Readily Available)

ALPINE STRAWBERRIES

Alpine strawberries are sold as seed by the following mail-order sources: (23,49,52,53,55). Some local nurseries sell plants. A number of varieties of Alpine strawberries exist, all quite similar to each other in fruit quality and growth habits.

'Alexandria'—medium-size red fruit; good flavor. (12,36,54)

'Baron Solemacher'—old-favorite variety. (5,23,37,45)

'Improved Rugen'—dark-red berry; improved quality. (7,49,54,57)

'Yellow Fruited'—small yellow fruits, sweet. (68)

Preserving

Strawberries can be made into jellies, jams, fruit leather and wine, or they can be frozen whole with sugar.

SUGAR PEA. See Peas and Snow Peas.
SUMMER SQUASH. See Cucumber, Squash, and Melon.
SUN CHOKE. See Jerusalem Artichoke.

Sweet Bay and California Bay

Sweet bay (bay laurel), *Laurus nobilis*
California bay, *Umbellularia californica*

Effort Scale
NO. 1, if informal
NO. 2, if sweet bay is clipped into a formal shape or
grown in containers
Some watering needed

Zones
8—10

Thumbnail Sketch
Sweet Bay
Evergreen shrub or tree
25—40 ft. tall
Propagated from seeds or cuttings
Needs sun or partial shade
Leaves are deep green, 3—4 in. long
Flowers are insignificant
Leaves are edible; used for seasoning; harvested year
round
Used as formal (topiary) shrub, hedge, screen, small
tree, and in containers

California Bay
Evergreen tree
25—80 ft. tall
Propagated from seeds
Needs sun or partial shade
Leaves are yellow-green, 3—5 in. long, and narrow
Flowers are insignificant
Leaves are used for seasoning; harvested year round
Used as street tree, shade tree, screen, or windbreak

How to Use
In the Kitchen
Both plants yield aromatic leaves that are similar to
each other in taste and are used as seasoning in stews,
soups, corned beef, and pickled herring. Some people
prefer the taste of sweet bay; California bay is more
potent, so must be used with discretion.

In the Landscape
Sweet bay is a slow-growing evergreen shrub or
medium-size tree, often multistemmed. Its oval leaves
are a deep, shiny green, 2 to 3 inches long. Its flowers
are insignificant, but the dark-purple berries are a nice
addition to the fall scenery. Bay lends itself to pruning

E. 112. *Sweet bay grows well in containers; it also takes well to
shearing for a formal style.*

and topiary clipping and, with its distinctly formal and
classic appearance, is an excellent container plant. In
containers, it can make a nice addition to your indoor
landscape.

California bay, a native of the redwood forests of
California, is a slow-growing evergreen tree that can
reach a height of 60—80 feet in the wild. In home gardens it is usually much smaller. It is often multistemmed. Its leaves are a bright yellow-green that can
reach 5 inches in length. California bay makes a neat-
appearing street or shade tree if properly pruned and
is also useful as a screen windbreak, or in a woodland
or creekside garden.

How to Grow, Purchase, and Preserve
Both plants are semihardy and can tolerate quite a
bit of shade. They can be excellent additions to your
landscape plans if they can grow in your climate. In
arid climates, water occasionally to keep them looking
fresh.

To harvest and preserve, pick leaves in late summer and allow to dry on a screen with good air circulation for 10 days to two weeks. Package in airtight
containers.

Sweet bay is sometimes available at local nurseries; in addition, plants are available from (65) and seeds are available from (2,6,12,18,65). California bay plants are available from an occasional West Coast nursery or from (6,48); seeds are carried by (1).

SWEET CHERRY. See Cherry.
SWEET ELDERBERRY. See Elderberry.
SWEET FALSE CHAMOMILE. See Chamomile.
SWEET MARJORAM. See Marjoram.
SWEET PEPPER. See Peppers.
SWEET POTATO. See Root Vegetables.
SWISS CHARD. See Greens.
TANGELO. See Citrus Fruits.

Thyme

Caraway-scented thyme, *Thymus Herba-barona*
Common thyme, *T. vulgaris*
Creeping thyme, *T. praecox arcticus*
Lemon thyme, *T. x citriodorus*

Effort Scale
NO. 1
Very easy to grow

Zones
All

Thumbnail Sketch
Evergreen shrub or mat-forming perennial
4—15 in. tall
Propagated from seeds, cuttings, and divisions, or by layering
Needs full sun
Leaves are gray-green, very small, 1/4—1/2 in. long
Flowers are lavender, white, or pink, grow in small spikes
Leaves are edible; used as seasoning; harvested all year
Used as a ground cover and in herb gardens, as edging plant, in flower beds, rock gardens, raised beds, containers

How to Use
In the Kitchen
The aromatic leaves of these shrublets are used to season soups, omelets, gumbos, poultry stuffing, and sauces for fish. They are often added to vegetable-juice cocktails and bring a subtle interest to green beans and carrots.

E.113. *Creeping thyme fills in between stepping stones. On the left is common thyme.*

In the Landscape
These evergreen plants vary in form from a matlike growth, as in creeping thyme, to that of a shrublet up to 15 inches tall, as in common thyme. Whatever the size of the plant, however, all thyme leaves are tiny, ranging from 1/4 to 1/2 inch long. The leaves can be gray-green, dark green, or variegated gold or silver. The tiny, lavender or pink flowers grow in short spikes and are attractive to bees.

The variations in plant form make thyme useful in several situations. Thyme plants belong both in an herb garden and a flower border and are handsome in containers, hanging or not. Creeping thyme is delightful when planted between stepping stones or in other areas with limited foot traffic.

All the thymes go well with chives, sage, saffron crocus, alyssum, ageratum, and small, pink zinnias.

How to Grow
Thyme is relatively easy to grow in most climates of the United States, but ideal growing conditions require a raised bed and rocky or sandy soil with excellent drainage. It prefers full sun. In areas with the hottest summers, plants need some watering, but it is easy to overwater thyme. Foliage should be pruned back in spring to make it stay compact and lush.

Thyme can be harvested at any time of the year for use fresh. However, if you are planning to dry it for the winter, harvest the leaves just as the plant has started to flower to ensure good texture and a rich flavor.

How to Purchase

The superior culinary thymes are the common and lemon thymes. Three nurseries (24,45,54) carry a large selection of thyme varieties. In addition, plants are available in small pots and as seed from local nurseries and mail-order firms. The four types are distinguished from one another by size, scent, and other characteristics noted in the following list.

Caraway-scented thyme—2—5 in. tall; leaves are dark green; flowers are rose-pink; good as ground cover; used as vegetable seasoning.

Common thyme—6—12 in. tall; leaves are gray; flowers are lavender.

Creeping thyme—2—4 in.; leaves are dark green; flowers are purplish-rose, purple, or white; good as ground cover.

Lemon thyme—4—12 in. tall; leaves are green; flowers are lavender; variegated silver and gold varieties available.

Preserving

See drying information under BASIL.

Tomato

Lycopersicon Lycopersicum [L. esculentum]

Effort Scale

NO. 3
Must be planted annually
Tying and staking usually needed
Vulnerable to some pests
Harvest is continual

Zones

Annual

Thumbnail Sketch

Perennial, treated as an annual
18 in.—6 ft. tall
Propagated from seeds
Needs full sun
Leaves are compound, medium green
Blooms in summer
Flowers are yellow, not showy, small
Fruits are edible; red, yellow, white; harvested in summer or fall
Used on fences and in hanging baskets, flower border, containers

How to Use
In the Kitchen

Tomatoes need no introduction. Still, have you ever tried a vine-ripened one, with the heat of the sun still upon it? If you have, you will know why the tomato is the most commonly grown vegetable in the United States. Whether your fruit is a 'Tiny Tim' or a 'Big Boy' does not matter. Once you have tried a fully ripened fruit, store-bought ones will seem a travesty. Enjoy them fresh all through the season—sliced, quartered, stuffed. Their flavor and color can enhance all summer meals.

Canned tomatoes add interest to winter meals in stews, soups, casseroles, and spaghetti sauce. It's hard to imagine cooking without catsup, chili sauce, salsa, tomato paste, and puree.

In the Landscape

When the tomato was first introduced to European gardens from the New World it was thought to be poisonous. Since the plant belongs to the nightshade family, the fruits were suspect, so tomatoes were used only as showy ornamentals. Now the reverse is true: the tomato has been relegated to the vegetable garden. How fickle we are!

The bright-green, lobed, hairy leaves and contrasting red or yellow fruits of the tomato plant are indeed ornamental. Now is the time to let the appearance of this plant increase the tomato's all-round usefulness. Plant tomatoes for beauty and function. The small-fruited varieties look nice in hanging baskets or decorative containers. The large vining types can be trained to cover a fence, where they might serve as the background for 'Red Cascade' petunias and green peppers.

When using tomato plants as part of the landscape, try to keep the use of wire cages to a minimum. Much can be done with less obtrusive stakes. When the plants begin to look spent and yellow, remove them.

How to Grow

Tomatoes are heat-loving plants. They grow best in warm summer areas and can tolerate no frost. Though perennials, they are grown as summer annuals. Buy tomato seedlings from your local nursery in spring or, for a larger selection of varieties, less expense, and more fun, start your own. About 6—8 weeks before your last frost, plant tomato seeds 1/4-inch deep in flats or milk cartons (be sure to make a few drainage holes) filled with good potting soil. Place under grow lites or in sunlight. Fertilize every 4 weeks. Place under grow lites or in sunlight. Fertilize every 4 weeks. When all danger of frost is past, transplant your tomatoes into the garden. Plant them in full sun and in well-drained soil amended with a generous

E.114. *Many of the cherry tomatoes are attractive in containers.*
Choose a container whose proportions suit the tall plant.

amount of organic matter. Plant the transplants deep; the soil should come up to the first set of new leaves. Most gardeners prefer to stake or trellis tomatoes to take up less room and keep the fruit from spoiling on the ground.

In addition to the organic matter, fertilize with fish emulsion, chicken manure, or a balanced fertilizer every 4-6 weeks. A form of calcium is often needed to prevent blossom-end rot.

Liming may be needed every few years if you live in an acid-soil area. Tomatoes prefer a soil pH of between 6.0 and 7.0. Keep your tomato plants evenly watered. Deep, fairly infrequent waterings are usually best. Mulching is beneficial to help retain moisture. A few major pests afflict tomatoes: tomato hornworms, cutworms, tobacco budworms, and whiteflies. The first three are easily controlled by hand-picking or Bacillus thuringiensis. See Part Two for more information. A number of diseases affect tomatoes. Control them by planting resistant varieties and rotating crops.

Pick tomatoes as they ripen.

How to Purchase

Hundreds of varieties of tomatoes are available. Check with your local nurseries for the plants or seeds that are best for your area.

Large, fruited varieties for planting in the ground are 'Ace', 'Better Boy', 'Big Boy', 'Pierce', and 'Ponderosa'. These are best for the Midwest and Eastern seaboard. Two yellow varieties, 'Jubilee' and 'Sunray', are sweet and have a low acid content. Varieties good farther nroth include 'Early Girl', 'Quick Pick' and 'Oregon Spring'. Heirloom varieties are available from (1,53,55).
ground are 'Tiny Tim', 'Patio', 'Pixie', 'Small Fry', and 'Toy Boy'. Good varieties for hanging baskets are 'Red Pear', 'Yellow Cherry', 'Yellow Pear', 'Red Cherry', and 'Sweet 100'.

Mail-order nursery with the largest selection of varieties for containers is (49). For unusual varieties contact (20,42,55); European varieties are carried by (57). (27,49,58) have a large number of varieties for gardens in the South. The nursery with the largest selection of tomato varieties (more than 100) is Tomato Growers Supply, P.O. Box 2237, Fort Myers, FL 33902.

Preserving

To preserve tomatoes, freeze or can them as catsup, sauce, paste, puree, juice, or stewed tomatoes.

Green (unripe) tomatoes can be pickled or made into chutney. Tomatoes can also be preserved for 4—8 weeks by harvesting the vines before fruit is fully ripe and hanging them—fruit and all—from the rafters of a cool garage or shed.

Walnut

Black walnut, *Juglans nigra*
Butternut, *J. cinerea*
California black walnut, *J. Hindsii*
Persian (English) walnut, *J. regia*

Effort Scale

NO. 3
Vulnerable to some pests, including squirrels
Mulching is beneficial
Raking is often necessary
Harvest is large

Zones

3—9

Thumbnail Sketch

Deciduous tree 20—80 ft. tall
Propagated from seeds and by grafting
Needs full sun

E.115. Even when bare in winter, the branches of a walnut tree make a handsome pattern.

Leaves are compound, leaflets are 4—5 in. long, medium green

Flowers are in catkins, not showy

Nuts are edible; harvested in fall

Used in very large yards as shade trees, street trees, and screens

How to Use

In the Kitchen

There are two distinct nuts here: Persian (English) walnuts, everyone's favorite; and black walnuts, which, like okra, gooseberries, and rhubarb, are an acquired taste. The latter, which are hard to shell, are used in the same ways Persian walnuts are—in breads, cakes, and frostings—but their flavor is quite strong and they should be used with more discretion.

Persian walnuts can be added to any food that calls for nuts. Their flavor is mild and they get crunchier with baking. These nuts add a richness that we probably do not need but that adds pleasure to the eating. Besides their uses in baked goods, walnuts can be used in place of pine nuts in pesto sauce. A subtly flavored oil made from walnuts, available in foreign- and health-food stores, provides a nice change from your regular oil on salads and in cooking. Some year when your crop is especially large, you might look into pressing your own.

A delectable hors d'oeuvre is walnut halves sandwiching a layer of softened Roquefort cheese.

In the Landscape

The term walnut comprises a number of closely related deciduous trees of great stature. These stately trees, with their compound leaves and handsome branching structures, are useful for screening an unwanted view or for casting cooling shade in hot weather. Large lots and country lanes are enhanced by their presence. Because of their size and because they are often bothered by aphids, whose secretion is a problem on cars or patios, walnut trees are difficult to use in small yards. Also, the trees drop catkins, leaves, and husks, which is no problem for an informal woodland path or an area with deep ground cover, but is not compatible with a tailored yard. Walnut trees are used as lawn trees in the East.

Note: Black walnuts exude an acid from their roots that inhibits the growth of many plants. Keep them away from vegetable gardens (particularly those containing tomato plants), flower beds, azaleas, and rhododendrons.

How to Grow

Climate

Different types of walnuts grow in different parts of the country.

Butternut is the most hardy. It will grow as far north as zone 3, New Brunswick, Canada; and south to Georgia, west to Minnesota, and in the Midwest, south to Arkansas.

Black walnut is also hardy. Its range includes southern Ontario, south to northern Florida, and west from South Dakota to Texas, as well as parts of the West Coast.

Persian walnut grows best in zones 6—9. One strain of Persian walnut, called Carpathian, has proved hardy to −25°F. Persian walnuts do not do well in very hot climates.

California black walnut is grown widely in California and is one of the major rootstocks for commercially grown Persian walnuts.

Exposure

These trees need full sun.

Planting

See HICKORY.

Soil

Walnut trees require well-drained, rich loam. They are at their best in deep alluvial soils. All walnuts have deep root systems. They prefer a soil with a pH of 5.5—7.0. Soils east of the Mississippi usually benefit from liming.

Fertilizing

Do not fertilize the first year. After that, supplemental nitrogen is usually needed. Keep walnut trees mulched but keep the mulch off the crown of the tree. If the trees are in a lawn, apply extra nitrogen to the lawn or use a root feeder.

Watering

In arid climates walnuts need deep-watering occasionally for the best nut production. If a tree is planted in a lawn, keep the grass cleared away from the trunk of the tree. Do not plant anything within 4 feet of a walnut's trunk. This is critical in western yards to prevent crown rot.

Pruning

Do not prune black walnuts from late winter through spring, because they bleed heavily at this time. For further pruning instructions, see HICKORY.

Pests and Diseases

Squirrels and jays are usually the pests most seriously affecting home plantings of walnuts. Other possible problems are aphids, walnut husk fly, fall webworm, walnut husk maggot, and walnut caterpillar. To control the latter two pests, try Bacillus thuringiensis. Occasionally, pyrethrum may be necessary on the others. Though aphids are seldom severe enough to threaten the tree and to require a spray, they are a nuisance because of the sticky substance they exude, which drips on anything below them. It is for this reason that you should avoid planting walnuts where they will overhang cars or patio furniture.

Harvesting

Harvest the nuts off the ground. Check daily to beat the squirrels. Persian walnuts usually fall from their husks; if the husks are still attached, remove them. In black walnuts the husk is usually still intact over the shell when it falls from the tree. Removing the husks will stain your hands, so use rubber gloves or, wearing heavy shoes, 'stomp' the nuts and roll the nuts out of their husks. Some people even drive their cars over black walnuts and let the tires do the job! Cure the nuts in a cool, dry place for two to three weeks before storing.

How to Purchase

Forms and Sources

Buy bare-root trees from local nurseries or from mail-order firms in late winter or early spring, or buy trees in containers through the fall. Nurseries with the largest selection of walnuts are (3,6,52,61,70).

Pollinators

Walnut trees are monoecious—that is they have male and female flowers on the same tree though often the two genders bloom at different times. Therefore, more than one variety of walnut should be planted for cross-pollination and a heavier yield. Most of the walnut species cross-pollinate.

Note: Some people are allergic to walnut pollen.

Varieties
BLACK WALNUTS

Black walnut can be planted from seed to produce in 4—5 years. Seedling trees already 2 or 3 years old are readily available from mail-order nurseries. Named cultivars are also available; the most common one is 'Thomas', which bears large nuts with a somewhat softer shell than most. A large selection is available from (60).

BUTTERNUTS

'Kenworthy' and 'Mitchell' yield good-size nuts of good flavor and good cracking characteristics. (60,70) has a large selection.

PERSIAN WALNUTS

The Carpathian type of Persian walnut is a hardy type for the coldest Persian walnut climates and most of the East. Nurseries with the best selection are (7,61,70).

The following Carpathian varieties are very similar to each other in quality; they have good flavor and the nuts crack well: Ashworth', 'Colby', 'Fateley', 'Hansen' (a small tree, considered the best), 'Helmle', 'James', 'Lake', 'Merkel', and 'Somers'.

One of the best Persian walnuts for the colder areas of the West is Ambassador', a smaller-than-usual walnut, 15—40 ft. tall, and self-pollinating. 'Chico', 'Ashley', 'Chandler', and 'Hartley' (the most commonly grown Persian walnut) are good for most areas of California. For the areas of the West with the mildest winters, plant 'Drummond', 'Payne', and 'Placentia'; (Readily Available).

Preserving

Store walnuts in a cool, dark place, or shell and freeze them.

PART TWO

PLANTING AND MAINTAINING THE EDIBLE LANDSCAPE

REGARDLESS OF your landscaping style, the planting and maintenance of your garden are as important as the original plan. This part of the book covers the basics of establishing and caring for a landscape, including soil preparation, seeding and planting, mulching, fertilizing, watering, pruning, composting, weed and pest control, and coping with plant diseases. For more detailed information on this vast subject I recommend The *Why and How of Home Horticulture* and many other books listed in the bibliography.

Analyzing and Preparing the Soil

Assuming that in designing your landscape you have located your plants properly and installed structural elements, you are now ready to execute your plan by planting. But to grow healthy plants, one more preliminary step is vital: proper soil preparation. Poorly prepared soil is difficult to improve after a plant is established. You should begin by identifying the type of soil on your property and any problems it might pose; then take measures to correct them.

Soil Types

Soil is composed of mineral particles of many sizes, organic matter in different stages of decay, water, and air. Soil is classified by the particle size of its mineral components into three major textural types: the designations are sand, silt, and clay. Sand is fairly large and the individual particles can be seen with the naked eye. Silt is smaller but can be seen with a microscope. Clay particles are so small they can only be seen through an electron microscope. Most garden soils are a combination of all these types.

Each soil type has its own specific characteristics.

1. Sandy soils are made up of a large proportion of relatively large, sometimes rough and sometimes rounded particles. These particles are primarily quartz, which is generally inactive chemically. Sandy soils have many pores—spaces containing air that allow roots to receive oxygen—but don't retain water well and therefore dry out quickly. In addition, nutrients are easily leached out of sandy soils so plants growing in this soil type often do poorly. The advantages of sandy soils are their ability to drain well and to warm up quickly in the spring. Very sandy soils benefit greatly from the addition of organic matter.

2. Silt soils are fine-textured soils that combine some of the features of both sandy and clay soils.

3. Clay soils are made up of extremely small, flattened, usually scalelike mineral particles. They contain few air spaces and pack down very easily. They retain water for long periods of time, and sometimes roots in clay soil get waterlogged and die. Drainage is very important in clay soils. Fertility is less problematic with clay soils than with sandy soils because most clay soil holds nutrients well; the chemical nature and large surface area of the particles, as well as the slow drainage, prevent nutrients from leaching. (Surface area, an important factor in soil science, refers to the surface area of each particle. Because of the fineness and platelike structure of the particles, there is more total surface area in clay soil than in a like volume of sandy soil.)

Good garden soil contains optimum amounts of all three types of soil particles and is called loam. Loam is the best soil type for growing most plants, particularly many of the more demanding edibles.

Use this rough test to determine your soil type. When slightly damp, clay soils can be squeezed between the thumb and fingers to make a continuous ribbon. Sandy soils are gritty, and when dry will run through your fingers. Dry silt has a talcum-powder feel to it and will have some plasticity or stickiness when damp. For more sophisticated tests consult your local university extension service.

The structure of soil as well as its texture is important. Soil structure is the arrangement of the soil particles into aggregates or "crumbs." These aggregations prevent the formation of brick-hard soil that crusts over. Soils with good structure are easily worked, and allow rapid water and root penetration.

The addition of large amounts of humus rectifies most soil-structure problems. Sandy soils do not form aggregates well, and the humus helps hold them together; it also improves water retention and adds fertility. In clay soils humus helps to create pore space and to prevent packing. Loams benefit in trace elements and improve structure from added organic matter.

Sometimes sharp contractors' sand (not smooth beach sand) is thoroughly incorporated to lighten clay soils. Perlite and vermiculite are also occasionally added, but if used for large areas they are quite expensive. None of these three additives is permanent. The sand tends to sift down into the subsoil, and the others gradually decompose. While humus also decomposes, annual applications of humus constitute the most effective and generally the most economical way to improve all types of soil.

In analyzing your soil situation, remember that plant roots breathe. Some need more air in the root zone than others. If your soil is a heavy clay and you choose not to modify it, your plant choices will be different from those for a sandy or loamy soil. See the encyclopedia for plants that tolerate heavy soil. If your soil is sandy and you choose not to add humus, you will need to fertilize and water more often.

Soil Problems

Few garden soils are perfect, but most problems can be identified and corrected without a major effort.

Acidity

Most plants grow well under slightly acidic conditions, but if the soil is too acidic, it will starve plants of vital nutrients and will have to be limed, or sweetened. Acid soil is a soil with a pH of less than 7.0 (see glossary), and is usually associated with areas of high rainfall, or sandy or very organic soils. If you suspect that your soil is too acidic, have it tested by your university extension service and follow their directions, or purchase a simple soil test-kit to confirm your suspicion. If the diagnosis proves correct, add limestone, following the directions on the bag for dosage. Some plants, such as blueberries and cranberries, require an acidic soil. See the encyclopedia entries for plants with special pH requirements.

Alkalinity

Soils with a pH of 7.0 or higher are considered alkaline. Some plants, particularly grasses, prefer a slightly alkaline soil. Alkaline soils are associated with areas of low rainfall and soils high in lime or sodium. For mildly alkaline soils, most organic matter helps, but the most helpful additives are powdered sulfur, peat moss, and pine needles. Applying a good amount of any of these materials is usually sufficient to allevi-

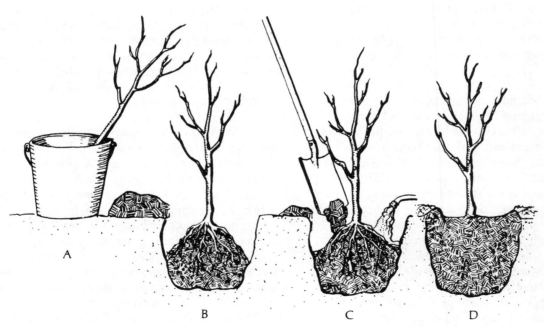

2.1. Planting bare-root plants. A. Soak plants in water overnight before planting. (Do not let them dry out while waiting to be planted.) B. Spread out the roots over a cone of soil. C. Cover the roots lightly with backfill and water well. D. Fill the hole with remaining backfill and tamp down lightly to eliminate large air pockets. Make a watering basin around the plant and water in well. Apply mulch.

ate an alkalinity problem. For highly alkaline soils, raised beds must be provided and supplemental chelated minerals added. (Chelated minerals are minerals in a special form that makes the nutrients available to the plants; they are available in nurseries.) Pomegranate and jujube are two edibles that can tolerate quite alkaline soils.

Salinity

Another common soil problem is salinity—a buildup of salts in the soil. This usually occurs in areas of the country that receive less than 30–40 inches of rain a year. Sometimes the salts occur in the soil itself, but often they come from the irrigation water or result from a buildup of chemical fertilizer or manure. Sometimes all three sources are present. The first sign of salt damage on plants is usually a browning on the leaf edges. Salt also causes leaves to wither, stunted growth, and poor seed germination.

If you have a salinity problem and your drainage is good, flood the soil thoroughly before planting and at regular intervals thereafter. If the problem is serious, drip irrigation, with the constant moisture it provides, is helpful; so are raised beds and planter boxes. Avoid using manure and chemical fertilizers with a high salt index, such as most nitrate types and urea, and don't choose plants that are particularly sensitive to salt burn, such as apples, peas, plums, pears, cabbages, lemons, oranges, avocados, and peaches. If you have serious salt problems, see your university extension service and consult Ortho's *All About Fertilizers, Soils, and Water* (see bibliography).

Hardpan

Occasionally, soil is packed down hard within the first few feet of topsoil or deeper. The result is called hardpan. Sometimes hardpan is a natural condition of the soil, and other times it is man-made-often created when heavy equipment is driven over wet clay soil and compacts it. Hardpan prevents roots from penetrating the soil properly and prevents water from draining off. If the hardpan layer is thin, you can usually break it up with a tractor or punch holes in it with a power auger. In serious cases you will need professional help to install sumps, drain tiles, or raised beds

Nutrient and Organic Matter Deficiencies

Plants need the major nutrients—nitrogen, potassium, and phosphorus—plus many trace minerals. Most soils are fairly fertile but are usually deficient In one or more of the nutrients needed by plants. Initial soil testing for nutrient levels can be helpful. In most parts of the country, most soils benefit from phosphorus added before new plants are planted, and some form of supplemental nitrogen must be added annually.

Organic matter deficiencies are prevalent throughout most of the country. Preplant applications of organic matter to improve the quality of the soil are usually needed. Manures, composts, and the majority of organic materials are quite low in the major nutrients, but they are used to improve soil structure, to add trace minerals, and to keep soil microbe activity high, which in turn makes nutrients more available to higher plants. See the "Plant Nutrients" section below for information on fertilizer and deficiency symptoms.

Soil Preparation

Once you have taken measures to correct any soil problems, you are ready to prepare the ground for planting. The first step is to remove large rocks and weeds from planting sites. Where large, established trees and shrubs are growing near a planting bed—plants that are deep rooted, not surface rooted like azaleas, blueberries, and camellias—prune off some of the large roots that intrude into the area; large shrubs and trees can usually tolerate the removal of some roots with no ill effects. Next, spade the areas over and, if you have not already done so, supplement your soil with organic matter, as most soils are deficient in humus, and lime if needed. Distribute the supplements evenly and incorporate them thoroughly into the soil by turning the soil over with a tiller or spade.

Finally, grade and rake the area. You are now ready to seed or dig planting holes. At this time, regardless of your soil type, it is particularly important to add phosphorus at the rate recommended on the package and mix it in. For food-producing perennials, trees, and shrubs, add phosphorus in the form of rock phosphate and manure, bonemeal or superphosphate (at recommended rates) to the planting holes so it will be near the root zone where it is needed. Mix it into the material, called backfill, that will be put back into the holes.

Seeding and Planting

Starting from Seed

Seeds can be started indoors in flats or other containers that have good drainage. Consider employing this method when you are concerned about giving your seedlings an early or safe start, since most young plants, especially warm-weather annuals, are susceptible to frost damage. Other reasons for starting plants indoors are to extend the growing season, to protect plants from pests, or to start vegetables and fruit production as soon as possible. When all danger of frost is past, the seedlings can be planted into the garden.

Propagation from seed is a complex subject because the cultural needs of seeds vary widely among species. Still, some basic rules apply to most seeding procedures. First, whether starting seed in the ground or in a container, make sure you have a loose, water-retentive soil that drains well. Good drainage is important, because seeds can get waterlogged and too much water can lead to the damping off of your seedlings. ("Damping-off" is a disease caused by several fungi that kill seedlings at the soil line.)

Smooth the soil surface and plant the seeds according to the directions on the package or information obtained from a book, such as *Plant Propagation Principles and Practices* (see bibliography). Pat down the seeds, and water carefully to make the seedbed moist but not waterlogged.

If you have started your seedlings in containers do not transplant them until they have their second set of true leaves and, if they are tender, until all danger of frost is past. Young plants started indoors or in a greenhouse should be "hardened off" before planting in the garden; that is, they should be put outside in a sheltered place for a few days to let them get used to the differences in temperature, humidity, and air movement. Transplanted seedlings should be protected by shading them with a shingle or other protective device for a day or two if it is windy or the sun is hot.

If your garden is small or if you are planting in containers only, buying a whole packet of some types of seed is often a waste. When you intend to grow only a few tomato, cabbage, or squash plants, for example, it is less work and cheaper to buy young plants from a reputable nursery. However, root crops such as carrots, beets, or parsnips and unusual varieties such as yellow tomatoes or red okra are not generally sold as transplants and must be bought as seeds.

Planting Annuals

Most varieties of annuals may be started from seed in place in the garden, or in containers and transplanted out into the garden. In both cases, the garden soil should be prepared as described above. In addition, large amounts of organic matter should be incorporated into the top 4—6 inches of the soil. Extra organic matter is particularly helpful for annuals, because most have shallow root systems, are heavy feeders, and need soil that is both light and high in organic matter.

Plant seeds according to the directions on the package, or set out transplants. When setting out transplants, if a mat of roots has formed at the bottom

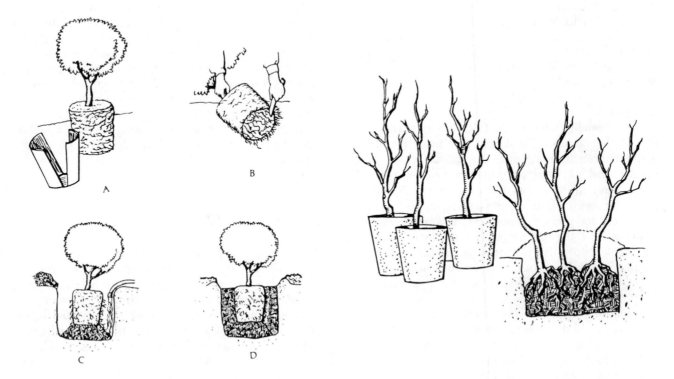

2.2. *Planting container plants. A. Remove plant from the container. B. Rough up the root ball and cut off large tangled masses, if present. C. Place the plant on a mound of backfill in the bottom of the hole. Partially fill the hole, and water. D. Finish filling the hole, make a watering basin, water well, and mulch.*
2.3. *Grouping two or three container plants in one hole can solve a small-space problem.*

of the root ball, you should remove it. In most cases, set the plant in the ground at the same height as it was in the container. Pat it in place with gentle hand pressure, and water it well. Tomatoes and members of the cabbage family should be planted deeper into the ground than they were in the container so that they will root more strongly.

Planting Trees and Shrubs

For years homeowners have been advised by experts to place soil amended with large amounts of light organic matter in planting holes for trees and shrubs to promote good growth. New evidence suggests that where the soil of the planting bed is heavy in density, this practice often causes the roots of trees and shrubs to remain confined in the original planting hole because they have trouble moving into the heavier surrounding soil after rapidly penetrating the fluffy amended soil.

In most medium to heavy soil, the following method is recommended: dig a hole two or three times the size of the root ball, add amendments to the backfill, and make a transition zone of half-amended and half-original soil, which will ease the roots' passage into the heavier soil of the planting bed.

In light to medium soils, this transition zone is usually not needed: just dig a fairly large hole, incorporate some organic matter and supplemental phosphorus, and plant the tree or shrub as shown in the accompanying diagrams.

If your soil is very heavy, consider using the following method with plants that will tolerate such soil. Dig a large hole to loosen the soil; place any needed fertilizer in the bottom of the hole and cover it with a small amount of soil, then place the plant in the hole and backfill with the loosened but unamended native soil. Use mulches around the plant to add organic matter to the soil.

Bare-Root Shrubs and Trees

Bare-root plants are deciduous shrubs and trees (and an occasional perennial) that are dug up while dormant and sold without soil on the roots. Many fruit-bearing shrubs and trees are best planted bare root (see Figure 2.1).

To plant bare-root plants, soak the roots overnight and, before planting, cut off any broken or withered roots. Dig a hole in the planting bed and make a cone of soil in the bottom. Set the tree or shrub so it rests a little high in the hole and carefully straighten and position the roots over the cone. The object is to plant the tree or shrub so that the original soil line (usually visible on the trunk) is visible above the new soil level. The tree will settle a little (about 10 percent) when it is watered and firmed into place; by placing the plant

a little high you will give it room to settle. Do not cover the graft (a bump or onionlike bulge on the lower trunk).

Cover half the root zone with backfill and firmly press it into place, then water. Add more soil to fill the hole completely; then make a watering basin around the plant and soak it thoroughly. The trunks of young fruit trees should be painted with tree paint or whitewash, or temporarily covered with burlap or other material, to protect them from sun. If rodent damage is a potential problem wrap with chicken wire or trunk wrap, a material manufactured specifically for protecting tree trunks. If you are planting some of the weak-rooted dwarf trees, or if you live in a windy location, stake the trees with sturdy supports and a flexible tying material that will not choke or bind the trunks. As a final step, mulch the plant.

Balled and Burlapped Shrubs and Trees

The term balled and burlapped, or B & B, refers to a method of preparing plants for sale whose roots cannot be exposed to air for any period of time. The technique is used most often for conifers and evergreen ornamentals.

Burlap is wrapped around the root zone to hold the soil in place after the plant is dug out of the ground.

See Figure 2.4 for the method of planting B and B. The root zone is fragile, so handle the plant gently. Dig a hole twice the width of the root ball and 6 inches deeper than the root ball is long. If the root zone contains heavy soil around it, create a transition area of soil with backfill, adding one shovelful of organic matter to every three of your garden soil. If the B and B contains soil of the same type as your garden, add no soil amendments.

Plant as shown in the illustration. Do not remove the burlap covering unless it has been especially treated to resist decay; ask at your nursery if this has been done. Fill the hole partially with soil. Adjust the plant so that the top of the ball will be 2 inches above the soil line. (It will settle to be even with the soil line.) Fill the hole three-quarters of the way up with soil. Untie the top of the burlap and loosen it. Water the root zone in well, and fill up the rest of the hole, tamping the soil in place with your foot. Make a watering basin around the plant and water deeply. Stake if necessary. Mulch to within a few inches of the trunk.

Container Plants

Evergreen plants and some deciduous plants are often sold in nursery containers, where they are usually planted in a light, porous planting mix. If such plants are planted in heavy soils, a transition zone must be created between the light soil mix and the

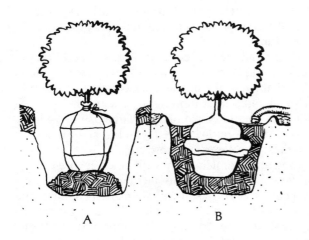

2.4 Planting balled-and-burlapped plants. A. Place the plant on a slight mound of backfill in the bottom of the planting hole. B. Partially fill in soil around the root ball. Loosen and peel back the top of the burlap, then finish filling the hole. Make a watering basin, water in well, and mulch.

heavy soil. In addition, rough up the sides of the hole, since smooth, straight-sided holes in clay soil act like containers and prevent roots from penetrating.

See Figure 2.2 for the planting method for container plants. Dig a hole at least twice as wide and 6 inches deeper than the container. Fill the first 6 inches of the hole with the mixture of garden soil and organic matter. Slip the plant carefully out of the can or use can cutters to split the can. Before planting, examine the root zone. Often there will be a mass of roots on the outside and bottom; use a knife or sharp spade to cut through these masses. Straighten the roots out onto the backfill in the hole. Never turn or twist the root ball in the hole; this will encourage the roots to grow in a circle. If you want to turn the plant around when it's in the hole, lift it up gently and reposition it. Fill the hole three-quarters of the way up with soil, water it well, and fill the rest of the hole. Tamp the soil in place with your foot. Make a watering basin and water the plant deeply. Stake if necessary and mulch.

Maintaining the Edible Landscape

A good plan and proper planting set the stage for good garden maintenance. Some of the plants mentioned in this book require a minimum of maintenance. But peaches, strawberries, Oriental plums, and a number of other favorite fruits need some tender, loving care in the form of mulching, fertilizing, pruning, pest control, and, in some instances, regular watering. Consult the encyclopedia for the effort

required to maintain individual species. Knowing what is required ahead of time, plus using superior hand tools, will help to keep maintenance chores manageable.

Horticultural consultants, nursery people, and landscape designers are often asked: How often do I water? What fertilizer should I buy? What spray can I use to kill all my pests? Most homeowners live busy lives and don't feel they have the time or inclination to learn the complexities of plant care. To simplify plant care, horticulturists and producers of garden products have tried to make all-purpose products and to specify unvarying application amounts. But there are many variables in plant care, and too often the allpurpose approach leads to wasting water and fertilizer and to the overuse of potentially harmful chemicals. Automatic watering systems have been devised that will water a yard once or twice a week whether the plants need it or not. Following the directions on an "all-purpose" fertilizer sometimes provides unneeded nutrients to plants in the yard. And pesticides formulated to kill numerous pests with a single spray will often kill useful predator species as well.

Because of our growing awareness of dwindling resources and the hazards and ineffectiveness of many pest controls, new products are being marketed and new methods developed. Water-saving systems such as drip irrigation are available; organic gardeners have renewed interest in natural fertilizers; and biological pest-control practices have been devised. These systems and methods require more involvement on the gardener's part, as well as some knowledge of soil chemistry and plant and insect physiology. The backbone of appropriate maintenance is your knowledge of your soil and weather, your ability to recognize basic water and nutrient deficiency symptoms, and as much information as you can amass about the plants you grow.

The goal of the following sections covering garden maintenance and pest control is to aid you in providing optimum conditions for plant growth in a manner which does as little damage as possible to the environment and its natural resources.

Plant Nutrients

Plant nutrition is a complex subject, and to maintain their gardens well, serious gardeners should understand basic soil chemistry and botany. The goal of fertilizing is to provide your plants with the nutrients that they may not be getting naturally, when they need them and in appropriate quantities. Obviously, in order to do this you must be familiar with both plant nutritional needs and with your own soil and its contents. If possible, get your soil tested for the primary nutrients and for pH. Some university extension offices will do this at no charge. Soil kits are also available to do a rough job yourself.

To live and be healthy, all garden plants need a number of nutrients. The three major nutrients and their chemical symbols are nitrogen (N), phosphorus (P), and potassium (K). In addition, ten minor nutrients are necessary for plant growth. These nutrients are discussed in detail in the following sections. Some of the plants listed in the encyclopedia have special nutritional needs; in such instances, the nutrients required are noted under the subhead "Fertilizing."

Nitrogen

Nitrogen stimulates shoot and leaf growth. It is important to supply the correct amount. Nitrogen deficiency is usually signaled by pale-green or yellowish leaves. This symptom first appears on the lower or older leaves, which might start to drop. Too much nitrogen can be as harmful as too little. Excess nitrogen can cause the leaves to become too succulent and thus more prone to disease and frost damage, and sometimes stimulates leaf production at the expense of fruit production.

Nitrogen renewal in the soil is accomplished via the decomposition of animal and plant wastes, the deposition of ammonium and nitrate salts from rain water, the action of the nitrogen-fixing bacteria that live on the roots of some plants, and the application of organic or synthetic fertilizers that contain nitrogen.

Nitrogen from organic sources is slowly made available to plants by means of bacterial action. That action is further slowed in cold, very acid, or poorly drained soils. Organic fertilizers are made from animal or plant residues, and most are quite low in nitrogen. While organic sources of nitrogen are extremely variable, some approximate percentages can be given: bloodmeal, 10—14 percent nitrogen; fish meal, 8 percent; cottonseed meal, 7 percent; and castor pomace, 4 percent. The rest of the organic fertilizers, such as most manures, bonemeal, leaf mold, pine needles, seaweed, and most compost, are quite low in nitrogen, containing only 3 percent at most.

Inorganic or synthesized organic sources of nitrogen, fertilizers such as sulfate and calcium nitrate, make high amounts of nitrogen readily available to plants. Many of these fertilizers contain as much as 30 percent nitrogen. Synthetic nitrogen is available in fast-acting forms, usually labeled nitrate or nitric, or in a slower and more controlled release form, labeled ammonic or slow-release. The fast-acting forms are directly available to plants and do not depend on bacterial action to make the nitrogen available.

Phosphorus

Phosphorus contributes to root growth, fruit development, and disease resistance. It is present in soil solutions (the microscopic film around the soil particles) in different forms, most of which are not available to plants. Microorganisms present in soils with sufficient organic matter help make phosphorus available to plants. Very acidic soils tie up phosphorus in a form unusable to plants.

The symptom of phosphorus deficiency in some plants, such as corn, tomatoes, and cabbage (not red cabbage), is a red-purple discoloration of the stems, leaf veins, and leaves.

Natural sources of phosphorus are finely ground phosphate rock, bonemeal, and fish meal. Small amounts of phosphorus can be found in cottonseed meal, bloodmeal, wood ash, and most manures. The most commonly used synthetic forms of phosphorus are superphosphate and ammonium phosphate. If you are growing high-yield vegetables or fruit crops, in addition to manure or compost you should add some form of supplemental phosphorus to the soil every year or two. Because phosphorus moves very little in the soil, it should be worked well into the soil to make it available to the roots or applied to the bottom of planting holes.

Potassium

Potassium, or potash, is the third major plant nutrient. Sufficient amounts of potash promote resistance to disease, cold, and drought. Potash deficiencies result in poor crop yields, uneven ripening, poor root systems, leaves streaked or spotted with yellow, and dried or burned leaf edges. Potash deficiency is usually hard to diagnose, and potash is usually added for safety because deficiencies often show up too late to be rectified.

More potash is available to plants in arid climates than in other climates. Natural sources of potash are manures, compost, plant residues, granite dust, and green sand. Commercial sources of potash are muriate of potash and sulfate of potash. In eastern sections of the country it is customary to add some form of potash in the spring.

The Minor Nutrients

Certain micronutrients are necessary in varying amounts for healthy plant growth. These are calcium, magnesium, sulfur, and the trace elements zinc, manganese, iron, boron, chlorine, copper, molybdenum, and for some plants cobalt. Most soils containing a sufficient amount of organic matter can supply enough micronutrients. The major exceptions are acid soils with calcium deficiencies and alkaline soils with iron deficiencies. Regular applications of some form of lime to renew calcium are necessary in acid-soil areas. Iron can be supplied by applications of chelated iron.

Other micronutrients are sometimes lacking in a few areas of the country. If you notice discoloration, stunted growth, chlorosis, or a die-back of the leaves and branches in your plants, it would be wise to have your soil tested for nutrient levels and pH.

Local authorities can alert you to nutrient deficiencies prevalent in your area.

Fertilizing

Fertilizers are available in many forms. So-called "organic" types may be powders, liquids, or fibrous materials such as manures. Synthetic fertilizers can be liquid, granules, or powder. Some are combination formulas and others contain only a single nutrient.

By law, synthetic fertilizers must be labeled to indicate the percentage of each of the three major nutrients they contain. This labeling consists of numbers which express these percentages, always designated in the following order: nitrogen, phosphorus, and potassium (N, P, and K). Thus the labeled formulation might read 16—20—0, meaning that the product contains 16 percent nitrogen, 20 percent phosphorus, and 0 percent potassium. Labeling also includes information about the sources of these primary nutrients, and the presence of other micronutrients in the product. The nitrogen may be in the form of ammonium sulfate or urea, for instance, and the product may also contain other nutrients such as iron or zinc.

The contents of organic fertilizers often are not labeled in the same manner because it is too difficult to determine and standardize the exact amounts of nutrients in most of these materials.

In the last few years, much has been written about organic, or natural, fertilizers versus synthetic fertilizers. There are advantages and disadvantages to each. The advantages of organics such as manures, bonemeal, bloodmeal, and fish emulsion include the following:

1. Many improve the structure of the soil and provide optimum conditions for soil microbes.
2. They recycle valuable materials.
3. They release their nutrients slowly and evenly.
4. Their nitrogen content is less likely to be leached from the soil (thereby wasting the nutrient and possibly polluting water sources).
5. They usually contain fewer soil contaminants.
6. Most are less likely to burn or overfertilize plants.
7. Some forms can be very inexpensive or free.

The disadvantages include:

1. Bulk and weight make some hard to store, handle, and apply.

2. Many are expensive and limited in quantity.
3. They are variable in nutrient content.
4. Most are slow to act.
5. Some of the nutrients are unavailable when the soil temperature is under 50°F.

The advantages of synthetic fertilizers are:

1. Most are less bulky and easier to apply and store.
2. They are often less expensive.
3. Amounts of nutrients are quantifiable.
4. They are generally fast acting.
5. Some can be used effectively under cool-soil conditions.

The disadvantages include:

1. In general, more petroleum is used in their manufacture than for organic types.
2. Many of the nitrogen forms leach from the soil relatively quickly.
3. Some contain soil contaminants and many are high in salt.
4. They provide little or no benefit to soil structure, microbes, or earthworms; some may be detrimental to soil inhabitants.

Organic-Type Fertilizers
BLOODMEAL

A powdered substance made from the blood from slaughterhouses; high in nitrogen, approximately 10—14 percent; can burn plants if applied too heavily; is expensive; uses petroleum energy in the drying process.

BONEMEAL

The steamed and ground-up bones from slaughterhouses; high in phosphorus, 15—25 percent; some nitrogen, 2—4 percent; releases its nutrients slowly; is expensive; reduces soil acidity.

COTTONSEED MEAL

Ground-up cottonseed; 6—7 percent nitrogen; 2—3 percent phosphorus; expensive; acidifying.

FISH MEAL AND FISH EMULSION

Ground-up fish by-products; fairly high in nitrogen and phosphorus; good for container plants; intense odor; expensive.

GREEN MANURES

Growing plants, usually legumes, are planted as cover crops and then tilled back into the soil to provide nutrients to subsequent crops and to increase the soil's content of organic matter. Types of plants generally used are rye grass (not a legume), clover, vetch, and alfalfa. Green manures are valuable providers of plant nutrients and can be used on vegetable garden areas, orchards, and for soil improvement on newly developed properties before lawns and gardens are installed.

MANURES

Animal excrement; varies widely in nutrient content from batch to batch approximate percentages are given. Poultry manure: (N) 2—4 1/2 percent, (P) 4—6 percent, (K) 1—2 1/2 percent; steer manure, (N) 1—2 1/2 percent, (P) 1—1 1/2 percent, (K) 2—3 1/2 percent. Generally inexpensive or free; must be weed free; generally should not be used fresh; some forms high in salts; valuable as soil conditioners as well as for nutrients provided.

PHOSPHATE ROCK

Finely ground rock; high in phosphorus as well as many micronutrients.
This substance is nearly insoluble in water and is made available by microbial action. The nutrient release is slow and steady. To encourage microbial action apply phosphate rock in conjunction with an organic substance such as manure. Incorporate the manure a few months before applying the phosphate rock.

SEWER SLUDGE

Granulated or fibrous wastes from municipal sewage treatment plants. Comes in two forms, activated and composted. Activated has a higher nutrient content: (N) 5—6 percent, (P) 3 percent, and (K) 5 percent. Potentially a valuable fertilizer, but contaminants from sources such as industrial processes and pesticide usage currently make it unsafe for use on edible plants. At some future time it may be possible to monitor for harmful contaminants.

Synthetic-Type Fertilizers
AMMONIUM-BASED FERTILIZERS

These include ammonium sulfate and urea; they are high-nitrogen fertilizers that are fairly stable in the soil and not as prone to leaching as the nitrate forms of nitrogen. These fertilizers have an acidifying effect on the soil and leave salt residues. Some ammonium sulfate is the by-product of coke manufacturing, but most ammonium-based fertilizers are made directly from petroleum products.

MURIATE OF POTASH (POTASSIUM CHLORIDE)

Leaves a fair amount of salt in the soil but produces no soil pH reaction; is easily dissolved in water; has a high percentage of potash.

NITRATES

These include ammonium nitrate, calcium nitrate, potassium nitrate. They are fast-acting nitrogen fertilizers that work in cold or sterile soils but should generally be avoided because they are easily leached by rain water or irrigation. Nitrates consume much energy in the manufacturing process.

SLOW-RELEASE NITROGEN FERTILIZERS

These fertilizers have special formulations or coatings designed to release some fast-acting forms of nitrogen in a more controlled way. They include IBDU, Ureaform, Mag-Amp, as well as some wax- or paraffin-covered fertilizers in granule form. These fertilizers are quite expensive initially, but less fertilizer is wasted and the dosages are more even.

SUPERPHOSPHATE

This is a rock phosphate treated with sulfuric acid, and is more quickly available to the plants than the parent material. In addition to providing phosphorus, it also provides sulfur and calcium.

Fertilizing Schedules for Major Fruits

All stone and pome fruit trees, as well as most young nut trees, gooseberries, blueberries, strawberries, and brambleberries, usually need supplemental fertilizing annually. A slow-release form of nitrogen plus phosphorus and potassium should be applied in the spring. These nutrients can be utilized best if applied in conjunction with some form of compost or manure mulch. In cold-winter areas, apply the mulch in late fall. In warm-winter areas, apply in late spring after the ground has warmed up. In many areas of the West, potassium is not needed for mature trees; have the soil tested to be sure. Watch for deficiency symptoms and consult local authorities to determine what is considered a normal amount of growth per year for your climate and the particular variety you are growing. In acid-soil areas, add lime every two years on normal soils and annually on light sandy soils.

Other Fruiting Perennials

On average soils, the following plants, once established, usually need little or no supplementary fertilizer: borage, caper, chamomile, chives, fig, jujube, Jerusalem artichoke, maple, marjoram, olive, oregano, pine, pomegranate, prickly pear, rosemary, sage, sweet bay, and thyme.

Annual Vegetables and Fruits

Annual fruits and vegetables have high nutrient needs. In vegetable gardens, cover crops such as winter wheat or rye are a valuable source of nutrients. In areas where cover cropping is not feasible, supplement the soil with large amounts of organic matter. In either case, incorporate phosphorus in the root zone. Supplemental nitrogen is usually needed, particularly for leafy vegetables. Tomatoes often need extra phosphorus, and root and tuber vegetables often need extra potassium.

The Environmental Impact of Fertilizers

Edible plants, as a group, use large amounts of fertilizer. Therefore it is important to be familiar with fertilizers and their proper use in order to minimize their environmental impact. The following guidelines should prove helpful.

1. Whenever feasible, use a recycled material such as compost or manure.
2. As a rule, avoid nitrate or nitric forms of nitrogen fertilizers unless they are treated to release slowly, as they are easily leached into underground water supplies. In addition to polluting the water, many nutrients are wasted.
3. Have your soil tested to determine what nutrients are needed.
4. For most plants, keep the soil pH between 6 and 7 so that soil nutrients can be utilized properly.
5. Keep the soil high in organic matter to encourage microbial action; this makes indigenous nutrients more available and enables added nutrients to be better utilized.
6. Cut down on lawn areas, as most lawn grasses are heavy feeders.
7. Don't plant heavy fertilizer users on a slope, as the fertilizer often washes off.
8. Incorporate the fertilizer into the top few inches of soil, so that it will not blow away or volatilize into the air.
9. Apply fertilizers where they will be used. Trees feed from "feeder roots." These are concentrated in an area from the drip line to within about 18 inches of the trunk. (The drip line is the perimeter on the ground directly under a tree's outermost branches.) Fertilizer placed much beyond the drip line or too near the trunk will be wasted.
10. Fertilizer should be watered in well, but don't flood the area and wash it away.
11. When the soil is cold, do not apply nitrogen fertilizers that depend on microbial action to break them down.

Fertilizer-related pollution problems are quite well known, but the energy implications of fertilizer use are just beginning to be explored, and some of the issues are quite complex. While it would be ideal if we could use only organic recycled material to fertilize our gardens, the fact is that there is not enough to go around.

In addition, given the reality that the United States will not become a nation of vegetarians in the near future, many experts feel that some of the high-nitrogen organic fertilizers such as bloodmeal, cottonseed meal, and fish meal, might be better used as animal feed. Furthermore, some of the organic fertilizers are not as energy efficient as one might think. Manures, for example, come primarily from midwestern feedlots and are bulky and energyconsuming to transport across the country. Others such as steamed bonemeal require heat in their processing and so do their share of energy consuming. However as a group the organic natural fertilizers use less energy, have fewer contaminants, and improve the health of the soil. While considerable study will undoubtedly result in future guidelines, for the time being use your best judgment based on what we know now.

Composting

Compost is the humus-rich result of the decomposition of organic matter, whether it be leafy kitchen waste, oak leaves, or lawn clippings. Organic materials will decompose whether or not they are in a compost pile-the breakdown of organic material takes place continually under every tree, shrub, and flower growing on the earth. The objective in maintaining a composting system is to speed up decomposition and centralize the material so you can gather it up and spread it where it will do the most good.

There need be no great mystique about composting. Basically, microbial action converts a pile of organic matter into the most beneficial soil amendment you can find. This section covers two different systems of composting: a very simple, cool, low-production method for dry wastes such as lawn clippings, leaves, and corn husks; and a more sophisticated high-production system for processing most kitchen waste.

Low-Production Systems

I have in my yard a very serviceable example of a low-production composting system. It is not a fast or high-production method, but it is simplicity itself. The materials it uses are dry and do not attract pests. All disease-free garden clippings are piled in a screened-off part of the yard. Excluded are weeds that have gone to seed, ivy clippings, or Bermuda grass clippings, because they do not always completely decompose and can lead to the growth of weeds, ivy, and Bermuda grass in the garden. Dry kitchen wastes, such as pea pods, egg shells, carrot tops, and apple peels, go in when I have them.

This system is a cool, slow-acting means of recycling needed organic matter; in its own small way it also helps to alleviate the pressure on our already full dumps. Because I do not often turn or water the pile,

2.5. A three-bin system is one of the most efficient ways of producing large amounts of compost. The first bin contains raw materials, the second contains partially decomposed organic matter, the last contains finished compost.

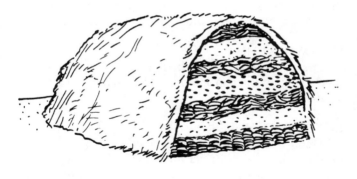

2.6. Compost piles are most efficient when layers of dry and green material are alternated.

microbial action is slow and does not produce enough heat to kill weed seeds or diseased material. Also, many of the nutrients are leached out before they reach the garden. But much organic matter that would have ended up wasted at the dump ends up in my yard instead, in the form of soil-building humus.

If you choose a low-production compost system and you feel ambitious, you can speed production by occasionally turning the pile, adding some form of nitrogen, and, in arid climates, watering it once in a while. The point to remember is that composting does not have to be a big production. Every yard should incorporate some method of developing this valuable material.

High-Production Systems

A well-designed high-production compost heap creates an environment in which decay-causing bacteria can live and reproduce at the highest possible rate. There are three requirements for providing this kind of environment: to keep a suitable amount of air in the pile; to keep the pile moist but not wringing wet; and to maintain a good balance of compatible material so that the microbes have sufficient nourishment. Much technical information has been circulated among experts regarding the optimum ratio between the available carbon and nitrogen. It is usually sufficient to know that if you build the pile with layers of fresh green material, alternating with layers of dried material and thin layers of soil, and occasionally add nitrogen in some form, you will have a successful compost pile. In warm weather the composting action will be much faster than in the winter. Omit or cut up large pieces of compost material, because they decompose very slowly.

An organized approach is necessary to maintain such a system. Two techniques exist: a series of bins (Figure 2.5) or the layered heap (Figure 2.6). The most efficient structure for composting in most yards is a wire bin 4—6 feet high. The wire siding can be supported on the sides by wooden posts. For ease in aerating and turning the compost, you might want to have two bins. Material can be transferred from one bin to the other once a week or more frequently, to speed up the composting process. Or you can use three bins: one for new material, a second for material being actively composted and frequently turned, and a third in which to store the finished product.

Once the organic matter is composted, apply it to the garden or cover it with a tarp to prevent valuable nutrients being leached out of the pile by rain water. Use whatever method you want, but do compost. It's the best possible thing you can do for the health of your plants. For further composting information, I recommend *The Gardener's Guide to Better Soil*, by Gene Logsdon, and *Let It Rot*, by Stu Campbell, *Organic Gardener's Composting*, by Steve Solomon listed in the bibliography.

Mulching

A mulch is any material laid on the soil to reduce evaporation and control weeds. Usually it is a material that will improve soil structure and fertility. Besides these primary functions, mulching can have a number of secondary roles in garden maintenance. Mulch helps keep soil from becoming packed down by foot traffic and rain. A mulch at least 3—4 inches deep helps smother many weed seeds. Mulch acts as insulation and helps keep weather extremes from affecting plants. The soil stays cooler in summer and stays warmer in winter. And organic mulches decompose and help improve the structure of the soil. Clearly, mulching is an important part of garden maintenance. Mulched plants are healthier, and weed control around them is much easier. In addition, mulches can be an attractive addition to the landscape.

How to Use Mulches

In mild-winter areas, apply mulches after the ground has warmed up in the spring. Dig the mulch in lightly in the late fall. In cold-winter areas where the ground alternately freezes and thaws, causing plants to heave out of the soil, apply a thick, 4—6-inch layer of mulch before the first heavy frost.

Near trees, mulches can cause some problems, so they should be kept at least 6 inches away from trunks. Mice make homes in the mulch, and when they venture out the tree trunks are handy for nibbling. Also, mulch too near trunks can cause fungus problems by keeping a constantly moist condition there. Finally, if the mulch covers the scion—the fruiting wood above the bud union—of a grafted tree, that tree may root above the graft. In such a case, a dwarf tree, for example, would become full size. In a very cold climate, however, the bud union should be mulched to protect it from hard freezing, but the mulch should be removed when the coldest part of the winter is past.

2.7. *Mulches of organic matter help conserve water, add nutrients to the soil, keep roots cool, and help keep down weeds.*

Mulching Materials

Mulches can be made from organic materials, such as compost, pine needles, or grass clippings, or from other substances, such as sheet plastic, rock, or gravel.

Where vegetable gardens are a good distance from the house and screened from view, the odor and appearance of a mulch are not particularly significant considerations; the best mulch there would be the one that promotes maximum production. But for landscaped areas of the yard, a foul-smelling or unattractive mulch is unacceptable. Manure near a front walk or black plastic near the patio just won't do, but many mulches actually enhance the appearance of the landscape. For example, earth-tone rock, peat moss, and well-rotted and screened compost are all attractive. The following are recommended mulches for landscaping situations. Availability varies from region to region.

BARK

Many different kinds of tree bark are available regionally. Bark is usually packaged and sold in garden supply houses, and comes in small-, medium-,and large-size chips. Large-size bark chips look coarser than the others, but they decompose more slowly and need to be replaced less often.

BUCKWHEAT HULLS

These hulls make a soft, beige-colored mulch, but they are lightweight so should not be used in windy locations.

COCOA-BEAN HULLS

This attractive mulch breaks down fairly quickly. Furthermore, it is a disaster for "chocoholics"—the delicious aroma of chocolate pervades the yard for weeks after application and inspires weak souls like me to sneak downtown for a chocolate bar. It is fairly expensive unless you can pick it up in quantity from a chocolate factory.

COMPOST

Well-aged compost, screened and spread around landscape areas, is both pleasing to the eye and valuable as a soil conditioner. The major problem is production. Most families do not produce enough compost to fill all their mulching needs, so I strongly suggest that you give priority to your new fruit trees and your vegetable garden when applying this valuable material.

GRAVEL OR ROCK CHIPS

Many different types and sizes of rock mulches are available. These mulches do not break down and improve soil structure. Rock mulches are attractive but are hard to rake. This is a particular problem under the most popular fruit trees, because decaying fruit and diseased leaves need to be removed. White, "sparkly" rock should generally be avoided, as it often looks dirty.

PEAT MOSS

Peat moss is one of the most expensive mulches. It is useful for acid-loving plants, such as blueberries and camellias. It has a good appearance but is hard to remoisten if it dries out, so it should be kept moist at all times.

PINE NEEDLES

These needles are attractive, lightweight, and add acidity to the soil. Use them for acid-loving plants, but do not use them if you have a soil-acidity problem. They work well on strawberry plants to keep the berries from rotting on the ground.

SAWDUST

Sawdust can be used raw, well aged, or treated. When treated, it is often called soil conditioner. If you use raw, fresh sawdust, treat it with ammonium sulfate or an organic, nitrogen-rich fertilizer, such as blood-meal or cottonseed meal. The decomposition of the sawdust by soil microbes takes available nitrogen from the soil that has to be replaced. (This aspect is valuable if you want to prevent plant growth. Raw sawdust applied 3 to 4 inches deep on garden paths is a valuable weed deterrent.) Well-rotted or treated soil conditioner can be used without supplemental nitrogen.

Watering

No easy formula exists for the correct amount or frequency of watering. Proper watering takes experience and observation. The needs of a particular plant usually depend on soil type, wind conditions, and air temperature, as well as what kind of plant it is. To water properly you must learn to recognize water stress symptoms (often a dulling of foliage color as well as the betterknown symptoms of drooping leaves and wilting); how much to water (too much is as bad as too little); and how to water.
Some general rules are:

1. Water deeply. Most plants need infrequent deep-watering rather than frequent light sprinkling. Shallow-rooted plants such as blueberries and azaleas are exceptions.
2. To ensure absorption, apply water at a rate slow enough to prevent runoff.
3. Do not use overhead watering systems when the wind is blowing.

2.8 A nozzle with a pistol grip that shuts the water off when not in use saves water.

4. Try to water early in the morning so that foliage will have time to dry out before nightfall, thus preventing some disease problems. In addition, because of the cooler temperature, less water is lost to evaporation.
5. Test your watering system occasionally to make sure it is covering the area evenly.
6. Use methods and tools that conserve water. When using a hose, a pistolgrip nozzle will shut the water off while you move from one container or planting bed to another (Figure 2.8). Canvas soaker hoses apply water slowly to shrub borders and vegetable gardens. Also see the following sections on sprinkler and drip irrigation systems.

Sprinkler Systems

In general, sprinkler systems have been responsible for wasting a good deal of water. Formerly, they were designed and used in accordance with the rule of the highest common denominator: the plants needing the most water got their share and everything nearby got the same amount, regardless. The plants that could not tolerate overwatering were eliminated and were often labeled "hard to grow" by homeowners. More sophisticated, modern sprinkler designs irrigate heavy water users on one system and more moderate water users on another system. Sophisticated automatic timers also enable the apparatus to water, say, one area once a week and another area twice a week.

Some systems, the digital type in particular, are sophisticated enough to water an area for five minutes at a time, shut off and allow the water to soak in, and then go on again for five minutes, repeating the cycle until the proper amount of water has been applied. The system prevents the runoff that twenty minutes of straight watering could produce, particularly on a slope. Automatic systems can also be programmed to water in the early morning when evaporation is at a minimum, since temperatures are lower and wind is less strong than later in the day.

Basically, the *proper use* of automatic sprinklers is consistent with the principles of water conservation. Still, the emphasis here is on the words proper use. One warning to be carefully heeded, particularly with specialized systems, is, *Remember to turn the sprinklers off during the rainy season*. If the automatic system is not adjusted for seasonal changes, the amount of water wasted can be enormous. My partner and I learned this the hard way. We installed an automatic system and new plants on a hot September day, gave the client instructions on how the system worked and how it was to be reset to water less often during late fall and turned off during the winter rainy season, and then we left. Six months later I ran into our client in the theater and asked how his yard was. He said, "Terrible! Everything is covered with gray slime." We went to check, and sure enough, it was. The client had forgotten to reset the system, and it had been pouring out the amount of water needed for a hot summer day all winter long, rain or shine!

To summarize, automatic systems must be set and reset to match water-saving schedules that do not overwater plants. They are not meant to set and forget! Most plants require less water than we want to give them. Set your system with that in mind and adjust it for seasonal conditions. And be sure to turn it off during the rainy season!

Drip Irrigation

Drip, or trickle, irrigation systems (Figure 2.9) are advisable wherever such systems are feasible. Many vegetable gardens, orchards, and perennial and shrub areas are often well suited to these systems. Drip irrigation systems deliver water a drop at a time through spaghetti-like emitter tubes or plastic pipe with nozzles that drip water right onto the root zone of the plant. Drip irrigation is the only water system devised for containerized plants (Figure 2.10). Another similar type of system called a porous-wall or ooze system (Figure 2.11) delivers water through porous plastic hoses along the whole length of a garden row. All of these systems are more efficient than furrow or overhead watering in delivering water to its precise destination. They deliver water slowly so it doesn't run off

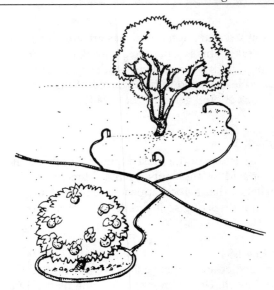

2.9. *Some drip irrigation systems have emitters on pegs that are pushed into the ground; others have porous tubing that oozes water in controlled areas. Both kinds of systems are prone to vandalism, but mulching sometimes can help camouflage the emitters.*

and they also water deeply, which encourages deep rooting.

However, though these methods often work well, I hesitate to recommend drip irrigation fully since it still has some problems. Drip irrigation can be frustrating because the tubes and emitter clog easily. Without a good filter system, often every emitter must be checked each time the system is used, especially if the water source has occasional grit in it. Obviously, this can be a chore in a system with 20 or 30 emitters. The porous wall or ooze systems, while not as versatile, have fewer clogging problems and are ideal for vegetable gardens and orchards. All these systems are, however, vulnerable to vandalism problems.

The future of drip irrigation looks promising, so examine all new systems and see if one comes along that is right for you. Check agricultural supply outlets for the best selection of systems. *Drip Irrigation For Every Landscape and All Climates* (see bibliography) gives detailed instructions on how to install all these drip or ooze systems.

Household Water Sources

Plan to plant heavy water users near the house so that all extra clean water can be used on them. By clean water I mean perfectly clean water that would otherwise go down the drain—for instance, cold water that precedes the hot water out of the shower or the water you rinse the teakettle with before you add fresh water. Such water has no foreign matter in it. Make sure, however, that no water softener containing harmful chemicals is added to your domestic supply. The waste water known as gray water—for example, dish water, rinse water, bath water, and so on—is usually produced in great quantities by most households, but gray water presents complicated health and soil problems and often needs processing before it is usable in the garden. For a thorough discussion of gray water, see *The Integral Urban House*, by the Farallones Institute.

2.10. *A drip system with tubes leading to each pot is an extremely efficient way to water containerized plants.*

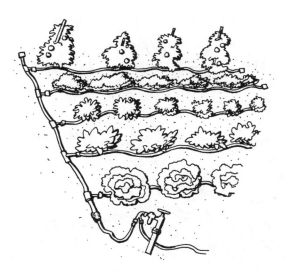

2.11 *Some ooze systems are particularly effective for the straight rows of a vegetable garden. Make sure that all the plants watered by one system have similar water requirements.*

Pruning

Plants are pruned to shape them for aesthetic reasons, to control size, to repair damage, to promote good air circulation, to provide light to the interior of the plant, and to control or promote fruit production in some species.

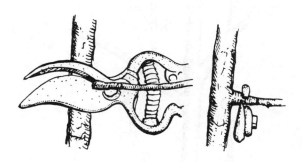

2.12 *An improper pruning cut leaves a stub that can become diseased.*

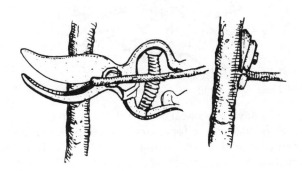

2.13 *A proper cut with a pruning shear is made cleanly, leaving no stub.*

The best way to learn to prune properly is to watch someone do it. If you have many plants that need to be pruned, it would be worthwhile to take a course or to ask a knowledgeable friend to show you how to train and prune them. Most university extension services, supply pruning information and can suggest courses offered locally. See the bibliography for books on pruning. What follows here are only the basics of pruning techniques and tools.

Your climate and the type of plant determine when and how to prune. In most areas, deciduous trees and shrubs should be pruned while still dormant. Set aside a few days for pruning plants and cleaning up your yard. Foodbearing evergreens should be pruned in spring after frosts are no longer expected.

When pruning, remove all dead wood. Do not leave stubs that can rot and invite disease organisms to enter. Do not use pruning paint; recent studies have

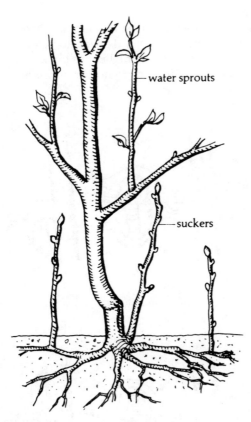

2.14 These suckers and water sprouts should be pruned off.

shown that wounds heal better if left unpainted. For tools, use hand clippers for twigs, lopping shears for small branches, and pruning saws for long heavy branches. Keep your tools sharp and make clean cuts close to the branch (Figure 2.13). If you are cutting off diseased tissue, be sure to sterilize your tools between cuts with denatured alcohol, mercuric chloride, or a 10 percent solution of household bleach to prevent the transfer of disease from one part of the plant to another.

When cutting a large branch, remember to make the first cut on the underside of the branch. Otherwise, as you saw through the top, the weight of the branch will pull it downward, tearing the bark on the trunk of the tree. Some types of trees produce suckers from their roots or, if grafted, from below the root graft. These should be removed. Upright-growing branches called water sprouts occasionally emerge from the main branches of a tree; these too should be removed. Some varieties of citrus are particularly prone to producing water sprouts.

Pruning Fruit and Nut Trees

Most deciduous fruit and nut trees are purchased as bare-root plants called "whips." When the young trees are planted, they are usually "headed back," or

shortened to between 24 to 30 inches. Most mail-order nurseries will have done the critical first pruning before they send the tree to you. They usually include with your order detailed drawings that show you how to continue training the tree. Local nurseries will usually prune the tree when you buy it. Watch closely and ask specifically what to do the next spring.

For the next two to three years, your aim will be to form the permanent framework of the tree. Three to five main branches that are evenly distributed radially are selected. Then you will choose among three major tree forms used by most fruit and nut growers. The first, called the *central leader* form, or system, is shown in Figure 2.16. This form is the strongest and is used for many nut trees, such as hickory, pecan, most walnuts, and occasionally for apples when they will be subjected to strong winds. The second form is a variation of the first and is called the *modified leader* or *delayed vase* shape. It is used with some fruit trees—most often apples and pears. The modified leader system has a short central trunk or leader that is headed back three or four years after planting when a strong system has developed. The modified leader system combines the strength of the central leader system with the advantages of more light and air circulation in the interior of the tree.

The third and most common training system for most fruit trees is called the *open center* or *vase* system. It is commonly used for peaches, nectarines, filberts, almonds, plums, apricots, and sour cherries. Figure

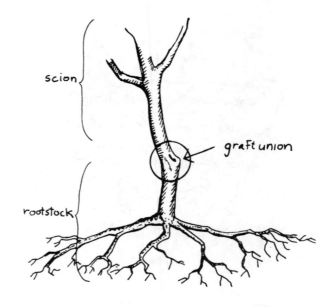

2.15. Diagram of a grafted fruit tree, indicating terms used in pruning.

2.17 shows the basic shape of this system. The center of the tree is open for good air circulation, ease of spraying, and to increase fruit production. The tree is shorter overall and easier to harvest than those produced by the other two systems.

After the first three to five years, depending on the species, fruit and nut trees have developed a permanent framework and will begin to bear their crops. Bearing trees of most species are pruned annually to shape them and to encourage fruit and nut production. Apples, pears, cherries, and most nut trees require little annual pruning to encourage fruiting. Peaches and nectarines need severe pruning yearly to encourage fruiting and to control fruit size and quantity. Apricots, sour cherries, Japanese plums, and filberts are intermediate between apples and peaches in the amount of pruning needed. See the individual entries in the encyclopedia.

Pruning Fruiting Shrubs

Some of the popular berries and fruits, such as blueberries, elderberries, gooseberries, currants, and pomegranates, grow on deciduous shrubs. For the first few years, these shrubs should be pruned lightly only to shape them. Once established they should be thinned annually, as shown in Figure 2.18. Old, diseased, or dead wood is removed and some of the healthy branches thinned to promote more fruiting, improve air circulation, and give a more pleasing shape. If fruits on blueberries and elderberries seem particularly small, tip pruning may be helpful. See the individual entries in the encyclopedia for more information.

2.17. Most fruit trees, including peaches, plums, apricots, and nectarines, as well as nut trees such as almonds and filberts, are generally trained to the vase, or open center, system.

2.18. Pruning a fruiting shrub.

Weeds, Pests, and Other Problems

Your garden may appear to be a quiet place, but in reality it is an arena where hundreds of life-and-death dramas are played out every day. Birth and death, killing and nurturing, even intrigue and cunning are all part of the complex community of life waiting to be discovered—and sometimes struggled with—in your garden.

This hidden world can add a new dimension to your gardening pleasure. For example, on an April day, I can turn flower pots over to find startled earwig mothers that wave their pincers at me, protecting their broods. And every June the baby katydids hatch and

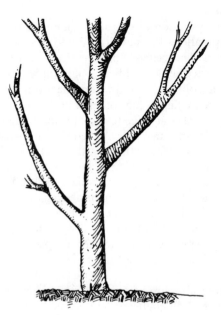

2.16. A few fruit trees and most nut trees are trained to the central leader system.

start chewing on the new leaves of my grapevine. Within a week three different species of spiders have divided up the territory around the grapes, and all day long they stalk the katydids. While not all pest problems are so easily solved, there are many ways in which you can use predator-prey relationships in garden maintenance. Knowledge of how plants and animals interact in the garden is at the heart of organic, or natural, gardening, and your chief tool for pest control will be your powers of observation of this mini-world around you.

Potential garden problems come in many forms: weeds, fungi, snails, slugs, insects, diseases, and even such wildlife as rabbits, deer, and birds. The list may seem overwhelming at first but most gardeners are actually faced with only a few pests. Everyone has to contend with weeds, however, so we'll consider weed control first.

Weed Control

The overuse of herbicides should be avoided in home gardening as well as in commercial agriculture. Because these products often cause environmental problems, and some may cause health problems as well, only the most serious weed problems should require herbicide use. In fact, routine use often backfires by damaging valuable plants and allowing free rein to resistant weeds. Remember that even though herbicides are labeled weed killers, when improperly used they kill most plants.

There are two major types of herbicides: selective herbicides, which are formulated to kill only a target weed without harming the crop or plant being weeded; and nonselective herbicides, which are designed to kill all vegetation. Read the package carefully to be sure that you are buying the type you want. If herbicides are to be used at all, selective herbicides are generally the better choice. Usually they kill fewer types of plants so the chance for harm is less. Some of the most serious problems I have seen in landscape work are due to herbicide damage. Sometimes the damage results from applying too much of the chemical, but plants are sometimes damaged even when directions are carefully followed. This may be due to an improper choice of herbicide or to residue buildup from previous applications.

My recommendation is to use herbicides only sparingly, for example, when establishing ground covers and when trying to control very persistent weeds, such as Bermuda grass, wild brambleberries, multiflora roses, and poison ivy. Do not use chemicals suspected of causing cancer or mutations, such as amino-triazole, atrazine, dicamba, 2,4,-D, and 2,4,5-T. And never use any herbicide near food plants.

There are a number of ways to control weeds with-out chemicals. If you don't like to weed very much, plan an informal yard with a minimum of garden-bed space that requires weeding. Woodland paths can be kept natural and should need only two or three weedings a year. Keeping small areas near the house weeded and trim will give a feeling of design and care to a yard left largely in woodland or meadow. A deep mulch, 4–5 inches, not only controls many weeds, but it also makes what weeds do grow easier to pull.

Of course, the most basic weed control uses hoe or hand. Hand-weeding can be tedious, and some people mind it more than others. I personally find working outside at a repetitive chore more enjoyable than working at an inside one such as dishwashing. I use weeding time to find out what is happening in my yard: I check for plant damage or new insect populations, and to see if plants are getting too crowded or dry. (Also, I find it more enjoyable to weed an edible planting such as Alpine strawberries, where I can help myself to an occasional berry, than to weed ornamentals.)

Take advantage of the best weeding tools available. Two of the tools I find most helpful are the scuffle hoe and the weeder. The scuffle hoe has a flat cutting blade that moves back and forth and a hoe-length handle. This tool is excellent for cutting young weeds off at the base. The weeder has a metal prong on the end of a 2-foot handle. It gets the long taproots of perennial weeds and can efficiently loosen the soil around more fibrous rooted weeds so whole root systems can be removed. Both of these tools are usually available at the nursery.

Pest Control

The application of synthetic chemicals to control pest populations has been routine for the last thirty or forty years. This reliance on chemical controls has many shortcomings. While big agriculture, because of economic constraints and its emphasis on monocrops, is still heavily dependent on chemical pesticides, home gardeners are free to look for more environmentally satisfactory methods. Armed with information and techniques rather than synthetic chemicals, most gardeners can maintain a productive, beautiful yard. Proper plant selection, proper plant and soil care, and minimal interference with natural systems will take care of most pest problems. In the event that a major pest problem surfaces, information at the end of this section on specific pesticides should prove useful.

Though a few insects and mites, sowbugs, snails, and slugs are potential garden pests, most insects are either neutral or are beneficial to your purposes. Given the chance, the beneficials will do most of your pest control for you. The insect world is a miniature version of the animal world. Instead of predatory lions stalking zebra, predatory ladybugs or lacewing larvae hunt and eat aphids. Many gardeners are not aware of predator-prey relationships and are not able to recognize beneficial insects. My students, who can quickly identify the adult ladybug as an ally, have been amazed when I bring ladybug larvae to class, because they realize that they have often killed them. The illustrated information about beneficial and pest insects later in this section will help you to identify and classify individual groups. Once you can identify the insects in your yard, you can help preserve the ones that are beneficial to you by knowing a few basic facts and definitions.

Predators and Parasitoids

Insects that feed on other insects are divided into two types, the predators and the parasitoids. Predators are mobile. They stalk the plants looking for such plant feeders as aphids, mites, and caterpillars. Many predators, the praying mantis, for example, consume any smaller insect they find. Others, such as ladybugs, consume aphids or mealybugs only.

Though predators are valuable insect enemies, they are usually less effective than parasitoids, which are insects that develop in the bodies of other, host, insects. Most parasitoids are minute wasps or flies, whose larvae (young stages) eat other insects from within. Some of these wasps are small enough to live within an aphid or an insect egg. In another case, one egg will divide into thousands of identical cells, which in turn develop into thousands of identical miniwasps, which then can consume an entire caterpillar. Most of the fly parasitoids are larger; a single bombex-fly maggot grows up within one caterpillar. In any case, the parasitoids are the most specific and effective means of insect control.

It should be obvious that indiscriminate use of broad-spectrum pesticides to kill pest insects will usually kill the beneficial parasitoids as well. In my opinion, many so-called organic gardeners who use organic broad-spectrum insecticides have missed this point. While using an "organic" pesticide, they may actually be eliminating a truly organic means of pest control.

Here is an example of predator pest control. Every spring, like clockwork, aphids appear on the growing tips of my ivy. Soon I begin to see syrphid flies (flower flies), whose larvae eat aphids, hovering around the ivy. They've come to lay eggs. Within a month there is none but an occasional aphid around. The hatched syrphid maggots have eaten most of them. In a case like this, patience is the key to pest control. If I had sprayed with a broad-spectrum insecticide to kill the aphids, I would have killed the syrphid flies as well as the target pest; the aphid population would have built up again, more quickly than the syrphid fly popula-

tion; and I would have had to spray again. This is often referred to as the pesticide merry-go-round.

The point is, you don't have to purchase a ticket for the pesticide merry-go-round to begin with. In my example, nature has the system arranged so that the hatching time for syrphid flies, and for most other predators, does not occur until a steady food supply is available. Furthermore, more prey organisms are provided than the predator can eat; thus, in this case, some aphids survive the predation of the flies. The system has to stay in balance, and the predator would not survive if all the prey were destroyed. Therefore, if you are committed to the idea of nonchemical pest control, you must be prepared to tolerate *some* insects on your plants.

Sometimes the natural system breaks down. For example, a number of imported pests have taken hold in this country. Unfortunately, when such organisms were brought here their natural predators did not accompany them. Two notorious examples are the European brown snail and the Japanese beetle; neither Organism has natural enemies in this country that provide sufficient controls. Where such organisms occur, it is sometimes necessary to use selective pesticides that kill only the problem insect and do not upset the balance of the other insects in a yard.

Another problem is that sometimes, for whatever reason, predator-prey relationships become extremely unbalanced. When this happens, you may want to spray with a selective insecticide or purchase live predators from insectaries. (Since the latter must usually be purchased in quantities too large for one household to use, its a good idea to try to collaborate with neighbors on the purchase.) Available predators are Aphytis wasps (for scale); *Cryptolaemus* beetles (for mealybugs); Encarsia wasps (for whiteflies); lacewings (for aphids, cabbage worms, mites, and mealybugs); and *Trichogramma* wasps (for cabbage worms and some other caterpillars). However, unless your problem is severe or you have a large acreage, it is doubtful if purchase of natural enemies is necessary or economical.

Making It Work

Here are some guidelines that will help make a system of biological pest controls work effectively in your garden.

1. Diverse plant materials.
   The chances are that this system will be more effective if you have a diverse assortment of plant material in your yard. This statement should be qualified, however, by the warning that not just any assortment will work. By analogy, in a random

grouping of species—such as a deer, a porpoise, and a robin—the animals would have little relationship to each other. But where a grouping consisted of, say, a wolf, a deer, and wild oats, the deer would eat the oats and the wolf would eat the deer. The same type of interrelationships exists in the insect world. The only problem is that we're just learning about this system. Who feeds on what or whom? For example, there is some evidence that syrphid flies, whose larvae feed on aphids, are attracted by members of the Composite family, such as daisies (the adults probably eat the daisy nectar), so it wouldn't hurt to grow daisies. It is probable that although you might not know about such intricate relationships, you will enable at least a few to flourish if you grow many different types of plants. Two plant groups that seem to be particularly good for this purpose are the Apiaceae family, which includes many herbs such as anise, dill, fennel, and angelica; and members of the Asteraceae family, such as asters, yarrow, artemesia, chrysanthemums, cosmos, black-eyed Susans, marigolds, and zinnias. Apiaceae and Asteraceae flowers appear to provide shelter and food for some stages of the insectfeeding insects.

2. Remove all rotten fruits and diseased leaves and plants.

    Good sanitation is important! Diseased leaves and fruits left under a fruit tree in the fall harbor disease organisms and eggs of pests, as do leftover annual plants. Compost these items in a hot compost heap or, to be extra safe, discard them.

3. Spray deciduous fruit trees with a dormant spray in the early spring if necessary. This spraying helps smother the eggs of young stages of some common pests. For many years gardeners have been routinely advised to spray all fruit trees with a dormant spray "to rid the garden of overwintering pests." Advice about timing or checking for pests was often not given. The value of dormant oil for pest, as distinct from disease, control is questionable in many situations. If your tree has a history of pear psyllid, scale, mite, or aphid infestations, it may be of value to apply a *light* oil just as the buds begin to swell in the spring. This oil will mechanically lower the populations of these soft-bodied insects or young scale crawlers by smothering them before their natural enemies are out in numbers. Again, remember that the predators usually don't hatch until their prey are present in numbers. If there is not a history of such pests, an oil spray for insect control is probably not appropriate. If you are spraying for fungus disease at the same season, most fungicides can be combined with the *light* oil; check the label to be sure.

4. Determine specific treatments for the pests in your yard.

    If plant-feeding insects are present in intolerable numbers, you may need to resort to chemical pesticides. But select those that are as specific as possible to the problem at hand. Carefully follow the guidelines in the section titled "Pesticides and How to Use Them" and in the encyclopedia.

Natural Control Agents

This and the following sections will help you to identify both helpful organisms and those that may give you problems. A more detailed aid in identifying both types of insects is *Rodale's Color Handbook of Garden Insects* by Anna Carr. It contains full-color pictures of the insects, both predator and prey, in all stages of development.

Most of the beneficials listed below are either predators or parasitoids of plant-feeding insects. Their preservation and protection should be a major goal of your gardening strategy. Sometimes waiting for insects to control pests may try your patience—like waiting for the cavalry to come to the rescue. In most cases, however, home gardeners will find their help invaluable.

BEES

2.19. *Bees are the primary insect pollinators of most fruits and many vegetables. If insecticides must be used during blossom time, choose your materials carefully, avoiding those that are particularly toxic to bees, and apply such materials after dusk when most bees are in the hive.*

While bees are not directly involved in pest control, as the major pollinators of fruits and vegetables they are probably the most valuable insect in the edible garden. Without them, our nation's food production would be severely affected. Attract bees to your garden by planting flowering plants, avoid spraying broad-spectrum insecticides at blooming time, and never use insecticides, such as Sevin, that are lethal to bees. If you have a number of fruit trees and live on a fairly good-sized piece of ground, and if no one in the vicinity is allergic to bees, a bee colony can increase your fruit crop and provide a bonus of honey. Many good books are available on the subject.

GROUND BEETLES

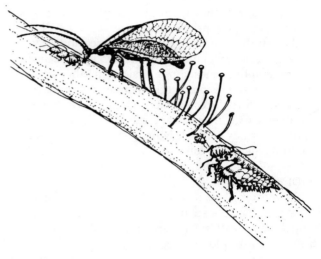

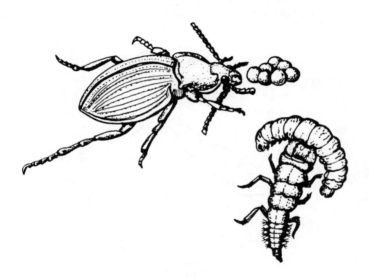

2.20. Many kinds of ground beetles, in both larval and adult stages, are helpful predators in the garden. Depending on the species, they eat snail and slug eggs, the larvae of tent caterpillars, gypsy moth larvae, cankerworms, and cutworms.

Ground beetles, members of the Carabidae family, are all predators. Some are small, but most are fairly large black beetles that scurry away when you uncover them. You will probably not see them the first year or two after planting a new garden. To encourage them, plant low-growing herbs under which they can hide, and keep an active compost pile, as these beetles thrive near them.

LACEWINGS

Lacewings are small green or brown gossamer-winged insects that in their adult stage eat nectar and pollen as well as aphids and mealybugs. In the larval stage they are fierce predators of aphids, psyllids,

2.21. Lacewings are voracious predators of aphids and mealybugs. Female green lacewings lay their eggs on stalks, and the larvae devour many soft-bodied pests.

mealybugs, and moth eggs and larvae. They are one of the most effective insect predators for the home garden. Unlike ladybugs, which often fly away when released, purchased lacewings stay in your garden. When purchased and put out at the appropriate time, the lacewing larvae can be expected to continue their development in the area in which they are released.

LADYBUGS

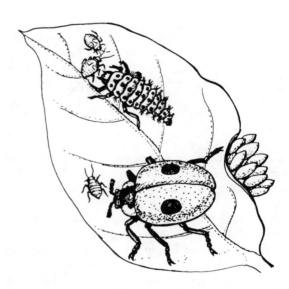

2.22. Many Species of ladybugs (ladybird beetles) and their larvae are predators of aphids, scale insects, mites, and mealybugs. These beetles are usually red, black, or white, and may be solid-colored or spotted.

Ladybugs are small beetles. There are about 400 types besides the familiar red one with black spots. Most people are familiar with ladybugs and know they are beneficial. Few people recognize the larvae of these beetles, on the other hand: they are fierce and ugly looking. Learn to identify them. Ladybugs and their larvae eat aphids, mealybugs, scale, and other small insects. I do not recommend buying ladybugs for garden pest control, because most studies have shown that they usually fly away and often don't eat more than a few pests before leaving. Use in greenhouses would be the exception.

SPIDERS

Spiders are close relatives of the insects. I don't know how they got such a bad name, since, in the United States, with the exception of Black Widows and Brown Recluse spiders, they are harmless, and these ever-present critters go about the business of eating up garden pests. We would be overrun with pests if it were not for their diligence.

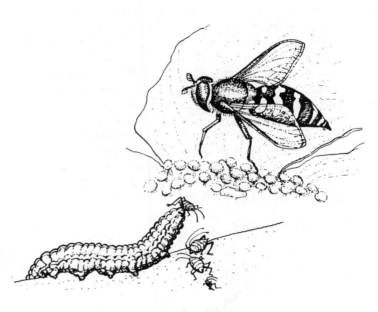

2.24. Syrphid flies are yellow and black, 1/3 to 1/2 in. long. The adults feed on flower nectar; the larvae of most species eat aphids and mealybugs.

2.23. Spiders, which come in many forms, are among the most common predators in the garden. On the left is a familiar daddy-long-legs; on the right is a web spider.

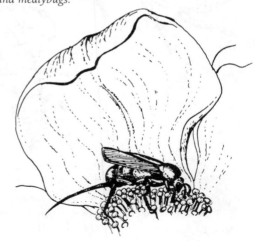

SYRPHID FLIES

Syrphid flies (flower flies or hover flies) are members of the Syrphidae family. They may look like small bees hovering over flowers, but they have only two wings, like other flies. Most have yellow and black stripes on the body. Learn to identify them. They are found all over the United States and Canada. Their larvae are small green maggots which live on leaves, eating aphids, mealybugs, other small insects, and mites.

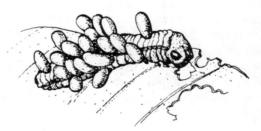

2.25. Many wasps are very small—1/10 to 1/4 in. long—and their larvae are parasites of insects, including caterpillars, scale insects, grasshoppers, and whiteflies. Shown is an adult braconid wasp obtaining nectar from a flower, and a caterpillar with wasp cocoons attached.

WASPS

Wasps are a large family of insects with transparent wings. Unfortunately, the few that sting have given wasps a bad name. In fact, all wasps are either insect predators or parasitoids. The parasitoid adult female lays her eggs in such insects as aphids and caterpillars, and the developing larvae devour the host. The predatory wasps feed on caterpillars, crickets, flies, and leafhoppers, among others. Encourage wasps whenever possible, and do not destroy caterpillars with brown cocoons attached, since these contain baby wasps or fly parasitoids.

OTHER BENEFICIAL INSECTS

Tiger, soldier, and rove beetles feed on insects and their eggs, or on snails and slugs. They may be found on foliage or on the ground. The color and appearance of the several species is varied but all three groups are large (1/2 −1 inch) and generally rectangular in shape. The last six segments of the adult rove beetles abdomen are exposed, giving it a nonbeetlelike appearance. All are valuable in insect control and should be protected.

Big-eyed and minute pirate bugs are valuable predators of soft-bodied destructive insects and mites. Both are small and blackish, oval to squarish in shape. Adult big-eyed bugs hibernate in garden litter—a good reason why the swept garden should sometimes be avoided.

Most assassin bugs and all damsel and ambush bugs are predators of plantfeeding insects. All are vase-shaped with small heads. Assassin and damsel bugs are large; ambush bugs are small. All may be found stalking insects on plants. Their colors are subdued; brownish, blackish, or greenish.
Snipe and robber flies are rapidly flying, predaceous flies of moderate to large size. The large head and thorax and the long curved abdomen of these flies give them a distinctive airplanelike appearance. The adults consume other flies, beetles, butterflies, and moths; the larvae prey on wood-dwelling, soil-dwelling, or aquatic insects.

Beefly adults are rounded, hairy, beelike flies, brownish in color, that often visit flowers. Their larvae are all insect feeding, some being predators and others parasitoids.

Tachinid flies look like large, bristly houseflies. The maggots are parasitoids of moths, butterflies, beetles, grasshoppers, and wasps. Usually only a single fly develops in each host.

Spider-mite populations (like their close relatives, spiders, mites are arachnids rather than insects) are generally controlled by predatory thrips (an insect), predatory mites, and syrphid fly maggots. Most of these natural enemies are more readily destroyed by insecticides than are the plant-feeding target mites. Pest mite outbreaks often follow the use of broad-spectrum insecticides.

AMPHIBIANS

Encourage toads and frogs to stay in your garden. When you know you have a resident toad, be careful you don't step on it. It takes steady nerves to weed the vegetable garden with a toad in it. When you least expect it, out jumps the toad from the beans or strawberries. But remember all the insects it eats, and go back to your weeding.

Mixed Blessings

Most of the world's insects are neither economic pests nor the pests' biological control agents. Thus they are usually of little concern to most of us. Unfortunately, a few such creatures that are usually beneficial may cause an occasional problem when they appear in the wrong place or in large numbers. Include ants, earwigs, and sowbugs (crustaceans) in this category.

ANTS

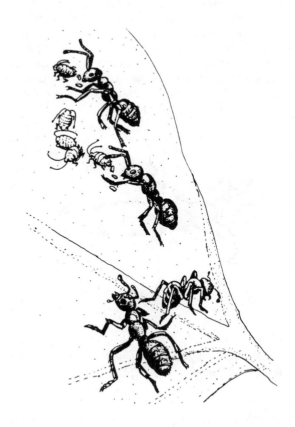

2.26. Ants usually are not garden pests but occasionally become troublesome when feeding on the honeydew excreted by aphids, because they are reputed to protect the aphids from their natural enemies.

Ants are general scavengers that remove dead insects and fallen fruit in the garden. Some species prey on such insects as small caterpillars, fruit flies, and fly larvae, and are natural enemies of termites. Other groups harvest weed seeds. Their nest-building activities may help to aerate the soil. However, many ants also feed on the honeydew exuded by aphids and mealybugs. The ants are believed to transport aphids and mealybugs from plant to plant. Their honeydew-collecting activities interfere·with the natural enemies of aphids and mealybugs, preventing adequate control of these pests.

If ants are contributing to your aphid or mealybug problem, use the commercial sticky substances that are available, such as Tanglefoot or Stickem. Apply these substances around tree trunks and places where the ants are traveling to prevent them from reaching the pests.

EARWIGS

Earwigs are fierce-looking brown insects with large pincers in the back. Earwigs prey on many bothersome pests, but they are occasionally a problem on young vegetable seedlings and ripe fruits. Observe them at night with a flashlight. If you have determined that they are eating your vegetables or fruits, trap them by laying rolled-up newspaper, bales of bamboo stakes, or corrugated cardboard around the garden. Earwigs will hide in these materials and you can destroy them in the daytime by shaking the collectors over soapy water.

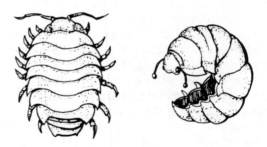

2.28. The sowbug, a gray crustacean whose outer covering resembles armor plate, often rolls up into a ball when disturbed. It is an occasional pest on strawberries and around seedlings.

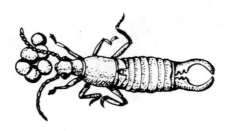

2.27. Unlike most insects, earwigs protect their eggs and young from predators. While usually not a problem, sometimes they eat the foliage and ripe fruits of edible plants.

SOWBUGS

Sowbugs (pillbugs) are not insects but crustaceans. They often roll up into a ball when they are disturbed. They prefer to eat decaying material, and if you mulch your garden you may see thousands. On occasion I have seen sowbugs eating young lettuce, bean

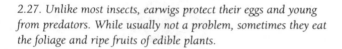

2.29. Aphids, which are plant-sucking insects, produce many generations a year and are the major food source or many predatory and parasitic insects.

seedlings, and tomato or strawberry fruits. Sufficient dry mulch under vulnerable crops helps prevent damage. There is also good evidence that sowbugs are secondary feeders. The initial damage to the fruits is likely caused by insects, snails, or slugs. Control of these other pests is the primary key to control of sowbugs.

Major Plant Pests
APHIDS

Aphids are soft-bodied, small, green, black, pink, or gray insects. They can produce many generations in one season. They suck plant juices and exude honeydew. If the leaves under the aphids turn black, a secondary mold is growing on the nutrient-rich honeydew. This unsightly mold will not directly harm the plant, though it does block sunlight coming to the leaves. The mold can be removed with a soapy spray (2 tablespoons of dishwashing liquid per gallon of water).

Aphids are a major food source for syrphid flies, lady beetles, lacewings, and wasp parasitoids. Among mammals, mice are analogous since they are a fast-reproducing food source for coyotes, owls, hawks, and the like. An aphid population can increase rapidly. If this happens, look for aphid mummies and other natural enemies mentioned above. Mummies are swollen, brown or metallic-looking aphids. They are valuable, so keep them. Inside the mummy a larval wasp parasitoid is growing. These aphids will never feed or reproduce again, and the wasp inside will hatch out and lay eggs in more aphids. If natural enemies are not present, or if the growth of the plant is impaired, or the leaf tips are curling (as often happens in citrus), you may need to intervene. Since aphids suck plant juices, large numbers of them can weaken a plant. In addition, some aphids spread viral or fungus diseases to vulnerable plants.

As in all control efforts, the simplest remedy should be tried first. Wash the affected plant with a strong stream of water. Some kinds of aphids will leave the plant under these conditions. If the aphids stick tightly, apply the soapy spray described above. The surfactant in the soap dehydrates aphids. Be sure to spray thoroughly the top and bottom of all leaves as well as the growing tips. Woolly and other especially waxy aphids may need to be treated twice at 24-hour intervals. Wash the plant with clean water 24 hours after the soap application. Usually, if the above steps are carefully followed, conventional pesticides are not needed for aphid control.

BORERS

Borers are the larval stage of a number of different insects. These larvae damage plants by boring through stems and trunks. The first sign of damage is usually wilted foliage or sawdust around a hole on the trunk. Control borers by cutting the damaged branch or leaf off. When the borer is in the main trunk, straighten a wire hanger and push up into the tunnels to crush the borers. Even one or two borers can be fatal to a young fruit tree. Inspect the young trunks often in summer and early fall, particularly near the crown of the tree (where the bark meets the root zone).

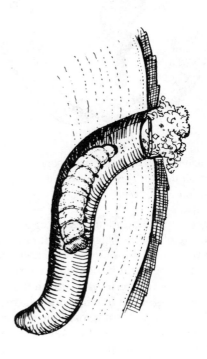

2.31. The lesser peach-tree borer burrows into the injured trunks and branches of apricot, cherry, and peach trees. Often this pest can be discovered by the gummy sawdust deposits it leaves on the bark.

2.30. Small parasitoid wasps lay eggs within aphids. The wasp larvae hatch out and parasitize other aphids.

Borers are a problem on apple, apricot, cherry, currant, peach, pear, pecan, plum, and raspberry. In addition, there are squash-vine stem borers. Cut off stems that have been affected below the entry hole.

CODLING MOTHS

The "worms" in wormy apples are often codling moth larvae. They usually develop in apples and pears, but sometimes attack quinces and walnuts. This European insect is now common worldwide. Because most growers want perfect fruit, codling moths are the "key pests" in many fruit-tree pest-control programs.

2.32. The codling moth is a major pest of apples throughout the U.S. The female deposits eggs that develop into larvae that burrow into the fruit.

First-generation adult females lay eggs on leaves or twigs near the blossoms; later-generation females lay eggs near the fruit. The young larvae enter and complete their development in the fruit. In spring, mature larvae pupate in crevices of bark and in hiding places on and near the ground. In fall, mature larvae spin cocoons in similar places and pass the winter there. They pupate only as the weather warms in spring. Overwintering larvae are preyed on by woodpeckers and other birds, as well as ants and other insect predators. Generally, none of these natural enemies provide enough control. Adult moths emerge from pupation over a 2—3-week period called a flight. Since optimum control of codling moths depends on strict

---

A Pheromone Trap for Codling Moths

These guidelines for controlling codling moths with a pheromone trap should enable you to keep your wormy apple count below 15 percent.

1. At blossom time place 1 pheromone moth trap about 6 feet up on the south side of each mature tree. Change pheromone caps and trap liners every 6 weeks.
2. Once a week, count and remove trapped moths. Record count. Rake up and destroy fallen apples.
3. When apples are the size of ping-pong balls, thin to 2 apples per cluster. Destroy wormy fruit.
4. When moth count on a particular week is lower than the previous week, add up total moths count ed for the entire moth flight. If moth total is less than 20, no spray is needed. If catch is greater than 20, and daytime temperatures exceeded 65°F on the previous 3 days, spray immediately. If daytime temperatures were lower than 65°F and the moth count still above 20, spray in 7 days (cool air slows egg hatch).
5. During a second or third flight, repeat steps 2—4. Between flights, the weekly count will drop to near zero. In step 4, add only moths caught in the most recent flight.

---

timing of pesticide sprays, pheromone traps should be used (see the accompanying box). These release the female codling moth's sex attractant. Male moths attracted to this fragrance, as to a female, are caught in the traps. Weekly counts of the trapped males help determine timing of sprays so that young larvae are killed just before they enter the fruit. If moth counts are low, no spraying is needed. The most selective codling moth spray is BT. The next best alternative is ryana. Neither of these pesticides kills all the natural enemies of aphids and mites. These pests tend to increase if broad-spectrum pesticides such as diazinon, methoxychlor, or carbaryl (Sevin) are applied. Because of the agricultural importance of codling moths, other control strategies are actively being studied. These include use of a viral disease and release of sterile male moths.

CUTWORMS

Cutworms are small chewing insects of the caterpillar family. They are usually found in the soil and will curl up into a ball when disturbed. Cutworms are a particular problem on annual vegetables when the seedlings first appear or when young transplants are set out. The cutworm often chews the stem off right at the soil line, killing the plant. Control cutworms by using cardboard collars or bottomless tin cans around the plant; be sure to sink these collars 1 inch into the ground. Severe infestations can be controlled with *Bacillus thuringiensis*. *Trichogramma* miniwasps and black ground beetles are among cutworms' natural enemies.

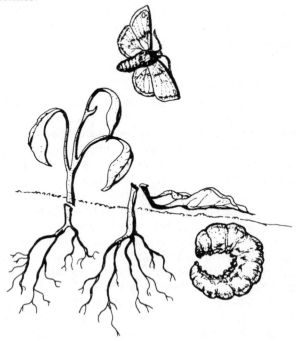

2.33. *Cutworms usually attack young annual vegetables and fruits. Look for them rolled up in the soil as you prepare the planting bed for seedlings. The seedlings can be protected with cardboard collars.*

JAPANESE BEETLES

2.34. *Metallic-looking Japanese beetles chew on the leaves, flowers, and fruit of many plants.*

Japanese beetles were accidentally introduced into the United States early in this century and are now a serious problem in the eastern part of the country. This metallic blue or green beetle with coppery wings chews its way through the leaves and flowers of apple, cherry, grape, peach, plum, quince, raspberry, rhubarb, and many other edible plants. The larval stage lives on the roots of grasses. In Japan a naturally occurring disease present in the soil controls these beetles in the larval stage. This disease, called milky-spore, has been produced for sale in this country and can be purchased at nurseries under the trade name Doom. The disease is slow to cut down the population, often taking three or four years to take hold. If serious infestations are a problem and you can't wait that long, hand-pick the beetles, knock them off into soapy water, or buy Japanese beetle bug traps that contain a pheromone (insect hormone) that attracts them. These traps seem to work most effectively if they are located at some distance from the plant to be protected, thus drawing the beetles away from the area. A good control for young transplants, vegetables and herb plants is to lay floating row covers over the beds. This prevents beetles from flying in to feed.

MITES

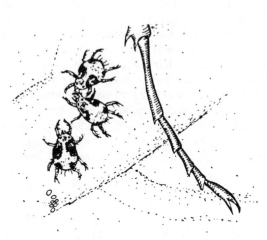

2.35. *Mites are minute members of the spider family. (They are dwarfed by an ants leg.) Most mite infestations result from applications of broad-spectrum insecticides that kill the mites' natural enemies. Mite damage makes foliage look dirty and parched.*

Mites are among the few arachnids (spiders and their relatives) that pose a problem in the garden. Mites are so small that a hand lens usually is needed to see them. They become a problem when they reproduce in great numbers and suck on the leaves of such plants as citrus, apples, beans, and strawberries. The symptoms of serious mite damage can be dried-looking silvery or yellow leaves, sometimes accompanied

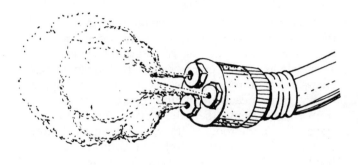

2.36. *A fogger attaches to the end of a hose and produces a strong mist when the water is turned on.*

by tiny webs. The major natural predators of mites are predatory mites. Mite-eating thrips and minute syrphids also help in mite control.

Mites are most likely to thrive on dusty leaves and in dry warm weather; thus plants near a dusty road, say, are likely to be mite-infested. The dust mechanically dehydrates delicate mite predators. A routine foliage wash and misting of sensitive plants helps mite control. I use a tool called a fogger, which produces a strong blast of misted water (see Figure 2.36). In spring, when the mite population on citrus may increase to large numbers, biweekly fogging is appropriate, if fungus diseases are not a problem. Mites are sometimes seen on beans and other vegetables but are seldom a serious problem, because large quantities of vegetables can still be harvested. If appearance is important, restrict these plants to the vegetable garden. Mites are sometimes described as serious fruit-tree pests. Usually, mite damage on such trees is caused by previous spraying with broad-spectrum pesticides. Sometimes such a problem can take several years to rectify after such spraying ceases.

SCALES

2.37. *Scale insects attach themselves permanently to the bark or leaves of a plant.*

Scales are plant-sucking insects that usually are covered with a shell or waxy coating. Adult females shed their legs and antennae and permanently attach themselves to a leaf or branch. The eggs are laid and the live young are born beneath the protective shell of the adult female. Generally, ladybugs and/or chalcid miniwasps keep scales in check, but since crawlers are especially susceptible to light oil sprays, you can use these in the dormant season if you have a problem. (See the section titled "Making It Work" for timing details.)

SNAILS AND SLUGS

My husband warns me teasingly that if snails are one of the Almighty's favorite creatures, then I'm in big trouble. I have killed thousands and thousands by hand. Gardeners of the East Coast battle Japanese beetles in the summer; gardeners on the West Coast battle snails all year round. It's said that a French gourmet brought the brown garden snail to this country for eating. He should have been baked in butter and garlic just like his beloved escargot!

Snails and slugs are not insects, of course, but mollusks. They eat most commonly grown fruits and vegetables. They feed at night and can go dormant for months in times of drought or low food supply. In the absence of effective natural enemies (a few snail eggs are consumed by predatory beetles and earwigs), several snail control strategies can be recommended. Since snails are most active after rain or irrigation, go out to hand-collect them on such nights. It is obviously impossible to find and collect all the snails, and only repeated forays will provide adequate control. In the more common situation where you do not have

2.38. *Snails and slugs will eat most edible plants. Look for their damage after irrigation or rain. The slime trails they often leave can help you identify them as the pest.*

time for such sustained collection, you may occasionally need to use metaldahyde bait. After a rain or watering, spread bait on pieces of cardboard, cover with another piece of cardboard, to keep the bait from children, birds and animals. Place baited cardboard where snails and slugs are the biggest problem. After a week or so dispose of the cardboard, including bait, slugs and snails, in the garbage. A good time would be in the early spring, when they are most active (February or March in California), and again in early summer when the majority of young hatch. Again, pelleted baits should only be applied to damp ground. If you wish to prevent buildup of large snail populations, consider removing (or avoid planting) such well-known snail harborages as ivy or vinca (periwinkle) ground covers, and sheltering strap-leafed plants such as agapanthus or iris.

WEEVILS AND CURCULIOS

Weevils and curculios are beetles with long snouts. The ones with particularly long snouts are called curculios. In both larval and adult stages, they can be serious pests. They feed on fruits, nuts, and roots, and are a particular problem on chestnuts, plums, apples, beans, cabbages, blueberries, cherries, and pecans. A few of these insects around are not a problem but large numbers should be controlled. Control includes the scrupulous cleaning up of old leaves, dropped fruits, and nuts. Throughout the growing season, whenever you see weevils or curculios around, place sheets under fruit or nut trees, and shake the trees to dislodge the adults. Dispose of them. Control moderate infestations by dusting the foliage with diatomaceous earth, the pulverized skeletons of small fossilized algae. The sharp surfaces abrade the insects' covering and cause death by dehydration. It is sold under the trade name Perma-guard.

WHITEFLIES

Whiteflies are sometimes a problem in mild winter areas of the country as well as in greenhouses nationwide. In the garden, *Encarsia* wasps and other parasitoids usually provide adequate whitefly control. Occasionally, especially in cool weather, whitefly populations may begin to cause serious plant damage (wilting and slowing of growth, flowering, or fruiting). Look under the leaves to determine whether the scalelike, immobile larvae and pupae are present in large numbers. Adults can easily be trapped using the following method. Apply Stickem or Tanglefoot to a mustard-yellow file folder. (No one knows why this color attracts whiteflies, but it does!) Hold the folder open near the affected plant, and give the plant an occasional shake. The adult whiteflies will fly to the folder and adhere to the sticky surface. Further devel-

2.39. *Weevils occasionally feed on the fruits and nuts of a number of popular edibles.*

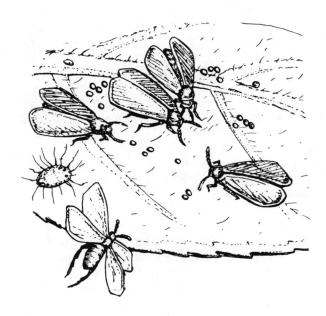

2.40. *Whiteflies generally live in colonies on the underside of leaves. They usually fly around only when disturbed.*

opment of the hard-to-control larvae can be stopped by any of several "houseplant sprays" containing methoprene, an insect-growth regulator appropriate for controlling several plant-sucking insects—but only on ornamental plants, not edibles. Since this compound readily degrades in sunlight, apply the spray at dusk. For edible plants, use a fogger if fungus diseases are not a problem. Safer's Soap can be effective as well.

GRASSHOPPERS

Grasshoppers occasionally are a garden problem, particularly in grassland areas in dry years. Try controlling them with a bait containing a grasshopper disease, *Nosema locustae*. It is available from (25).

NEMATODES

Nematodes are microscopic worms, sometimes called threadworms or eelworms. These organisms inhabit the soil in most of the United States, particularly in the Southeast. Most nematode species live on decaying matter or are predatory on other nematodes, algae, and bacteria. A few types are parasitic, attaching themselves to the roots of plants. Edible plants particularly susceptible to nematode damage include many annual crops such as beans, cantaloupe, eggplant, lettuce, okra, pepper, squash, tomatoes, and watermelon, as well as the perennial fig and brambleberries. The symptoms of nematode damage are stunted-looking plants and small swellings or lesions on the roots.

If nematodes are a problem in your area, prevent nematode damage by planting trees that are grafted onto nematode-resistant rootstock, if available. Rotate annual vegetables with less susceptible varieties, keep your soil high in organic matter (this encourages fungi and predatory nematodes that help keep them under control), and, before planting, try the soil solarization procedure outlined later in the box under "Disease Control."

Marigolds are sometimes planted to control nematodes. The limited documentation available has shown that some species of the plant do contribute to nematode control, but further documentation is needed. There are many species of both marigolds and nematodes, and a number of the combinations are not effective.

Pesticides and How to Use Them

Weather, good cultural techniques, and natural enemies are the most important elements in controlling pests. As you gradually learn how these natural controls operate, you will find that pesticides are seldom required. If additional help is needed, try a non-chemical control method such as water, soapy water sprays, or traps, if available. If all these attempts fail and pests are doing substantial damage, you may have to resort to something stronger.

Because of the toxicological and other tests required before registration, pesticides are enormously expensive to produce. So pesticide manufacturers usually choose to market only those chemicals that will kill a great variety of organisms, or, in the case of selective pesticides, those that offer enormous sales potential. Such choices give them a chance to recover developmental costs and make a profit. Pesticides which kill many kinds of organisms have been dubbed "broad spectrum." Broad-spectrum pesticides include some of the so-called "organic" pesticides such as nicotine and rotenone and sabadilla as well as the synthetic organophosphates such as malathion, chlorinated hydrocarbons such as DDT, and carbamate pesticides such as Sevin (carbaryl).

Your pest-control strategy should differ from that of the pesticide manufacturer If chemical aids are needed, use them as selectively as possible. For example, never spray the entire yard or treat for insects on a calendar basis. You should seek techniques and chemicals which affect Only the target pest, allowing its natural enemies to survive. Sometimes you will use a truly selective pesticide. At other times you can apply a broad-spectrum material at an optimum time when it will kill the pest but preserve the most natural enemies. To give your strategy the best chance for success, you should learn as much as possible about the life cycles of the insects, mites, and mollusks in your garden. In addition you will need to know something about the pesticides themselves so you can choose those with the least potential to harm you and the environment.

Since most insecticides are designed to kill living insects quickly, few are truly nontoxic to humans. Though the compounds I have recommended are among those that are the least toxic to humans, you should always carefully follow the directions for use. Some people believe a little more is always better. Not so! When you use a little extra pesticide, you not only increase your personal risk, you may also injure your plants and unnecessarily kill natural enemies. While in a few situations it may be appropriate to use less, it is never appropriate to increase the dose.

Wear protective clothing when spraying pesticides. A long-sleeved shirt, pants, closed shoes, gloves, and even goggles and a face mask are often appropriate. Pesticides can penetrate your skin or enter your lungs. To avoid drift, spray when the air is still.

Pesticides are usually classified under two major categories: inorganic and organic. Until the 1940s, the majority of pesticides were inorganic. Examples of inorganic pesticides still in use are sulfur, Bordeaux solution, copper oxide, and boric acid. Many of these inorganics do not kill insects on contact. Those being used today function mainly as fungicides and stomach poisons.

Beginning with DDT in the 1940s, a variety of synthetic organic pesticides have been introduced. (Chemicals are called organic when they contain carbon, the element which is basic to life.) Most of the new synthetic organic insecticides kill insects on contact. Some organic insecticides are based on natural plant products. However, the fact that they are plant extracts does not necessarily make them any more "organic" or safer in use than the synthetic carbon-based insecticides. Some well-known plant-based organic pesticides are ryania, nicotine, sabadilla, pyrethrins, and rotenone. Nicotine is extremely toxic to humans.

Some of the newer organic materials should not be considered insecticides in the normal sense, since they do not kill insects directly. Instead they change insect behavior or development in such a way that the insect dies, primarily from starvation or exposure. Most of these compounds are classified as either behavior modifiers or as insect-growth regulators. Many of the behavior modifiers are antifeedants (chemicals which stop insects from eating). The insect-growth regulators include cuticle synthesis inhibitors (which stop development of insect skin), juvenile hormone analogues (which resemble a normal insect hormone), and perhaps in the future, anti-juvenile hormones (which would remove a normal insect hormone). Finally, specific insect disease-causing organisms—bacteria, fungi, viruses, and nematodes—are now formulated as sprays to aid in insect control.

In addition to differences in structure and in activity, pesticides differ in stability. If they are readily changed to simpler compounds by microorganisms or animal enzymes, they are said to be nonpersistent or biodegradable. If they remain unchanged or little changed by natural processes, they are called persistent. In general, persistent pesticides have been proven to cause environmental problems. The persistent, inorganic, heavy-metal pesticides containing lead, arsenic, or mercury tend to build up in the soil, poisoning plants growing there and animals that eat the plants. The persistent chlorinated hydrocarbons are readily stored in the fatty tissues of fish, mammals, and birds; they may later cause death or reduce reproduction in these animals. In addition, several of these, including DDT, chlordane, aldrin, dieldrin, and heptachlor, have been partially or totally banned because they are suspected carcinogens (cancer-causing compounds). As an organic gardener, you should avoid all persistent pesticides whose limited use is still permitted—these include the chlorinated hydrocarbons lindane and toxaphene—as well as those that include arsenic, lead, or mercury.

RECOMMENDED INSECTICIDES

No pesticide can be recommended unequivocally. Environmental effects and eventual toxicity sometimes take years to surface. The following substances have the least potential for harm as of this writing. Your best defense is to stay informed.

If a pesticide is called for, your first choice should be a selective pesticide, since these do not directly kill beneficial insects. Of the available materials, the most selective are not chemicals but microorganisms. *Bacillus thuringiensis* (BT) contains bacterial particles that cause a caterpillar disease. It kills no other group of insects. BT is sold under the trade names Dipel, Thuricide, and Orcon Caterpillar Control. Milky-spore disease (*Bacillus popilliac*) is a soilborne bacterial disease that helps control Japanese beetle grubs. And grasshoppers are being controlled by a bait containing a grasshopper disease called *Nosema locustae*. All are available from (25). Remember that even these very selective disease-causing materials should be used sparingly. It has been experimentally demonstrated that repeated use can disrupt garden ecology by destroying the prey (food source) of the beneficial insects and causing them to starve.

Among the most selective and biodegradable materials are the juvenile hormone analogues (JHAs). They are suitable for use on homopteran insects (scales, whiteflies, aphids, and mealybugs) and on insects that are a problem as adults (some flies, fleas, and mosquitoes). Though they potentially affect all kinds of insects, in practice they tend to be very specific. To control adult pests JHAs must be applied to *late larval* stages. Further development stops at the beginning of the pupal stage. Currently two products containing methoprene (Altosid) are available for home use (though not, as mentioned previously, on edible plants): Dexol Whitefly and Mealybug Spray and Chacon House Plant Mist. Methoprene and other JHAs do not kill immediately, so wait a few days for the results. Another useful JHA, kinoprene (Enster) is currently registered for commercial greenhouse use to control some of the same pests. It probably will be available in the future for home use. Both of these JHAs are nontoxic to birds and mammals.

The proper timing of sprays is a useful way to increase pesticide selectivity. For example, light oil sprays are not intrinsically selective. However, when applied as a dormant spray just as buds begin to swell in the spring, they give good control of thrips, scale crawlers, and pear psylla, all of which begin to be mobile then. But they do not affect most natural enemies of these pests, since the beneficials, which hatch later, will still be protected in bark crevices and under bud scales. Conversely, a dormant oil spray to control insects in winter will actually control nothing, and a spray in late fall might kill important natural enemies that are still around. Dormant oil spray is available at nurseries. Generally this product cannot be used while plants are in foliage, but scale infestations on citrus or on some house plants can be controlled with a light oil formulated for this purpose. Follow directions carefully.

The use of pheromone traps to determine the need for and the proper timing of sprays is another way of minimizing pesticide use. In addition to the codling moth traps mentioned earlier, traps are available for apple and other fruit-feeding maggots, and for several scales. Pheromone traps are available from (25). They generally come in three-station kits, so it's a good idea to cooperate with neighbors when ordering.

Spraying in the evening allows you to use some broad-spectrum insecticides (those that biodegrade rapidly) while still protecting many beneficials. Resmethrin, a synthetic pyrethroid, disappears in a few hours, leaving day-active beneficials such as bees, wasps, and parasitic flies unaffected; other natural enemies will come back rapidly. Naturally, this technique should be used sparingly.

Because they function primarily as stomach poisons, the effects of some pesticides are limited mainly to plant-feeding insects. This is the case with ryania, the material recommended for codling moth control. Ryania degrades within a few days, so if you follow the directions on the container, residues on your fruit will not be a problem.

Neem oil is extracted from the foliage and seeds of the neem tree (*Azadirachta indica*) and is an effective control for dozens of insect pests, including Japanese beetles, leafminers, Colorado potato beetles, mealybugs, whiteflies, caterpillars, crickets, and grasshoppers.

Neem oil acts as both a contact pesticide and a systemic. When bitter, strong-smelling neem oil is added to the soil, the essential ingredients become systemic, entering the plant's stems and foliage. Pests then either pass up the bitter, strong smelling plant parts, or eat them and die before maturing.

Neem oil has very low toxicity to mammals. The active ingredients break down rapidly in sunlight and within a few weeks in the soil.

A broad-spectrum pesticide can become selective when it is formulated to attract the pest. For example, the short-lived organophosphate metaldahyde is marketed in a bran bait that attracts snails and slugs. These baits should be used with care, however, since they can kill animals or children that eat them (see the section on snails and slugs for application directions).

Soap solutions are valuable in insect control because they remove some of the insects waxy coating, causing dehydration and death, or they break the surface tension of water so that insects drown. Hold a jar of soapy water (1 tablespoon dishwashing liquid per quart of water) under plants laden with plant-feeding beetles or bugs, flip them into the solution, and they drown immediately. This is a good technique to rid your yard of earwigs, adult *Diabrotica* (cucumber) beetles, Japanese beetles, asparagus and harlequin bugs, and other hard-to-control, mobile pests. If aphids cause severe curling of leaves, as can occur on citrus or cherries (a few curled leaves on fruit trees are not important), do not wait for natural controls. Spray your tree with 2 tablespoons of dishwashing soap in a gallon of water, and the aphids will be gone in a day. The next day, wash the plant with clear water to remove the soap. Plants infested with woolly aphids should be drenched with two soapy water applications at 24-hour intervals; be sure to wash the soap off a day after the last treatment.

A number of widely available and popular insecticides should be avoided. These include: carbaryl (Sevin), which is relatively persistent, extremely toxic to bees and wasps, and can sometimes lead to aphid and mite outbreaks; two plant extracts, nicotine and rotenone, because they are broad-spectrum contact insecticides toxic to humans; and methoxychlor, which is the least persistent of the chlorinated hydrocarbons but which also can cause pest problems.

A word about homemade insecticides. They are not necessarily safer or more effective than commercial products. Remember that they have not undergone long-term toxicology tests, have not been formulated to protect you and your plants (the wrong formulation can be irritating to your skin or kill your plants), and have not been tested for effectiveness. The fact that no pests are seen after their application may be coincidence rather than cause and effect.

Disease Control

Plant diseases are potentially far more damaging to your crops than are most insects. Diseases are also more difficult to control because they usually grow inside the plant, and plants do not respond with immune mechanisms comparable to those that protect animals. Consequently, most plant disease control strategies feature prevention rather than control.

Plant Resistance

Research on plant diseases that have plagued commercial agriculture has resulted in the widespread availability of disease-resistant cultivars of several important vegetables and fruits. Certain varieties of wilt-resistant tomatoes and blight-resistant pears are examples of plants that resist diseases by genetic means. Always choose disease-resistant varieties whenever they are available

In other instances—raspberries are an example—strict inspection and quarantine help to ensure that most commercially available plants are disease free. You should avail yourself of these products whenever possible. In addition, it is advisable to plant two or three different varieties of a particular vegetable in your garden to help prevent total crop wipeout from an invading disease.

Cultural Techniques

Changing the location in your garden of some disease-prone plants on a regular basis is helpful, as pests and diseases often build up in the soil. This is called crop rotation. Light, exposure, temperature, fertilizing, and moisture are also important factors in disease control. The entries for individual plants in the encyclopedia give specific cultural information.

Seriously diseased plants should be discarded. Diseased fruits should be picked up from the ground or pulled off the plant itself, and placed in a hot compost pile (risky) or in the garbage. In the fall, rake up all leaves and fruit from around disease-prone varieties. Apply dormant sprays when appropriate.

Soil Solarization

It has recently been discovered that a variety of soil-borne fungi, nematodes, and weeds can be controlled by a plastic mulch technique called soil solarization. (Katan, J. "Solar Pasteurization of Soils for Disease Control: Status and Prospects." Plant Disease Journal 64, 1980.) If you have problems with any of the serious soil-borne plant diseases such as verticillium or fusarium wilt, or if you have a serious nematode infestation, soil solarization is appropriate. (A significant reduction in weed growth can also be expected.)

How to Use Soil Solarization

This complete process takes one month during the warmest season of the year.

1. Obtain sufficient clear polyethylene plastic film (4-mil thickness) to cover the treatment area.
2. Irrigate the plant 1 week before laying down the plastic tarping.
3. After 1 week, cultivate and level the treatment area. Install drip emitters or ditches on 3-foot centers for irrigation during treatment.
4. Place plastic film tightly over treatment area. Do not leave air spaces. Weight edges of plastic with soil.
5. Thoroughly irrigate area under plastic once a week.
6. One month later remove plastic and plant as desired.

Plant Diseases

The most common diseases of edible plants are described below. Conditions related to deficiencies and their symptoms are covered earlier under "Plant Nutrients" and "Soil Problems." Symptoms and cures, if any, are suggested. (Recommended fungicides are listed in a table at the end of this section.) For fruit trees, supplement this information with a regular pruning program.

BROWN ROT

There are two types of brown-rot fungi. One causes blossom blight and the dieback of shoots; the other causes spoilage of such stone fruits as apricots, peaches, cherries, and plums. Just as the fruit ripens, round brown spots appear which eventually affect the entire fruit. Unless removed from the tree, these fruits often stick tightly to the branches; the dried-up diseased fruits are known as "mummies." Prevention is helpful in some situations. Avoid planting these trees in lawns, where conditions are usually moist.

If the disease develops, remove and destroy all spoiled fruit. Do not leave it on the tree or the ground. If the spoilage level is intolerable fungal sprays may be required. For apricots and cherries spray with Bordeaux at pink-bud stage and full bloom. Use again two or three weeks before harvest. For peaches, nectarines, and plums, if blossom blight has been a problem, spray with Bordeaux or wettable sulfur at pink-bud stage and full bloom. Preharvest treatment for fruit rot is usually needed for peaches and nectarines; use sulfur three weeks, and again one week, before harvest. (Never use sulfur compounds in hot weather or on apricots, since they damage the trees.)

FIRE BLIGHT

Fire blight is a serious bacterial disease of fruit trees. In fact, in some warm, humid areas, some species should not be grown at all because of the fire-blight risk. Such members of the rose family as pears, quinces, loquats, and apples are particularly prone to this disease. During the blooming period you must remain constantly vigilant for fire-blight symptoms. At this time check weekly for blossoms, twigs, leaves, or branches that look burned and blackened. Act immediately; the disease spreads rapidly. Trim the diseased tissue off, cutting at least one foot into healthy tissue, and sterilizing your tools between cuts with a 10 percent solution of bleach in water. Choose blight-resistant varieties if you live in an area where fire blight is a serious problem. See the encyclopedia for fire-blight-resistant varieties of individual species.

LEAF-SPOT FUNGI

A number of fungus plant diseases are associated

with warm, wet weather: among them are anthracnose, scab, and shot-hole fungus. Plant resistant varieties, clean up all diseased leaves, and apply dormant sprays if possible. (See table for recommended fungicides.)

MILDEWS

Mildews are fungus diseases that affect plants under certain conditions. There are two types of mildews: powdery mildew and downy mildew. Powdery mildew appears as a white powdery dust; downy mildew makes a velvety or fuzzy patch. Both affect leaves, buds, and tender stems. The poorer the air circulation and the more humid the weather, the more apt your plants are to have mildew. Make sure your plant has plenty of sun and is not crowded by other vegetation. Train your fruit trees to a vase shape, as described earlier in the pruning section. If you must use overhead watering, do it in the morning so the water will evaporate by nighttime. Use sulfur and dormant sprays to control mildew on grapes, currants, and fruit trees.

PEACH LEAF CURL

Peach leaf curl is a serious fungus disease of peaches, nectarines, and sometimes almonds. It causes unnatural swelling, discoloration, and curling of the foliage. The injured leaves fall prematurely and are replaced with new healthy leaves. The need to replace the leaves twice annually seriously weakens the tree, and few fruits are produced. What fruits that are produced often become sunburned. The fungus overwinters in the bark, twigs, and fallen leaves. All leaves should be raked from the ground and prunings destroyed. All peaches and nectarines should be sprayed annually with a dormant lime sulfur spray, as described below under "Scab." Almonds do not require treatment unless the disease is seen.

SCAB

Scab is a serious disease of apples, crabapples, and sometimes pears in rainy climates. It results in deformed Leaves and blotched and cracked fruit. Whenever possible plant scab-immune apple varieties such as 'Priscilla' or 'Prima'. If you already have an established apple tree that suffers from scab, spray with lime sulfur just before the flower buds open in the spring. After the blossoms have fallen, spray with wettable sulfur. In summer and fall, clean up all leaves and fruits from the ground and destroy them. If it is a very rainy season and more control is needed, spray with one of the recommended fungicides.

VERTICILLIUM WILT

Verticillium wilt is a soil-borne fungus that is destructive in many parts of the country. The symptom of this disease may be sudden wilting of one part of the plant. There is no cure, but the soil solarization procedure described earlier should help prevent it. Plant resistant species or varieties if this disease is in your soil. In general, apples, asparagus, bamboo, beans, citrus fruits, figs, mulberries, pears, walnuts, and certain varieties of tomatoes and strawberries are naturally resistant to verticillium wilt.

VIRUSES

A number of viruses attack plants. There is no cure for viral conditions, so most affected plants must be destroyed. Deformed or mottled leaves or stunted plants are symptoms of virus diseases. Grapes, raspberries, figs, tomatoes, strawberries, and beans are particularly susceptible. Buy virus-resistant plants, and order certified virus-free plants by mail whenever possible.

Some gardening books recommend using tobacco or cigarette extracts as a source of nicotine for use in controlling insects. This is a poor idea, since tobacco itself is susceptible to many viral diseases that will readily spread to such plants as peppers, tomatoes, and potatoes.

SOIL-BORNE FUNGI

Certain fungi become active and attack plants when drainage is poor. This problem is particularly severe in warm weather. One destructive disease associated with warm and wet soils in the West is *Armillaria*, or oak-root fungus. If oak-root fungus is a problem, choose resistant species of plants. Edibles known to be resistant include avocado, carob, chestnut (Spanish), fig ('Kadota' and 'Mission'), pear, peach, persimmon, plum (Japanese), and walnut (California black). The agricultural extension service of the University of California can supply a list of resistant plants, ornamentals as well as edibles.

Recommended Fungicides

NAME	TYPE	LEVEL OF TOXICITY[1]	USE[2]	DISEASE CONTROLLED	HAZARDS AND PRECAUTIONS
Bordeaux	Inorganic sulfate and lime)	Very low	D and G	D: brown rot, peach leaf curl, apple scab; G. fire blight, anthracnose, leaf spot	Corrosive to (copper iron or steel - do not mix with other materials except oil
Lime sulfur	Inorganic	Medium	D	Peach leaf curl, apple scab, mildews, anthracnose	Same as Sulfur
Sulfur	Inorganic	Very low (protect eyes)	G	Brown rot, mildews, apple scab, peach scab; also mites, and thrips	Harmful to apricots, D'Anjou pears, raspberries, and cucurbits; scales, do not apply in hot weather.

[1]Acute oral to-city.

[2]D = Dormant; G = Growing season.

Problems with Wildlife

Rabbits and mice can be problems for gardeners. If you suspect these animals of disturbing your young fruit trees, wrap the trunks with the plastic guards made for the purpose or use aluminum foil or chicken wire. With the latter, keep the wire at least 6 inches from the bark.

Gophers and moles are problems in some areas. Plant trees and shrubs in chicken-wire baskets. Make sure the wire sticks out of the ground at least a foot to keep the critters from reaching over the wire. Trapping usually is needed as well. Cats help with all the rodent problems but seldom provide adequate control.

Because of their omnivorous eating habits, squirrels are a serious problem for many gardeners. Nets over the fruit trees sometimes help, but trapping which could result in squirrel stew-might be the only solution.

In rural areas, deer can cause such severe problems that edible plants cannot be grown without 9-foot fences or a trained dog. You can somewhat control summer deer problems by getting lion manure from a zoo or spreading dried blood or mothballs. In winter, however, the odors of such substances are ineffective, and it is in winter that the deer problems are the most severe.

Such birds as starlings and finches can be major pests of berries and cherries. Dwarf trees and bushes can be effectively covered with black nylon bird netting. Radios playing, aluminum pie pans hung in trees, and scarecrows are somewhat effective, but they should not be used until just before harvest so the birds do not become desensitized to them.

This section, by necessity, has covered a large number of pests, diseases, and other garden problems. An individual gardener, however, will encounter few such problems in a lifetime of gardening. Good garden planning, good hygiene, and an awareness of major symptoms will keep problems to a minimum and give you many hours to enjoy your garden and feast on its bounty!

PART THREE
RESOURCES AND REFERENCES

APPENDIX A
A COMPREHENSIVE CHECKLIST OF EDIBLE SPECIES

Perennials Planted for Food

COMMON AND LATIN NAME	SOURCES+	ZONES	NOTES
*Almond *Prunus dulcis* var. *dulcis*	E	6-9	Medium-size deciduous tree; to 30 ft. White or pink showy flowers. Semidwarf and dwarf available. Use for interest and shade. Nut edible.
*Apple *Malus* species	E	3-9	Medium-size deciduous tree; to 30 ft. White to pinkish flowers. Comes in many sizes. Use for interest and shade. Fruit edible.
*Apricot *Prunus Armeniaca*	E	5-9	Medium-size deciduous tree; to 25 ft. White or pink flowers; bronzy new growth. Dwarf available. Use for interest and shade. Fruit edible.
*Artichoke *Cynara Scolymus*	E	8,9	Tall herbaceous perennial; to 5 ft. Striking gray foliage. Flowers are lavender thistles. Use in herbaceous borders. Flower bud edible.
*Asparagus *Asparagus officinalis*	E	4-9	Herbaceous perennial; to 5 ft. Small, fine-textured foliage. Use as background for herbaceous border. Shoot edible.
*Avocado *Persea americana*	E	10-11	Large evergreen tree; to 40 ft. Dwarf available. Handsome foliage. Good shade tree. Fruit edible.
Azarole *Crataegus Azarolus*	Locally available	7-9	Deciduous 30-ft. ornamental tree. Attractive foliage, white flowers, yellow or red fruits. Fruit edible. *
Bamboo *Bambusa* and species		7-11	Large perennial grasses; to 60 ft.; most smaller. *Phyllostachys* Decorative form. Use as hedge or interest plant. Shoot edible.

*   Starred items are included in the encyclopedia.

+ "E" indicates sources noted in encyclopedia; "s" indicates available in seed form only; numbers refer to sources listed in Appendix B.

*Banana
Musa species   10-11   Tall herbaceous perennial; to 25 ft. Large dramatic
                                                                 leaves. Use as interest plant or in atrium. Fruit edible.

*Bitter melon
Momordica Charantia   E   5-10   Perennial or annual large vine; to 20 ft. Decorative leaves and
                                                                 fruit. Use on arbors and fences. Fruit and leaf edible.

*Blueberry and huckleberry
Vaccinium species   E   3-9   Deciduous shrubs; to 18 ft.; most types shorter. White flow
                                                                 ers, Colorful fall foliage. Use as hedge, interest plant, and in
                                                                 containers. Fruit edible.

*Brambleberry
Rubus species   E   3-9   Deciduous thorny cane plants; 5-25 ft. Attractive white flow
                                                                 ers. Use as barrier and fence plants. Fruit edible.

Breadfruit
Artocarpus altilis   Locally   10-11   Evergreen tree; to 60 ft. Striking cut-leaf foliage. Use for
                                  available   shade, interest. Fruit edible.

*Butternut
Juglans cinerea   E   3-9   Deciduous tree; to 80 ft. Use as shade tree. Nut edible.

*Calamondin
Citrus reticulata x   E   8-11   Small to 20 ft.) evergreen tree. Handsome foliage, *Fortunella*
sp. *mitis*   colorful fruits. Use as hedge and interest plant. Fruit edible.

Carambola
Averrhoa Carambola   s, 2;   10,   Evergreen tropical ornamental tree; to 30 ft. Yellow fruits
                                  plants 53   11   large and decorative. Use as shade and interest tree. Fruit
                                                                 edible.

Cardoon
Cynara cardunculus   s, 12,18,   6-9   Large herbaceous perennial; to 8 ft. Gray handsome foliage.
                                  45,65   Blanching process unattractive. Use as back ground for
                                                                 herbaceous border. Often grown as an annual. Can become a
                                                                 weed in mild winter areas. Stalk edible.

Carob
Ceratonia Siliqua   9, 10   Large shrubby evergreen tree; to 40 ft. Handsome foliage and
                                                                 form. Use as screen and interest tree. Roots invasive. Pod edi
                                                                 ble.

Chayote
Sechium edule   Buy fruit   9, 10   Large herbaceous vine; to 40 ft. Use from to cover large from
                                  produce   arbors. Plant more than one to ensure pollination. Shoot,
                                  market   seed, and fruit edible.

Cherimoya
Annona Cherimola   s, 15;   10-11   Medium-size shrubby evergreen tree; to 25 ft. Velvety large
                                  plants, 48   leaves. Use as interest plant and screen. Fruit edible.

*Cherry, sour
Prunus Cerasus   E   4-9   Small deciduous tree; to 20 ft. Showy white flowers. Use as
                                                                 interest plant. Fruit edible.

*Cherry, sweet
Prunus avium   E   5-9   Medium-size deciduous tree; to 35 ft. Showy white flowers.
                                                                 Use as interest or shade tree. Dwarf available; use as shrub.
                                                                 Fruit edible.

*Chestnut
Castanea species   E   5-9   Large spreading deciduous trees; to 100 ft. White, showy
                                                                 flowers, decorative burrs. Use as shade and interest trees.
                                                                 Nut edible.

Coconut
Cecos nucifera   Locally   10-11   Graceful palm tree; to 80 ft. Use as available interest tree in
                                  available   areas where falling nuts will not cause damage. Nut
                                                                 edible.

*Crabapple
Malus species   E   3-9   Medium-size deciduous tree; to 25 ft. Showy white to pinkish
                                                                 flowers. Use as interest and shade tree. Fruit edible.

Cranberry		3-8	Low-growing evergreen vine; to 1 ft. White flowers, showy red fruit. Use as ground cover. Fruit edible.
Vaccinium macrocarpon			
*Currant	E	3-8	Deciduous shrub; to 5 ft. Showy red fruit. Use as foundation plant and in shrub borders. Fruit edible.
Rib sativum			
Date	s, 14,	10	Handsome palm tree; to 100 ft. Use as interest and shade tree. Fruit edible.
Phoenix dactylifera	15,53		
*Elderberry	E	2-9	Deciduous shrubs; to 3 ft. Showy white flower clusters. Use as screen and background shrub. Some species are very weedy. Fruit edible.
Sambucus species			
*Fig	E	8-11	Dramatic deciduous tree; to 30 ft.; semidwarf available. Use as shade and interest tree. Fruit edible.
Ficus carica			
*Filbert	E	4-8	Deciduous shrub or tree; to 25 ft. Handsome foliage and seed covering. Use as hedge, interest tree. Nut edible.
Corylus Avellana			
*Gooseberry	E	3-8	Deciduous shrub; to 5 ft. Attractive foliage. Use as foundation plant and in shady borders, pendulous types to drape over retaining walls. Fruit edible.
Ribes species			
*Grape, American	E	4-9	Woody deciduous vine; to 50 ft. Handsome foliage. Use on arbors and fences. Fruit edible.
Vitis Labrusca			
*Grape, European	E	5-9	Woody deciduous vine; to 50 ft. Handsome foliage. Use on arbors and fences, and as small weeping trees. Fruit edible.
Vitis vinifera			
*Grape, Muscadine	E	7-9	Woody deciduous vine; to 50 ft. Handsome foliage. Use on and fences. Fruit edible.
Vitis rotundifolia arbors			
Grapefruit	E	10-11	Evergreen tree; to 40 ft.; dwarf available. Use for hedge and interest. Fruit edible.
Citrus paradisi			
Guava, Chilean	s, 53	9, 10	Small-leaved ornamental evergreen shrub; to 6 ft. Small lily-of-the-valley-type white flowers, bronzy new growth. Use as foundation shrub, in containers, and in shady shrub borders. Fruit edible.
Ugni Molinae			
Guava, common	s, 15,36;	10-11	Medium-size tree; to 30 ft. Use as plants, shade tree and hedge. plants,Fruit edible.
Psidium Guajava	53		
*Guava, pineapple	E	9-11	Large evergreen shrub or small tree; to 18 ft. Gray foliage, showy dark-red flowers. Use as multistemmed interest tree, screen, and hedge. Fruit edible.
Feijoa Sellowiana			
Guava, strawberry	s, 15, 36	10-11	Evergreen shrub or small tree; .to 25 ft. White flowers, deep-red fruit. Use as hedge or multi-stemmed tree. Fruit edible.
Psidium littorale			
*Hickory	E	5-9	Deciduous trees; to 120 ft. Trunk and foliage attractive. Use as shade and interest tree. Nut edible.
Carya species			
Hops		10	Large to (25 ft.), deciduous, herbaceous vine. Use on arbors and trellises. Flower and shoot edible.
Humulus Lupulus			
*Jerusalem artichoke	E	2-9	Herbaceous perennial; to 10 ft. Showy yellow flowers. Use as screen and background for large flower borders. Can become a weed. Tuber edible.
Helianthus tuberosus			

Jicama (Mexican potato)

Pachyrhizus tuberosus   s, 15, 24,   9, 10
33,53

Large herbaceous perennial vine; to 20 ft. Handsome foliage, white or purple flowers; but should not be allowed to bloom. Use on arbors and fences and in large containers. Seeds are poisonous. Tuber edible.

*Jujube

Ziziphus Jujuba   E   10

Deciduous semiweeping tree; to 30 ft. Attractive shiny foliage. Suckering can be a problem. Use as shade and interest tree. Fruit edible.

*Kiwi kiwifruit

Actinidia chinensis   E   9,10

Deciduous, woody vine; to 30 ft. Attractive foliage; showy, cream-colored flowers. Use on arbors, fences. Fruit edible.

*Kumquat

Fortunella species   E   9,11

Small evergreen tree; to 25 ft.; dwarf available. Attractive foliage and fruit. Use as hedge, interest tree, or shrub. Fruit edible.

*Lemon

Citrus Limon   E   9, 11

Small evergreen tree; to 20 ft.; dwarf available. Attractive foliage and fruit. Use as hedge, interest tree, or shrub. Fruit edible.

*Lime

Citrus aurantiifolia   E   10, 11

Small evergreen tree; to 20 ft.; dwarf available. Attractive foliage and fruit. Use as hedge, interest tree, or shrub. Fruit edible.

*Limequat

Citrus aurantiifolia   E   9-11
Eustis' x *Fortunella margarita*

Small shrublike evergreen tree; dwarf available. Attractive ' foliage and fruit. Use as hedge, interest tree, or shrub. Fruit edible.

Lingonberry
(mountain cranberry)   s, 36   6-9
Vaccinium Vitis-idaea var. minus

Evergreen shrub; to 1 ft. Dark-green leaves, showy red fruits. Use as ground cover. Fruit edible.

Litchi

Litchi chinensis   53   10-11

Evergreen tree; to 40 ft. Handsome foliage and red fruit clusters. Use as interest and shade tree. Fruit edible.

*Loquat

Eriobotrya japonica   E   8-10

Handsome evergreen tree; to 25 ft. Beautiful woolly foliage and colorful orange fruits. Dramatic form. Use for shade and interest. Fruit edible.

Lotus

Nelumbo nucifera   5-11

Large herbaceous water plant. Dramatic leaves to 3 ft. wide; pink flowers 12 in. across. Use in pools and water containers. Rhizome, seed, and leaf edible.

Macadamia (Queensland nut)

Macadamia species   s, 2,15;   10, 11
plants, 48

Large spreading evergreen tree with handsome foliage; to 50 ft. Use as shade tree. Nut edible.

*Mandarin
orange *Citrus reticulata*   E   9, 11
fruit.

Small evergreen tree; dwarf available. Attractive foliage and Use as hedge, screen, interest tree, or shrub. Fruit edible.

*Mango

Mangifera indica   10-11

Striking evergreen tree; to 50 ft. Fruits colorful. Use as shade tree, screen, and interest plant. Fruit edible.

Maple

Acer species   3-6

Large deciduous, graceful trees; to 100 ft. Dramatic fall foliage. Use as street and shade tree. Sap edible.

Medlar

Mespilus germanica   s, 36;   6-9
59

Small deciduous tree; to 20 ft. Handsome large foliage, white plants, flowers. Use as shade or interest tree. Fruit edible.

Mulberry

Morus species   E   5-10

Medium-size deciduous trees; to 30 ft. Use limited to background plant and screen. Fruit edible.

*Mulberry, black *Morus nigra*	E	5-10	Medium-size deciduous tree; to 30 ft. Use limited to back ground plant and screen. Fruit edible.
*Mulberry, white *Morus alba* 'Pendula'	E	5-10	Weeping deciduous tree; 6-8 ft. tall. Dramatic form. Variable fruit quality. Use as accent or interest plant. Fruit edible.
*Natal plum *Carissa grandiflora*	E	10-11	Evergreen shrub; to 18 ft. Handsome foliage and white flow ers, showy fruits. Use as hedge, interest plant, and ground cover. Fruit edible.
*Nectarine *Prunus Persica*	E	5-9	Small deciduous tree; to 20 ft.; dwarf available. Some varieties have var. *nucipersica* showy pink flowers. Use as background tree or interest shrub. Fruit edible.
*Olive *Olea europaea*	E	9, 10	Medium-size evergreen tree; to 30 ft. Gray foliage, interesting gnarled shape. Use as interest multistemmed tree, screen, or large shrub. Fruit edible.
*Orange *Citrus sinensis*	E	9-11	Attractive evergreen tree; to 30 ft.; dwarf available. Decorative fruit. Use as hedge, screen, interest tree, or shrub. Fruit edi ble.
Papaya *Carica Papaya*	s, 15,53; 48	10-11	Evergreen tree; to 25 ft.; dwarf available. Large palmate leaves 2 ft. plants, across. Awkward form. Landscaping use limited to background. Fruit edible.
Passion fruit (granadilla) *Passiflora* species	s, 2,48	10-11	Large twining evergreen vine. Attractive foliage and some have plants,showy flowers. Can be used on fences and arbors. Fruit edible.
*Pawpaw *Asimina triloba*	E	4-9	Deciduous tree or shrub; to 25 ft. Interesting pyramid shape; attractive foliage. Use as small tree and interest plant. Fruit edible.
*Peach *Prunus Persica*	E	5-9	Small deciduous tree; to 20 ft.; dwarf sizes available. Some varieties have showy pink flowers. Use as back ground tree or interest shrub. Fruit edible.
*Pear, common *Pyrus communis*	E	4-9	Medium-size deciduous tree; to 25 ft.; dwarf sizes available. Showy white flowers. Upright form. Use as shade and inter est tree or shrub. Fruit edible.
*Pear, Oriental *Pyrus pyrifolia*	E	5-9	Medium-size deciduous tree; to 40 ft., with upright growth. Showy white flowers. Use as shade and interest tree. Fruit edible.
*Pecan *Carya illinoinensis*	E	6-9	Large deciduous tree; to 100 ft. Use as shade or street tree. Nut edible.
*Persimmon, American *Diospyros virginiana*	E	5-9	Deciduous tree or shrub; to 40 ft. Attractive foliage and fruit. Use as shade tree, large shrub, and interest plant. Fruit edible.
*Persimmon, Oriental *Diospyros kaki* foliage and	E	6-10	Deciduous tree or shrub; to 40 ft. Attractive red-orange fruit. Use as shade tree and interest plant. Fruit edible.
Pineapple *Ananas comosus*	48; or start from grocery store fruits	10-11	Herbaceous perennial; 3-4 ft. tall. from leaves in rosettes. Used in hobby grocery gardens clustered with bromeliads. Limited use. Fruit edible.

Pine nut
(pignola or pinon)   3-10   Needled evergreen trees; size varies with species; 10 to 100 ft
Pinus species   Use as interest plants, shade trees, windbreaks. Seed edible.

*Pistachio
Pistacia vera   E   7-9   Deciduous tree; female to 30 ft., male taller. Limited use.
                                                                Screen orstreet tree. Nut edible.

Plantain
Musa species   10-11   Tall (to 25 ft.), herbaceous perennial. Large dramatic leaves.
                                                                Use as interest plant or in an atrium. Fruit edible.

*Plum, beach
Prunus maritima   E   5-7   Deciduous shrub or small tree; to 10 ft. Showy white flowers.
                                                                Use for beach planting, interest plant, hedge. Fruit edible.

*Plum, bush
(Nanking and Western   E   3-5   Small deciduous shrub; to 6 ft. Showy white flowers. Use as
sand cherries)   hedge, foundation, and interest plant. Fruit edible.

*Plum, European and prune
Prunus domestica   E   4-9   Medium-size deciduous tree; to 20 ft.; dwarf available. Showy
                                                                white flowers. Upright form. Use as screen or interest plant.
                                                                Fruit edible.

*Plum, Japanese
Prunus salicina   E   6-9   Medium-size deciduous tree; to 20 ft.; dwarf available.
                                                                Uprightform. Showy white flowers. Use as screen or interest
                                                                plant. Fruit edible.

*Pomegranate
Punica granatum   E   9, 10   Deciduous shrub or small tree; to 20 ft. Leaves have bronzy
                                                                new growth, turn yellow in fall; flowers red and showy. Use
                                                                as multistemmed tree, large shrub, and interest plant. Fruit
                                                                edible.

*Pomelo (shaddock)
Citrus maxima   E   9-11   Rounded evergreen tree; to 30 ft. Attractive foliage and dec
                                                                orative fruit. Use as screen and interest plant. Fruit edible.

*Prickly pear
Opuntia and *Nopalea* species E   6-11   Large cactus; to 15 ft. Thorny pads. Flowers orange or yel
                                                                low, showy. Use as interest or barrier plant. Fruit and pad
                                                                edible.

*Quince
Cydonia oblonga   E   5-9   Small deciduous tree; to 20 ft. Pale pink showy flowers. Use
                                                                as interest tree or shrub, screen. Fruit edible.

*Rhubarb
Rheum Rhabarbarum   E   1-9   Perennial herb; to 5 ft tall. Large dramatic leaves and red
                                                                stems. Use as interest plant in herbaceous borders. Stalk edi
                                                                ble.

Rose hips
Rosa species   2-9   Deciduous shrub to 8 ft. Lovely crinkled leaves; showy white,
                                                                red, or pink flowers. Can get invasive. Use as barrier, hedge,
                                                                and interest plant. Hips edible.

Salal
Gaultheria Shallon   6-9   Evergreen shrub; to 6 ft. Small leaves, attractive white to pink
                                                                flowers. Use as hedge or in shrub border. Fruit edible.

Sapote
Casimiroa edulis   s, 15;   10   Large evergreen tree; to 50 ft. Use as shade tree and screen.
                                48   Fruit plants, edible.

Sea grape
Coccoloba Uvifera   10-11   Small evergreen tree or shrub; to 20 ft. Large decorative
                                                                leaves and attractive fruit. Use as windbreak, in seaside gar
                                                                dens, as hedge and interest tree. Fruit edible.

*Sorrel
Rumex species   E   5-9   Small herbaceous plant; to 3 ft. Upright growth. Use for herb
                                                                gardens and perennial borders. Can become a weed. Leaf
                                                                edible.

*Strawberry
Fragaria species | E | 3-10 | Herbaceous perennials; most have runners; 9 in. tall. Handsome foliage, decorative fruit. Use in flower beds and as ground cover. Fruit edible.

Strawberry tree
Arbutus llnedo | s, 1, 15; plants, 48 | 8, 9 | Lovely evergreen tree; to 30 ft. Attractive pinkish flowers, showy orange and scarlet fruits of variable quality. Use as screen, multistemmed tree, and interest plant. Fruit edible.

Surinam cherry
(pitanga) *Eugenia uniflora* | | 10-11 | Shrub or small tree; to 15 ft. Showy red or yellow fruits. Use as hedge, screen, multistemmed interest plant. Fruit edible.

Tamarind
Tamarindus indica | s, 2, 15, 36; plants,48 | 10-11 | Evergreen tree; to 80 ft. Ornamental pinnate leaves and yellow flowers. Shade tree. Pod edible.

*Tangelo
Citrus paradisi x *Citrus reticulata* | E | 9, 10 | Evergreen tree or shrub; to 30 ft. Attractive foliage, colorful fruit. Use as screen, hedge, interest plant. Fruit edible.

*Tea
Camellia sinensis | | 8-10 | Variable-size (to 15 ft.) evergreen shrub or tree. Shiny green foliage, showy white flowers. Use as hedge, interest plant. Leaf edible.

Tree tomato
Cyphomandra betacea | 15,36, | 10 | Evergreen shrub or small tree; to 10 ft. Large leaves, colorful fruits. Awkward form. Landscape use limited. Fruit edible.

*Walnut
Juglans species | E | 3-9 | Large deciduous tree; to 80 ft. Use as shade and street tree. Nut edible.

Water Chestnut
Eleocharis dulcus | E | 7-11 | Herbaceous reedlike water plant; to 3 ft. tall. Use in pools and water containers. Corm edible.

Herbs, Spices, and Condiments-Perennials

COMMON AND LATIN NAME	SOURCES+	HARDINESS	NOTES
Angelica *Angelica Archangelica*	s, 45; plants, 45	Hardy	Tall, tropical-looking plant; to 6 ft. Compound green leaves, white flowers in large umbels. Biennial or perennial plant. Use as background in herb garden or flower bed. Stem edible.
*Bay, California *Umbellularia californica*	E	Tender	Large evergreen tree; to 80 ft. Small leaves, bushy form. Use as street or shade tree. Leaf edible.
*Bay, sweet *Laurus nobilis*	E	Moderately hardy	Evergreen tree or shrub; to 40 ft. Glossy green leaves. Use as hedge, shrub, or small tree. Leaf edible.
Bee balm *Monarda didyma*	s, 26,36, 45	Hardy	Upright, bushy plant; 3-4 ft. tall. Showy red, pink, or lavender flowers. Use in herb and flower gardens. Leaf edible.
Burnet *Poterium sanguisorba*	s, 36,45, 49,65	Hardy	Decorative small plant; to 18 in. Leaves grow in a rosette; pinkish flowers. Use in herb and flower gardens. Can become a weed. Leaf edible.
Caper *Capparis spinosa*		Tender	Sprawling, large shrub; to 5 ft. Roundish leaves; flowers white with showy pink or lavender stamens. Use in large rock gardens and on dry banks. Flower bud edible.
Catnip *Nepeta Cataria*	Readily available	Hardy	Medium-size, spreading plant; to 3 ft. Gray-green leaves, lavender flowers. Pretty in herb gardens, but attracts neighborhood cats to come roll in your garden. Leaf edible.

*Chamomile, Roman *Chamaemelum nobile*	E	Hardy	Low-growing, spreading mat; to 12 in. Fine-cut leaves; small, buttonlike yellow flowers. Can be used as ground cover and in rock gardens. Flower edible.
Chicory *Cichorium Intybus*	s, 49,53	Hardy	Tall, rangy, gray-green plant; to 4 ft. Blue dandelionlike flowers. Use in back of flower gardens. Can become a weed. Leaf and root edible.
*Chive *Allium* species	E	Hardy	Tubular, grasslike leaves in clumps; to 2 ft. Attractive, cloverlike lavender or white flowers. Use in herb garden or flower border. Leaf edible.
Comfrey, Russian *Symphytum* peregrinum	16,29,48	Hardy	Large, attractive, leafed plant; to 3 ft. Use in herb garden. Leaf edible.
Costmary *Chrysanthemum Balsamita*	18,45	Hardy	Straggly plant; to 3 ft. Gray-green leaves, tiny yellow flowers. Keep trimmed; use in herb garden. Will spread. Leaf edible.
Geranium *Pelargonium* species	s, 36,49; plants, 65	Tender	Variable plants-some upright, some vining; some have gray-green leaves, others have variegated ones. Flowers red, pink, or lavender. Use in herb gardens. Leaf edible.
Horehound *Marrubium vulgare*	s, 36, 49,53	Semi-hardy	Small, gray, round, fuzzy-leafed plant; to 18 in. Small white flowers. Can look rangy. Use in herb gardens. Leaf edible.
Horseradish *Armoracia rusticana*	Readily available	Hardy	Stout, wavy-edged, leafed plant; to 15 in. Not particularly attractive; can get weedy. Landscaping use limited. Root edible.
Lemon balm *Melissa officinalis*	s, 36,45; plants, 18,65	Hardy	Erect plant; to 2 ft. Mintlike leaves, flowers insignificant. Use in herb gardens. Leaf edible.
Licorice *Glycyrrhiza glabra*	65	Tender	Medium-size, upright-growing plant; to 3 ft. Attractive small, cut leaves; small light-blue, pealike flowers. Use in herb gardens. Root edible.
Lovage *Levisticum officinale*	Readily available	Hardy	Large, upright plant; to 6 ft. Celerylike leaves, yellow flowers in umbels. Ornamental; good for back of herb gardens. Leaf edible.
*Marjoram *Origanum Majorana*	E	Semi-hardy	Short plant; to 2 ft. Tiny gray-green leaves, small white flowers. Use in herb gardens. Leaf edible.
*Mint *Mentha* species	E	Most are hardy	Most mints are erect, medium-size plants 1/2-3 ft. tall, with crinkled leaves, white or lavender flowers. One variety with a creeping mat form is good for ground cover. Use upright forms in herb gardens. Can become invasive. Leaf edible.
*Oregano *Origanum vulgare*	E	Hardy	Upright plant; to 2 1/2 ft. Medium size, gray-green leaves; lavender flowers. Use in herb gardens. Leaf edible.
*Rosemary *Rosmarinus officinalis*	E	Semi-hardy	Evergreen shrub with gray-green needlelike leaves. Different varieties have different shapes, from erect, 6 ft. tall, to ground hugging. Showy blue flowers on some varieties. Use on dry banks and in herb gardens. Leaf edible.
*Saffron *Crocus sativus*	E	Hardy	Small grasslike foliage; to 4 in. Large mauve flowers. Use in rock garden, flower border, and herb garden. Stigma edible.
*Sage *Salvia* species	E	Varied	Small, shrubby plants; to 2-3 1/2 ft. Most with gray-green leaves, red or blue flowers. Use in herb garden or flower garden. Leaf edible.
Savory, winter *Satureja montana*	Readily available	Hardy	Small, erect, green-leafed shrub; to 12 in. Small white flowers. Use in herb gardens. Leaf edible.
Sweet woodruff *Galium odoratum*	s ; plants, 18,65	Hardy	Ornamental low-growing plant; to 12 in. Lovely deep-green leaves, clusters of tiny white flowers. Use as ground cover in shady places. Leaf edible.
Tarragon, French *Artemisia dracunculus*	45	Tender	Creeping narrow-leafed plant; to 2 ft. Use in herb garden. Preferred French variety only available as cuttings, not seed, from (42). Leaf edible.
*Thyme *Thymus* species	E	Hardy	A number of very small-leafed plants; to 15 in. Various foliage colors-yellow, variegated, silver, green. Use as ground covers and in herb gardens. Leaf edible.
Turmeric *Curcuma domestica*	Specialty produce markets	Tender	Rhizomatous, tropical-looking plant; to 1-1/2 ft. Attractive leaves. Use in shady borders and containers. Rhizome edible.

| Wintergreen *Gaultheria procumbens* | 52 | Hardy | Ornamental creeping plant; 6 in. tall. Dark-green, shiny leaves; white flowers and scarlet berries. Use as ground cover in shade. Leaf and berry edible. |

Annuals, and Perennials Commonly Treated as Annuals, Planted for Food

COMMON AND LATIN NAME	SOURCES+	NOTES
Amaranth (Chinese spinach) *Amaranthus gangeticus*	s, 1,45,51,53	Tall, upright, succulent green- or red leafed plant; to 3 ft. Cloverlike blossoms. Ornamental plant. Use in the background of perennial borders. Leaf edible.
Asparagus bean (Chinese yard-long bean) *Vigna sinensis sesquipedalis*	s,21,24,38,63,71	Tall, vining plant with medium-green leaves. Insignificant flowers. Very long beans, to 3 ft. Limited landscape use; can be used on trellises. Pod edible.
Asparagus pea (Goa bean or winged bean) *Lotus tetragonolobus*	s, 24,49,66	Short twining herb; to 1 ft. Beanlike bright red flowers. Attractive plant. Use in hanging baskets and in front of flower beds. Pod edible.
Bean, fava (broad bean) *Vicia Faba*	s, 29,60	Erect plant; to 6 ft. Gray-green leaves, fragrant white flowers. Dwarf available. Attractive plant, but can get straggly. Use in back of flower borders. Leaf and seed edible.
Bean, garbanzo (chick pea) *Cicer arietinum*	s, 37,42	Bushy plant; to 2 ft. Undistinguished. Limited landscape use. Seed edible.
*****Bean**, green snap (bush) *Phaseolus vulgaris humilis*	E	Small (to 2 ft.), open, bushy plant. White or purple leguminous flowers. Some varieties are more ornamental than others. Purple varieties are attractive in flower borders. Pod edible.
*****Bean, green** snap, kidney, pinto, romano, and wax (pole) *Phaseolus vulgaris*	E	Vining plant; to 6 ft. Most varieties have small white flowers; some have large white or purple flowers. Some varieties have decorative red, yellow, or purple pods. Use decorative varieties on arbors, fences, and trellises. Pod and seed edible.
Bean, hyacinth (Bonavista bean) *Dolichos Lablab*	Locally available	Large woody climber; to 20 ft. Attractive available purple flowers and pods. Use on arbors and trellises. Pod and seed edible.
Bean, lima (bush) *Phaseolus limensis* var. *limenanus*	Readily available	Small, bushy plant; to 2 ft. Undistinguished. Use limited in landscape. Seed edible.
Bean, lima (pole) *Phaseolus limensis*	Readily available	Vigorous vine; to 6 ft. Undistinguished. Use on trellis or screen for color, inter-plant with morning glories. Seed edible.
Bean, mung *Vigna radiata*	s,37,63,71	Hairy bushy plant; to 3 ft. Small, purplish yellow flowers. Undistinguished. Limited landscape use. Seed edible.
*****Bean, runner** *Phaseolus coccineus*	E	Tall, twining vine; to 10 ft. Showy red or white leguminous flowers. Decorative on fences, arbors, and trellises. Pod and seed edible.
Bean, soy *Glycine Max*	Readily available	Hairy; grows 1-6 ft. Undistinguished. Limited landscape use. Seed edible.
*****Beet** *Beta vulgaris*	E	Short (to 18 in.) herbaceous plant with red veined green leaves. Yellow and white varieties available. Attractive, but hard to use in a landscape. Harvested beets leave empty spaces; try interplanting with flowering annuals to cover the holes after harvest. Leaf and root edible.
Black-eyed pea (cow pea) *Vigna unguiculata*	Readily available	Small bushy plant; to 3 ft. Undistinguished. Limited landscape use. Seed edible.
Broccoli *Brassica oleracea*-Botrytis Group	Readily available	Short (to 2 1/2 ft.), compact plant with gray green leaves. Some varieties have purple flower buds. Somewhat decorative, but hard to keep looking neat. Limited landscape use. Use in containers. Flower and stem edible.

Brussels sprouts *Brassica oleracea*-Gemmifera Group	Readily available	Awkward-looking, blue-green leafed plant; to 3 ft. Harvesting sprouts makes plant look scruffy. Limited landscape use. Leaf edible.
Buckwheat *Fagopyrum esculentum*	s,5,37	Triangular-leafed plant; to 3 ft. Small clusters of fragrant white flowers. Landscape use limited. Use in informal yard adjacent to a meadow. Seed edible.
Burdock (gobo) *Arctium Lappa*	s,38,54	Tall plant; to 8 ft. Leaves 20 in. long. Harvested primarily for its root; use in vegetable garden. Can become a weed. Leaf and root edible.
*****Cabbage** - *Brassica oleracea*or Capatata Group	E	Compact (to 2 ft.), large-leafed plant; grows in tight head. Gray red foliage. Attractive form. Useful in flower beds and red foliage. Attractive form. Useful in flower beds and red foliage. Attractive form. Useful in flower beds and containers. Leaf edible.
Cabbage, Chinese (Pe Tsai) *Brassica Rapa*- Pekinensis Group	E	Compact, glossy-green plant; to 20 in. Growth similar to chard. Use in herbaceous borders with other greens. Leaf edible.
*****Cantaloupe** (melons) *Cucumis* species	E	Trailing vines, 5 ft. long; dwarf available. Attractive ivylike leaves. Dwarf varieties used in flower borders; vining types used on fences. Mildew can make them scruffy looking. Fruit edible.
*****Carrot** *Daucus Carota* var. *sativus*	E	Graceful, ferny foliage; to 1 ft. Plant attractive, but hard to use in landscape. Harvested carrots leave empty spaces. Try in containers or interplant with violas or other flowering annuals. Root edible.
Cauliflower - *Brassica oleracea* Botrytis Group	Readily available	Short (to 2 ft.), compact plant with wide green leaves. Compact flowerhead forms a ball. Blanching of the head and its tendency to flop over makes its use limited in a landscape. Try in containers. Flower edible.
Celeriac *Apium graveolens* var.	Readily available	Open plant; to 3 ft. Attractive pinnate leaves. Limited landscaping use. Harvesting leaves empty spaces. Use in containers or *rapaceum* interplant with nasturtiums. Swollen crown edible.
Celery *Apium graveolens* var. *dulce*	Readily available	Upright plant; to 3 ft. Attractive bright green, pinnate leaves. Blanching and harvesting of individual stalks deforms plant. Use in the background or in containers. Leaf and stem edible.
*****Chard, Swiss** *Beta vulgaris* var. *cida*	E	Handsome, large, foliage plant; to 18 in. Red-stemmed varieties very attractive. Use in flower beds. Leaf edible.
Collard *Brassica oleracea*- Acephala Group	Readily available	Compact foliage plant; to 18 in. Use in landscape combined with other greens in herbaceous borders. Leaf edible.
Corn (and popcorn) *Zea Mays*	Readily available	Tall, broad-leafed grass; to 15 ft.; dwarf varieties available. Hard to use in a landscape; dwarf types have some possibilities as background plants in informal gardens. Seed edible.
Corn salad (lambs lettuce) *Valerianella Locusta*	s, 12,26,57	Compact foliage plant; to 1 1/2 ft. tall. Use in landscape combined with lettuces in herbaceous borders. Leaf edible
*****Cucumber** (Armenian, bush, pickling) *Cucumis sativus*	E	Trailing vines with ivylike leaves; to 6 ft. Bush varieties available. common, Oriental, and Trailing types used on trellises and fences; bush types used in flower gardens. Fruit edible
Dandelion *Taraxacum officinale*	Readily available	Compact plant with long leaves; to 1 ft. Can be interplanted with greens in an herbaceous border. If it is to be blanched, it should be relegated to the vegetable garden. Can become a weed (surprise!). Leaf edible.
*****Eggplant** *Solanum Melongena* var. *esculentum*	E	Compact bush to 3 ft. tall with fuzzy gray-green foliage; some varieties have purple stems. Handsome purple flowers and glossy purple or white fruit. Very ornamental. Use in herbaceous borders and herb gardens. Fruit edible.
*****Endive**, chicory, curly, and escarole *Cichorium* species	E	Attractive, compact (to 2 ft. tall), foliage plants with large variety of foliage textures and colors. Use in herbaceous borders with other greens. Leaf edible.

Fennel *Foeniculum vulgare* var. *azoricum*	Readily available	Fernlike foliage; to 5 ft. Rounded clusters available of yellow flowers. Use in back of herbaceous borders. Can become a weed. Leaf edible.
Ground cherry (dwarf Cape gooseberry) *Physalis pruinosa*	s,20,37	Sprawling, bushy plant; to 3 ft. Fruits have papery husks. Limited landscape use. Fruit edible.
Huckleberry, garden *Solanum melanocerasum*	s,16,24,29,62	Undistinguished plant; to 2 1/2 ft. Small white flowers and black berries. Rangy plant with limited landscaping use. Can become a weed. Fruit edible.
Husk tomato (tomatillo) *Physalis ixocarpa*	s, 33,45,53	Upright plant; to 4 ft. Weak stemmed and tends to sprawl; needs staking. Landscaping use limited. Fruit edible.
***Kale** *Brassica oleracea-* Acephala Group	E	Compact (to 20 in.) plant with decorative foliage; pink and white ornamental varieties available. Use in herbaceous borders. Leaf edible.
Kohlrabi - *Brassica oleracea* Gongylodes Group	Readily available	Low (to 20 in. tall), leafy plant with available bulbous stem. Some varieties have purple coloring. Landscaping use limited. Harvesting leaves empty spaces, and the form is awkward. Stem edible.
Leek *Allium ampeloprasum* var. *porrum*	Readily available	Narrow-leafed plant with handsome fanlike form. Landscaping use limited. Harvesting leaves empty spaces. Try containers or interplant with forget-me-nots or other flowering annuals. Bulb and leaf edible.
Lentil *Lens culinaris*	s, 36	Many-branched open plant; to 1','i ft. tall. Interesting small pinnate foliage. Attractive, but tends to become sprawly. Limited landscaping use. Seed edible.
***Lettuce**, curly, head, and romaine *Lactuca sativa*	E	Short, compact (6-12 in. tall), leafy plant; many textures and colors available. Use in herbaceous borders. Keep new plants coming to fill in harvested sections. Leaf edible.
***Melon, casaba, honeydew** *Cucumis* species	E	Trailing vines; to 5 ft. long; dwarf varieties available. Dwarf varieties used in flower borders; vining types used on fences. Attractive ivylike leaves. Mildew can make them scruffy. Fruit edible.
***Mustard, black** *Brassica nigra*	E	Large, upright plant; to 6 ft. Bright yellow flowers. Attractive in meadow garden. Can become a weed in confined situations. Seed edible.
***Mustard green** *Brassica juncea*	E	Compact (to 18 in. tall), leafy plant with attractive foliage; numerous forms. Combine with greens in an herbaceous border. Leaf edible.
Oat *Avena sativa*	s,5,28,37 health food stores	Tall grass; to 3 ft. Landscape use limited to informal yards adjacent to meadows. Seed edible.
***Okra** (gumbo) *Abelmoschus esculentus*	E	Tall, upright plant; to 6 ft.; dwarf varieties available. Large leaves and lovely hibiscus type cream or yellow flowers. One variety has red stems. Use in herbaceous borders. Pod edible.
***Onion, scallion,** and shallot *Allium Cepa*	E	Tubular, upright plant; to 18 in. Gray-green leaves. Limited landscaping use. Bulb types must die down before being harvested. Harvesting scallion types leaves empty spaces. Try in containers or interplanting with dwarf nasturtiums or marigolds. Bulb edible.
Orach *Atriplex hortensis*	s,28,45,55	Tall, upright, showy plant; to 5 ft. Leaves usually green but can be bright red or yellow. Use in back of herbaceous borders. Leaf edible.
Parsnip *Pastinaca saliva*	Readily available	Short (to 18 in.), clumping plant with cut leaves. Landscaping use limited. Harvesting leaves empty spaces; try containers or interplanting with flowering annuals. Root edible.
***Pea** (bush) *Pisum sativum*	Readily available	Bushy, sprawling plant; to 2 ft. Gray green foliage, white flowers. Mildew occasionally disfigures foliage. Landscaping use limited. Seed edible.
***Pea** (pole)* *Pisum sativum*	Readily available	Large, twining vine; to 6 ft. Gray-green foliage, white flowers. Landscaping use limited. Mildew occasionally disfigures foliage. Seed edible.

*Pea, snow (bush) (Chinese pea pod) *Pisum sativum var macrocarpon*	E	Bushy, sprawling plant; to 2 ft. Gray green foliage, white or purple flowers. Mildew occasionally disfigures foliage. Purple-flowered variety attractive in herbaceous borders. Pod edible.
*Pea, snow (pole) (Chinese pea pod) *Pisum sativum var. macrocarpon*	E	Large, twining vine; to 6 ft. Gray-green foliage, white flowers. Landscaping use limited. Mildew occasionally disfigures foliage. Pod edible.
*Peanut (goober) *Arachis hypogaea*	E	Compact plant; to 2 ft. Cut leaves and yellow flowers attractive. Use for temporary ground covers. Seed edible.
*Pepper, sweet, chili, Tabasco *Capsicum* species	E	Ornamental, upright plant; to 3 ft. Decorative red or yellow fruits. Use in herbaceous borders and in containers. Fruit edible.
*Potato *Solanum tuberosum*	E	Ornamental, dark-green-leafed, sprawling plant; to 2 ft. Landscape use limited. Vines must turn yellow and die down before harvesting. Try containers. Tuber edible.
*Radish and daikon *Raphanus sativus*	E	Short, clumping plant; to 12 in. Landscaping use limited. Harvesting and very short life leave empty spaces. Try interplanting with sweet alyssum. Root and tuber edible.
Rutabaga (swede) *Brassica Napus*-Napobrassica Group	Readily available	Clumping plant, to 20 in. tall, interesting foliage. Landscape use limited. Harvesting leaves empty spaces; try containers or interplanting with petunias or other flowering annuals. Root edible.
Rye *Secale cereale*	s,5, health food stores	Tall grass; to 5 ft. Landscape use limited. Try using it in informal yards adjacent to meadows. Seed edible.
Salsify (oyster plant) *Tragopogon porrifolius*	Readily available	Upright, grasslike, leafed plant; to 2 ft. Limited landscaping use. Can become a weed. Root edible.
Sesame *Sesamum indicum*	s,12,28,45,49	Upright plant; to 3 ft. Pleasant foliage, white or pink flowers. Use in herbaceous borders. Seed edible.
*Spinach, common *Spinacia oleracea*	E	Small foliage plant, to 2 ft., with a rosette form. Use with other greens in an herbaceous border. Spinach has a short growing season. Try interplanting with flowering annuals to prevent holes in the garden. Leaf edible.
*Spinach, New Zealand *Tetragonia tetragonioides*	E	Fleshy-leafed, sprawling, ornamental plant; to 2 ft. Use in hanging baskets and over walls. Leaf edible.
*Squash, summer and zucchini *Cucurbita Pepo* var. *melopepo*	E	Large (to 2 ft.), prickly, deep-green leaves. Most varieties are bushlike and have strong, upright growth; to 3 ft. Some varieties have showy yellow flowers. Can become mildewed. Use in herbaceous borders. Fruit edible.
Squash, winter, pumpkin *Cucurbita* species	Readily available	Large, sprawling vines; to 12 ft. Some varieties have ornamental flowers and fruits. Plants usually become yellow and withered-looking before harvest. Rampant vines generally unmanageable in the average landscape. Fruit edible.
Sunflower *Helianthus annuus*	Readily available	Tall, upright-growing plant; to 10 ft. Giant yellow flowers. Unwieldy. Seed edible.
*Sweet potato (yam) *Ipomoea Batatas*	E	Large, attractive, spreading vines; to 1 1/2 ft. tall. Blooms occasionally, pink flowers. Use to spill over a wall or as temporary ground cover. Tuber edible.
*Tomato *Lycopersicon Lycopersicum*	E	Tall, sprawling, upright vine; to 6 ft. Cut leaves, decorative red or yellow fruits. Small varieties available. Use in hanging baskets and on fences. Fruit edible.
Turnip *Brassica Rapa*-Rasifera Group	Readily available	Short, clumping plant; to 18 in. Limited landscape use. Harvesting leaves empty spaces. Try containers or interplanting with dwarf nasturtiums or pansies. Root and leaf edible.
Watercress *Nasturtium officinale*	s,12,49	An aquatic plant to 6 in. with attractive foliage. Landscape use limited to stream sides. Can become a weed. Leaf edible.
*Watermelon *Citrullus lanatus*	E	Ivy-leafed, sprawling vines; to 10 ft. Dwarf plants available. Large varieties unwieldy; small varieties ornamental, hanging over retaining walls or trained on a fence. Fruit edible.
Wheat, bread *Triticum aestivum*	s,5,37	Tall grass; to 4 ft. Landscaping use limited. Try planting in health food stores informal yards adjacent to meadows. Seed edible.

Wild rice *Zizania aquatica*		Tall aquatic grass; to 10 ft. Landscape use limited to lakes and streamsides. Seed edible.
Winged bean (Goa bean) *Psophocarpus tetragonolobus*	s,15	Tall tropical vine; to 10 ft. Experimental in the United States, probably best in Florida. Use on arbor or fence. Seed, leaf, and tuber edible.

Herbs, Spices, and Condiments-Annuals, Perennials Commonly Treated as Annuals, and Biennials

COMMON AND LATIN NAME	SOURCES+	NOTES
Anise *Pimpinella Anisum*	Readily available	Dainty, cut-leaf plant to 2 ft. Flowers white, in small umbels. Use in an herb garden or a flower bed. Seed edible.
*****Basil** *Ocimum Basilicum*	E	Upright, shiny green-leafed plant; to 2 ft. White flowers. Purple-leafed varieties with pink flowers are available. Use in herb garden or flower bed. Leaf edible.
***Borage** *Borago officinalis*	E	Large, prickly, gray-green leafed plant; to 2 ft. Bears handsome blue flowers in clusters. Use in herb garden or flower bed. Can become a weed. Leaf and flower edible.
Caraway *Carum Carvi*	Readily available	Many-branched biennial; to 2 ft. Decorative pinnate leaves, white flowers in umbels. Use in herb garden or flower bed. Seed edible.
***Chamomile**, sweet false (German) *Matricaria recutita*	E	Medium-size, ferny, spreading plant; to 2 1/2 ft. Small, daisylike flowers. Use in herb garden or flower bed. flower edible.
Chervil *Anthriscus Cerefolium*	Readily available	Small, parsley-leafed plant; to 2 ft. Ornamental foliage. Use in a shaded herb garden or flower bed. Leaf edible.
Chia *Salvia hispanica*	s,33,49	Small, delicate-looking plant; to 20 in. Small blue flowers stand above leaf clusters. Use for dry rock gardens. Seed edible.
Coriander *Coriandrum sativum*	Readily available	Medium-size, graceful plant; to 3 ft. Compound leaves, small white flowers in umbels. Use in herb garden or flower bed. Leaf and seed edible.
Cumin *Cuminum Cyminum*	Readily available,	Tiny plant with threadlike leaves; height, 6 in. Flowers white or pink in small umbels. Use in front in herb garden or flower bed. Seed edible.
Dill *Anethum graveolens*	Readily available dwarf available s,18,49	Medium-size plant; to 3 ft.; dwarf available. Ferny threadlike foliage, yellow dwarf flowers in umbels. Use in herb garden or flower bed. Seed and leaf edible.
Garlic *Allium sativum*	Readily available	Tubular, upright plant to 2 ft., gray-green leaves. Awkward-looking plant; becomes unkempt; must die down before harvesting. Limited landscape use. Bulb edible.
Ginger *Zingiber officinale*		Perennial rhizome, usually planted as an annual. Tall, upright stems grow to 4 ft. and have grasslike leaves. Flower insignificant. Pleasant foliage plant for shady borders. Rhizome edible.
***Nasturtium** *Tropaeolum* species	E	Climbing vine, to 10 ft., with round leaves and bright red, yellow, or orange flowers. Dwarf bush varieties available. Very ornamental. Use in hanging baskets, on fences; bush types in flower gardens. Flower, bud, and leaf edible.
***Parsley** *Petroselinum crispum*	E	Compact, curly-leafed, dark-green, biennial plant; 18 in. to 3 ft. \ Use in herb garden or flower bed. Leaf edible.
Savory, summer *Satureja hortensis*	Readily available	Small, upright, bushy, somewhat hairy, green plant; to 18 in. high. Small lavender flowers. Use in herb garden and flower bed. Leaf edible.

APPENDIX B
SOURCES OF EDIBLE PLANTS

How to Obtain Plant Materials

Plants are available from many sources: a gardening friend or neighbor, horticultural organizations, supermarkets and discount stores, and local and mail-order nurseries. From your friends and horticultural societies the plants will come as seeds, cuttings, or divisions. From commercial sources you can buy them as seeds, started seedlings, tubers, and bare-root or container plants. The information in this section will help you find a wide variety of healthy plants at a reasonable price. Included, in addition to the commonly available edible plants, are old-fashioned vegetables and fruits that are no longer commercially available but that can be found outside the usual channels, and varieties that are commercially available but difficult to obtain. Nearly every plant mentioned in this book is available from at least one of the sources given in this section or in the encyclopedia.

Storing and Saving

One of the great joys of gardening is sharing our bounty with others. Whether we give or receive these edible plants, the plants will be acclimated to our area, will have been proven successful, and sometimes will be a variety that is no longer commercially available. The extra seed from an old-time bean that Aunt Folly grew or budding stock from an out-of-fashion fruit tree can add diversity to a garden. Many edibles are plants that need dividing, so there are many opportunities to pick up an artichoke plant, Jerusalem artichoke tubers, or a creeping rhizome of a banana.

Many edible plants set great quantities of seed that most gardeners enjoy sharing. But remember that no matter how delicious the product or how sturdy the plant, if it is from hybrid seed it is usually not worth saving or givingæthat seed will not develop the plant you want next year. Many commercial seeds are now hybrids because of their improved hardiness, a special flavor quality, or a particular growth habit. Plants designated as hybrid or F-1 hybrid on the seed package cannot reliably reproduce themselves. Hybrid seed is produced by crossing parents with different characteristics and this same combination of parents must be continually rebred to produce the hybrid offspring. Another group of plants to avoid when saving seed is the cucurbit family (the cucumbers, melons, pumpkins, gourds, and squashes). Unless planted in complete isolation these plants cross-pollinate with each other and produce strange second generations.

However, many plants do have open-pollinated varieties that will come true from seed. Seeds of plants that can be saved because they will come true from seed are beans, peas, and carrots, as well as select cultivars of many other vegetables. If you have a favorite, share it and cherish it. Some seed companies also make a point of providing a good selection of varieties of seed whose second generation can be saved by the homeowner. They are: (1,7,32, 40,57,60,62,64).

To save money, you can also grow fruit and nut trees from seed. These trees take a few years longer to bear and will give a variable productæsometimes better than the parent, sometimes worse, and sometimes the same. Or you can grow your seedling tree and then graft onto it wood from a known cultivar. For information on growing fruit and nut trees from seed and for grafting and budding, see relevant titles in the bibliography. Its also worthwhile to join the fruit and nut societies named in Appendix C, as they are knowledgeable in this area. Sources of seed for fruit and nut trees are: (15,36, 37,60,63).

A pamphlet called *Growing Garden Seeds*, by Robert Johnston, Jr., available from (40), is a valuable source of information on seed saving.

Caution: No matter what the form of the shared cropæseeds, cuttings, or divisionsæbe sure the source is disease free. Virus-infected bean seeds or strawberry roots with nematodes are no bargain. If you save your own seed you must keep only seed that is healthy. Learn to identify virus symptoms in plants (see Part Two) and discard seed from plants so affected. Commercial plants are usually pest free because they have been grown under controlled conditions, and have been inspected or handled by people who know how to recognize the problems.

Horticultural Organizations and Seed Exchanges

Horticultural organizations are excellent sources for obtaining antique or unusual edibles. Membership in these organizations is usually required to receive their products, but the dues are minimal and the advantages are many. Besides offering uncommon seeds, or scion or budwood, they usually publish newsletters and offer cultural and historical material on plants of interest.

A popular way of obtaining seed is through seed exchangesæpublished lists of gardeners willing to share their seeds. Two of the sources listed at the end of this appendix (36,60) offer this service, as do some of the gardening magazines and a number of organizations devoted to different aspects of food growing, including:

California Rare Fruit Growers, Inc.,

Home Orchard Society,

North American Fruit Explorers. (See Appendix C for addresses.)

There is one organization devoted solely to the exchange of seeds: Seed Savers Exchange, c/o Kent Whealy, 203 Rural Ave., Decorah, Iowa 52101.

State Forestry and Agricultural Departments

Many states have programs to encourage tree planting and provide young trees for reforesting woodland areas and for erosion control at a nominal fee. Inquire at your local extension service office to see if there is such a program in your area. This service is aimed not at homeowners who want to put in one or two trees, but at those who need a number of trees to help control erosion or to establish woodland or windbreak areas.

Cut-Rate Plants

In general, the plants sold at local discount houses, groceries, and hardware stores cannot be considered good buys. These plants usually have been given only sporadic care, with minimal attention to their light requirements and pest problems. The salespeople in these stores usually cannot give you advice on care or suitability.

These stores sometimes carry inferior seeds and occasionally indulge in some questionable practices. For example, they will sell at "bargain" prices rose bushes that were originally used for florist production and have consequently lost their vigor. These discounted plants may also have many health problems. In plants, as in other things, the old adage holds true: you get what you pay for.

A Word About Nurseries

Nurseries, both local and mail-order, reflect the people who run them some are honorable and well informed, some are not. Most are run by people who love plants and want you to have a successful garden. They take courses to keep current. Well-informed neighborhood nursery people are aware of local soil, pest, and climate problems and new plant introductions. They often know the best variety for your areaæplants resistant to diseases in your area or that have been bred for local soil conditions. They take pride in their knowledge and sell a superior product.

On the other hand, most mail-order houses will not know your area well. You must do your homework diligently to see which species and varieties grow well in your area. If you live in Florida and order a peach variety that has a high chilling requirement, you will probably be sent that variety and it will not do well. Mail-order nurseries seldom have information specific to your area.

Why do people use mail-order firms? Because they offer a much larger selection of plants than any local nursery could provide. Just remember that you must take the responsibility for learning about a plant's usefulness in your area.

Note: To help control pests and diseases, many states have laws covering the importation of plants. Some plants, such as currants, are banned altogether in a few states. Inspection requirements or agricultural crop protection in a state determines if the mail-order nursery can send you what you want. Read the catalog carefully; it usually tells what can be sent where.

Local Retail Nurseries

The average local nursery is your most valuable plant source because it has information for your area, is handy, and enables you to pick out merchandise yourself. Following are some things to notice in judging a nursery:

Do the plants look healthy?

Do they sell plants for the wrong season? For example, are they selling marigold or pepper plants a month before frost is due? (Seeds do not seem to be sold for a particular season. Seeds for all seasons are often sold at one time, so, again, do your homework.)

Will they order things for you?

Is the person behind the counter able to give you information about the plant you buy?

Do they continually push chemical pesticides and herbicides?

The majority of local nurseries carry deciduous fruit trees and a few perennial vegetables such as asparagus and artichokes in bare-root form during late winter and early spring. Bare root is the least expensive and most beneficial way to buy these plants. Some nurseries will give you a 10-20 percent discount if you order your fruit trees in the fall before they put in their order to the wholesaler.

Many of the retail nurseries I have visited around the country have two shortcomings. The first is their lack of knowledge about edibles, ornamental edibles in particular. This is primarily due to the fact that inedible ornamentals have been stressed by the industry as well as by customers for the last 20 or 30 years. Second, information about garden chemicals (pesticides, fungicides, herbicides, and fertilizers) is not always balanced with information about nonchemical alternatives. The reason for this one-sidedness is that much of the nurseries' knowledge about pest control comes from the companies selling the chemicals. Moreover, money is made when a pesticide is sold to control aphids, whereas an alternative method of control, such as spraying with a heavy jet of water, would entail no sale. The temptation, therefore, is for the nursery to recommend the pesticide.

When you find a good nursery, frequent it and appreciate it. Like a good car mechanic or dentist, it is a valuable resource.

Mail-Order Nurseries

The many mail-order nurseries in the United States are a valuable resource for the home gardener. They are a varied group. There are nurseries like Stark Brothers that specialize in a wide selection of fruit trees, and the grandfather of the mail-order seed business, the Burpee Seed Company, which sells most seeds for vegetables and flowers. Most nurseries carry standard edibles, but a few, such as Exotica Seed Co. or Kitazawa Seed Co., carry the unusual. There are even bamboo, pistachio, and bean specialty nurseries. Some, Johnny's Selected Seeds and Nichols Garden Nursery, for example, are particularly interested in organic gardening. Peruse the list, and you will find many that interest you.

How to Use a Mail-Order Firm

Write for a catalog; they all have one (some charge a fee that is subject to change). Read it carefully and do your homework. Be leery of "miracle plants." Some mail-order nurseries seem to hire fiction writers to compose their catalogs. There are no climbing strawberries! Zoysia grass is durable and needs little mowingæbut it's also almost impossible to get rid of, and it can eat up your flower or vegetable border. The egg tree is really just a white eggplant. I have included some of these imaginative nurseries on my list because they carry some of the plants not carried by any other source, but let the reader beware.

Most mail-order catalogs come out in late winter or early spring. Write for your catalog early so that you can take advantage of bare-root shipping if possible. Send in your order early so you can be assured of the best and most complete selection.

Most seeds and small plants are sent by first-class mail; the majority of large plants and trees are sent parcel post.

Sources: An Annotated List

The numbers appearing after plants listed in the encyclopedia and under "Sources" in Appendix A refer to the numbers assigned to the following nurseries. For example, the number (10) after 'Ambrosia' cantaloupe indicates it is available from Burpee Seed Company.

1
Abundant Life Seed Foundation
P. 0. Box 772
Port Townsend, WA 98368
    An organization dedicated to preserving heirloom veg-

etables and self-sufficient living. Specializing in plants for the Northwest, it carries many varieties of vegetable, herb, and wildflower seeds.

2
The Banana Tree
715 Northampton St.
Easton, PA 18042
    This nursery carries a large selection of banana plants as well as seed of many tropical and subtropical edibles. Catalog $3.

3
Bear Creek Nursery
P.O. Box 411
Northport, WA 99157
    This nursery specializes in full-size fruit and nut trees for cold climates, including a particularly large selection of apples, filberts, hickory, chestnuts, and walnuts.

4
Boston Mountain Nurseries
Box 405-A, Rt. 2
Mountainburg, AR 72946
    Specialists in berries.

5
Bountiful Gardens
Ecology Action
18001 Shafer Ranch Road
Willits, CA 95490
    A seed company specializing in open-pollinated vegetables and supplies for organic gardeners. In addition to a large selection of vegetables, it carries seeds for herbs, grains, and cover crops.

6
Burnt Ridge Nursery
432 Burnt Ridge Road
Onalaska, WA 98570
    Good selection of nut trees, fruit trees and some ornamentals.

7
Burpee Seed Company
300 Park Avenue
Warminster, PA 18991-0004
    180-page general seed catalog, including flowers, vegetables, garden aids, nursery stock; 10 pages on fruit. Of special interest are 'Dwarf Gray Sugar' peas; tampala; 'Bush Porto Rico' sweet potato; miniature watermelons; Ambrosia' cantaloupe; Oriental persimmon; genetic dwarf fruit trees; filberts; and bush cherries.

8
California Nursery Company
Niles District
Box 2278
Fremont, CA 94536
    Many standard fruit trees plus tender species, including citrus, pomegranate, persimmon, avocado, and some California wine grapes.

9
Chestnut Hill
"Rt. 1, Box 341"
Alachua, FL 32615
    Specializes in chestnuts, persimmons and figs.

10
Columbia Basin Nursery
POB 458
Quincy, WA 98848
    Colored brochure and price list. Seeding rootstock, dwarfing apple rootstock, dwarf and standard budded fruit trees.

11
The Cook's Garden
Box 535
Londonderry, VT 05148
    A seed company that carries numerous superior varieties of vegetables, many of which are European. If you are particularly interested in lettuce, this company carries more varieties than any other.

12
DeGiorgi Company, Inc.
6011 'N' Street
Omaha, NE 69117-1537
    Seed company. Many Italian varieties of vegetables, plus red okra, sorrel, and cardoon.

13
Edible Landscaping Nursery
POB 77
Afton, VA 22920
    This nursery specializes in kiwis, both the standard and hardy types, but also carries many other edibles.

14
Exotica Seed Company
POB 160
Vista, CA 92083
    Seeds of many unusual edibles, including bamboo, pistachio, pinon, kiwi, pineapple guava, pawpaw, unusual chili peppers, black mulberry, pomegranate, prickly pear, olive, carob, persimmon, loquat, and natal plum.

15
F. W. Schumacher Company
36 Spring Hill Rd.
Sandwich, MA 02563
    This company carries only seeds. While it is primarily a wholesale nursery, it will sell seed to the public in bulk. Available are pecan, hickory, natal plum, salal, pineapple guava, walnut, mulberry, olive, piñon, and seeds for common fruits.

16
Farmer Seed & Nursery
818 N.W. 4th St.
    Faribault, MN 55021
    Large general seed catalog. Ornamentals, vegetables, and 8 pages on fruit, including a good selection of cherry plums.

17
Fowler Nurseries, Inc. & Garden Center
525 Fowler Rd.
Newcastle CA 95658
    Good selection of fruit trees and berries, including genetic dwarf fruit trees, Oriental persimmons, pomegranates, Oriental pears, and some California wine grapes. The company also carries filberts, Western pecans, and walnuts. Free 4-page price list of 200 varieties. Catalog $4

18
Fox Hill Farm
Box 9
Parma MI 49269-0009
    This nursery carries one of this nation's largest selections of herb plants. For example, it carries 32 types of thyme, 11 kinds of rosemary, and 17 varieties of mint.

19
Garden City Seeds
1324 Red Crow Road
Victor, MT 59875-9713
    Good selection of lettuce and herbs.

20
Glecklers Seedmen
Metamora, OH 443540
    This nursery carries standard vegetable seeds, including the 'Peron' tomato, which is disease and crack resistant and reputed to be immune to hornworms.

21
Good Earth/Tsang and Ma International
P.O. Box 294
Belmont CA 94002
    Large selection of Chinese vegetable seeds, including Chinese chive, bitter melon, and Chinese parsley.

22
Good Seeds
"Star Route, Box 73a"
Oroville (Chesaw), WA 98844
    Good selection of vegetables, flowers and herbs.

23
Gourmet Gardener
4000 W. 126th St.
Leawood KS 66209
    An excellent selection of gourmet vegetables and herbs. Catalog $2.

24
Gurney Seed & Nursery Co.
110 Capital St.
Yankton, SD 57078
    Large general seed catalog including flowers, vegetables, and nursery stock that includes blueberries, rugosa rose, Jerusalem artichoke, hop plants, red okra, Alpine strawberry, ginger root, pawpaw, Chinese chestnut, Nanking cherry, dwarf lemon, orange, lime, grapefruit, and banana. In addition, this nursery sells *Trichogramma* wasps, red worms, and organic fertilizers.

25
Harmony Farm Supply
3244 Hwy 116 No.
Sebastopol, CA 95472
    Specialist in fruit trees and supplies for organic gardeners. The company carries many of the varieties of fruit and nut trees recommended in this book. and continue to carry new varieties. In addition, it also carries drip irrigation supplies.

26
Harris Seeds
POB 22960
60 Saginaw Drive
Rochester, NY 14962-2960

This company carries a large selection of standard vegetable varieties and some herbs.

27
Hastings
POB 115535
1036 White St. SW
Atlanta, GA 30310

Specialist in fruit, nut, and vegetable varieties for the South. Fruits include: rabbiteye blueberries, persimmon, pomegranate, and muscadine grapes.

28
Heirloom Gardens
10365 Hwy 116
Forestville, CA 95436

This company carries a large number of open-pollinated varieties of vegetables as well as many herbs.

29
Henry Field Seed & Nursery Company
415 N. Burnett
Shenandoah, IA 51602

'Extensive general seed catalog. Ornamentals, vegetables. 14 pages of fruit, including seedling pawpaw, 'Allred' plum, hardy nut trees, currants and gooseberries, figs, and a large selection of bush cherries.

30
Henry Leuthardt Nurseries, Inc.
Montauk Highway   Box 666
East Moriches, Long Island, NY 11940

This company specializes in grapes and espaliered hardy fruit trees and ships to most parts of the country. Guidebook on dwarf and espalier-trained fruit trees for $1.00.

31
Hidden Springs Nursery
Rt. 14, Box 159
Cookeville TN 38501

Good selection of fruit trees.

32
High Altitude Gardens
POB 4619
Ketchum ID 83340

A good selection open-pollinated vegetable and wildflower varieties that grow well in cool, short seasons at high latitudes.

33
Horticultural Enterprises
P.O. Box 810082
Dallas, TX 75381-0082

Specializing in peppers, this nursery has 30 varieties of sweet and hot peppers. In addition, it has tomatillos, jicama, and epazote.

34
Interstate Nurseries
POB 208
Hamburg, IA 51640-0208

Large catalog, including 12 pages on fruits and nuts.

35
J. W. Jung Seed Company
335 S. High St.
Randolph, WI 53957-0001

Large general seed catalog, with 16 pages on vegetables, 6 pages on fruits. The company carries scab-immune apples, peanuts, bush and climbing cucumbers, and dwarf cantaloupe.

36
J. L. Hudson, Seedsman
P.O. Box 1058
Redwood City, CA 94064

Carries a wide selection of different types of vegetables. The very large catalog is known for its extensive selection of seeds collected from all over the world. Around 4,000 varieties of seeds are listed, some of them very unusual, including cacti, succulents, ferns, ornamental grasses, alpines, and wild edibles. This nursery carries seeds for many of the unusual edibles mentioned in Appendix A. A $1.00 charge for this catalog is well worth it. The nursery also has a seed exchange.

37
Johnny's Selected Seeds, Organic Seed & Crop Research
Albion, ME 04910

A large selection of organically grown vegetable seeds, with special emphasis on northern gardens. Also available are seeds of Oriental vegetables, including edible chrysanthemum; herbs; sorrel; Alpine strawberry; white clover; and 'Stampede' Jerusalem artichoke tubers. This seed company carries open-pollinated varieties of vegetables that allow you to save your own seeds. Inquire about 'seed swap."

38
Kitazawa Seed Company
356 West Taylor St.
San Jose, CA 95110

Oriental vegetables, including bitter melon, spinach mustard, and edible chrysanthemum.

39
Liberty Seeds
POB 806
New Philadelphia OH 44663

Good selection of root vegetables, tomatoes, greens and peppers.

40
Lilypons Water Gardens
6800 Lilypons Road
P.O. Box 10
Lilypons, MD 21717

This nursery offers a complete supply of water-garden accessories and water plants, including lotus and water chestnut. Catalog: $5.

41
Lockhart Seed Company
POB 1361 - 3 N. Wilson Way
Stockton CA 95205

Largest selection of onion seeds

42
Long Island Seed and Plant
P.O. Box 1285
Riverhead, NY 11901

Organization interested in seed-saving, heirloom vegetables, and self-sufficiency Seed for vegetables and fruits.

43
McLaughlin's Seeds
POB 550
Mead, WA 99021
    A very large selection of herb seed.
44
New York State Fruit-Testing Cooperative Association
P.O. Box 462
Geneva, NY 14456
    Very large fruit catalog. $5.00 membership fee, refunded
    on first order. Many new varieties of standard fruits. The
    association carries antique varieties of apples, a large
    selection of rootstock material, dwarf pears, and dessert
    and hardy wine grapes. A large selection of experimental
    fruits being tested for disease resistance and hardiness
    are also available.
45
Nichols Garden Nursery
1190 North Pacific Highway
Albany, OR 97321
    Extensive list of herbs, including plants as well as seeds;
    unusual vegetables; miniature flowering kale; Japanese
    climbing and Armenian cucumbers; and hops.
46
Northwoods Nursery
28696 S. Cramer Road
Molalla OR 97038
    Outstanding selection of exotic fruit trees, kiwis and
    berries that will grow in cool climates.
47
Northern Groves
POB 86291
Portland OR 97286
    Super selection of bamboos that will grow in cooler cli-
    mates.
48
Pacific Tree Farms
4301 Lynwood Drive
Chula Vista, CA 92010
    One of the largest selections of mail-order tropical and
    subtropical plants, including citrus, guava, pomegranate,
    sapote, surinam cherry, banana, kiwi, and mango.
    Catalog: $2.00.
49
Geo. W. Park Seed Company, Inc.
P.O. Box 31
Greenwood, SC 29647
    Park's is one of the major suppliers of vegetable and
    flower seeds in the United States. This company has a
    very large selection of vegetable seeds, including many
    varieties for small gardens.
50
Pinetree Garden Seeds
Route 100
New Gloucester ME 04260
    Excellent selection of vegetables, herbs and flowers.
51
Plants of the Southwest
Agua Fria, Rt. 6, Box 11-A
Santa Fe, NM 87501

A good selection of southwestern native plants, plus vegetable varieties for the cool growing seasons of the
mountains and high plains of the West.
52
Raintree Nursery
391 Butts Road
Morton, WA 98356
    This nursery carries many of the varieties of fruits and
    nuts mentioned in this book, including: Oriental pears,
    salal, antique apples, quince, and nuts. Many of its vari-
    eties are particularly suited to the Northwest.
53
Redwood City Seed Co.
P.O. Box 361
Redwood City, CA 94064
    Seeds of many of the unusual plants mentioned in this
    book are offered in this company's "Catalog of Useful
    Plants." The company specializes in seeds of vegetables
    and herbs from Europe, Mexico, and the Orient. It also
    has a large selection of seeds for fruit and nut trees and
    berry bushes. Catalog:$1.
54
Richter's
Goodwood, Ontario
Canada L0C 1A0
    Herb seed specialist carrying many unusual varieties.
55
 Seeds Blüm
Idaho City Stage
Boise, ID 83706
    Carries seeds of ornamental, heirloom, and open-polli-
    nated vegetables. Great information on seed saving, edi-
    ble flowers, landscaping with ornamental vegetables.
    Catalog: $1.50.
56
Seeds of Change
1364 Rufina Circle, # 5
Santa Fe NM 87501
    All organically grown seeds. Excellent selection of veg-
    etables (specialty tomatoes,and peppers) herbs, grains
    and flowers.
57
Shepherd's Garden Seeds
6116 Hwy 9
Felton, CA 95018
    This nursery carries one of the best selections of superi-
    or varieties of European vegetables available. It also car-
    ries collections of vegetables from France, Italy, and
    Germany. Catalog: $2.00.
58
Southern Exposure
POB 158
North Garden, VA 22959
    Superb selection of heirloom vegetables, multiplier and
    topset onions, rare tomatoes and other vegetables.
59
Southmeadow Fruit Gardens
Bx. SM
Lakeside, Ml 49116
    Probably the largest collection of major fruit varieties-

old, new, and rare-in the United States. The large illustrated catalog is $6.00 but worth it; a small price list is available free. This company carries plants of antique apples; numerous varieties of grapes, plums, peaches, pears, cherries; Oriental pears; beach plum; quince; a large selection of gooseberries; medlar; and a selection of hardy native fruits.

60
St. Lawrence Nurseries
RR 5, Box 324
Potsdam, NY 13676
   A large selection of hardy fruits and nuts, including over 100 varieties of apples and a number of varieties of half-high blueberries.

61
Stark Brothers Nursery
Louisiana, MO 63353
   Stark Brothers is one of the largest growers of fruit trees in the United States, carrying many of its own varieties. It has an illustrated catalog and guide offering fruit trees as well as a few vegetables, ornamentals, and nuts.

62
Stokes Seeds, Inc.
183 East Main St.
Fredonia, NY 14063
   One of this nation's largest seed companies. It carries a vast collection of vegetable and flower varieties with a particular emphasis on northern gardens.

63
Sunrise Enterprises
BOX 330058
West Hartwood, CT 06110-0058
   Specialist in Oriental vegetables and herbs. In addition to vegetable seeds, the company carries ginger and taro tubers and Chinese chive plants.

64
T & T Seeds Ltd.
Box 1710
Winnipeg, Manitoba
Canada R3C 3P6
   This nursery carries vegetable and fruit varieties for northern gardens. It has a good selection of cherry plums, hardy apples, and berries.

65
Taylor's Herb Gardens, Inc.
1535 Lone Oak Road
Vista, CA 92083
   Very large selection of herb plants, including many that are quite unusual. Catalog $3

66
Territorial Seed Company
20 Palmer Avenue
Cottage Grove, OR 97424
   A marvelous regional seed company that specializes in vegetable varieties that grow well in the Northwest Cascade Mountain range.

67
The Pepper Gal
POB 23006
Ft. Lauderdale, FL 33307
   Specializes in all types of peppers.

68
Thompson and Morgan, Inc.
P.O. Box 1308
Jackson, NJ 08527
   This seed company specializes in unusual vegetables and flowers. The seed is expensive. The company carries seed for everything from Alpine strawberries to bananas.

69
Tomato Grower's Supply
POB 2237
Fort Myers, FL 33902
   Most complete selection of tomatoes available, plus an extensive list of peppers.

70
Ty Ty south Fruit & Berry Nursery
Box 130
Ty Ty, GA 31795
   Good selection of fruits and berries.

71
The Vermont Bean Seed Company
Garden Lane
Bomoseen, VT 05732
   Extensive list of beans and peas but the company also carries seed of many other vegetables.

72
The Wayside Gardens Company
1 Garden Lane
Hodges, SC 29695-ooo1
   Primarily specializes in ornamentals but carries some fruits.

APPENDIX C
SOURCES OF INFORMATION

Organizations

The following organizations are sources of information on many of the subjects covered in this book. Your county extension service can tell you of local groups such as native plant societies, historical societies, and botanic gardens.

Brooklyn Botanic Garden
1000 Washington Ave.
Brooklyn, NY 11225
An organization with a large worldwide membership interested in all aspects of growing plants. Monthly journal published; back issues, available as booklets, contain valuable information for gardeners. See list in the bibliography.

California Rare Fruit Growers, Inc.
The Fullerton Arboretum
California State University, Fullerton
Fullerton, CA 92634
An organization devoted to experimenting with and spreading information about unusual fruits. Has a worldwide membership. Newsletter available.

Herb Society of America
9019 Kirtland Chardon Road
Mentor, OH 44060
Organization devoted to promoting the culture of herbs. Membership $35.

Home Orchard Society
POB 776
Clackamas, OR 97015
An organization to promote the culture of fruit-bearing plants and to preserve historic varieties. Newsletter available.

National Audubon Society
950 Third Ave.
New York, NY 10022
A venerable organization devoted to the study and preservation of birds.

National Wildlife Federation
1412 16th St., N.W.
Washington, DC 20036
This national organization is devoted to the preservation of wildlife.

New York State Fruit-Testing Cooperative Association
POB 462
Geneva, NY 14456
The association provides information about old and new varieties of hardy fruits. It also has trees for sale.

North American Fruit Explorers
Route 1, Box 94
Chapin, IL 62628
Members of the Fruit Explorers exchange ideas about fruit growing. Newsletter available.

Northern Nut Growers Association
9870 S. Palmer Road
New Carlisle, OH 45344
An excellent source of information on nut growing.

Seed Savers Exchange
c/o Kent Whealy
Rural route 3, Box 239
Decorah, IA 52101
Seed Savers is dedicated to preserving heirloom vegetable varieties. Newsletter and seeds available.

Sierra Club
730 Polk St.
San Francisco, CA 94109
A national organization devoted to conservation causes.

Publications

The following publications provide up-to-date and in-depth information on food growing.

The Avant Gardener
P.O. Box 489
New York, NY 10028
> Marvelous potpourri of gardening information. The goal of the magazine is to provide unto-date gardening information. Published twice monthly. Subscription rate: $18. a year.

Environment
4000 Albemarle St., N.W.
Washington, DC 20016
> This magazine explores environmental issues, from nuclear power to pesticides. Published monthly, except bimonthly Jan./Feb. and July/Aug. Subscription rate: $12.50 a year.

Harrowsmith
Camden House Publishing Ltd.
Camden East
Ontario, Canada K0K 1J0
Fabulous magazine for northern gardeners. Self-sufficiency, environmental issues, and gardening information covered in a bimonthly format. Subscription rate: $24. a year.

National Gardening
180 Flynn Ave.
Burlington, VT 05401
One of the best gardening magazines for home food gardeners. Published monthly.
Subscription rate: $18. a year.

Organic Gardening
33 East Minor St.
Emmaus, PA 18049
The publishers of this magazine have been one of the motivating forces behind the organic gardening movement. The magazine carries articles on organic methods of food production and pest control. Published monthly. Subscription rate: $18. a year.

Sunset Magazine
Menlo Park, CA 94025
This "magazine of western living" emphasizes gardening, interior decoration, cooking, and travel. Published monthly. Subscription rates: $14.00 or $18.00 a year depending on state.

GLOSSARY OF GARDENING TERMS

Acid soil. A soil with a pH of less than 7.0. Soil bacteria and most plant growth are inhibited in a soil high in acidity. Some plants thrive in it, however-for instance, blueberries and azaleas. Acid soils are usually associated with rainy climates. Acid soils are low in limestone, and limestone is applied to reduce acidity (raise pH). See *pH*.

Alkaline soil. A soil with a pH of more than 7.0. Strongly alkaline soils are harmful to plants. They are associated with arid or desert conditions. Jujube and pomegranate are edibles able to grow in strongly alkaline soils. See *pH*.

Annual. A plant that grows, flowers, sets fruit, makes seeds, then dies-all in one season. Many vegetables are annuals-for example, peas, corn, and squash.

Auxin. A type of plant hormone, natural or synthetic. Auxins affect cell enlargement, branching, root development, fruit development, and fruit set.

Bare root. A term used for plants that are sold without their roots in soil. These trees, shrubs, or perennials are usually deciduous and are dug up while they are dormant. This is the least expensive and usually the healthiest way to buy deciduous fruit trees and shrubs. Most types of stone fruits, cane berries, asparagus, and artichokes are sold this way.

Biennial. A plant that requires two growing seasons to flower. The first year only leaves develop; the second year the plant flowers, makes seed, and dies. Parsley is a biennial.

Biological control. Pest control by natural means, such as parasites, predators, or disease organisms, instead of chemicals. For example, importing lacewing larvae to a yard, instead of spraying malathion, is a biological means of controlling aphids.

Budding. See Grafting and budding.

Chelate. An organic agent which, when added to certain plant nutrients such as iron, aids in making these nutrients available to the plant.

Chilling requirement. Many fruit trees, bulbs, and herbaceous perennials need a certain number of hours under 45°F before they will break dormancy, grow, bloom, and fruit. The number of hours can vary from 400 to 2000 for different plants. Gardeners must choose types and varieties of plants with this requirement in mind. If a plant has a low chilling factor it can be grown in a mild winter climate; a plant with a high chilling factor is used in a location with harsh winters. Local nurseries usually carry the plants for their areas; some research is needed when you order by mail.

Chlorosis. A general term referring to a loss of chlorophyll in plant foliage, resulting in a yellowing of the leaves. Lack of nitrogen or iron can cause this condition. Iron deficiency is usually signified by pale-yellow leaves with darker veins. Iron chlorosis is usually treated with chelated iron or iron sulfate applied to the soil, or in some formulations as a foliage spray. Many herbicides restrict the production of chlorophyll and create a chlorotic condition.

Deciduous. Plants that lose their leaves all in one season, every year. Most temperate zone fruit trees are deciduous.

Dormant spray. A chemical applied in late fall, winter, or early spring, when the plants are dormant. It is one of the most effective controls of fungus diseases and some pests. See Fungicide.

Drought tolerance. The ability of a plant to survive under water-stress conditions. Plants have different mechanisms to help them live through drought conditions: some go dormant; some take up water more efficiently; some, like cacti, adapt to low water supplies; others escape by living only through the rainy season. Pomegranate, olive, and fig are drought-tolerant edibles.

Espalier. The art, dating from medieval times, of training a tree, shrub, or vine in a flat plane. Many plants can be trained in this way, against a wall or a fence or as a free-standing divider.

Evergreen. Plants that retain their leaves or needles for more than one season. Examples of some evergreen edibles are citrus, carob, tea, avocado, and pinon pine.

Floating row cover. Spun polyester fiber used to cover plants to protect them from pests and harsh weather; available under the brand names Reemay™ and Agronet™. Remove floating row covers when the temperature exceeds 80° F.

Fungicide. A chemical used to control fungus diseases, such as mildew and apple scab. Some of the most effective fungicides are applied when the plant is dormant.

Genetic dwarf. A plant that is naturally dwarf; in contrast to induced dwarfs, which are dwarfed by grafting or budding a standard fruit tree on dwarfing rootstock. See Grafting and budding.

Grafting and budding. A means of attaching a preferred plant (the scion) to a rootstock (understock) so the resulting plant gives the flower or fruit desired, with the advantage of roots that withstand more types of stress. It is also practiced for dwarfing. Budding is a special kind of grafting.

Groundwater. Water under the surface of the earth. It is in a saturated layer that supplies wells and springs. In some areas the groundwater is near the surface, and in others it is down very deep.

Hardy. Term to describe plants able to winter over without artificial protection. The term is generally used for plants that survive severe winters.

Herbaceous. Soft plants, as contrasted to woody plants. Herbaceous plants are generally annuals but some are perennials. Herbaceous perennials usually die to the ground each year. Examples are artichoke, chives, and rhubarb.

Herbicide. A chemical used to kill weeds. Some herbicides act on contact with the leaf surface; others are taken up through the roots of the weed. Some are selective; others kill most plants.

Humus. The end product of the decomposition of organic materials, best exemplified by forest duff. Composting is a gardener's method of developing humus. Humus is an important soil additive to help keep bacterial and other microorganism activity high, to add to the general fertility of the soil, and to improve soil structure. Hybrid. Term to describe a plant that results from the crossing of parent plants differing in one or more genes. Plant hybridization aims at increased productivity, flavor and disease resistance, as well as size and floriferousness of ornamental plants. Seed from hybrid plants will usually not "come true" (be identical to its parents), so it is not saved for another year. Most modern vegetable seeds are hybrids. By law, hybrid seed must be identified as such in catalogs.

IPM (integrated pest management). A process of controlling pest populations by monitoring; timing pest treatment to be most effective and least damaging to natural controls; and using selective, not broad-spectrum, pesticides.

Liming. A process of 'sweetening' the soil-that is, reducing its acidity. For most plants, if a soil has a pH below 6, a soil conditioner, usually dolomitic limestone, is added. Sometimes your county agricultural agent can do a soil test to determine if you need it. Soil-testing kits are also available. Acidic soils are associated with rainy climates; soils in arid climates rarely need liming. To determine the dosage follow the instructions on the package.

Microclimate. The climate specific to a small local area, such as your yard or a small part of your yard. Your yard may have either a cold or a warm microclimate, depending on sun, wind protection, or position on a slope.

Mulch. A cover that is put over soil to lessen evaporation, maintain even temperature, and keep down weeds. Mulches can be organic-grass, hay, leaves, wood chips, etc.; when decomposed, these can add humus to the soil. Mulches can also be inorganic-aluminum foil or plastic, for example-keeping weeds down but adding nothing to the soil.

Multistemmed. A shrub or tree that is trained to more than one trunk to make it more decorative. A number of young trees can be placed in one prepared hole to achieve the same effect.

Perennial. A plant that lives for an indefinite number of years. The term usually refers to herbaceous plants; strictly speaking it includes all woody plants as well. Examples of edible perennials are artichokes, asparagus, and rhubarb.

pH. An index denoting the acidity or alkalinity of biological systems. The logarithmic scale runs from 0, acid, to 14, alkaline, with 7 being neutral. For gardeners pH is a soil factor to consider when choosing plants. Most plants grow well in a range of 5.5-7.0. The pH of most garden soils falls within this range.

Pollination. A necessary part of the fertilization process, whereby pollen from the stamens, the male flower parts, is transferred to the pistil, the female flower part. Pollination is accomplished naturally by the wind, bees, and other insects. Some plants, instead of having male and female organs on the same plant, have separate female and male plants-kiwi, for instance-so both plants are always necessary for fruit to develop. Other plants, such as 'Bing' cherries, have to be pollinated by another variety of cherry tree, because though the male and female organs are both present, the pollen of the 'Bing' is dissipated before the pistil is ready to receive it.

Self-fertile. A plant able to pollinate itself and produce fruit without another plant of the same species nearby. Also called self-fruitful or self-pollinating.

Self-sterile. A plant unable to pollinate itself; it must have cross-pollination from another plant or another variety. For example, 'Bing' cherry needs another variety, such as 'Van', for pollination and fruit set.

South wall. A south-facing wall; the warmest wall for plants that need heat and sun.

Spur. Short, specialized twig on which some fruit trees, such as apples and pears, bear their blossoms and fruit.

Stone fruits. A group of commonly grown fruits, known as drupes, that have a stony covering over the seed; includes apricots, cherries, nectarines, peaches, and plums.

Sucker. Growth originating from rootstock or underground stems. On a grafted plant the suckers from the root growth will take over the plant if not removed. Some plants sucker more readily than others; pawpaws and jujube sucker heavily and can form new plants in that way.

Taproot. A large central root that grows straight down from the crown. Some plants have a fibrous, spread-out root system; others a strong central taproot. Plants with taproots are usually quite drought resistant, but they transplant poorly. Most nut trees have taproots.

Tender. A term to describe plants unable to withstand low winter temperatures.

Thinning. A term with a number of horticultural meanings, including reducing the number of plants in a seed bed so there are not too many of them competing for the available nutrients and moisture. Also, reducing the number of immature fruits on a branch so the remaining fruit will be Larger, or removing fruits from trees, such as some peach trees, that are inclined to overbear. In pruning terms, thinning means reducing the number of branches.

Topiary. The practice of shearing and pruning a plant to make unnatural geometric or fanciful shapes.

Windward. The side from which the wind blows.

ANNOTATED BIBLIOGRAPHY

General Information

American Society of Landscape Architects Foundation. *Landscape Planning for Energy Conservation*. Charles McClenon, ed. Reston, VA: Environmental Design Press, 1977.

Bailey, L. H., and staff. *Hortus Third*. New York: Macmillan Publishing Co., 1976.
This 1300-page book is a basic reference for horticulturists. The Latin names and botanical descriptions used in this book are based on *Hortus Third*.

Bienz, Darrel R. *The Why and How of Home Horticulture*. San Francisco: W. H. Freeman and Co., 1980.
A comprehensive collection of information needed for the average home gardener. The book covers basic botany, plant propagation, and growing techniques. It also includes information on how to preserve harvests and landscape planning. An excellent supplement to this text.

Brady, Nyle C. *The Nature and Properties of Soils*. 8th ed. New York: Macmillan Publishing Co., 1974.
A basic textbook on soils. Valuable for serious gardeners.

Brooklyn Botanic Garden Handbooks. Brooklyn, NY: Brooklyn Botanic Garden.
Are available for a charge from Brooklyn Botanic Garden, 1000, Washington Ave., Brooklyn, NY 11225.
The Environment and the Home Gardener, no 39.
Biological Control of Plant Pests, no. 34.

Carr, Anna. *Rodale's Color Handbook of Garden Insects*. Emmaus, PA: Rodale Press, 1979.
300 color close-ups of insects. Valuable for identifying insects, good and bad.

Crockett, James. *Crockett's Tool Shed*. Boston: Little, Brown & Co., 1979.
A comprehensive book on garden tools. Specific brands of tools are discussed.

Farallones Institute. *The Integral Urban House*. San Francisco: Sierra Club Books, 1979.
Extensive information on self-reliant living in the city. It includes suggestions for conserving water and energy, managing household waste, raising food plants and animals, and using solar technology. Rich in practical knowledge.

Hartmann, Hudson T., and Dale E. Kester. *Plant Propagation-Principles and Practices*. 3rd ed. Englewood Cliffs, NJ: Prentice-Hall, Inc., 1975.
Detailed information on the propagation of plants from seed, by grafting, layering, and cuttings. 50 pages on specific propagation for edible species.

Logsdon, Gene, and the editors of *Organic Gardening and Farming*. *The Gardener's Guide to Better Soil*. Emmaus, PA: Rodale Press, 1975.
Very helpful for composting, mulching, soil amendments, and cultivation.

Ortho Books, Chevron Chemical Company Editorial Staff. San Francisco: Ortho Books, Chevron Chemical Co.
All About Fertilizers, Soils, and Water. A. Cort Sinnes, 1979.
A basic illustrated text on the complex subject of soil, fertilizer, and water management in the home yard.
All About Pruning, 1978.
A basic illustrated text on the pruning of ornamental and edible plants.

Olwkowski, William, Sheila Darr, and Helga Olkowski, *Common-Sense Pest Control*. Newton, CT: The Tauton Press, 1991.
A valuable reference for integrated pest management.

Powell, Thomas, and Betty Powell. *The Avant Gardener*. Boston: Houghton Mifflin Co., 1975.
Marvelous potpourri of gardening information, including suggestions for edible landscaping and native plant use.

Reilly, Ann. Park's *Success with Seeds*. Greenwood, SC: Geo. W., Park Seed Co., 1978
A classic text for starting seeds.

Smith, J. Russell. *Tree Crops: A Permanent Agriculture*. New York: Harper Colophon Books, Harper & Row, 1978.
A classic in its field (original edition, 1950), providing information on chestnut, mulberry, persimmon, walnut, oak, and carob, among other trees. Permanent agriculture is suggested as an answer to hunger and environmental problems.

Sunset Books Editorial Staff. *New Western Garden Book*. Menlo Park, CA: Lane Publishing Co., 1986.
A comprehensive western plant encyclopedia. Zoned for all western climates. 1200 plant identification drawings; plant-selection guide in color. Popularly known as the bible of West Coast gardening. Don't garden without it if you're in the West.

Landscaping Information

Creasy, Rosalind, *The Complete Book of Edible Landscaping*. San Francisco, CA: Sierra Clubs Books, 1982.
The basic text on edible landscaping from which this book is based.

Gessert, Kate Rogers. *The Beautiful Food Garden Encyclopedia of Attractive Food Plants*. New York: Van Nostrand Reinhold Co., 1983.
This book is an excellent companion to *The Complete Book of Edible Landscaping*. Gessert shares her vast knowledge on how to landscape with beautiful vegetables.

Ireys, Alice Recknagel. *How to Plan and Plant Your Own Property.*
    New York: William Morrow & Co., 1975.
    Complete plant lists and information for landscaping a small
    property-including approaches, garden rooms, terraces,
    paths, hedges, poolside and woodland sites all practical,
    with low upkeep. Little or no information on edible plants.
Johnson, Hugh. *The Principles of Gardening.* New York: Simon &
    Schuster, 1979.
    A delightful guide to the art, history, science, and practice of
    gardening. Very well illustrated.
Kourik, Robert. *Designing and Maintaining Your Edible Landscape
    Naturally.* Santa Rosa, CA: Metamorphic Press, 1986.
    An extremely helpful book on maintaining your edible gar-
    den.

Information on Edible Plants

Baron, Lloyd C., and Robert Stebbins. *Growing Filberts in Oregon.*
    Extension Bulletin 628, rev. ed. Corvallis, OR: Oregon State
    University Extension Service, 1978.
    A valuable aid for growing filberts. Available for a charge
    from Oregon State University Extension Service, Oregon
    State University, Corvallis, OR 97331.
Bennett, Jennifer. The Harrrowsmith Book of Fruit Trees.
    Camden House Publishing, 1991
    A complete reference book for northern fruit growers.
Bianchini, Francesco, Francesco Corbetta, and Marilena Pistoia.
    The Complete Book of Fruits and Vegetables. Translated from
    the Italian by Italia and Alberto Mancinelli. New York:
    Crown Publishers, 1976.
    Magnificently illustrated book. Gives history of edible plants
    around the world and some basic botanical information.
Bianchini, Francesco, Francesco Corbetta, and Marilena Pistoia.
    Health Plants of the World. English adaptation (from the
    Italian) by M. A. Dejey. New York: Newsweek Books, 1979.
    Beautifully illustrated book that gives medicinal information
    on many plants, including some edibles.
Bond, M. D. *Peanut Production Handbook.* Circular P-7. Auburn,
    AL: Alabama Cooperative Extension Service.
    Extensive information on growing peanuts, including insects
    and diseases. Heavy on pesticides. Available from Alabama
    Cooperative Extension Service, Auburn University, Auburn,
    AL 36830.
Brooklyn Botanic Garden Handbooks. Brooklyn, NY: Brooklyn
    Botanic Garden.
    Each handbook discusses one subject thoroughly. All are
    particularly helpful. Available for a charge from Brooklyn
    Botanic Garden, 1000 Washington Ave., Brooklyn, NY
    11225.
    Fruit Trees and Shrubs, no. 67.
    Handbook on Herbs, no. 27.
    Herbs and Their Ornamental Uses, no. 68.
    Japanese Herbs and Their Uses, no. 57.
    The Home Vegetable Garden, no. 69.
California Rare Fruit Growers. *California Rare Fruit Growers
    Yearbook.* 17 vols. Bonsall, CA: California Rare Fruit
    Growers, 1969-1993.
    The yearbooks for this organization include valuable
    research on many fruits grown in subtropical climates. Back
    issues are available.

Clark, John C. *The Pecan Tree.* Publication 475, rev. ed.
    Knoxville, TN:
    University of Tennessee, Agricultural Extension Service,
    1975.
    Extensive information on growing pecans in the East. Heavy
    emphasis on pesticides.
Clark, John C. *Quality Sweet Potato Production.* Publication 420,
    rev. ed. Knoxville, TN: University of Tennessee, Agricultural
    Extension Service, 1976.
    Extensive information on growing sweet potatoes, including
    illustrations of disease problems.
Gibbons, Euell. *Stalking the Wild Asparagus.* New York: David
    McKay Co., 1962.
    Complete guide to edible plants in the wild.
Hill, Lewis. *Fruits and Berries for the Home Garden.* New York:
    Alfred A. Knopf, 1977.
    The best all-round fruit-growing book for the East Coast. It
    offers extensive cultural information for the major fruits,
    identifies common diseases and pests, and offers pest con-
    trols that are largely organic. A must for eastern and mid-
    western home fruit gardeners.
James, Theodore, Jr. *How to Grow Fruit, Berries, and Nuts in the
    Midwest and East.* Tucson, AZ: H. P. Books, 1983.
    An excellent resource book covering varieties and cultural
    information specific to the Midwest and East.
Jaynes, Richard A., ed. *Nut Tree Culture in North America.*
    Hamden, CT: The Northern Nut Growers Association, 1979.
    Up-to-date information on nut growing in the United States.
    A valuable resource for serious nut growers.
Jeavons, John. *How to Grow More Vegetables.* Palo Alto, CA:
    Ecology Action of the Midpeninsula, 1982.
    A primer on the biodynamic/French-intensive method of
    organic horticulture.
Larkcom, Joy. *The Salad Garden.* New York: Viking Press, 1984.
    Fabulous book filled with detailed information on all of the
    routine, as well as unusual, salad vegetables.
Larcom, Joy. Oriental Vegetables - *The Complete Guide for the
    Garden and Kitchen.* Toyo: Kodansha International, 1991.
    A truly comprehensive look at the vast subject of Oriental
    vegetables.
Maxwell, Lewis S. *Florida Vegetables.* Tampa, FL: Lewis S.
    Maxwell, Publisher, 1974.
    Valuable book for Deep South vegetable gardeners. Many
    unusual varieties included, as well as descriptions of dis-
    eases prevalent in Florida.
Organic Gardening and Farming Editorial Staff. *Unusual
    Vegetables.* Anne Moyer Halpin, ed. Emmaus, PA: Rodale
    Press, 1978.
    The book discusses how to grow and where to obtain 79
    unusual vegetables, including bamboo, prickly pear, jicama,
    tomatillo, Jerusalem artichoke, sorrel, and peanut. A valuable
    resource.
Ray, Richard, and Lance Walheim. *Citrus-How to Select, Grow,
    and Enjoy.* Tucson, AZ: H. P. Books, 1980.
    A beautifully illustrated book covering all aspects of citrus
    growing.
Riotte, Louise. *The Complete Guide to Growing Berries and Grapes.*
    Charlotte, VT: Garden Way Publishing, 1974.
    Extensive information on all types of berries and grapes.
    Includes drawings of most berry pests.
Seymour, John. *The Self-Sufficient Gardener.* Garden City, NY:
    Dolphin Books, Doubleday & Co., 1979.

Emphasis on deep-bed method of growing more food in less space. Production, not aesthetics, stressed.

Schneider, Elizabeth. *Uncommon Fruits and Vegetables - A commonsense Guide.* New York: Harper and Row, Publishers, 1986.
A comprehensive guide to hundreds of unusual fruits and vegetables.

Simmons, Adelma Grenier. *Herb Gardening in Five Seasons.* New York: Hawthorn Books, 1964.
Extensive information on growing and harvesting herbs in the garden.

Underhill, J. E. *Wild Berries of the Pacific Northwest.* Seattle: Superior Publishing Co., 1974.
Helpful information on edible and poisonous berries, including juniper, Oregon grape, gooseberry, service berry, wild strawberry, crabapple, rose hips, blackberry, salmonberry, mountain ash, arbutus, wintergreen, huckleberry, mountain cranberry, elderberry, and salal.

Walheim, Lance, and Robert L. Stebbins. *Western Fruit, Berries, and Nuts: How to Select, Grow, and Enjoy.* Tucson, AZ: H. P. Books, 1981.
A valuable book for westerners who are serious about growing their own fruits, berries, and nuts. The hook includes detailed information on varieties and cultural techniques.

Whealy, Kent, ed. *Fruit, Berry, and Nut Inventory.* Decorah, IA Seed Saver Publications. 1989
This catalog identifies and helps you locate hundreds of fruits, berries, and nut trees.

Whealy, Kent, ed. *Garden Seed Inventory,* second edition. Decorah, IAA: Seed Saver Publications, 1988
This catalog identifies and helps you locate hundreds of open-pollinated vegetable varieties.

Wickson, Edward J. *California Vegetables in Garden and Field.* San Francisco: Pacific Rural Press, 1897.
One of the classic books for California agriculture.

Will, Albert A., Eric V. Golby, and Lewis S. Maxwell. *Florida Fruit.* Tampa, FL: Lewis S. Maxwell, Publisher, 1973.
Filled with excellent information for tropical fruit growing.

Recipes and Food Preserving

Ball Corporation. *Ball Blue Book,* no. 29. New rev. ed. Muncie, IN: Ball Corp., 1974.
A well-written manual for canning and freezing put out by the makers of Ball canning equipment. It may be ordered for a nominal charge from Ball Blue Book, Dept. PK-2A, Box 2005, Muncie, IN 47302.

Brennan, Georgeanne. *Potager - Fresh Garden Cooking in the French Style.* San Francisco: Chronicle Books. 1992
A lovely book full of delicious dining.

Creasy, Rosalind. *Cooking From the Garden.* San Francisco, CA: Sierra Club Books, 1989.
A compendium of information on growing and cooking many familiar and unusual garden produce.

Greene, Bert. *Greene on Greens.* New York: Workman Publishing, 1984
A great selection of recipes for vegetables.

Hawkes, Alex D. *A World of Vegetable Cookery.* New York: Simon & Schuster, 1968.
A very rich selection of 188 usual and unusual vegetables, with 500 recipes from Akee to Zucchini.

Hutson, Lucinda. *The Herb Garden Cookbook.* Austin, TX: Texas Monthly Press, 1987.
A large selection of information on culinary herbs.

Lappé, Frances Moore. *Diet for a Small Planet.* New York: Friends of the Earth and Ballantine Books, 1974.
A must for all cooks. How to feed your family while being less of a burden on the world's resources.

Morash, Marian. *The Victory Garden Cookbook.* New York: Alfred A. Knopf, 1982.
The garden cookbook. If you can only have one cookbook, this should be your choice. Morash covers how to harvest and prepare all the garden vegetables.

Ogden, Shepherd and Ellen. *The Cook's Garden.* Emmaus, PA: Rodale Press, 1989
Lot's of recipes for your garden harvest.

Peirce, Pam. *Golden Gate Gardening.* Davis, CA: AgAccess. 1993.
Organic food gardening for the San Francisco Bay Area.

Supplementary Reference Material

All of the books mentioned previously were used in gathering material for this book. The following references are less useful to the individual home landscaper but were valuable resources for the author.

Choudhury, B. *Vegetables: India-The Land and the People.* New Delhi: National Book Trust, India, 1967.
Cultural information on vegetables grown in India.

Council on Environmental Quality. *Environmental Quality-1979.* Washington, DC: U.S. Government Printing Office, 1979.
Up-to-date information on pesticides, toxic substances, energy, groundwater problems, conservation. For sale from Superintendent of Documents, U.S. Government Printing Office, Washington, DC 20402.

Harler, C. R. *Tea Growing.* London: Oxford University Press, 1966.
Basic information on tea growing.

Hoyt, Roland S. *Ornamental Plants for Subtropical Regions.* Los Angeles: Livingston Press, 1938.
A basic text for landscape designers. It has detailed lists of Landscaping uses for a majority of ornamental plants grown in subtropical regions.

Jackson, Michael, ed. *The World Guide to Beer.* Englewood Cliffs, NJ: Prentice-Hall, 1977.
Comprehensive guide to beer tasting and brewing.

Masefield, G. B., M. Wallis, S. G. Harrison, and B. E. Nicholson. *The Oxford Book of Food Plants.* London: Oxford University Press, 1975.
Background information on a majority of the world's food plants. Superb illustrations.

Plant Growth Regulators: Study Guide for Agricultural Pest Control Advisers, 1978.
Basic information on plant growth regulators in California agriculture. Available from Agricultural Publications, University of California, Berkeley, CA 94720.

Study Guide for Agricultural Pest Control Advisers on Plant Diseases, 1972.
Basic information on plant diseases of agricultural plants in California. Available from Agricultural Publications, University of California, Berkeley, CA 94720.

Index